D0893313

PROUST & THE ART OF LOVE

PROUST & THE ART OF LOVE

THE AESTHETICS OF SEXUALITY IN THE LIFE, TIMES, & ART OF MARCEL PROUST

J. E. RIVERS

NEW YORK
COLUMBIA UNIVERSITY PRESS
1980

Library of Congress Cataloging in Publication Data

Rivers, Julius Edwin, 1944–
Proust and the art of love.

Bibliography: p.
Includes index.
1. Proust, Marcel, 1871–1922—Criticism and inter-
pretation.   2. Love in literature.   3. Sex in
literature.   4. Homosexuality in literature.
I. Title.
PQ2631.R63Z8352   843'.912   80-24103
ISBN 0-231-05036-4

Columbia University Press
New York   Guildford, Surrey

One must never be afraid of going too far, for truth lies always beyond.

—Marcel Proust. From a letter to E. R. Curtius, written to accompany "the gift of *Sodome et Gomorrhe II.*"

CONTENTS

THE FOLLOWING study began as an attempt to understand the thirty-two pages that constitute the first part of Proust's *Sodome et Gomorrhe*, pages that come at the midpoint of *A la recherche du temps perdu* and are, as I try to show, in every sense central to the novel's artistic vision. Those pages introduce an aspect of *A la recherche* that has received only slight attention from Proust's critics. And yet an understanding of the material they contain is, I think, crucial to an understanding of Proust's genius. I have, accordingly, tried to place this section of *A la recherche* in its proper biographical, historical, and literary context and to explain the resonance it sends throughout the novel's search for lost time. The result is an extended explication of *Sodome I*, though it does not involve a formal "close reading" of it. Instead, the book uses *Sodome I* as a point of reference and a recurrent theme in an attempt to show how the sexual paradoxes it expresses are also the personal, cultural, and aesthetic paradoxes of Proust's life, times, and art.

Some readers will detect in the book, particularly in the final chapters, critical techniques and perspectives similar to those employed by structuralists, by the Geneva school of literary critics, and by exponents of the so-called *nouvelle critique*. There is also a good deal of attention in the final chapters to what is now called "intertextuality." Though I have occasionally employed approaches associated with these recent critical trends, I have not used the specialized terminology to which the trends have given rise nor attempted to align my argument with any particular school of literary analysis. I believe that Proust is unlikely to yield up his deepest meanings to any single critical method and that the multiplicity of Proust requires a multiplicity of approach. My emphasis throughout the book is on the human dimensions and the cultural implications of Proust's artistic struggle and literary achievement. This emphasis does not exclude formalistic inquiry, but I hope that nowhere in the book is there formalism without humanism.

In preparing the book I have incurred a great debt to writers
who have preceded me, critics of Proust as well as students of cultural
and literary history. That debt is acknowledged as fully as possible in
the footnotes. There are debts of another sort, however, that should
be acknowledged here. I should like first of all to express gratitude to
my teacher Randi Birn, who showed me the beauty and complexity of
Proust's work and who has been over the years a constant source of
help and encouragement. She read the manuscript in an earlier version and made valuable comments, as did Bruce Kawin, Siegfried
Mandel, Marcel Muller, Roger Shattuck, and George Stambolian.
Many of the ideas expressed in the book first took shape in conversations about Proust with my friend and colleague William Walker, who
was also the most careful and demanding reader of the final version
of the manuscript. Maresa Fanelli, John Hall, Elyane Jones, V. A.
Kolve, Jim Rivers, and the late Professor George Clemens also offered valuable advice and encouragement. Lee Baker served variously,
and superbly, as research assistant, typist, and critic of style and
substance. Aladeen Smith and Colleen Anderson gave skillful assis-
tance with typing and editing. Joan Brewer of the Institute for Sex
Research at Indiana University made my work there both pleasant
and profitable. My parents, Mr. and Mrs. J. E. Rivers, Sr., have
given encouragement and support for as long as I have been reading
and writing and were especially helpful during my work on this book.
Warm and special thanks are due to Philip Anderson for the time, advice, and criticism he contributed at every stage of the project. If the
study is successful in what it attempts to do, these people deserve a
great deal of the credit. Any errors or shortcomings are mine alone.

For the convenience of English-speaking readers and in the interest of consistency of language, I have quoted Proust in English
throughout the study. Titles of French works, however, remain in the
original. In English *A la recherche du temps perdu* is known as *Remembrance of Things Past* (a title with which, despite its Shakespearean allusion, Proust was none too happy). The English equiva-
lents for the French titles of the novel's seven volumes are, in the
familiar translations by Moncrieff, Blossom, and Mayor: *Swann's Way
(Du côté de chez Swann); Within a Budding Grove (A l'ombre des
jeunes filles en fleurs); The Guermantes Way (Le Côté de*

Guermantes); *Cities of the Plain* (*Sodome et Gomorrhe*); *The Captive* (*La Prisonnière*); *The Sweet Cheat Gone* (*La Fugitive*); and *The Past Recaptured* (*Le Temps retrouvé*). When referring to *A la recherche* I follow the standard practice of citing volume and page number of the Pléiade edition in parentheses immediately following the quotation or reference. References to other works by Proust are given in the footnotes by title and page number. A list of these works, which includes complete bibliographical information, will be found in the first part of the bibliography at the end of the book.

All translations of Proust and other writers are my own, unless otherwise indicated. The book contains, in the form of long excerpts from Proust's correspondence, a good deal of writing by Proust which has not been previously translated into English.

Part of the research and writing for the book was supported by a Younger Humanist's Research Fellowship from the National Endowment for the Humanities, for which I should like, in conclusion, to express my thanks.

J. E. R.

London, England
Boulder, Colorado
1979–80

ACKNOWLEDGMENTS

I AM grateful to the following publishers and authors for permission to quote or translate for this volume extracts from the following works:

Maurice Bardèche and Les Sept Couleurs for Maurice Bardèche, *Marcel Proust, romancier*, 1971

Chatto and Windus, Ltd. (publishers of Proust's *Remembrance of Things Past*, © 1922) for *A la recherche du temps perdu*, 1951

Editions Gallimard for Marcel Proust, *"Jean Santeuil" précédé de "Les Plaisirs et les jours*," © 1971, and Marcel Proust, *A la recherche du temps perdu*, © 1954

Editions Robert Laffont for Céleste Albaret, *Monsieur Proust*, 1973

Librairie A. G. Nizet for Henri Bonnet, *Marcel Proust de 1907 à 1914*, 1971, and Marcel Plantevignes, *Avec Marcel Proust*, 1966

Librairie Plon for Marcel Proust, *Correspondance, 1880–1895*, 1970, Marcel Proust, *Correspondance générale*, 1930–36, and Marcel Proust, *Lettres retrouvées*, 1966

Random House, Inc. (publishers of Proust's *Remembrance of Things Past*, copyright © 1934 and renewed 1962 by Random House, Inc.) for *A la recherche du temps perdu*

Simon and Schuster, Inc., for *"Jean Santeuil" précédé de "Les Plaisirs et les jours*," 1971

Dr. C. A. Tripp for C. A. Tripp, *The Homosexual Matrix*, 1975

Weidenfeld and Nicolson for *"Jean Santeuil" précédé de "Les Plaisirs et les jours*," 1971

Portions of the book first appeared as an essay, "The Myth and Science of Homosexuality in *A la recherche du temps perdu*," in *Homosexualities and French Literature*, ed. George Stambolian and Elaine Marks, 1979. Permission to use portions of that essay has been granted by the publisher, Cornell University Press.

PROUST & THE ART OF LOVE

CHAPTER ONE

PROBLEMS AND PERSPECTIVES

*S*HORTLY AFTER Proust died in 1922, Ortega y Gasset declared that Proust's novel embodies nothing less than "a new way of seeing." Ernst Robert Curtius, in another tribute, wrote that "a new era in the history of the great French novel . . . begins with Proust. . . . he surpasses Flaubert in intelligence as he surpasses Balzac in literary excellence and Stendhal in understanding of life and of beauty." And Joseph Conrad stated that "there has never been in all of literature such an example of analytical power, and I can say with a good deal of assurance that there will never be another."[1]

Since the time of these early tributes Proust's reputation has not ceased to grow. His masterpiece, the vast and sprawling novel *A la recherche du temps perdu*, is now universally acclaimed as one of the greatest works of the twentieth century and of all time. Inevitably an enormous body of criticism has gathered around *A la recherche*. Proust's work is encyclopedic, and so is the interpretation it has generated. There are book-length studies of the Proustian conception of time, art, and the self. There are books on Proust and religion, Proust and music, Proust and painting, Proust and medicine, and Proust and the theater. There are critical articles which consider Proust's affinities with such figures as Plato, Dante, Shakespeare, Beethoven, and Einstein and still others which analyze Proust's treatment of such recondite and diverse topics as cooking, military science, and sport.

There is, however, a major lacuna in this profusion of analysis: there has never been an extended inquiry into Proust's treatment of human sexuality. Any investigation of this topic must, of course, revolve around the complex issues raised by Proust's homosexuality and

1

his uses of this theme in *A la recherche*, partly because this theme has received very little critical commentary and partly because, as I hope to show, it implies and contains Proust's vision of sexuality in general, which, in turn, implies and contains his vision of life and of the world.

The reason Proustian criticism has had so little to say on these matters is not far to seek. Until recently homosexuality was considered a taboo subject, no less among literary critics than among the general public, one that was discussed reluctantly and then, perforce, amid a host of circumlocutions, apologies to the reader, and protestations of the critic's distaste. Such an approach does not lend itself very well to analysis and understanding, and for the first three decades after Proust's death homosexuality was given short shrift in discussions of his work. It was considered impolite and embarrassing to bring the subject up. And it was assumed, besides, that this was a phenomenon which intelligent people understood already and which therefore needed little elaboration. Proust's homosexuality was seen as an unfortunate flaw in a character otherwise possessed of great genius and insight, a tragic moral failing, a degrading sexual perversion, an illness.

These views produced one of the paradoxes of modern literary history. Proust is the first major novelist to deal extensively with homosexuality and is, more than any other writer, responsible for introducing the theme into the mainstream of modern literature. Indeed, Proust's name and novel are so intimately connected with homosexuality that for a long time the epithet "Proustian" served in literary circles as a euphemism for "homosexual." Critics sensed the importance of homosexuality in Proust's life and art, but out of shame, embarrassment, prejudice, and deference to decorum they refrained from discussing the idea publicly and according it the study it deserves.

One of the first critics to give serious attention to homosexuality as a shaping force of Proust's art was Justin O'Brien, who in December of 1949 brought out an article called "Albertine the Ambiguous: Notes on Proust's Transposition of Sexes."[2] O'Brien's thesis, which has since passed into the popular lore about Proust and *A la recherche*, is that Proust draws upon his homosexual memories in portraying the heterosexual love affairs of the novel and thus "transposes" the sexes in creating several of his female characters, principally Albertine. This, O'Brien asserts, accounts for the boyish appearance and demeanor of certain of Proust's female characters and for Proust's dark view of love as illusory and doomed to failure. O'Brien concludes that A la recherche is a "subterfuge," which Proust carries out at the price of "largely falsifying the entire psychology of love and depicting that universal emotion in a form unfamiliar to most readers."[3]

In arriving at this view O'Brien makes several assumptions about homosexuality that nowadays would not be so readily granted. During the past three decades empirical sex research has made significant progress in understanding homosexuality and placing it within the general spectrum of human sexual response. Also during this time, and especially during the past decade, Western society has become more tolerant of homosexuality and less ready to view it as conforming to the negative stereotypes of the past. These stereotypes acted on Proust and have acted on Proustian criticism, but our growing awareness of the potential richness and complexity of all forms of sexual experience should encourage us to avoid some of the pitfalls of O'Brien's article. Though O'Brien warns against making sweeping generalizations about "the homosexual" (p. 944), he himself does precisely this in certain sections of his argument. O'Brien assumes, for instance, that homosexuality is unworkable as a sexual or emotional arrangement and that homosexually oriented people automatically have a pessimistic view of love. This leads him to his conclusion that any attempt to pretend that homosexuality is comparable to heterosexuality is a "subterfuge" at best.[4] What O'Brien is really saying in this conclusion is that A la recherche is not about love because it is about homosexuality, a point of view that has been echoed and reechoed in criticism since O'Brien. O'Brien constantly suggests that the homosexual experience Proust recasts in the narrator's affair with Albertine is an inferior kind of experience and is unworthy of literature. This point of view is perverse, since one of the goals of Proust's novel is to show what homosexual experience has in common with human experience in general and to use it, finally, as an image for perennial human problems and aspirations. Furthermore, recent sex research has made it increasingly difficult to dismiss homosexuality as being, in and of itself, fundamentally different from or inferior to heterosexuality. Some of this research has suggested that the two kinds of love can and often do involve comparable feelings of tenderness, comparable problems of adjustment, and a comparable potential for mutual respect and enrichment. As this book goes to press, a new and important voice has been added to this research, the book *Homosexuality in Perspective* by William Masters and Virginia Johnson (Boston: Little, Brown, 1979), a carefully researched empirical study, which concludes, among other things, that the physical processes of lubrication, erection, ejaculation, and orgasm are identical in heterosexual and homosexual experience. The book also suggests that homosexually oriented people may actually have a better understanding of some of the physical and emotional intricacies of sex than heterosexually oriented people. We may doubt the suggestion that one group is, qua group, more sensitive or knowledgeable about sex than the other. The work of Masters and Johnson is, nonetheless, symptomatic of a growing awareness in sex research of the common ground linking modes of sexual expression formerly thought to be diametrically opposed.

Other empirical research has called into question O'Brien's view that homosexuality is "a form [of love] unfamiliar to most readers." At about the same time O'Brien wrote, Kinsey published his finding that 50 percent of American males are likely to have a history of homosexual feelings, behavior, or both. Kinsey's statistics have been attacked, but they have never been disproved.[5] And regardless of whether Kinsey's figures are strictly true, they have led to a heightened appreciation of the prevalence of homosexuality both now and in the past. To affirm that it is a rarity, as O'Brien does, and that "most readers" will have no experience of it is to adopt an extremely naive point of view. The dichotomy between "homosexual" and "heterosexual" on which much of O'Brien's argument rests is also an oversimplification. As Kinsey's work argued and as common sense tells us, these terms do not represent mutually exclusive modes of identity but are simply the extremes of a scale on which many nuances and combinations of sexual feeling and behavior are to be found.[6]

Many critics of Proust, however, continue to dress their arguments in the full panoply of popular stereotypes about homosexuality:

that it is a disease, a type of moral insanity, a crime against nature, and so on. Milton Hindus, for instance, discussing the cruelty sometimes evinced by Proust's characters, writes that "Morel is exhibited in perhaps the greatest variety of such actions, possibly because homosexuality, being itself the quintessential perversity, naturally attaches itself to creatures more morally obtuse than any that can be found among the more normal lovers."[7] Hindus's argument begs the question. It reasons that since all homosexually oriented people are morally obtuse, it is natural that a character who is criminally inclined should also be homosexually inclined. And yet a few pages earlier Hindus praises Proust for the "morality of [his] vision of the world."[8] Hindus tries to condemn homosexuality as a manifestation of moral degeneracy and at the same time praise the morality of an author whose homosexuality helped to create the book under discussion.

Hindus embarrasses himself by forgetting—or ignoring—Proust's homosexuality. Justin O'Brien, who remembers Proust's homosexuality, strides into another, even more common pitfall: the fallacy that it necessarily produces a warped and erroneous perspective on human experience. Since O'Brien published "Albertine the Ambiguous," his idea that Proust falsified love with a surreptitious transposition of the sexes has been reiterated so often that it now amounts to a critical cliché. MacDonald Allen, for instance, recently wrote that "the important difference between Joyce and Proust is that the first could look both ways psychologically, but Proust, the invert, failed. His females, such as Albertine, are but males in transvestist [sic] garb, and the device wears thin. They react like male lovers, as did their models and their creators [sic]."[9] This well-worn stricture on Proust's sexual transpositions has even found its way into fiction. In Vladimir Nabokov's *Pale Fire* Charles Kinbote asserts that the principal love affair of *A la recherche* is a "sexual *travestissement* . . . [involving] an absurd, rubber-and-wire romance between a blond young blackguard (the fictitious Marcel), and an improbable *jeune fille* who has a pasted-on bosom, Vronski's (and Lyovin's) thick neck, and a cupid's buttocks for cheeks."[10] And in Nabokov's *Ada* Van Veen says:

I would like your opinion, Ada, and yours, Cordula, on the following literary problem. Our professor of French literature maintains that there is a grave philosophical, and hence artistic, flaw in the entire treatment of the Marcel and Albertine affair. It makes sense if the reader *knows* that the narrator is a pansy, and that the good fat cheeks of Albertine are the good fat buttocks of Albert. It makes none if the reader cannot be supposed, and should not be required, to know *anything* about this or any other author's sexual habits in order to enjoy to the last drop a work of art. . . . The professor concludes that a novel which can be appreciated only by *quelque petite blanchisseuse* who has examined the author's dirty linen is, artistically, a failure.[11]

The context is different, but the thought is the same, namely, that the image of love presented in *A la recherche* is invalid, because the author "is a pansy" who attempts to deceive his readers by describing homosexual experience in heterosexual terms.

This idea, which has come dangerously close to universal acceptance, is badly in need of detailed reexamination. In a reply to Justin O'Brien's original article on the subject, Harry Levin outlines some of the weaknesses in the position. Levin begins by pointing out that O'Brien's investigation of Proust's homosexuality "makes it henceforth possible to discuss on the plane of scholarly inquiry what has heretofore subsisted on the level of literary gossip." But he goes on to challenge the notion that we must retranspose the sexes in order to understand the real meaning of *A la recherche*. "I respectfully submit," Levin writes, "that, when mere acquiescence in a novelist's own designation of the sex of his heroine is held to be erroneous, we have reached a confusing epoch in the history of criticism." It may be true, Levin continues, that Proust's homosexuality contributes to "certain equivocations, confusions, and improbabilities in his treatment of heterosexual relationships." But he also points out that "to press such points very far . . . is to assume that Proust is never improbable or confused or equivocal when he addresses himself to other themes; and that relationships between the sexes, as described by heterosexual writers, are invariably convincing." As for the idea that Proust's pessimism about love springs from his homosexuality, Levin reminds us that "literature would tell us, if life did not, that other men have reached similar conclusions by way of the normal channels." If Proust indeed recasts his homosexual experience in heterosexual form, he has, according to Levin, a legitimate aesthetic reason: "His intention was not to conceal what no one could have expected him to reveal, but rather to appeal—as writers, regardless of their

peculiar traits, must always do—to the norms of human experience."
And simply because Proust may have employed sexual transposition
in creating some of his characters is, Levin argues, no reason for us to
visualize Albertine as a man. If we read "Albert" for "Albertine" and
"Gilbert" for "Gilberte," consistency would require, in Levin's view,
that we also read "François" for "Françoise." But this would be an absurdity, since Françoise is obviously and unquestionably female, as
are many other characters in the book (Levin also cites the Duchesse
de Guermantes). And he continues:

Once we commit ourselves to this process of *travestissement*, the work reduces itself to a travesty. What of Andrée, the chief object of the narrator's
jealous suspicions? Is she to be transposed into André? In that case, the situation is turned into an unrelieved homosexual triangle. But if, as Professor
O'Brien seems to think, Albert remains bisexual (to which I would agree,
with the qualification that Albertine remains herself), it follows that Andrée
must then be regarded as a normal young woman in love with Albert—
despite the pains that Proust takes to establish her reputation as a Lesbian.
Further questions might be multiplied, but these may suffice to back my
original contention that a change in the sex of Albertine introduces more difficulties than it settles.

Levin concludes with some general thoughts on the complexities
raised by any writer's imaginative portrayal of a gender other than the
writer's own. Dorothy Richardson, he points out, thought that no
man, no matter how talented and no matter what his sexual experience, could ever give a convincing portrait of a woman. Indeed,
Baudelaire once declared that Emma Bovary, who is usually regarded
as one of the most fully realized portraits of a woman in literature, is
really a man. And, Levin adds, "when Flaubert said, '*Madame Bovary, c'est moi*,' he explicitly acknowledged the transposition." The
upshot of all this, in Levin's estimation, is not that we, as readers and
critics, should think of Madame Bovary and Albertine as males in
disguise. The fact of the matter is that Flaubert, like Proust, is simply
displaying "the talent of all great novelists for imaginatively projecting
themselves into other lives than their own, and thereby calling upon
us to meet them half-way." [12]
　　Levin's objections to O'Brien's article are well taken; but so is
O'Brien's reply to Levin:

Everyone would agree with Professor Levin that criticism has no right to forbid the creative writer to use his imagination in order to evoke life beyond
his own experience. Yet criticism sometimes reaches the point where it
profits from a study of the quality and the working of that imagination. Certainly Proust had the right . . . to create an unquestionably feminine Gilberte or Albertine as the object of Marcel's passion, but the fact remains that
he did not do so. My colleague believes that "the effect of narrative art . . .
depends upon a literal acceptance of characters and situations as stated." But
surely he would not forbid a second, *critical* reading to examine just how, and
perhaps even why, the artist's world differs from the reader's?[13]

Levin and O'Brien both have a point. It is indisputable that Albertine, Gilberte, and certain other female characters in *A la recherche*
have some characteristics that are traditionally regarded as masculine;
and it is also indisputable, as we shall see, that Proust draws on his
homosexual experiences to create certain parts of the heterosexual
love affairs in the novel. O'Brien's argument fails not at this point but
rather in his insistence that insofar as *A la recherche* is based on
homosexual experience, it provides a distorted image of love. To this
Levin supplies a corrective by reminding us that other writers who are
not homosexual have shared Proust's conclusions about love and that
since we readily grant other authors the license of imaginative recon-
struction of their private lives (including, at times, sexual transposition), there is no reason to deny this same license to a homosexual author such as Proust.

But this does not settle the matter. We still want to know why
Proust, who obviously has the ability to create unambiguously female
characters, does not consistently do so. It is not, as O'Brien thinks,
because Proust's understanding of love is limited by his homosexuality, since sexual proclivity per se has nothing to do with the potential breadth and depth of one's human understanding.

A somewhat better reason for Albertine's sexual ambiguity is
given by Maurice Sachs: "Proust's heroine does not have a well-
defined sex: she is Love itself, and each reader can lend her the
image which is dearest to him."[14] This is true as far as it goes, and it
is likely that such open-endedness of characterization is part of
Proust's conscious intention (cf. 3: 910–11). But on the question of
gender Sachs's interpretation tells us, finally, only what Albertine is
not.

Eric Bentley, in a recent interview, comes closer to discovering what Albertine is:

Proust admitted to Gide that Albertine was modelled on a boy. He also said he wished he'd been bold enough to make her a boy. But are artists always the ultimate authority, the highest court of appeal, on their own work? I think Proust sold himself short there. Albertine is more of a creation than he's allowing. She may be "modelled on a man," but she still is *not* a man. There is *creativity* in the characterization. Proust is not so successful as Tennessee Williams in creating a woman, but it's too thoughtless just to say, well, since we have Proust's authority for it, we could call the character *Albert,* and it would make sense. It wouldn't. Proust has not tried to give the character what a man would have said and done on all occasions. Albertine is a creation of the imagination, not completely successful, and therefore not completely feminine, but, since it isn't completely masculine either, a sort of half-finished statue. Now even if Albertine is a man without a penis, that still isn't a woman. But it isn't Albertine either: she has positive feminine traits. . . . But I'm going to stop talking about this before I become hopelessly entangled in the words "masculine" and "feminine." [15]

It is possible, however, that Proust wants his readers and critics to do precisely what Bentley avoids doing: to become entangled in the concepts of "masculine" and "feminine." Or, to put it another way, perhaps Albertine and Proust's other ambiguous females are not, as is often supposed, unsuccessful attempts to deceive the readers of *A la recherche* about the nature of the author's sexual experience. Perhaps they are, on the contrary, a more truthful embodiment of that experience than would have been the case had Proust made them stereotypically male or female. And perhaps these characters are not the *pis aller* of a writer incapable of creating or understanding women. Perhaps they are, on the contrary, products of conscious artistry, carefully planned and executed to serve aesthetic goals more complex and far-ranging than have heretofore been imagined. These, at least, will be the contentions of the present study and specifically of the section of the fifth chapter entitled "The Androgynous Vision."

THE FREUDIAN FALLACY

Critics have generally assumed that once we have pointed out that Proust "is a pansy," we have said all that needs to be said about androgyny and sexual transposition in *A la recherche*. This is an odd trait in Proustian criticism, for in practically every other respect Proust's critics have been quick to praise, and even to overpraise, the careful, conscious design of Proust's novel. When it comes to Proust's homosexuality, however, we are told that Proust is now controlled by, rather than controlling, the material of his art, material which blurs his vision and causes certain characters to appear as "half-finished statues."

The longevity of this approach to Proust is in large measure due to the Freudian influence on literary criticism and on Proustian criticism in particular. Most of the writing which has been done about Proust's sexuality has been done either from an overtly Freudian perspective or with the Freudian position on human sexuality tacitly taken for granted. The result has been to obscure the complexities of Proust's experience and to oversimplify the relationship of his experience to his art.

As is well known, psychoanalysis holds that the creation of art is a symptom of neurosis. The artist creates in obedience to repressed, subconscious urges and in an attempt to compensate for various personality defects or traumata of early life. In the Freudian view the artist has very little conscious control over his choice of symbols and themes: they are dictated to him by his subconscious fears, desires, and aspirations. The Freudian position is one of psychological determinism. A failure to resolve the Oedipus complex, toilet training which comes too early or too late, a child's inadvertently spying on the "primal scene" of the parents in the act of sex—all of these early events can, in the Freudian scheme, leave an imprint on the subconscious which will determine not only the shape of one's personality but the course of one's entire life.

Freud assumed (an assumption which has since been discarded by many experimental psychologists) [16] that there is an innate instinct or drive which guides us toward heterosexuality and procreation. He also postulated various pitfalls which must be avoided if one is to reach this supposed goal of personality development. Among these pitfalls there is, above all, the Oedipus complex, in which the male child perceives his father as a rival for the affections of his mother. For a time the child will subconsciously desire to kill his father and marry his mother. But in a healthy development the child will pass through the Oedipal phase and find a substitute for his mother by taking another woman as wife.

The child is also said to evolve through various stages of sexual organization: first an "oral," then an "anal" stage, in which the erotic interest is focused on the mouth and the anus respectively. From the oral and anal stages he goes on to the "phallic" stage. Then, after a period of "latency," his interest turns to members of the opposite sex, and he is ready to procreate.

According to Freudian theory most people retain some vestiges of the early stages of development. The desire to kiss, for instance, is an extension of the pleasure derived from breast-feeding in the oral stage. When development is arrested in one of the early stages, however, the result is neurosis and a pathological personality structure. If one fails to grow out of or reverts to the anal stage, for example, he develops an "anal personality" and may become miserly and overly fastidious. Such an anal personality forever repeats the pattern of his early toilet training, compulsively trying to clean himself and hoarding his money the way he once wanted to hoard his childish feces.[17]

If a child fails to resolve the Oedipus complex and remains intimately attached to his mother, he is likely to develop a homosexual orientation. In this case he may be compulsively repeating any of several early patterns. Indeed, the Freudian theory of homosexuality has, as C. A. Tripp points out, "interchangeable parts that can be rearranged to 'explain' any instance one might encounter." And Tripp continues:

Thus, it is still widely believed that a boy turns out to be homosexual when he identifies with his mother and becomes effeminate. . . . Or, by identifying with his mother, he later wants to repeat the joys he experienced with her by choosing boys whom he can treat as his mother treated him. Or without identifying with her at all, his wish to have sex with his mother becomes transformed into a wish to enjoy the kind of sex she enjoys. Or maybe he is really heterosexual after all, but is in love with his mother and wants to stay true to her, so he gives up all other women. Or simply by loving her too much he can have his sexuality prematurely aroused at a time when it has nowhere to go but toward other boys. Or if she is a mean mother, he comes to hate her, ever afterward disliking and distrusting all women. Or whether he loves her or hates her, on discovering she has no penis he develops a "castration complex" that forces him to turn to other males in a need for sex-with-safety. . . .[18]

These are some of the ideas which Freudian psychology has developed concerning the causes and nature of homosexuality. And they have, of course, filtered down by now to popular thinking, where, as Tripp says, "they continue to satisfy the curiosity of the unwary."

The trouble with the Freudian ideas is that they are based more on theory than on empirical observation. There is not, and there never has been, any satisfactory proof that homosexuality is caused by the influence of a dominant mother or that it is accompanied by identity problems, a flight from the opposite sex, or any of the other traditional Freudian notions.

One famous study by Irving Bieber and associates claimed to offer clinical proof of the Freudian position.[19] In this study Bieber and associates examined 106 psychiatric patients who were homosexually inclined. They concluded that such people generally have a family history containing a "detached-hostile father" and a "close-binding-intimate mother." Bieber's study, however, has been discredited. Its methods of research are faulty and its scope severely limited. Wainwright Churchill writes:

From a study of only 106 individuals, all of whom are seriously neurotic and most of whom represent a highly select population in a number of other important respects, we can hardly feel certain that these generalizations may be applied to every individual who is homosexually oriented. . . . When, in addition, these generalizations seem to have little or no applicability to a number of important data on homosexuality—consider, for example, their lack of relevance to the homosexual behavior of subhuman primates and other of the lower mammals—we are forced to be skeptical of them. . . . Nor can we see any general applicability of the factors stressed in the Bieber study to the homosexuality of most non-Judaeo-Christian peoples. To imagine, for example, that all Siwian males participate in homosexual relations and enjoy them because of the damaging effects of a relationship with a detached-hostile father and close-binding-intimate mother is a bit strained.

It may be, Churchill says, that the Freudian explanation of homosexuality has "limited applicability in certain isolated instances." But the Bieber study fails to produce satisfactory proof of even this limited applicability. Churchill concludes that "the assumption that homosexuality is but a symptom of some pervasive disturbance within the total personality and that homosexual interests can only develop in a pathogenic context is based, no doubt, upon the fact that homosexuality is studied by clinicians in people who are, in fact, neurotic and emotionally upset."[20]

Bieber also claimed in his study that homosexuality could be cured with the methods of psychoanalysis. When challenged by Wardell Pomeroy (an associate of Dr. Alfred C. Kinsey) to produce tangible proof of cured homosexuality, Bieber finally, as C. A. Tripp relates, "confessed to Pomeroy that he had only one case which he thought would qualify but that, unfortunately, he was on such bad terms with the patient he did not feel free to call him up." And Tripp continues:

One possible case?—then what about his 358-page book claiming from 19 to 50 percent cures? Whether or not it qualifies as an outright misrepresentation is, in part, a matter of definition. The psychiatrist did not actually say in his much-quoted book that he, personally, had cured anybody, nor did he claim to have actually seen or personally examined anybody else's successful results. There were numerous implications of a firsthand knowledge, to be sure (along with elaborate statistical citations) but legalistically speaking, the psychiatrist was, and is, in the clear.[21]

The Bieber study, in short, illustrates how Freudianism often operates as a self-fulfilling prophecy, discovering only what it has decided in advance it will discover. Bieber and his associates try to prove, among other things, that homosexuality is a pathological condition; so they conveniently choose their subjects from among psychiatric patients who have, in the first place, a history of serious psychological maladjustment. Obviously in its choice of this particular study group the Bieber research assumes what it sets out to prove, namely, that homosexuality and neurosis are directly related. It then adds another loop to the circular reasoning by surmising that since homosexuality is a psychological illness and since psychiatry is in the business of curing psychological illnesses, then psychiatry must be able to cure homosexuality. The fact that there are no convincing data to support any of Bieber's conclusions does nothing to temper the authoritative tone with which they are put forward.

But the surest indication of the scientific bankruptcy of the

Bieber study and of the Freudian position in general is, as Churchill points out, their total lack of relevance to cross-species and cross-cultural data on homosexuality. It would be ridiculous to argue that cultures which accept and encourage homosexuality do so because all members of those cultures have undergone injurious parental influences. Furthermore—and contrary to popular belief—homosexuality is a regular occurrence among animals. In a chapter called "The Phylogenetic Basis of Homosexuality" Churchill summarizes an extensive body of research documenting homosexual behavior "among monkeys, dogs, bulls, rats, porcupines, guinea pigs, goats, horses, donkeys, elephants, hyenas, bats, mice, lions, rabbits, cats, raccoons, baboons, apes, and porpoises."[22] Are we to assume the existence of close-binding-intimate porcupine mothers and detached-hostile porpoise fathers? Or of young lions who introject the image of their mother and thereby become effeminate sexual inverts? Hardly. The fact is that homosexuality is a perennial adjunct of mammalian sexuality, neither a pathological condition nor a biological perversion. It has always existed, both among humans and among animals; and no doubt it always will exist. It cannot, of course, be cured, because it is not an illness in the first place. "Over the years," writes C. A. Tripp, "there have been literally dozens of second-party accounts of 'cured' homosexuality. . . . they very often appear, but without the presence of the elusive beast."[23] This does not mean, of course, that once homosexual, always homosexual; as George Weinberg points out, one may have a homosexual orientation "for a minute, an hour, a day, or a lifetime."[24] It simply means that to attempt to eradicate behavior that is natural and universal is both irrational and self-defeating.

Why has the Freudian view of homosexuality persisted for so long in psychiatric circles and in popular opinion? Perhaps because it helps to support, in the name of science, the social status quo. The onus of guilt in the Freudian drama of homosexuality consistently falls on a domineering mother, a detached father, or both at the same time. By portraying the assertive female as a symptom of incipient pathology, Freudianism neatly reinforces the sexual prejudices of Western society: in a healthy situation, according to psychoanalysis, the female is passive, not domineering. The Freudian view that healthy sexual development involves a teleological progress toward heterosexuality also lends obvious support to the cultural and moral biases of the Judaeo-Christian tradition.

The Freudian theory of homosexuality is useful to the social establishment, because it bestows the blessings of science on long-established cultural standards and thereby helps to ensure their survival. It defines disease as deviation from the standard, and treatment consists of attempts to alter the subject's behavior and attitude to accord with those of the presumed majority. From an objective, scientific point of view, however, the Freudian approach to homosexuality has little to recommend it. Indeed, C. A. Tripp claims that the recent discoveries of empirical psychology and sex research have led to "the utter embarrassment of every formal psychiatric theory [of homosexuality] without exception."[25] Not that we have now replaced a body of myths with a body of inalterable truths. The progress of knowledge is unfortunately not that simple. We have a great many new facts about homosexuality, but the way we collect and juxtapose those facts raises its own problems of interpretation. Many things about homosexuality—and heterosexuality—remain mysterious. But we have at least recognized the flaws in the Freudian view, and that view is slowly being abandoned by those who used to propound it most vociferously.[26] Recently, for instance, the American Psychiatric Association reversed a position it had held since its very inception and removed homosexuality from its list of mental disorders.[27]

PROUST'S SEXUALITY AND FREUDIAN CRITICISM

Proust's life fits a good many of the Freudian stereotypes of homosexuality. Several of Proust's friends found an air of the feminine about him. And though he obviously loved and respected his father, he was, as is well known, much closer to his mother. When around the age of thirteen or fourteen Proust was asked on a questionnaire, "Your idea of misery?," he responded, "Being separated from Mother."[28]

Proust's relationship to his mother was exceptionally deep and intimate, becoming, at times, stormy and ambivalent, with quarrels and reconciliations worthy of a pair of bickering lovers. He seems, moreover, to have regarded his homosexuality as a betrayal of his mother's image of him. In the discussion of homosexuality at the beginning of *Sodome et Gomorrhe,* homosexually oriented men are described as "sons without mothers, to whom they are obliged to lie all their life long and even in the hour when they close her eyes" (2: 615).

Most critics assume that the scene of the good-night kiss in the *Combray* section of *Du côté de chez Swann* is based upon Proust's real-life relationship to his own mother. In this scene the young narrator is made to go to bed without the customary kiss from his mother, who is entertaining M. Swann downstairs. But the boy finds that he cannot get to sleep without the peace and security provided by his mother's presence. He rebels against his parents, causing them finally to capitulate. As a result the mother does more than simply kiss her son good night: she spends the night in his room, while the father goes to bed alone.

Freudian critics have made the scene of the good-night kiss into a locus classicus of the Oedipus complex in literature, and the Freudian interpretation of the scene has contributed greatly to the widespread conception of Proust as the typical homosexual "mama's boy." The narrator of *A la recherche* is, of course, presented as heterosexually inclined. But to critics steeped in Freud it has seemed all too obvious that Proust's homosexuality stems from a real-life relationship to just such a "close-binding-intimate" mother and "detached-hostile" father. Milton Miller has given us the full Freudian line in his *Nostalgia: A Psychoanalytic Study of Marcel Proust.*

Proust's homosexuality, Miller writes, "definitely seems related to the pattern of a love he felt toward his beautiful, sensitive, somewhat nervous and domineering mother. This love was unbearable, partly because of jealous rivalries (with the father at the most repressed level, with his brother on a more conscious or preconscious level). The torments of this love resulted in introjection of his mother image, identification with her femininity, her sensitivity, ambition and talent." At a later point Miller discusses "the father's frequent absences which left [Proust] mainly female images with which to identify." This, according to Miller, "upset his development and prevented masculine identification." So when Proust fell in love with other males, he was motivated by a desire to love them as his mother loved him; he was, Miller states, "emotionally like a domineering woman with a younger one."[29]

Miller's formulations make sense only if we grant the Freudian view that homosexuality results from identification with a woman, arrested development, and Oedipal identity conflicts. But we cannot grant Miller that view, because he gives us no good reason for granting it: he simply appeals to Freudian tradition, as if that tradition represented a body of unquestioned and unquestionable fact. It is true that Proust admired his mother and was very close to her (this does not mean, however, that he had an Oedipus complex). It is also true that Proust had a homosexual orientation, at least during certain periods of his life. But Miller does not supply enough epistemological grounding to establish a convincing cause-and-effect relationship between these two facts, especially since the Oedipus complex is a theoretical construct whose existence has never been proved. Miller's reasoning is circular (Proust was homosexual, he therefore had an Oedipus complex that caused his homosexuality), and it does not get us very far. Nonetheless, Miller's interpretation of Proust's sexuality, possibly because it offers simple answers to some very complex questions, continues to be widely read and widely echoed in Proustian criticism (a French translation of Miller's book appeared in 1977).[30]

George Painter, in his biography of Proust, also finds no explanation for Proust's sexuality but the Freudian one. Of Proust's mother Painter observes that "her blood made him a tribesman of Abraham, her overanxious love a native of the Cities of the Plain."[31] Painter's often acute analysis of Proust's life is marred by this simple faith in the dicta of psychoanalysis. There is a well-known and perhaps apocryphal story that Proust frequented a Paris brothel where he paid to watch rats tortured and killed by young men of the working classes. After arguing that the story is true Painter explains its meaning with the assertion that "rats . . . are regarded with special libido and dread by homosexuals as emblems of anal aggression and anal birth."[32]

Painter thus asks us to believe that all homosexually oriented men harbor a fear of rats. But the idea is based on a quadruple absurdity: (1) The assumption that one can generalize about all homosexually oriented men (2) The assumption that the fear of rats is more acute among, or more characteristic of, homosexually oriented men than other human beings (3) The assumption that rats automatically suggest "anal aggression" and "anal birth" to a homosexually oriented man (4) The assumption that homosexuality always revolves around an interest in or a fixation on the anus. Painter offers no evidence to support any of these ideas, which are nothing more than a free fantasy on certain Freudian myths and stereotypes. The passage rivals even Ernest Jones's insistence in his psychoanalytic study of *Hamlet* that Claudius's murder of the king is a "homosexual assault," because to Shakespeare's subconscious mind the king's ear represents the king's anus.[33]

Throughout these psychoanalytic interpretations of Proust's homosexuality runs the characteristic Freudian determinism: the conviction that Proust, simply because he has homosexual tastes, is compelled to act according to certain stereotyped patterns from which he is incapable of diverging. His image of love, we are told, is the image automatically produced by someone with a homosexual orientation. "Under the name of love," writes J.-B. Boulanger, "Marcel Proust described nothing but a guilty sexual inversion. Love as he understands it and as it is practiced by his heroes always presents homosexual characteristics: a fundamental narcissism, dissociation between tenderness and physical desire, morbid jealousy, absence of woman and permanence of the mother figure."[34] For Edmund Bergler the cruelty and suffering of Proustian love are projections of Proust's "oral-masochistic" tendencies, tendencies of which "Proust's *homosexuality* in itself was a proof." And Bergler continues:

All homosexuals labor—as pointed out in *Neurotic Counterfeit-Sex*—under the "mechanism of orality," the tripartite unconscious process in which an individual misuses a reality situation (or creates one to order) so that he can appear to be unjustly treated, retaliates with pseudo-aggression which will rebound to his own disadvantage, and then concludes on a note of profound self-pity. In the homosexual, and in the homosexual *specifically*, this mechanism is strongly accentuated by the presence of an enormous narcissistic substructure. It is the combination of overwhelming narcissism with oral-masochistic regression that makes the homosexual.[35]

Oral-masochistic regression? But we have just been instructed by George Painter that men with homosexual inclinations labor under *anal* fears and compulsions and that it is this which explains Proust's sadomasochism. In Freudian criticism, as in psychoanalysis itself, the parts of the theory can be subjectively rearranged to serve any argument the theorist wishes to make. But whatever the specific contentions of Freudian criticism, the image of the homosexually oriented artist is usually the same. He has no individuality and no originality: he belongs to a subcategory of the mentally ill, and his view of life is the same as that of all other people with homosexual tastes. He has, furthermore, no artistic free will: his characters, situations, and symbols are dictated to him by his abnormal psyche and are, in fact, predictable to the psychoanalytic observer (though the predictions are conveniently made, of course, after the fact).

Thus Milton Miller asserts that Proust creates androgynous characters because "he wanted to assure himself that women had phalluses and men were really not potent; then he could identify, safely, with either one, and there was no danger of impregnating or being made pregnant, no identification with the completely submissive women or sadistically domineering men."[36] But another Freudian critic draws upon psychoanalysis to argue precisely the opposite. For Lisa Appignanesi Proust's Albertine is not a disguised homosexual lover or androgynous in any way. She is an image of the eternal feminine, and the proof is that in the affair of the narrator and Albertine:

The rhythm of the mother-son relationship has been transposed to the rhythm of the lovers. This, in itself, would seem to imply that Proust desires to make Albertine a woman and not a disguised homosexual lover. It is only the woman who can incorporate the maternal role. The homosexual lover is, rather, an extension of the male: in his love object he is seeking for himself and in this other male, he loves himself. As Freud tells us, inverts 'proceed from a narcissistic basis and look for a young man who resembles themselves and whom they love as their mother loved them'. Marcel may have narcissistic tendencies, but Proust reveals how this pattern of narcissism is broken up by the very fact of a heterosexual relationship [with Albertine].[37]

Appignanesi is obviously unaware of the recent body of research that suggests, as C. A. Tripp puts it, that "notions to the effect that the homosexual is looking for some 'narcissistic' reflection of his own image are as mythical as was Narcissus himself."[38] Once we break free of stereotyped modes of thinking, common sense tells us that homosexual love is no more narcissistic in and of itself than heterosexual love. A man can be attracted to a man who seems in every way his opposite, just as a man can be attracted to a woman who seems to be his equal and his double. And in both cases, of course, there can be admixtures of feelings and multiple motivations. Freudian theory disregards these complexities of real life in its desire to fit all cases of homosexual (and heterosexual) love into mythological prototypes and rigid theoretical categories. The literary criticism engendered by this theory is, at best, a mass of tangled syllogisms; at worst, a welter of self-contradictions. It illuminates little and ignores much about human sexuality and its role in Proust.

To mention a final example, we constantly hear from Freudian critics about the "passivity" of Proust's personality and writing. The reasoning is: (1) Homosexually oriented men have feminine personalities. (2) The feminine personality is a passive personality. (3) Proust, being homosexually oriented, has a passive approach to experience and to art. Lisa Appignanesi states that "Freud marks passivity as one of the chief elements in the make-up of the feminine principle and he is seconded in this by a host of later psychologists. It would appear from this that there is a certain validity in using the term 'feminine' in referring to Proust or Marcel when proof of a refined sensibility and a passive nature can easily be found throughout Proust's biography and A la recherche."[39] Similarly, Milton Miller holds that "something happened, in Proust's development, to impede his masculine, procreative function. . . . We note the passivity in his writing, typified in the description of the three steeples and three trees, where movement is the result of his being drawn along in a carriage, seeing stationary objects which appear to change their own positions."[40]

Such analyses overlook an extremely important, perhaps the most important, dimension of Proust's aesthetic philosophy. In A la recherche Proust's narrator sets out to do nothing less than recreate the world of his experience in a monumental undertaking which will at once record, interpret, and transform the world he has known. The task will require an aggressive assault on reality and a heroic challenge to time and to death. It will, moreover, demand long periods of labor and vast amounts of energy. At Balbec the painter Elstir tells the narrator that "we are not given wisdom; we must discover it on our own, after a long journey which no one else can take for us, which

no one can spare us" (1: 864). The novel to which this advice ultimately leads will, the narrator says, be "long in the writing. The most
I could hope for would be a little sleep during the day. If I worked, it
would be only at night. But I would need many nights, perhaps a
hundred, perhaps a thousand" (3: 1,043).

Is this the typical "passivity" of homosexuality? The narrator
makes it clear that his novel will have to be the product of, among
other things, demonic industry and tenacious self-dedication. Gilles
Deleuze points out that "the *Recherche* is not simply an effort of
remembering, an exploration of memory: *recherche* ['research,'
'quest'] must be taken in the vigorous sense, as in the expression 'the
quest for truth.' "[41] And Serge Doubrovsky writes at the beginning of
another recent book on Proust: "I believe Proust has been . . . made
too aseptic. I would like to give him back his aggressive charge, re-
store to him his violence."[42] The quest, the search, the aggressive
charge, the violent assault on reality are just as important to Proust's
aesthetic as are "passive" contemplation and "involuntary" memory.
But this is something we would never know if we heeded only those
who portray Proust in Freudian stereotypes of "passivity" and "femininity."

The Freudian approach to Proust's sexuality has had a long and
not very profitable run; to pursue the Freudian line further could
only add to the general clutter of distortions and falsifications. It is
time for Proustian criticism to move on to areas which offer greater
possibilities for the discovery of meaning: to cross-cultural and cross-
species data on homosexuality; to the discoveries of empirical sex
research; to Proust's remarks about his plans for dealing with the
theme; and to a close consideration of the biographical, historical, and
cultural context in which those plans took shape.

THE THEME OF HOMOSEXUALITY

Proust is a novelist who transforms his homosexual experience into
art, and this fact must be reckoned with in any assessment of his genius. Many of the major and minor characters of *A la recherche*—
Charlus, Saint-Loup, Morel, the Prince de Guermantes, Jupien, Le-
grandin, Nissim Bernard—turn out to have homosexual tastes. And

lesbianism is, of course, one of the narrator's major preoccupations: he spends nearly a third of the great novel pondering the implications of female homosexuality and trying to discover whether Albertine has ever loved other women. Surrounding the homosexual experiences of these characters are complex and influential theories of homosexuality, which need to be evaluated in their own right.

Some critics have been offended by the presence of so much homosexuality in Proust's novel and have complained about Proust's penchant for "tainting" his characters with unconventional sexual tastes. This is, to some, a near-fatal blow to the novel's verisimilitude and attractiveness as work of art. One common criticism asserts that homosexuality is simply not as widespread as its proliferation in A la recherche suggests. If Kinsey is correct in his finding that 50 percent of the male population has a history of homosexual feelings or behavior (and many sex researchers think he is correct), this argument is untenable on the very grounds of verisimilitude from which it is proffered. But the criticism is questionable in any case, since a writer of fiction is not under any obligation to maintain a strict one-to-one correspondence between the world as it is and the world he creates in his fiction. Proust often has his own special reasons for distorting this or that aspect of reality, and true or false does not always equal good or bad in a work of literature. A second criticism, related to the first, involves a matter of taste. This second criticism asserts that A la recherche is a bad book in proportion to its homosexual content—not that it describes more homosexuality than actually exists but that it commits the sin of dwelling on a subject that is distasteful to the critic in question. These two objections are not always clearly disentangled in the minds of those who make them. Both, for instance, seem to be present in A. L. Rowse's complaint about the "too large place homosexuality occupies as the work unfolds" and his assertion that "if Proust had been able to accept homosexuality easily and naturally, it would have fallen into place."[43]

These ideas have received a serious hearing only because they appeal to a Western cultural bias of puritanism and of homophobia (the irrational fear and rejection of homosexual experience and homosexually oriented people). No one has ever criticized Proust, or any other author, for putting too much heterosexual love into a novel.

The other complaint is equally absurd and equally irrelevant. It is made by critics who have refused to look below the surface of the narrative to see what Proust is doing with the theme.

A few critics have even wondered out loud whether *A la recherche* might not have been a better book without any mention of homosexuality at all. Jocelyn Brooke writes:

if Proust's treatment of sex had been as orthodox as that of, say, Galsworthy, *A la Recherche du Temps Perdu* would still remain a great novel; for that matter, when one compares *Swann* and the *Jeunes Filles*—in which the theme of homosexuality remains latent—with the shoddiness of the later volumes, one is inclined to wonder whether it might not, in fact, have been even greater. True, it is hard to imagine *A la Recherche* without Charlus; yet it is at least arguable that, if Proust had made Charlus a womanizer, and Albertine a perfectly normal heterosexual girl, the novel would have been, *qua* novel, neither better nor worse than it is.[44]

This is a statement with which Proust would have strongly disagreed. Proust's correspondence shows that he regarded the treatment of homosexuality in *A la recherche* as inseparable from—indeed, as undergirding—both the long-range structure and the principal aesthetic objectives of the novel.

Be that as it may, Proust received complaints about the presence of homosexuality in his work from the time of its first publication. When the poet and novelist Francis Jammes read *Du côté de chez Swann,* he was so shocked by the scene of lesbian love that he urged Proust to remove it from his book. Jammes's particular bias was religious. After Proust's death Jammes wrote to a friend: "Proust died, a man for whom I had been taking communion and praying for several months. He had for my work in general and for my *Mémoires* in particular an unbounded admiration. But, alas, I could not return that admiration in kind, because the virtues he possessed were spoiled by a kind of complaisance for certain morals he depicted. For people of my sort this kind of thing produces an insurmountable malaise. . . . What Saint Paul calls an abomination and consigns to hell remains for me an abomination."[45]

When the critic Paul Souday also objected to certain "gloomy" and "useless" scenes in *Du côté de chez Swann,* he provoked a letter from Proust defending the presence of homosexuality in the first volume of the novel. The letter has become a classic, and it is one of the sources most frequently quoted by critics interested in showing the control Proust exercises over his wide-ranging artistic materials. That Proust here offers his treatment of homosexuality as an example of that control is a fact whose implications have been too often ignored. Proust wrote to Souday:

> My composition is veiled and all the less quickly perceptible in that it develops on a large scale (excuse the style, for a long time I have not even had the strength to sign a dedication, my first interminable letter feels the effects of my fatigue); but in order to see how rigorous it is, I have only to recall one of your reviews, ill founded in my estimation, where you censured certain gloomy and useless scenes in *Swann*. If it was a question, in your mind, of a scene between two girls (M. Francis Jammes ardently begged me to remove it from my book), it was, indeed, "useless" in the first volume. But its remembrance is the foundation of volumes IV and V (through the jealousy it inspires, etc.). In suppressing this scene, I would not have changed very much in the first volume; I would have, in return, because of the interdependence of the parts, caused two entire volumes, of which this scene is the cornerstone, to fall down around the reader's ears.[46]

This remark is typical of Proust's attitude toward the role of homosexuality in his masterpiece. It was, for him, a theme of capital importance, one on which he lavished a great deal of careful reflection and painstaking craftsmanship. There is, in fact, evidence which suggests that *A la recherche* began as a nonfiction essay on homosexuality, which gradually grew into a novel, as Proust saw broader and broader implications in his subject. We shall examine that evidence later on. For now it is sufficient to emphasize the disparity between Proust's own statements about the importance of homosexuality in his work and the condescending treatment critics have sometimes accorded the theme.

Proust lived, of course, in an era when any mention of homosexuality was likely to produce a shocking effect, and he feared that his readers and critics might be so appalled by their initial encounter with homosexuality in *A la recherche* that they would not go on to perceive the aesthetic importance of the theme. Consequently, he wrote many letters in which he tried to pave the way for the revelations of *Sodome et Gomorrhe*, announcing to friends and potential publishers that the later volumes of *A la recherche* would explore in detail the delicate subject which makes a brief appearance in *Du côté de chez Swann*. In November of 1912, a year before the publication of *Du côté de chez Swann* by Grasset, Proust wrote such a letter to Gaston Gallimard, the man who was eventually to become his publisher. In the letter Proust warned Gallimard that homosexuality would take on increasing importance in the later volumes of the novel, and he made one of the first allusions on record to the character who was to become M. de Charlus. Proust wrote, in part:

Since I have written you such a long letter and since it fatigues me to write too often, I would like very much . . . to tell you about the shocking things in the second volume. . . . At the end of the first volume (third part) you will see a M. de Fleurus (or de Guray, I have changed the names several times), who has already been vaguely discussed as the supposed lover of Mme Swann. But, as in life, where reputations are often false and where it takes a long time to know people, only in the second volume will it be seen that the old gentleman is not the lover of Mme Swann but a pederast. He is a type of character I think is rather new, the virile pederast, in love with virility, detesting effeminate young men, detesting, to tell the truth, all young men, as men who have suffered from women are misogynists. This character is so scattered through absolutely different parts that the volume has in no way the appearance of a special monograph, such as the *Lucien* of Binet-Valmer, for example. . . . Moreover, there is no coarse exposition. In sum, you can rest assured that the metaphysical and moral point of view predominates throughout the work. But in the end this old gentleman will be seen picking up a concierge and keeping a pianist. I prefer to warn you in advance about everything that could discourage you.[47]

Proust is very diplomatic on the subject of homosexuality in his unpublished novel. He tells Gallimard that even though the theme is a shocking one, it is not handled with "coarse exposition" (and this is, of course, true). He is also careful to point out that he does not use homosexuality simply for its shock value, and to this end he shows how the homosexual motif relates directly to other recurrent ideas of the novel: the now well-known Proustian concepts (here greatly simplified) that "reputations are often false" and that "it takes a long time to know people." He assures Gallimard, in other words, that homosexuality, though it is an important theme, is only one theme among many and that all the themes are interdependent. Indeed, says Proust, the fact that the novel discusses homosexuality does nothing to alter the fact that "the metaphysical and moral point of view predominates throughout." Most significantly, perhaps, Proust shows that although he is aware that there will be resistance to any novel which accords a major role to homosexuality, he has no intention of changing his plans for the theme. Proust simply warns Gallimard of what is to come; he does not ask whether it will be acceptable or whether it might be advisable to change it in some way to facilitate publication.

We should bear in mind, in order to appreciate the delicacy of Proust's position, that he is at this time a nearly unknown writer with little literary influence, casting around for a publisher for a strange, new, and (in Proust's own word) "shocking" work. By emphasizing to Gallimard the homosexual dimension of his novel Proust is taking a calculated risk. It could be that Gallimard would think such a work too hot to handle and immediately lose interest. But a part of Proust's strategy in his overture to Gallimard is to exploit the recent exposure given homosexuality in works such as Binet-Valmer's *Lucien,* a novel which attracted a great deal of attention and unleashed a furor of denunciation in the French press. Proust hopes to stimulate Gallimard's interest in *A la recherche* by pointing out that his novel will also treat this controversial theme but, Proust emphasizes, in a unique and original way. Obviously Proust is aware that the pendulum of official and public taste can swing either way with respect to homosexuality and that the reception of *A la recherche* can suffer for it. Even so, he makes it clear to Gallimard that his plans for the novel have crystallized and that homosexuality is there to stay.

Proust had, as the letter to Gallimard testifies, a keen sensitivity to literary timing and literary politics. Nine years later, when Proust was the respected and lionized winner of the Prix Goncourt, we find that sensitivity emerging once again. By this time the book-publishing arm of the *Nouvelle Revue Française* under the direction of Gaston Gallimard was bringing out Proust's immense novel in a gradual succession of volumes. On 30 April 1921 the *NRF* issued a book containing the second part of *Le Côté de Guermantes* and the first part of *Sodome et Gomorrhe.* Up until this point in *A la recherche* the homosexual theme, aside from the lesbian scene in *Du côté de chez Swann,* had lain more or less dormant. But in *Sodome et Gomorrhe I* the narrator discovers the homosexuality of the Baron de

Charlus, a discovery which drastically alters his perception of Charlus's character and of society at large. *Sodome I* also contains the narrator's famous essay on the nature of homosexual love, an essay which many critics have seen as both an indirect confession of Proust's own homosexual tastes and a covert plea for understanding and tolerance of the homosexual way of life.

The appearance of *Sodome I* was, then, an event charged with profound artistic and personal meaning for Proust. He did not let it pass without writing another apologia for homosexuality as a literary theme. It has been truthfully said that Proust, even when he writes about other authors, is really writing about himself. And this is in many ways true of Proust's article "A propos de Baudelaire," published in the *Nouvelle Revue Française* in June of 1921, only a month after the publication of *Sodome I*. The Baudelaire article was cleverly timed. For although Proust discusses several ideas in his evaluation of the great poet who was in many ways his precursor, he accords a central place to Baudelaire's fascination with homosexuality. Proust writes:

When *Les Fleurs du mal* appeared, Sainte-Beuve wrote naively to Baudelaire that the collected poems produced "an altogether different effect." This effect, which seems favorable to the critic of the *Lundis*, is frightening and grandiose to anyone who, like those of my generation, knew *Les Fleurs du mal* only in its expurgated edition. Certainly we knew that Baudelaire had written the "Femmes damnées" and we had read them. But we thought this was not only a forbidden but also a different kind of work. Many other poets have also had their secret little publications. Who has not read the two volumes by Verlaine—which are as bad as the "Femmes damnées" are beautiful—entitled *Hommes* and *Femmes?* And at school the pupils passed around works of pure pornography they thought were by Alfred de Musset, though I haven't thought since to check to see whether the attribution is justified. It is an altogether different case with the "Femmes damnées." Looking into an edition of Baudelaire which is faithful to the first edition (for example, the *Baudelaire* of M. Féli Gautier), those who were not in the know are stunned to see that the rawest, most licentious pieces about love between women are to be found there, and that in his brilliant innocence the great Poet assigned in his book as much importance to a piece such as the "Delphine" as to the "Voyage" itself. . . .

[It is true] that these magnificent pieces, when added to the others, produce, as Sainte-Beuve wrote, not knowing how truly he spoke, an "altogether different effect." They take their place among the greatest poems of the book, like lofty, crystal waves which rise up majestically after evening storms and broaden with their intercalated summits the immense tableau of the sea. Our emotion is heightened still further when we learn that these pieces were not simply assigned an importance equal to the others but that for Baudelaire they were the most important pieces, so much so that he wanted at first to call the whole book not *Les Fleurs du mal* but *Les Lesbiennes*.[48]

Just as Proust himself, we might add, assigned either the title or the subtitle *Sodome et Gomorrhe* to three volumes out of the seven which comprise *A la recherche du temps perdu*.[49]

Proust's treatment of homosexuality is analogous to Baudelaire's and is subject to the same sorts of misunderstanding.[50] It does not represent a scandalous diversion, an irrelevant digression, a vulgar caprice in a writer otherwise serious and profound. Homosexuality, in Proust as in Baudelaire, is integrally related to the overall enterprise of artistic creation, and in both cases that enterprise cannot be fully understood without understanding the role of homosexuality within it. In both Proust and Baudelaire we confront passages which seem at first mutually exclusive. In Baudelaire the homosexual love of "Lesbos" and the "Femmes damnées" stands on equal footing with the sublime aesthetic summa of "Le Voyage." In Proust outrageously prancing *tantes* and bizarre activities in male brothels vie for attention with the metaphorical visions of an Elstir and the anagogic flights of a Vinteuil. And Proust insists in his correspondence and suggests in his article on Baudelaire that it is all an organic whole.

There is, in fact, a sense in which the theme of homosexuality implies *A la recherche* and *A la recherche* implies the theme of homosexuality. How we get from one to the other is a question Proustian criticism has never answered—or really even asked. It is the fundamental question posed by this study.

CHAPTER TWO

THE PRIVATE LIFE
OF A GENIUS

—For what fault have you most toleration?
—For the private life of geniuses.

*T*HE YOUNG Proust's answer to the question about tolerance on Antoinette Faure's questionnaire seems not only precocious (Proust was at this time in his early or mid teens) but strangely prophetic, both of the genius he was to become and of the highly unconventional private life in which his genius would be nurtured. The principal elements of the Proustian mythology are, of course, well known: the cork-lined room, the upside-down schedule of sleeping all day and working all night, the fur coat in which the asthmatic invalid bundled up in even the sultriest weather. And we have also heard of furtive excursions into the byways of sexual pleasure, into male brothels where the bizarre was the commonplace and where Proust supposedly organized and witnessed spectacles of sadism. "Proust," asked his friend Paul Morand in a poetic apostrophe, "to what revels do you go by night / That you return with eyes so tired and lucid?"[1]

For a long time it was fashionable to pretend that Proust's life is irrelevant to his art, and one mark of the astute Proustian critic was thought to be the extent to which the critic was able to avoid biographical references.[2] This odd state of affairs arose partly from the influence of Proust's idea that art issues from a hidden, creative self and not from the everyday, social self[3] and partly from the influence of New Criticism and other critical schools which held that literary meaning resides in the text itself and not in the history, the culture, or the biography which surround it. It is also possible that certain critics avoided biographical inquiry because of the scandalous things it could reveal about homosexuality and its relation to Proust's art, a topic with which Proustian criticism has traditionally felt uncomfortable.

But it is, of course, naive to suppose that a writer's life and art are not related to each other. Proust himself used biographical materials in his criticism, though he excoriated Sainte-Beuve for doing the same thing.[4] Proust probably overstated his arguments against biographical criticism in order to emphasize that his own writing, though it is at times autobiographical, is at other times fictional. But whether we are dealing with fiction or with thinly disguised autobiography—and in A la recherche we have to deal with both—we naturally want to know what kind of man wrote Proust's novel and what kind of personal experience went into it. As Maurice Bardèche asks, "How can we account for the genius of Marcel Proust without beginning with the sensibility of Marcel Proust, in order to show how it became thought?"[5]

Since the publication of George Painter's biography of Proust, a great deal of additional biographical material has come to light. New letters have been found and published, new reminiscences have appeared, and smaller-scale biographical studies have been attempted. The purpose of this chapter is to review and reinterpret what is known about Proust's sexuality and to flesh out the story by adding to it material that has recently become available. We shall see in this chapter that in order to discuss the question of love in A la recherche a firm grasp on the relevant facts of Proust's life is indispensable. But we shall also see that biographical criticism has its own special problems and limitations.

These problems and limitations are especially acute in Proust's case, since anyone who studies Proust's life eventually realizes that what Proust says about his character Morel is also true of Proust himself: "He resembled an old book of the Middle Ages, full of errors, of absurd traditions, of obscenities; he was extraordinarily composite" (2: 1,032). And at another point: "His nature was, in truth, like a piece of paper folded so many times and in so many directions that it would be impossible ever to straighten it out" (2: 1,034). Complicating the problems posed by Proust's multifarious personality is the fact that some of the stories told and retold about Proust—his sadism in male brothels, his profanation of his mother's picture—have obvious analogues in A *la recherche,* raising the possibility that these stories were inspired by fictions in the novel rather than actual events in Proust's life. Did Proust write about such things because he really did them? Did he write about them precisely because he would not do them? Or did he perhaps both do them and write about them? How do we distinguish between the facts of the man's life and the legends the work has helped to create?

Very often it is not possible to distinguish. But the question of Proust's private life and its bearing on his art is nonetheless important. The legends that have gathered around Proust and his novel, regardless of whether or not they are true, tell us something about what Proust and A *la recherche* have come to symbolize for later generations. Legends do not have to be true in order to be interpreted. And the legends surrounding Proust's sexuality are in special need of reinterpretation.

A DUEL FROM AN OPERETTA BY OFFENBACH

That Proust was homosexually inclined there can be little doubt. He seems to have confessed as much to André Gide in a conversation which Gide recorded in his *Journal* and which has since become a celebrated literary anecdote:

> . . . as soon as I arrived [Proust began] talking with me about homosexuality. . . .
> Far from denying or hiding his homosexuality, he flaunts it, and, I could almost sáy, brags about it. He says he has never loved women except spiritually and has never known love except with men.
> . . . I am willing to believe . . . that homosexuals are a little more numerous still than I at first thought. In any case, I didn't think Proust was so exclusively so.[6]

Some critics and biographers have questioned the veracity of this anecdote. Céleste Albaret, who served as Proust's housekeeper, suggests that Gide never made this visit to Proust and that he fabricated the story in order to portray Proust as a brother in homosexuality. Céleste says that Gide did pay a visit to Proust to apologize for rejecting *Du côté de chez Swann* when it was submitted to the *Nou-*

velle Revue Française. But she goes on to say that "I know Gide talks somewhere about notes he supposedly took after two other visits to Monsieur Proust, taking place, according to him, in May of 1921. . . . It's odd that, as for me, I have no recollection of a second visit, especially from him. . . . If Gide did not come, he has the excuse of not being the only one who claims to have visited Monsieur Proust but didn't. If he did come, I fear he took advantage once again of his supposed accord with Monsieur Proust concerning 'uranism.' "[7] Throughout her book Céleste says she never saw any evidence of homosexual inclinations in Proust but saw a great deal of evidence of heterosexuality. In short, Céleste wants to convince us that there was no homosexual component in Proust's personality, a position which is hardly tenable in light of the cumulative evidence and one she probably adopts (although she denies this) in an attempt to protect the reputation of the man to whom she was, and continues to be, fiercely loyal.

On the other hand, it is easy to understand how even someone as close to Proust as Céleste could receive the impression that Proust had no personal interest in "uranism." Proust was extremely defensive on the subject of homosexuality and always officially posed as heterosexually inclined. On 4 November 1920 Paul Souday published in *Le Temps* a review of Proust's *Le Côté de Guermantes I,* and in it he attributed to Proust a "feminine" sensibility. Proust wrote to Souday:

One thing upset me, something I'm sure you didn't mean maliciously. At a time when *Sodome et Gomorrhe* is about to appear—a time when, since I will be talking about Sodom, no one will have the courage to come to my defense—you are blazing the trail (without malice, I am sure) for those who *are* malicious by treating me as being "feminine." From "feminine" to "effeminate" is only one short step. Those who served me as seconds in my duel will tell you whether I have the softness of effeminates. Once again, I'm sure you said it without premeditation.[8]

Proust alludes menacingly to a duel he fought twenty-three years earlier under similar circumstances, when another journalist, Jean Lorrain, implied in print that Proust was having an affair with Lucien Daudet, son of the novelist Alphonse Daudet. Lorrain's insinuation figured in a review of Proust's first book *Les Plaisirs et les jours,* which Lorrain criticized for its effeteness of tone and subject matter.

Proust immediately issued a challenge, and the two combatants met in an old-fashioned *rencontre,* where both fired one shot (probably into the air), and neither was injured. For the rest of his life Proust remained extremely proud of the way he had proved his mettle and his masculinity on the field of honor.[9]

And he remained always ready to issue another challenge to anyone who implied that he had homosexual tastes. Marcel Plantevignes recounts a remarkable episode, which took place in Cabourg, the Norman seacoast town where Proust was fond of vacationing. Marcel Plantevignes was a sensitive, intelligent boy of nineteen when he met Proust in Cabourg in August of 1908. The two quickly became close friends. Plantevignes paid regular evening visits to Proust's room at the Grand Hotel, and Proust favored him with long hours of conversation and read to him passages from his novel in progress. Henri Bonnet, who has carefully chronicled Proust's early work on *A la recherche,* believes that Plantevignes and the boys with whom he associated in Cabourg served Proust as models for the little band of young girls with whom, in *A la recherche,* the narrator falls in love in the fictional seacost town of Balbec.[10]

Proust's relationship with Plantevignes reveals a good deal about the public image Proust strove to maintain in connection with homosexuality. One day in Cabourg Marcel Plantevignes received a strange and unexpected letter from his older friend:

Monsieur,

Since you used to lavish upon me with a tenacity and persistence which sometimes worried me—because I used to wonder whether one day these qualities would not touch upon perfidy—indications of the most sincere attachment, I was very far from imagining that you were preparing yourself for the dastardly act of stabbing me in the back.

Having always had very little regard for these customs of the Renaissance, I am informing you right away of my disdain and of the fact that I shall never see you again.

You have clumsily spoiled a friendship which might have been very beautiful.

And I feel no regret in not even telling you goodbye.

Marcel Proust

Plantevignes was stunned and was unable to recall anything he could have said or done to offend Proust.

And then an intricate and revealing comedy of manners and

morals began to unfold. Plantevignes and his father made several attempts to discover how Proust had been insulted and how reparation could be made. First Plantevignes *père* called on Proust at the Grand Hotel, only to return twenty minutes later and announce, "Proust wants to fight a duel with me!" He explained that Proust had received him icily, saying: "I was waiting, in fact, for your visit, Monsieur. Your son is a minor, and you are acting as his substitute. That is your right, and it is entirely natural, and I am at your disposition. Moreover, in view of the friendship I had for your son and the esteem, Monsieur, I have for you, I must tell you that although I am the aggrieved party, I have decided to leave you the choice of weapons, of the date, and of the place of the encounter." When Plantevignes *père* protested that he and his family had never felt anything but friendship for Proust and that there should be no grounds for a duel, Proust said: "Please, Monsieur, I have no explanation to give you. Your son is big enough to know what he is saying and doing, and it is to him that you will have to turn for an answer."

But Plantevignes *fils* could not remember doing anything to cause injury. His worried parents sent him to his room alone, thinking that would perhaps improve his memory. But after an entire afternoon of reflection the boy could still think of no way in which he could have offended Proust. So Plantevignes *père* set out again for the Grand Hotel and another interview with the bristling writer. Proust would say only that it was necessary to choose seconds immediately and that no other explanation would be forthcoming from him.

Plantevignes *père*, resigned to the duel, began to look for seconds. He called for this purpose on the Vicomte d'Alton, only to discover that Proust had already asked d'Alton and the Marquis de Pontcharra to serve as his seconds. D'Alton said he would try to smooth things over and avoid the confrontation. He said this kind of behavior was nothing unusual for Proust and that Proust could be easily mollified. "He acted on false impressions," d'Alton declared. "His imagination and his dandyism did the rest."

But Pontcharra viewed the proceedings more darkly. "It's a ridiculous affair," he told Plantevignes *fils*, "and I am surprised that a man such as M. Proust, whom I scarcely know but who is said to be intelligent, would have a hand in it. It is absolutely absurd on the part of someone who sees you every evening. He had only to sum-

mon you urgently and ask you frankly, man to man, to explain yourself on the matter he thinks gives him grounds for reproach. This outburst is absurd and can only become an even more absurd scandal if
d'Alton and I don't work things out right away. . . . Ah, if my
mother-in-law and my wife knew about it, they would be outraged. I
don't have to tell you I'm not breathing a word about it, and that you
should do likewise. It's so ridiculous, this outburst, and we don't even
know what caused it, because Proust refuses to say anything, and it
appears that you don't know anything about it."

But when d'Alton and Pontcharra met with Proust, Proust appeared determined to carry through with the duel. He threatened to
dismiss d'Alton and Pontcharra and to ask the Duc de X. and the
Prince de Y. to come over from Deauville to serve as his seconds.

"You see the snobbery that's involved," d'Alton remarked to the
Plantevignes family. "So we looked ashamed, thinking of you, because we must avoid at all costs having people from Deauville come
over here to get mixed up in the affair. Pontcharra was furious. So we
have to be careful and wait for the wind to change."

"It's all the more ridiculous," d'Alton continued, laughing, "in
that Proust openly declares that if the duel is fought with pistols, he
will fire into the air."

"As will I," said Plantevignes *père*.

"Well, it's a duel from an operetta by Offenbach, with the two
adversaries shooting into the air. I tell you, we're in the middle of an
operetta by Offenbach. We could call it 'The Duel of Cabourg.' We're
locked in a veritable comic convulsion; we'll have to wait for it to
pass."

But the Plantevignes family thought the affair had already
dragged on too long, and that it was by no means comical. Several
more days passed, and finally d'Alton arrived to inform the family that
Proust had dropped a hint about the source of the offense. Proust had
heard that Marcel Plantevignes had met on the Cabourg promenade a
woman who had implied that Proust had "special morals" and that
Plantevignes had endorsed this accusation. "Suddenly all the veils
were rent for me," Plantevignes remembers.

Suddenly I saw that brief scene again. The encounter on the promenade had
been so quick and fortuitous that I had never thought about it. She was a
young woman very fond of teasing, who often teased Proust about homosex-

uality and who, when she had met me on the promenade, had stopped me again to warn me and cast her terrible aspersions. "I know, I know, Madame, what you're going to tell me," I had answered quickly, "but it has no importance as far as I'm concerned. Excuse me, Madame, goodbye, I'm in a big hurry." And I had fled as quickly as possible.

"Ah, you should have contradicted her," said Plantevignes *père*, when his son told him the story. "That's the reproach Proust will bring against you."

And so the whole story gradually emerged. On the day following her encounter with Marcel Plantevignes the woman had gone for a walk with Proust and had begun teasing him about his supposed homosexuality, adding: "What's more your favorite, your darling, your cicisbeo, this charming boy about whom you're constantly belaboring us with your stories, is of a similar mind. I met him, brought up the subject, and he said, 'Yes, I know all about it, but it's all the same to me.' "

Having thus discovered the source of the offense, Plantevignes *père* made yet another visit to Proust. This time Proust agreed to receive the boy himself, whom he had interdicted from the Grand Hotel, and hear his explanation. When the young Plantevignes arrived, Proust issued his accusation.

"One morning on the promenade," Proust declared, "you met Mme X., who teased you about our friendship, saying that you see me every evening, and warning you about my reputation for having special and very dangerous morals. Then, instead of contradicting her, you acquiesced, answered that you, in fact, agreed, that you had been sufficiently warned, and that it had no importance as far as you were concerned. Is this indeed the case?"

"No," answered the boy. "I did not acquiesce. I answered with the curt phrases anyone uses when wishing quickly to get rid of an importunate person: 'I know, I know what you're going to tell me, but it has no importance as far as I'm concerned, goodbye, Madame, excuse me, I am in a big hurry.' And I went away."

"Just like that, without contradicting her! Really, Marcel, have you ever had any occasion to complain about me? Have I ever said one word, have I ever committed a single act which might have shocked you?"

"Absolutely not."

"Well, someone accuses me in your presence of dangerous morals, warns you about me, and you don't protest. . . . But look here, you should have remained and protested violently. . . . You said, 'I know, I know.' But, after all, what do you know? Upon what evidence do you base this 'I know, I know'?"

Plantevignes repeated that what he had said to the woman was, "I know, I know what you're going to tell me."

"Why, yes," said Proust. "You acquiesced in what she was going to tell you. But, once again, how did you know what she was going to say?"

"Proust and I were now at a deadlock," Plantevignes remembers. "The time had come to deliver the key to the incident, if I wanted to save our friendship. I had for some time resigned myself to the inevitable, and I stated with cold emotion, 'Because that's what everybody's whispering on the promenade.' "

"Proust's face," Plantevignes continues, "which was already ivory colored, seemed to grow even paler and to take on the tint of polished marble. Visibly shaken, he remained silent with emotion. Then, in a tone which was half sorrowful, half bantering and sarcastic, he said, 'How charming to arrive somewhere preceded by one's reputation.' "

In an attempt to lessen Proust's shock and to smooth things over, the young Plantevignes pointed out that it was, after all, fashionable to accuse people of homosexuality. And he reminded Proust that this kind of gossip was a favorite pastime at the court of Louis XIV and was the sort of thing frequently said about the great and the famous. Proust remained pensive for awhile, then suddenly said, "But you, Marcel, what do you think of all this?"

"I don't believe a word of it," the boy answered. "Otherwise, I would not be here."

"And your parents?"

"My parents don't believe a word of it either. Otherwise, they would not allow me to see you."

At last Proust seemed mollified. "Well, Marcel," he said, "I offer you my hand, and I owe all my apologies to your father. . . . But look here, Marcel, this affair is partly your fault. You tell everybody too openly and with too much enthusiasm about your evening visits to me. You aren't secretive enough. . . . Society is so constructed that it has to destroy at all costs anything which was created without it. Our friendships, our loves, are made in order to be mocked and vilified. Don't tell anyone you come to see me. Even better, declare that you don't see me any more."

After another interval of silence Proust exclaimed, "Well, Marcel, naturally you'll come to see me tomorrow evening, as always."

The boy answered, "Oh, yes."

"And our mutual enthusiasm," Plantevignes recalls, "suddenly released from all constraint, became so boyish and comical that we burst out laughing simultaneously, drowning our recent estrangement in a resolution sumptuous with joy."[11]

This story affords significant insight into Proust. In life and to some extent in art Proust accepted and submitted to the social prejudice against homosexuality and kept his homosexual proclivities cautiously concealed. He feared that if the truth were known, he would be mocked, snubbed, and branded a pariah. Indeed, the possibility that someone had discovered his homosexual tastes was enough to make his always pale complexion take on, as Plantevignes says, "the tint of polished marble." So Proust let it be known that he stood ready to revert, at the least suggestion that he was anything other than exclusively heterosexual, to the ancient French code of honor (ostentatiously choosing French noblemen as his seconds). But the Plantevignes anecdote shows that Proust's elaborate masquerade fooled hardly anyone. Rumors about Proust's homosexuality flew thick and fast in Cabourg, to the extent that Proust was openly teased about it on the promenade. (The woman who teased him was on relatively safe ground, since women could not be challenged to a duel).

Proust's need for constantly striking postures of self-denial must have exacted a heavy toll of suffering. As Henri Bonnet points out,[12] it was around the time Proust underwent the homosexual scare in Cabourg that he wrote an early draft of the essay on homosexuality which begins *Sodome et Gomorrhe*, an essay to which this experience may have contributed and one to which similar experiences certainly did. In this version of material later included in *A la recherche* Proust calls people with homosexual tastes a *race maudite*, a "race accursed":

A race accursed, because its ideal of beauty and its nourishment of desire also embody a source of shame and a fear of punishment, and because it is forced to live . . . in deceit and perjury . . . like criminals, it is forced to hide its secret from those it loves most, fearing the grief of a family, the contempt of friends, the chastisement of a country; a race accursed, persecuted like the race of Israel and like that race ending, in the common opprobrium of an undeserved abjection, by taking on common characteristics . . . excluded from the family, with whom they can never be totally honest, from the fatherland, in whose eyes they are covert criminals . . . excluded from friendship, because their friends might suspect motives other than friendship where there is friendship alone and would not understand when there is friendship and something more. . . .[13]

In his own experience of sexual exile Proust found the inspiration for one of the most moving aspects of his novel: his heartfelt portrayal of and implicit protest against the "undeserved abjection" experienced by the *race maudite*.

But Proust—and here is one of the marks of his genius—was also keenly attuned to the comic potential of human sexuality. He viewed sexuality as he viewed the human condition in general, as tragic from this perspective, comic from that. And just as he examined his own heart to discover the tragic dimensions of the theme, so he used himself as a model in extracting the theme's comic possibilities. It is often said, and truthfully so, that Proust satirized his own hypochondria in the character of Tante Léonie, his own Jewishness in the character of Bloch, and his own homosexuality in the character of the Baron de Charlus.

In this vein of self-satire and self-parody Proust exploits in *A la recherche* the humorous implications of his conduct in "The Duel of Cabourg" and similar affairs where he called someone out (or threatened to do so) in an overstated attempt to deny his homosexuality. As Marcel Plantevignes points out, the letter he received from Proust announcing an immediate end to friendship bears a striking similarity to a letter in *A la recherche* sent by Charlus to Aimé, the headwaiter at the Grand Hotel in Balbec. Quite involuntarily (for Aimé's interests lie elsewhere) Aimé has caught the Baron's eye and aroused his interest. The Baron has, consequently, sent for Aimé on three occasions, only to be told that Aimé is indisposed and unable to come. Miffed at the idea that he is being ignored by someone whose social standing is lower than his own, Charlus sends Aimé a letter in which he states that Aimé, having denied him three times ("if I can speak thusly without committing sacrilege") has now relinquished all hope of ever meeting him and taking advantage of the many benefits which would accrue. But no sooner has Charlus announced this break in relations which never existed than he coyly mentions his address and the hours when he can be found at home. And he concludes:

it is a mistake to imagine that boorish conduct ever adds to charm, in which, moreover, you are entirely lacking. . . . Goodbye, Monsieur. . . . We are like those ships you must have seen at Balbec, passing each other for a brief moment; it might have been to their mutual advantage to stop for awhile; but one judged differently; soon each is out of sight on the horizon, and the meeting is forever effaced; but, before this definitive separation, each salutes the other, as does here, Monsieur, wishing you all good fortune,

The Baron de Charlus (2: 991–93)

The language is very similar to that of Proust's letter to Plantevignes: "I shall never see you again. You have clumsily spoiled a friendship which might have been very beautiful." Perhaps the motives behind the two letters are also similar and Proust's break with Plantevignes, like Charlus's break with Aimé, was partly a stratagem for attracting the young man's attention by starting a quarrel with him and thus becoming, at least for a time, the center of all the young man's thoughts and worries.

There is another echo of "The Duel of Cabourg" in *A la recherche,* also in a comic passage and also in a homosexual context. It is the scene where Charlus concocts a sham duel for the purpose of ensuring that Morel will cancel other plans he has made and spend an evening with him. The episode begins on a tragicomic note. Charlus stands on the train platform where Morel has left him, weeping huge tears and melting his makeup like Canio (2: 1,064). But tragicomedy soon gives way to comedy of the broadest sort. Charlus, recovering himself and conceiving a diabolical plan, writes to Morel informing him that two officers of Morel's regiment have made insinuations about their relationship and that he, Charlus, is sending seconds to call upon them. Morel, horrified that his relationship with Charlus might become a public issue, hastens to Charlus's side, just as Charlus has planned, to try to persuade him to call off the duel.

Meanwhile Charlus, in order to make his fiction more verisimilar, has actually written to seconds asking them to serve him in an affair of honor. One of the chosen seconds is the clinically brilliant but socially and verbally blundering Dr. Cottard.

Cottard is so excited by the prospect of a *rencontre* that he "finally arrived, although very late, because . . . he had been obliged to stop at all the cafés and farms along the way and ask to use the 'you-know-what' and 'the little boys' room' " (2: 1,071). As Cottard makes halting progress toward Doncières, Charlus, who has invented so convincing a fiction that he has started to believe in it himself, begins doing farcical warm-up exercises for the duel that will never be:

a taste for battle, which he naively thought he inherited from his ancestors, filled him with such sprightliness at the thought of a fight that although he had originally invented the duel for the purpose of making Morel come to him, he could not now give it up without regret. Always in an affair of this sort he took on an air of valor and identified himself with the illustrious High Constable de Guermantes, though when anyone else went upon the field of honor he regarded it as an act of utter insignificance. "I think it will be really fine," he told us sincerely, and in recitativo intonations. "To see Sarah Bernhardt in *L'Aiglon*, what is that? Caca! Mounet-Sully in *Oedipe*? Caca! . . . How can any of this compare to the unprecedented spectacle of the lineal descendant of the High Constable going into battle?" And at this thought M. de Charlus, who could not contain himself for joy, began to strike fencing stances which recalled Molière, making us carefully draw our beer steins closer to us on the table and raising the fear that the first crossing of swords would wound not only the adversaries but the doctor and the seconds besides. (2: 1,070)

When Cottard finally arrives, Charlus abruptly calls off the fictitious duel, claiming that he has now discovered that the insulting remark was probably never made in the first place (a resolution not unlike that of the quarrel with Plantevignes). And then Proust spins another bit of high comedy, turning this time on the fact that everyone already knows about the Baron what the sham duel is designed to conceal—that is, that he has homosexual tastes—and on the counter fact that Cottard, even though he is a doctor and potentially an expert on the subject, has quite an imperfect understanding of what Charlus's homosexuality entails. Cottard rightly interprets the duel as a homosexual stratagem but wrongly regards himself as the object of Charlus's desires:

Once the danger had passed, Cottard was disappointed. . . . [But] the doctor repressed an expression of vexation, which would have changed nothing, and having muttered (he, the most cowardly of men) that there are some things one simply does not let go by, added that it was better thus, and that he was pleased with this solution. M. de Charlus, desirous of showing his gratitude to the doctor . . . brought his chair closer to that of Cottard, in spite of the disgust the latter inspired in him. And it was not only without any physical pleasure but also in having to overcome a positive physical repulsion—as a Guermantes, not as a homosexual—that in order to say goodbye to the doctor he took his hand and caressed it a moment with the goodness of a master rubbing the muzzle of his horse and giving it a lump of sugar. But Cottard, who had never so much as let the Baron know that he had heard vague rumors about his morals, but nonetheless classified him privately as belonging to the category of "abnormals," a type with which he had little experience (he even, in his habitual impropriety of terminology and in the most serious tone of voice, said of one of M. Verdurin's footmen, "Isn't he the Baron's mistress?"), imagined that the caress on the hand was the immediate prelude to rape, for the accomplishment of which, with the duel serving as a pretext, he had been lured into an ambush and conducted by the Baron to this solitary room, where he was now to be taken by force. Not daring to leave his chair, where he had been riveted by fear, he rolled his eyes in terror, as if he had fallen into the clutches of a savage and was not quite sure but what the savage feasted upon human flesh. (2: 1,071–72)

Thus ends this other "duel from an operetta by Offenbach"—or, to use Proust's own metaphor, a comedy by Molière. When we come upon such episodes in *A la recherche*, we know what Roger Shattuck means when he speaks of reading Proust and laughing aloud.[14] These passages, with their clear biographical reverberations, embody one of Proust's most attractive and winning traits: his ability to laugh at himself.

Homosexual humor, like Jewish humor, often serves as a shield against the prejudice and hostility to which the members of the group in question are subjected. Sometimes it does so by reiterating the stereotypes of society at large, thereby helping to mock them and make them less painful. So it is in the work of Proust, who was, we recall, Jewish on his mother's side and who often compared the "chosen race" and the "race accursed." By showing a learned man of medicine quaking with fear at the touch of someone he knows to be homosexually inclined (because he has placed all such men in the category of "abnormals"), Proust at once satirizes the blinding effect of all prejudice and deftly alludes to the traditional antagonism between established medicine and homosexuality. The episode of the sham duel is one of the most powerful bits of satire in *A la recherche,* because no one emerges from it unscathed. In it Proust laughs at ignorance and prejudice about homosexuality—but he also laughs at homosexuality. It is as good an example of the universal vision sometimes attributed to Proust as it is possible to find.

Having moved only this little distance into the sexual aesthetics of *A la recherche,* we have already gone far beyond the Freudian conception of Proust's novel as a manifestation of rigid homosexual compulsions over which the author has little control. Far from involuntarily dramatizing the symptoms of a mental illness or writing under the sway of repressed, subconscious urges, Proust consciously weaves a variegated tapestry of human comedy around the sexual motif. Through characters such as Charlus he analyses his own failings and aspirations and thereby shows that he has little need of armchair or professional psychoanalysis. It is true that he sometimes indulges in self-pity and self-hatred. Given the times and the social circumstances in which he lived, it would be surprising if this were not the case. But he is also able to look at his own personality with humor and with complex irony. And of all the traits of the human mind these are the most foreign to the Freudian scheme of things, which, among its other faults, views life and literature much too soberly. As D. A. Begelman remarks, "Psychoanalysts take sex too seriously and have gulled everyone else into doing likewise."[15] This is a danger from which Proust, at his best, can save us, if we will let him.

HE WHO LOUISA CANNOT WIN/ NO REFUGE HAS BUT ONAN'S SIN

Marcel Proust was by no means immune to the attraction of women. Some writers (principally Céleste Albaret) have argued that his preferences were, in fact, heterosexual. Such conflicting testimony recalls the mysterious erotic currents of *A la recherche* itself. Consider

Morel, for instance. Is he "a homosexual" or "a heterosexual"? There is evidence to support either case. And Albertine? Is she "a lesbian"? Although the narrator engages in some of the most careful detective work in literature, he never finds out for certain, and neither does the reader. Even Charlus, we recall, was married, was devoted to his wife, and visited her grave regularly after her death (though he claimed to have asked a choirboy for his name and address at his wife's funeral). As with Proust's characters, so with Proust himself. One cannot contemplate the story of Proust's life for very long before the traditional sexual categories begin to lose their meaning.

The problem with most biographical studies of Proust is that they assume that sexually Proust must have been either this or that and nothing else. In popular (and in Freudian) belief taxonomy is paramount, and there is no bestriding the traditional sexual pigeonholes and polarities.[16] And so Proust's biographers usually attempt to shrink him to the size of some sexual label derived from Freudianism or from other medical theory. Robert Soupault, for instance, denies that Proust was a "true invert" (whatever that may be) but speculates that he had a hormonal imbalance and a "biological taint" which led him to love other men.[17]

The categories of homosexuality and heterosexuality are usually treated in the same way. Most biographers are not comfortable until they have decided to which of these Proust "really" belonged. But no matter what label is applied, Proust eludes it in one way or another. A critic who argues that Proust was heterosexual—or even bisexual— has to discount the confession of exclusive homosexuality Gide says Proust made to him, to say nothing of the profound sense of homosexual identity Proust felt and reflected in his portrait of the "race accursed." Critics who argue that Proust was exclusively homosexual must, on the other hand, explain away Proust's romantic attachments to women.

And these are not easy to explain away, for Proust was extremely sensitive to female charm and paid court to women of all ages and social classes. His letters are filled with a keen appreciation of female beauty. The remarks on this subject range from the parenthetical ("The other day at Larue's I saw . . . a little woman with beautiful eyes who pleased me very much")[18] to the dithyrambic. To Louisa de

Mornand he sent an account of his encounter in Cabourg with Lucy Gérard, an actress who had appeared in a play with Louisa three years earlier:

I met Lucy Gérard on the promenade in Cabourg. It was a ravishing evening when the sunset had forgotten only one color: pink. But her dress was all in pink and from far off placed upon the orange sky the complementary color of twilight. I stayed there a very long time watching this delicate patch of pink, and I came back in with a cold when I saw her blend into the horizon, at the extremity of which she disappeared like an enchanted sail.[19]

Proust's admiration for women was not always so aesthetic. He responded to the erotic appeal of young girls, of women d'un certain âge, and of the full range of types in between. In 1908, after he had purchased some pornography (both heterosexual and homosexual) at the sale of a wealthy Protestant banker, he wrote to Georges de Lauris and offered to lend the pornography to him—"if," he impishly added, "your innocence is finally getting to be a burden to you." And he continued: "As for me, I scarcely like anything . . . but young girls, as if life were not already complicated enough as it is. You will say that's why marriage was invented, but then she's no longer a young girl, you can only have a young girl once. I understand Bluebeard, he was a man who liked young girls."[20]

In the same spirit Proust once paid a midnight visit to his old friends Gaston and Jeanne de Caillavet and begged them to introduce him to their beautiful, sixteen-year-old daughter Simone. The girl had already gone to bed, but at Proust's entreaty she was awakened and brought down to meet Monsieur Proust. Though sleepy, she managed to smile at Proust, and she immediately won his heart. Proust later wrote to Jeanne de Caillavet: "It's true that one can love opposite physical types. For now I find myself in love with your daughter. How cruel she is in her kindness, because her smile lent its meaning to her entire person and made me fall in love. If she had been grumpy, I would be at peace. I'm trying to remember a species of flower whose petals are exactly like her cheeks when she smiles. I would like very much to see her smile again."[21]

The narrator of A la recherche shares Proust's admiration for budding femininity. The title of one whole volume of the novel—A l'ombre des jeunes filles en fleurs—alludes, among other things, to the narrator's fascination with the charm and mystery of the adolescent girl. "It comes so soon," the narrator remarks in this volume, "that moment when there is nothing left to anticipate, when the body is fixed in an immobility which holds no more surprises . . . it is so short, this radiant morning of youth, that one ends by loving only the youngest girls, those in whom the flesh, like the leaven of a precious dough, is still at work" (1: 905). And though the narrator is himself an adolescent in *A l'ombre,* he never outgrows his attraction to girls of the age of the little band (cf. 3: 432, 443–44, 1,028 ff.). So marked is the narrator's appreciation for young girls that it led Nabokov in *Lolita* to include Proust along with Edgar Allan Poe and Lewis Carroll in a series of allusions to literary precursors of Humbert Humbert.[22]

The heterosexual aspect of Proust and of his narrator is not limited to an admiration for young girls. Proust admired all types of women, and he drew upon his experiences with them in creating the love affairs he describes in *A la recherche.* In the summer of 1887, when Proust was sixteen, he fell in love with Marie de Benardaky, a Polish girl with whom he played on the Champs-Elysées in the afternoons after school. He made her one of the models for Gilberte. And throughout his life, up until the time of his death, he remembered her as "one of the two great loves of my life."[23] Another Marie in the young Proust's life was Marie Finaly, the sister of Proust's school friend Horace Finaly and one of the models for Albertine. Proust romanced this Marie by quoting poetry to her, and especially Baudelaire's haunting line "J'aime de vos longs yeux la lumière verdâtre."[24] According to Céleste Albaret there was yet a third Marie in Proust's life—his mother's maid, for whom the young Proust developed a puppy love which lasted only until his mother became suspicious and discharged the girl.[25]

Then there was Jeanne Pouquet, to whom Proust paid court as a young man at afternoon tennis parties in Neuilly. A famous photograph immortalizes one of these parties. It shows Jeanne standing on a chair holding a tennis racquet, while Proust kneels at her feet and strums another racquet as if it were a guitar or mandolin. Much later, in a letter to Jeanne, Proust revealed that these afternoon meetings contributed to the description of the narrator's anxiety about whether he will find Gilberte on the Champs-Elysées when he goes out to play.[26] Still later, reminiscing about Jeanne with Céleste Albaret, Proust remarked, "I was in love with her as one can never love again."[27] But Jeanne was betrothed to Proust's friend Gaston de Caillavet, and Proust's love, however ardent, was not returned. After Jeanne's marriage to Gaston, Proust was to become, as we have seen, infatuated with her daughter Simone, just as he had once loved the mother.

As a young man Proust also fell in love with Laure Hayman, a famous original for Odette. Like Odette, Laure Hayman was a genteel cocotte. In addition to serving Proust as a model for Odette, she also inspired Paul Bourget's story "Gladys Harvey." Soon after they met, Laure gave Proust a volume containing this work, bound in silk taken from one of her petticoats. Proust met Laure Hayman at his great-uncle Louis Weil's, when he was seventeen and she was around thirty-seven—the meeting which becomes, in A la recherche, the narrator's encounter with "The Lady in Pink" (Odette) at Uncle Adolphe's. Proust told Céleste Albaret: "Uncle Louis was glad to give Laure Hayman anything that would make her happy. I had a great deal of admiration for her, and I spent so much on flowers for her that she warned Papa about it. He scolded me for my extravagance—I was very young. But Papa himself had some admiration for Laure Hayman on account of her sensitivity and intelligence, and he encouraged me to keep up a friendship with her because of it."[28] Proust's friend Jacques-Emile Blanche later implied that Laure Hayman granted Proust, as the French say, her ultimate favors.[29]

One of the most intensely erotic of Proust's flirtations with women was his relationship with Louisa de Mornand, an actress who was the mistress of Proust's friend Louis d'Albufera (the pair served as models for Rachel and Saint-Loup). Proust's opinion of Louisa as an actress was rather low. But he had great admiration for her as a woman, and there is evidence that she and Proust carried on a brief but passionate love affair.[30] Soon after he met Louisa, Proust sent her a copy of his translation of Ruskin's The Bible of Amiens, along with a highly suggestive inscription which included the lines: "He who Louisa cannot win / No refuge has but Onan's sin."[31] Soon Louisa issued an invitation to visit. George Painter thinks that during this visit Proust's relationship with Louisa took on a physical dimension and offers as evidence a poem Proust sent Louisa to commemorate their evening together. The poem, entitled "Pour Louisa," goes in part as follows:

> The sky-colored canopy of the bed,
> Azure streaked with white cloud,
> Floats over Louisa who is reading
> Before going to sleep, on her side.
>
> Her attention must be wandering:
> Her sleepy head nods,
> She is looking at, but not seeing, a branch
> Painted by Madeleine Lemaire.[32]
>
> On the pretext that it's Sunday
> Marcel Proust, in this paradise
> From which an angel is leaning,
> Remained so long . . . that it's Monday!
>
> If I said that an angel was leaning
> From this paradise so disturbing,
> Descending from the blue and white sky
> To the pink and white maiden,
>
> I was no doubt mistaken
> Because it's really two Sèvres cupids
> Who, delightful and surprised,
> See lips united
> And two hearts intertwined.[33]

The language is typical of the tone of erotic playfulness and double entendre Proust customarily took with Louisa. He once wrote to her that he wanted to kiss "her two cheeks, and even the beautiful nape of her neck, if she will allow it (I'll tell you later why I struck out my first nouns and replaced them with others)."[34] And in a letter thanking Louisa for a New Year's gift of a watch, Proust wrote as follows:

I contemplated the case without dreaming that so pretty a thing could enclose something prettier still, since it had such an air of being sufficient unto itself. However, a certain secret button (no suggestive reference intended) seemed persistently to invite me to push it softly. Never was there a button (again, no suggestive reference intended) that held so much promise, and never one that kept its promise more perfectly, since it gave access to such a paradise. I opened the case . . . and I saw something so adorable that I don't know how I have been able to live without it. . . .[35]

Of her relationship with Proust Louisa later remarked, "Ours was an *amitié amoureuse* in which there was no element of a banal flirtation nor of an exclusive liaison, but on Proust's side a strong passion tinged with affection and desire, and on mine an attachment that was more than comradeship and really touched my heart."[36]

Occasionally Proust contemplated marriage to the women with whom he was smitten. Maurice Duplay reports that Proust once fell in love with a young woman who was a friend of the Duplay family, one Mlle Hélène d'Ideville, and that she "inspired in him ideas of marriage."[37] But Proust's most famous brush with marriage involves the mysterious "Girl of Cabourg." Proust's letters suggest that in Cabourg in 1908 he met a young woman with whom he fell very quickly in love and with whom he maintained a relationship later in Paris. Soon after his return from Cabourg in 1908 Proust wrote to Georges de Lauris, "I had a few little pleasures with a woman who is new and dear to me."[38] By the early part of 1909 Proust was making plans for marriage, but he had doubts. Again he wrote to Lauris: "Georges, I will perhaps have some news for you soon or rather I will ask your advice. To make a very young, delightful girl share my horrible life, even if she is not afraid to do it—wouldn't that be a crime?"[39] This engagement, or near engagement, is echoed in *A la recherche*, when Gilberte encourages the aging narrator to get married:

"By the way, Robert and I were just saying that you ought to get married. A wife would be good for your health, and you would make her happy." "No, I have too bad a character." "Nonsense!" "I assure you it's true. Besides, I was engaged once, but I wasn't able [to go through with it]." (3: 706–7)

In life, too, Proust's plans for marriage to the "Girl of Cabourg" never came to fruition. Who was this girl? "I suppress the identity of the person concerned," wrote Proust's friend Antoine Bibesco several years after Proust's death, "since she has begged me not to print her name."[40] And, indeed, her name remains unknown to this day.

According to Céleste Albaret, Proust also considered marrying one of his distant cousins, a granddaughter of his great-uncle Abraham Alphonse Weil. Céleste says that Proust used to meet the girl at Uncle Louis Weil's place in Auteuil and that he found her "very pretty and even beautiful." But Proust's mother was opposed to the marriage, and so it never took place. When, years later, Céleste asked Proust whether he harbored any regrets about having lost this girl, he replied, "No, not a single regret."[41]

We could continue to review examples of Proust's love for and appreciation of women: his half-snobbish, half-sexual pursuit of the Comtesse Laure de Chevigné, for example, or his early, extravagant courtship of Mme Straus.[42] But the point should by now be clear: there is extensive evidence that Proust was capable of heterosexual feeling and that it represented an important part of his personality.

It is often argued, however, that since Proust was also capable of homosexual feeling, his love for women was spurious. The operative assumption—which stems, again, from Freudianism—is that one must be either heterosexual or homosexual, with no room for nuances or admixtures of preference and behavior. The psychiatrist Irving Bieber states: "From a theoretical point of view, I conceive of two distinct categories—heterosexual and homosexual. Heterosexuality is part of normal biosocial development, while homosexuality is always the result of a disordered sexual development. The two categories are, therefore, mutually exclusive."[43] This kind of thinking is responsible for the widespread misconception that someone who is homosexually inclined is incapable of understanding or responding to a member of the opposite sex, a misconception which has often led Proust's biographers to conclude that his affairs with women were nothing but empty charades. Jocelyn Brooke, for instance, dismisses Proust's heterosexual loves as being of "that romantic, sentimental kind to which a certain kind of homosexual is sometimes addicted"; and he concludes that Proust must have been "profoundly and exclusively homosexual."[44] Proust's friend Antoine Bibesco, in a rather perfidious memoir, advances a similar argument:

Proust experienced the natural pleasures of love neither through marriage nor through any *liaison* worthy of the term. I am reluctant to enlarge upon his emotional abnormality. He liked to encourage the idea that he might have been in love with Louisa de Mornand and Jeanne Pouquet, and skilfully insinuated that he had adored them without obtaining any recompense. Better still, I have been shown a letter that promises to try the sagacity of critics and biographers, in which he debates whether he shall not marry a certain young girl whom he had met at Cabourg. . . . At all events it was merely another whimsy, as when he had persuaded my friend Bertrand de Fénelon to conduct him to a *mauvais lieu*—an adventure that had a disappointing sequel. The women were not as attractive as he had expected. Moreover, it was excessively cold. The place had to be turned upside down, hot-water bottles ordered and additional coverings brought up, to comfort the chilliest of professional invalids.[45]

Bibesco apparently feels that one failure means perennial failure and that only eyewitness proof that Proust was able to perform heterosexual intercourse will suffice to show that he was capable of erotic feeling for women.

George Painter takes a similar approach. Painter describes in detail some of Proust's heterosexual love affairs, and he takes pains to prove that Proust slept—and performed adequately—with women (the evidence here, of course, is unclear, as is the evidence bearing on how, when, and where Proust slept with men). These heterosexual affairs, according to Painter, furnish proof that "Proust's picture of heterosexual love is valid and founded on personal experience."[46] But Painter undermines his own argument by insisting throughout his biography that Proust's heterosexual attachments were always based on homosexual motives. Using the Freudian theory he deploys at every opportunity, Painter asserts that Proust pursued only women who would be impossible to marry because they were too old for him, too far above or below him in society, or already spoken for by one of his friends, and that in this he followed a typical homosexual pattern of flight from the opposite sex. After describing Proust's early love for Marie de Benardaky and the manner in which it was broken up by Proust's mother, Painter writes:

No doubt [Proust] was doomed even before he met Marie de Benardaky—if not by some antenatal predisposition, then by tensions whose work was done for ever in his early childhood—to lifelong homosexuality. Perhaps, too, as not infrequently happens in the puberty of a future homosexual, his unconscious mind had deliberately made a heterosexual choice which was certain to fail, in order to set itself free for its true desire. In every homosexual, perhaps, there is a heterosexual double, uppermost at first, who must be impris-

oned and made powerless before his strronger brother can come to life. . . .
Almost to the end of his life he continued, now and then, to fall in love with
women; but somehow his choice always happened to be a respectable married lady, twenty years older than himself, or a high-class, equally safe and
unattainable cocotte; or if he loved an unmarried woman of his own age or
younger, then she was usually the fiancée or mistress of a friend. The married
ladies or the cocotte, Freudians would say, were mother-images; and they
would rightly add that a preference for women already bespoken to male
friends is a typical symptom of homosexuality. These were substitutes for his
mother; those were substitutes for his friends. But there was a rejected part
of himself . . . for which the young girls were also substitutes for Marie de
Benardaky; and when he migrated to the Cities of the Plain he took with
him a prisoner crushed beneath the weight of Time and Habit, a buried heterosexual boy who continued to cry unappeased for a little girl lost.[47]

Painter's melodramatic prose does little to redeem the hollow theory
on which it rests. He tries hard to prove that Proust had valid heterosexual experiences; but he works against himself by adopting at the
same time the Freudian notion that homosexuality can appear only in
someone who has perverted or destroyed his heterosexual urges. Irving Bieber succinctly states the psychoanalytic dogma that underlies
Painter's analysis: "In our view every homosexual is, in reality, a 'latent' heterosexual."[48] Again we find that psychoanalytic theory needs
a strong injection of common sense, which tells us that sexual tastes,
like any tastes, can arise for many reasons, some of which may be personal, some of which may be physical, and some of which may be cultural. To say with Bieber and Painter that "every homosexual" (take
note of that "every") would really have been heterosexual if only he
had followed the path of "normal biosocial development" (take note of
that "normal") is to appeal to private mythology rather than to
address the complexities of the real world. Such declarations are not
only useless but detrimental to an understanding of Proust's—or anyone's—life. It may seem that a possible escape hatch for Freudian
critics who wish to argue the genuineness of Proust's heterosexual experience would be to appeal to the concept of bisexuality. Unfortunately, this concept does them no good, since in the psychoanalytic
view bisexuality is also a perversion: it is a subcategory not of heterosexuality but of homosexual maladjustment.[49]

   It is not as difficult as it may at first seem to cut the Gordian knot of homosexuality versus heterosexuality in Proust's biography. We need only discard the burdensome and misleading idea that heterosexuality and homosexuality are antagonistic and mutually exclusive. The discoveries of inductive sex research afford us abundant justification for so doing. The statistical surveys conducted by Kinsey and his associates demonstrate that:

Males do not represent two discrete populations, heterosexual and homosexual. The world is not to be divided into sheep and goats. Not all things are black nor all things white, [for] nature rarely deals with discrete categories. Only the human mind invents categories and tries to force facts into separated pigeon-holes. The living world is a continuum in each and every one of its aspects. The sooner we learn this concerning human sexual behavior the sooner we shall reach a sound understanding of the realities of sex.[50]

Kinsey's work showed that sexual preference and behavior can be meaningfully discussed only in these terms. Accordingly, he and his associates devised a 7-point scale on which o stands for a history of exclusive heterosexuality and 6 for a history of exclusive homosexuality. The numbers 1 through 5 represent the many and varied degrees in between. And, as Kinsey emphasized, there are "individuals in the population occupying not only the seven categories which are recognized here, but every gradation between each of the categories, as well."[51] Among Kinsey's greatest contributions to the understanding of sex was the emphasis he placed on the large group of men ratable 1 through 4 on the scale—men who have occasional homosexual contacts and feelings. Before Kinsey, studies of homosexuality had focused on the upper extremes of the scale, on people whose tastes are exclusively homosexual, or very nearly so. This practice contributed to the misconception that homosexuality appears only in a certain type of individual with predictable characteristics and behavior patterns. Kinsey demonstrated that there is no homosexual type and that homosexuality is found everywhere people are found. His study also revealed that a man can respond simultaneously to homosexual and heterosexual stimuli or can be homosexually oriented at one point in life and heterosexually oriented at another. This means—and this was Kinsey's most startling revelation—that most men who have homosexual experiences also continue to function well heterosexually.[52] It should be emphasized that these are not theories but are inductive findings based on careful statistical surveys. Furthermore, in a review of Kinsey's work by the American Statistical Association, undertaken in the wake of the moral outcry which followed the publication of *Sexual Behavior in the Human Male,* both Kinsey's methods of research and his contribution to science were judged to be of the highest caliber.[53] Kinsey concluded that "in view of the data which we now have on the incidence and frequency of the homosexual, and in particular on its co-existence with the heterosexual in the lives of a considerable portion of the male population, it is difficult to maintain the view that psychosexual reactions between individuals of the same sex are rare and therefore abnormal or unnatural, or that they constitute within themselves evidence of neuroses or even psychoses."[54]

Kinsey's findings mean, among other things, that it is misleading to use the terms "homosexual" and "heterosexual" as nouns. Wainwright Churchill explains:

It does not seem that there is any worthwhile purpose served in the promiscuous use of the word "homosexual" as a substantive referring to persons. Whatever convenience there may be in the habitual use of this word as a substantive is offset by the confusion and abuse to which such a habit inevitably leads. Talk about the "homosexual" encourages generalizations that usually cannot be substantiated by reality. . . . Instead of being used as nouns the words "homosexual" and "heterosexual" are better used as adjectives to describe the particular nature of a sexual contact. Thus, a sexual contact between male and female is a heterosexual contact, though one cannot be absolutely certain that either partner is necessarily always a "heterosexual." Similarly, a sexual contact between two males or between two females is a homosexual contact, although once again one cannot be absolutely certain that either partner is necessarily a "homosexual."[55]

Or, as Mark Freedman writes: "the use of the word 'homosexual' as a noun [should be] avoided as much as possible. The dichotomy of 'homosexuals' and 'heterosexuals' is highly artificial because man is inherently a *pansexual* creature, capable of responding to a variety of sexual stimuli. . . . In fact, shifts in sexual preference and sexual outlet often occur within an individual's lifetime. Thus, labeling the person a 'homosexual' or 'heterosexual' implies a permanent, irreversible pattern of preference and behavior that is not substantiated by available evidence."[56] In other words, we can safely say that Proust was, at certain times and with certain people, homosexually inclined or homosexually oriented; and we can safely speak of Proust's homosexuality, or of the homosexual component in his personality; but we cannot safely say that Proust was *a* homosexual or *a* heterosexual. The distinction is not trivial: it is necessary and fundamental to a true understanding of human sexual nature.

It could be that Proust sometimes overstated or exaggerated his heterosexual feelings in an attempt to camouflage his homosexuality. Like his own mysterious and multifaceted characters, he seems to have talked in different ways to different people—homosexually to André Gide, heterosexually to Céleste Albaret. Several things may be simultaneously true: that Proust actually did love women, that he also loved men, that he sometimes loved women more than men and at other times men more than women, that he sometimes pretended to be keener on women than he actually was in order to conceal from certain people his homosexual tastes. But none of these things necessarily undermines the authenticity he claimed for his experiences with both women and men. The evidence for Proust's attraction to women is so great that the burden of proof is finally on those critics who claim that his feelings for women do not count as genuine heterosexuality. One would like to hear more from these critics about what counts as genuine heterosexuality. Some of them feel, along with Jocelyn Brooke, that in order to enter the ranks of "heterosexuals," Proust would have to show us that he "had complete sexual intercourse with a woman [and] enjoyed it" (p. 17). But for what person, living or dead, do we have such proof? Do we have it for Petrarch? For Dante? We assume the heterosexuality of these writers, because they adopt heterosexual personae in their writings. It seems that we are willing to take a writer's word for his heterosexuality as long as his life and work do not also require us to accept a homosexual component in his personality. It is only after the question of homosexuality arises that people begin to ask for affadavits testifying to "complete sexual intercourse with a woman" and enjoyment of it. But these same critics do not feel that such proof is necessary for homosexuality. All that is necessary on that score is a soupçon of scandal. This stereotyped thinking has blinded many people to the sexual richness of Proust's life and writing. Proust is one of our greatest poets of sexuality, and evidence for his appreciation of female sexuality is everywhere in his correspondence and in A la recherche (as when he roguishly writes to Louisa de Mornand of the little button which, when softly pushed, gives access to paradise).

Maurice Bardèche points out that "Proust at twenty-five years old, thirty years old, forty years old is no longer the little Proust of the Lycée Condorcet. Proust's sentimental biography probably needs to be entirely redone, because his first biographers did not take account of the contradictions in him. A more complete and less rigid biography might still hold some surprises."[57] It is doubtful, however, that it will ever be possible to assay and quantify the precise admixture of homosexuality and heterosexuality in Proust's character at every stage of his life. There comes a point past which precision is unattainable, and critics and biographers should not be embarrassed to admit that such a point exists. If Proust teaches us anything, he teaches us the ultimate elusiveness of human identity. But he also teaches us that certain things about the personality can be known. If we can accept that homosexuality and heterosexuality coexisted in Proust's character and made equally important contributions to it, we can take an important step forward in understanding his life and art.

HE IS THERE, IN A ROOM, ATTACHED TO THE WALL WITH PADLOCKED CHAINS

Proust's homosexual affairs, friendships, and experiences contributed in many ways to his development as a man and an artist. But exactly when Proust first became cognizant of the homosexual side of his personality is not clear. Certainly he had passionate schoolboy crushes on two of his classmates at the Lycée Condorcet, Jacques Bizet and Daniel Halévy (the sons, respectively, of the composer and the co-librettist of Carmen). To them he wrote two remarkable love letters which survive but which for many years have been suppressed in Proustian biography. The letters were apparently unknown to George Painter, and André Ferré was denied authorization to publish them in Les Années de collège de Marcel Proust.[58] Recently, however, they have been edited and published by Philip Kolb, whose publisher,

Librairie Plon, has granted me permission to translate them here. Proust was around seventeen years old when he wrote the letters. He composed the letter to Jacques Bizet in the class of M. Choublier, his geography and history teacher:

I have just read your letter at frightened and breakneck speed, under the watchful eye of M. Choublier. I admire your circumspection but also regret it. Your reasons are excellent, and I am glad to see how alert and strong, lively and penetrating your mind is becoming. But the heart—or the body— has reasons of which Reason is scarcely aware. I therefore accept with admiration for you (I mean for your mind, and not for the matter you refuse, for I am not [vain] enough to think my body is such a precious treasure that one needs great will power to do without it) but also with sadness the superb yet cruel yoke you impose upon me. Perhaps you are right. However, I still think it is unfortunate not to pick the delightful flower which very soon we shall no longer be able to pick. Because by that time it will have turned into . . . forbidden fruit. I realize that even now you think of it as a poisonous flower. So let's not think about it or talk about it any more: prove to me through a very long and very affectionate friendship—as will be, I hope, mine for you—that you were right. [59]

Evidently Proust has made a sexual advance to Bizet, and Bizet has refused. So Proust says he has decided to let the friendship proceed on a nonphysical basis. But at the same time he advances cogent reasons for "picking the flower" while he and Bizet are still schoolboys, a time when these sorts of affairs are more or less expected and tolerated. As they get older, Proust warns, the flower of youth will turn into forbidden fruit.

In the letter to Daniel Halévy—written during M. Darlu's philosophy class—Proust once again uses floral imagery to allude to sex (one recalls that to "do a cattleya" becomes, with Swann and Odette, a euphemism for making love). Proust writes to Halévy:

You have administered to me a slight chastisement, but your switches are so laden with flowers that I cannot hold it against you: the brilliance and the fragrance of those flowers have so sweetly intoxicated me as to soften the cruel sting of the thorns. You have administered a beating with a lyre. And your lyre is enchanting. I would therefore be enchanted if. . . . But I am going to explain my idea to you or rather talk with you, as a refined boy, about things most worthy of interest, although one does not like to talk about them even privately. I hope you will be grateful to me for this modesty. I think immodesty is a horrible thing. It seems to me much worse than debauchery. My ethical beliefs allow me to believe that sensual pleasure is a very good thing. They prompt me also to respect certain feelings, certain refinements of friendship, and especially the French language, an amiable and infinitely gracious lady whose melancholy and voluptuous qualities are equally exquisite but upon whom one should never impose unclean affectations. That would be to dishonor her beauty.

You take me for a blasé, worn-out person, but you are wrong. If you are delightful, if you have clear, beautiful eyes which reflect the fine grace of your mind so purely that it seems to me that I do not love your mind completely unless I also kiss your eyes, if your body and your eyes are, like your mind, so graceful and supple that it seems to me that I can mingle better with your mind while sitting on your lap, if, finally, it seems to me that the charm of your you, the you in which I cannot separate your lively mind from your nimble body, would refine for me, by increasing it, "the sweet joy of love," there is nothing in all that which causes me to deserve these contemptuous phrases which would be more properly addressed to a man tired of women and seeking new pleasures in homosexuality. I know some very intelligent boys of—and I pride myself on this—a high moral refinement, who once had a good time with another boy they knew. That was when they were very young. Later they turned back to women. If that was their end what— great gods!—do you think they are, and what do you think I am, and especially what do you think I will be if I have already finished with love pure and simple! I will gladly speak to you of two Masters possessed of refined wisdom who all their lives picked only "the flower," Socrates and Montaigne. They allow very young men to "have a good time" in order to gain a little familiarity with every kind of pleasure and to find release for the fullness of their affection. They believed that friendships which are at once sensual and intellectual are better than relations with stupid and corrupt women when one is young and yet also has an acute awareness of beauty and also of the senses. I think these old Masters were mistaken, and I'll explain why later. But I retain only the general character of their advice. So don't treat me like a homosexual, that causes me pain. Morally I try, if only by means of elegant conduct, to remain pure. You can ask M. Straus what kind of influence I have had on Jacques [Bizet]. And it is by one's influence that his morality should be judged.

M. Darlu is warning me that he is going to ask me a question, so I'll stop here, having only begun the letter. But just tell me what this means: that your hands are not pure? . . .[60]

I . . . send you a kiss, if you will allow this chaste declaration.[61]

Again the letter seems to be written in response to a rebuff of Proust's sexual advances, and again Proust pretends to accept the rebuff while simultaneously deploying additional reasons for gathering rosebuds while they may. Moreover, we can detect in this letter echoes of the philosophy of homosexual love expounded in Plato's *Symposium*, which Proust was probably studying at about this time in his philosophy class.[62] Proust seems to have taken to heart Plato's description of how the homosexual lover attains the spiritual and mental ideal of beauty. In the *Symposium* Diotima tells Socrates that "by right boy-loving [one mounts] for that beauty's sake ever upwards, as by a flight of steps, from one to two, and from two to all beautiful bodies, and from beautiful bodies to beautiful pursuits and practices, and from practices to beautiful learnings, so that from learnings he may come at last to that perfect learning which is the learning solely of that beauty itself, and may know at last that which is the perfection of beauty."[63] To be sure, the young Proust's recasting of these ideas—"I can mingle better with your mind while sitting on your lap"—is clumsy and unintentionally comical. But the letter to Halévy is, nonetheless, a testimony to the philosophical and aesthetic importance Proust attached to homosexual love even at this early stage of his life.

Halévy and Bizet played hard to get, and Proust was hurt. He concluded a letter to another friend, Robert Dreyfus, with this comment:

And now, since you want to write to me, here, to tell the truth, is the subject which will interest me the most. First, what you are doing. And then give me all the details about "the congenial personality who masquerades unconvincingly behind the initials D. H." [Daniel Halévy]. . . . Why, after being on the whole very nice to me, does he abandon me *entirely*, making me feel the abandonment very clearly, and then a month later come to say hello to me, at a time when he was supposedly not speaking to me? And his cousin Bizet? Why does he tell me that he is my friend and then abandon me even more than before?

What do they want from me? To get rid of me, to bother me, to mystify me, or what?

I thought they were so nice![64]

Proust's experiences with the elusive Halévy helped him to formulate an early version of his famous concept of multiple personality. He answered a letter from Robert Dreyfus as follows:

Did you mean to tell me in a polite way that Halévy thinks I am scatterbrained and crazy? I confess I did not understand very well.

I don't think a type is a character. I think that what we think we divine about a character is only the effect of associations of ideas. I'll explain myself, at the same time letting you know that my theory is perhaps false, since it is entirely personal.

Suppose that in life, or in a literary work, you see a man who weeps over the misfortune of another. Since, each time you have seen someone feel pity, it has been someone who was good, kind, and sensitive, you deduce from this that this man is sensitive, kind, and good. For we construct a character in our minds only in accordance with certain visible lines which imply others. But this construction is very hypothetical. . . . Thus Halévy abandons me, taking care to arrange things so that I know he's done it on purpose, then a month later comes and says hello to me. Well, among the various men who make up my personality, the romantic one, whose voice I seldom heed, tells me: "He's done it to tease you, to play a game, to test you. Then he was sorry, since he didn't want to leave you altogether." And this man portrays Halévy's attitude toward me as that of a friend who is capricious but who still desires to know me.

But the suspicious man, whom I prefer, tells me that it's simpler than that, that Halévy finds me unbearable, that he—since he is so circumspect— found my ardor at first ridiculous, then, very soon, oppressive, that he wanted me to know this and also to know that I was sticking too close to him, and to get rid of me. And once he definitely saw that I would no longer importune him with my presence, he spoke to me. This man does not know whether this little scenario was motivated by pity, by indifference, or by moderation, but he is well aware that it is without importance and worries about it very little. Moreover, he only worries about it as a problem in psychology.[65]

Thus does the dual personality of the observer struggle with the dual personality of the person observed. Two decades later such problems in psychological relativity would become a fundamental concern of *A la recherche.*

After Proust left the Lycée Condorcet, he put in a year of service in the French army. Considering the strong homoerotic feelings which had already begun to well up in him, it is not difficult to understand why he later remembered this year of barracks life as "a paradise."[66]

Then in 1891 Proust met a young Swiss named Edgar Aubert. The two formed an immediate attachment, which was cut short when Aubert died of appendicitis on 18 September 1892. At about the same time Proust began another friendship with a sensitive young Englishman named Willie Heath. With Willie he made youthfully grandiose plans to "live more and more together, in a chosen group of magnanimous men and women, far enough away to be sheltered from the vulgar arrows of stupidity, vice, and evil."[67] But Willie also died before the relationship had had a chance to develop, succumbing to typhoid on 3 October 1893. Soon afterwards Proust wrote to Robert de Billy, alluding to the imminent publication of his first book *Les Plaisirs et les jours:* "This year I am going to publish a collection of little pieces, most of which you have already seen. I immediately had the idea of dedicating this little book to the memory of two people I knew only a little while but whom I loved, and still love, with all my heart: Edgar Aubert and Willie Heath."[68] As it turned out, *Les Plaisirs et les jours* contained a moving if somewhat melodramatic dedication to Willie Heath alone, a dedication which began with this epigraph: "From the breast of God where you repose . . . reveal to me those truths which conquer death, render it less fearsome, and make it almost loving." Meanwhile, Proust had started another friendship, this one destined to last for several years, with a young man who shared his interest in both the history and the craft of literature, one who was to become himself a writer of minor fame: the person Proust described as "the young, charming, intelligent, kind, affectionate Robert de Flers."[69]

There has been a good deal of argument over the precise nature of these early friendships. Were they "homosexual" or merely spiritual? On the latter side it has been suggested that Proust might not have been aware at this tender age (Proust was now in his early twenties) that homosexuality existed[70]—an argument that collapses in light of the letters to Jacques Bizet and Daniel Halévy. Furthermore, Proust published a story with a homosexual theme ("Avant la nuit") in *La Revue Blanche* for December of 1893. Proust was well aware of the existence of homosexuality during his school days at the Lycée Condorcet and during the later period of Edgar Aubert, Willie Heath, and Robert de Flers. The nicer question of whether there was a physical dimension to Proust's relationship with these friends is, to a certain extent, beside the point. Proust cared for these young men deeply, spoke of them and to them in language which blurred the distinction between friendship and love, and romanticized them in his writing and in his correspondence. From Proust's perspective, at least, the relationships clearly went beyond simple camaraderie.

The year Willie Heath died Proust met the person who was to exert perhaps the greatest influence on his eventual treatment of homosexuality in *A la recherche*. This was the famous, and infamous, Comte Robert de Montesquiou-Fezensac, an aesthete and dandy of limitless vanity, unbelievable cruelty and snobbery, and almost exclusively homosexual tastes: it was said that he once slept with Sarah Bernhardt and vomited for a week afterwards. Montesquiou had already served Huysmans as a model for Des Esseintes in *A rebours;* and eventually he was to contribute significantly to Proust's portrait of the Baron de Charlus. Proust met Montesquiou at a reception at Madeleine Lemaire's in April of 1893. It may be that Montesquiou initially made sexual advances to Proust; but Proust and Montesquiou did not become lovers. Their relationship, which was to last for many years, was ostensibly one of master and disciple, with Proust playing, but not taking very seriously, the role of protégé. At first Proust was interested in Montesquiou principally because he had entrée to exclusive salons which Proust, who was not innocent of snobbery himself, also wished to visit. And so Proust flattered Montesquiou and fed his ravenous vanity with fawning letters and sycophantish gifts. Privately, however, Proust made fun of Montesquiou and was famous in Parisian society for his highly comical and lethally accurate impersonations of Montesquiou's voice and bearing. As George Painter points out, Charlus's speeches in the scene of the narrator's visit in *Le Côté de Guermantes* are in places outright parodies of Montesquiou, including some actual quotations of Montesquiou's favorite turns of phrase.[71]

Montesquiou had a male secretary and lover named Gabriel d'Yturri, a South American who had emigrated to Paris as a teenager and who lived with the Comte for twenty years in what amounted to homosexual marriage. Given the mercurial nature of Montesquiou's personality, the relationship was extraordinarily stable and long-lived; it ended only with the death of Yturri in 1905. Céleste Albaret recalls that "certainly one of the things that fascinated Monsieur Proust the most in the character of the Comte was the particularity of his loves.

He followed and observed step by step . . . the strong feeling Montesquiou had for his secretary Yturri, a South American who lisped and who called his master 'Moussou lé Comté.' The affair was the talk of Paris, and I am sure Monsieur Proust found in it an inexhaustible source for his Baron de Charlus."[72] From the enduring relationship of Yturri and Montesquiou Proust may have gotten the idea for the unstinting devotion of Jupien to Charlus in A la recherche, a relationship which is among the most lasting and successful of all those described in the novel.

Gabriel d'Yturri probably provided Proust with characteristics for Morel as well as for Jupien. But Morel owes a more direct debt to Léon Delafosse, a young pianist who was also for a time a protégé and friend of Montesquiou. Proust rather shamelessly played the role of go-between in introducing Delafosse to Montesquiou, in a typical effort to please the Comte and curry his favor. Proust's friend Fernand Gregh says:

Proust's Morel was called Léon Delafosse. He was an excellent pianist, composed music occasionally, and was one of the prettiest young men of his generation. Of humble stock—Proust makes Morel the son of a valet de chambre and Delafosse was, I believe, the son of a concierge—he was not long in penetrating the highest society, thanks to his talent and to his pretty, almost too pretty, face. It was Montesquiou who paved the way for him. Proust, Louis de La Salle, another friend of ours (Bertrand de Fénelon?), and I had lunch at his place several times, in a very elegant apartment near the Avenue du Bois, which people were always a little surprised to find inhabited by this extremely young musician who had at that time given only a few concerts and who laid an excellent table. After breaking up with Montesquiou, he withdrew to Switzerland, whence he sent us reviews in which he was called a great artist. These notices appeared almost regularly: I imagine he had publicity contracts with certain newspapers. When people asked Montesquiou, "Whatever happened to Delafosse?" he would answer, "He fell down his own name." [French fosse 'hole' or 'pit'][73]

Céleste Albaret reports that of all the people Proust knew Robert de Montesquiou was the one about whom he talked the most in their private conversations. She says that one night when she and Proust were discussing Montesquiou, Proust suddenly became silent and withdrew into himself, as he frequently did when meditating on his characters and his novel. Then, coming back to the conversation about Montesquiou, Proust remarked, "He's the nucleus of the whole business."[74]

Though Montesquiou was the principal model for Charlus, he was not the only one. Proust also drew inspiration from a certain Baron Doasan, whom he met in the salon of Mme Aubernon. It was said that Doasan had been the protector of Gabriel d'Yturri, before Yturri went to live with Montesquiou. And Doasan had also had a relationship with a Polish violinist, an ill-fated affair which perhaps contributed to the Charlus-Morel relationship in A la recherche.[75]

After Robert de Montesquiou and Baron Doasan, speculation about the real-life models for the Baron de Charlus becomes more nebulous. It has been suggested that the portrait of Charlus contains traces of Oscar Wilde, and this may in fact be the case. Proust met Wilde when Wilde came to Paris in 1891. Their social paths crossed again when Wilde returned to Paris in 1894, the year before his trial for homosexuality. Proust had dinner with Wilde one evening at Mme Arman de Caillavet's, and Wilde also paid a visit to Proust. Of this potentially momentous visit many versions exist; but the one reported by Philippe Jullian is perhaps the most amusing and most typically Wildean:

by dint of paying [Wilde] innumerable compliments [Proust] prevailed on him to accept an invitation to dine at his house. That evening Proust arrived back late and at once asked of the family valet: 'Has the English gentleman arrived yet?' 'Yes, monsieur, ten minutes ago. He is in the bathroom.' Proust hurried to the door. 'Mr. Wilde!' he called. 'I hope that you are not ill.' Wilde emerged: 'Not in the least, dear, charming Monsieur Proust. But I was under the impression that I was going to dine alone with you, and when I saw the drawing-room and your good parents awaiting me in that drawing-room, I realized that the ordeal would be too much for me. So goodbye, dear Monsieur Proust—goodbye!'[76]

It is conceivable that Wilde's relationship with Lord Alfred Douglas, who accompanied Wilde to France in 1894, may have been yet another source for the affair of Charlus and Morel. The Wilde-Douglas affair could have suggested to Proust the tragic pattern of fall from grandeur through fatal hamartia, which he assigns to Charlus in A la recherche; for just as Wilde's career was destroyed by his passion for "Bosie," so Charlus's fall from social eminence is precipitated partly by his love for Morel.

In an allusion to Wilde in *Sodome et Gomorrhe* Proust pays tribute to him as a martyr to homosexual love. People with homosexual
tastes are, Proust writes, "without position except the most unstable,
like the poet one day celebrated in all the salons, applauded in all the
theaters of London, the next day unable to find even a room to rent
or a pillow whereon to lay his head" (2: 615–16). There exists a letter
from Mme Arman de Caillavet to her son which hints that Proust
made regular visits to Wilde when, after his imprisonment and disgrace, Wilde was living in Paris, sick and dying. "[Proust once] told
me he was going to the Passage des Beaux-Arts, where he was writing
a novel at the home of an obscure friend. . . . Now Oscar Wilde was
living at the Passage des Beaux-Arts when he died under an assumed
name! What a mystery. . . ."[77] It would have been entirely natural
for Proust, while writing a novel which touched upon homosexuality,
to seek out the man who had suffered the most for his homosexual
tastes (the novel in question would have to be the early, unfinished
Jean Santeuil, since Wilde died before Proust began *A la recherche*).
But there is no proof that these visits to Wilde ever took place.

There are several other traits Proust could have adopted from
Wilde for his portrait of Charlus: the admiration for Balzac; the stu-
pendous egomania; the genius for conversation and for the cutting,
witty epigram; and the conception of life as an art.[78] But these are, of
course, traits Proust could just as easily have borrowed from Montesquiou. As with Proust's other characters, the more we consider the
possible models for Charlus, the more composite the picture appears
to be. There is, as we have seen, something of Proust himself in the
character of Charlus. And Léon Guichard suggests that Proust, with
his intimate knowledge of and admiration for the Ballets Russes,
based the Charlus-Morel affair partly on the celebrated relationship
between Diaghilev and his protégé Nijinsky.[79] Céleste Albaret reveals another possible source, a relationship between a man named
M. Goldsmith (or Goldschmidt) and a younger man, an Englishman
known as Charlie (the name Proust assigns to Morel in *A la recherche*). Goldsmith, according to Céleste:

pursued Monsieur Proust with invitations to dinner. Monsieur Proust didn't
like to go; he told me that the fellow was a frightful bore and that it was a
waste of time. . . . He did not conceal the fact that the gentleman was of the
"Sodomite persuasion." He himself never received him or invited him. . . .

But he was fascinated by the young Englishman's way of dressing . . . and especially by his vests. That is the only reason he accepted two visits from him—to study his outfits for possible inclusion in his book. Afterwards, he never saw them again, neither the young one nor the old one.[80]

From the grand pattern of Wilde's tragic fall to a detail of an outfit worn by a young man named Charlie—we know, it seems, everything, and nothing, about the origins of Charlus and his love affairs. The possible models continue to proliferate; but the exact traits Proust took from each model and the workings of the imagination which fused them into the unique personalities of A la recherche are mysteries about which we can only speculate.

In 1894 Proust began a love affair with the nineteen-year-old, Venezuelan-born pianist and composer Reynaldo Hahn, whom he met in Madeleine Lemaire's salon. Hahn was, in the description of William Sansom, "pale brown, handsome, gifted, Jewish, moustached."[81] At Mme Lemaire's he played and sang his compositions to great applause and became a star of the salon. He and Proust were immediately attracted to each other, and in the summer of 1894 Mme Lemaire gave her blessing to their friendship by inviting them to stay at Réveillon, her château in the Marne. Proust's first book Les Plaisirs et les jours contained illustrations by Madeleine Lemaire as well as musical compositions by Reynaldo Hahn.

Proust's affair with Reynaldo lasted until Proust fell in love with Lucien Daudet in late 1895 or early 1896. (Proust would soon fight a duel with Jean Lorrain for suggesting in print what was, in fact, true of the new relationship, just as it had been true of the old.) When Proust's affections turned toward Lucien, he and Reynaldo underwent a period of quarreling and mutual jealousy. Proust wrote to Reynaldo:

I had an impulse of bad temper this evening, and you shouldn't be surprised or hold it against me. You told me: I'll never tell you anything again. If this were true, it would amount to perjury; not being true, it is still the most painful blow for me. To have you tell me everything has been, since the 20th of June, my hope, my consolation, my support, my life. In order not to cause you pain I hardly ever speak to you about it; but in order to avoid suffering too much myself I think about it always. So you see, you have said the only thing which could really wound me. I would prefer a thousand insults. Very often I deserve them, more often than you think. If I don't deserve them, it is in those moments of painful effort when watching a face, linking one name with another, reconstructing a scene, I try to fill in the gaps in a life which is dearer to me than anything but which will cause me the most painful anxiety so long as even its most innocent parts are unknown to me. Alas, it is an impossible task, and your kindness undertakes a Danaid's work by helping my affection pour a little of the past into my curiosity.[82]

This letter contains the germ of Proustian jealousy as it is described in A la recherche—the agony the lover experiences over the impossibility of knowing and understanding all the details of another's life. Indeed, in a passage in La Prisonnière describing the narrator's jealousy over Albertine, Proust returns to the metaphor of the Danaids he first used to describe his jealousy over Reynaldo Hahn: "Jealousy, which wears a blindfold, is not only powerless to discover anything in the shadows which surround it: it is yet another of those torments whose task is to begin forever anew, like that of the Danaids, like that of Ixion" (3: 151).

Despite this period of tension and bitterness, Proust and Reynaldo made a successful transition from passion to friendship, and for the rest of Proust's life Reynaldo remained one of his closest friends. When Proust died in 1922, Reynaldo Hahn was the one who contacted the inner circle of acquaintances to convey the sad news. And, along with Céleste Albaret, Reynaldo watched over the deathbed for part of the night following Proust's death, finally withdrawing to another room to continue—as Proust would have understood—working on his musical compositions.[83]

Aside from the letters of mutual reproach which were exchanged in 1896, Proust's letters to Reynaldo embody a playfulness, an intimacy, and a tenderness not found anywhere else in his correspondence, not even in his letters to his mother. Proust and Reynaldo spoke a private language consisting of invented words and playfully distorted spellings. Their pet names for each other continually multiplied. Marcel was the "pony" and Reynaldo was the "master." Or Reynaldo was Puncht, Binibuls, Binchnibuls, Hibuls, and Guncht, while Marcel was Buncht, Buninuls, or Cornouls. Proust regaled Reynaldo with comical drawings, poems, and parodies of the epistolary style of their friends, interspersed with serious discussions of classical music and French literature. The correspondence is childlike and at the same time sophisticated and intellectually acute. It shows us, almost better than *A la recherche* itself, what Maurice Sachs must have had in mind when he remarked that *A la recherche* is "the work of a sort of monster child, whose mind had all the experience of a man and whose soul was ten years old."[84]

Not surprisingly homosexuality is a recurrent topic in Proust's letters to Reynaldo. Only a part of that correspondence survives, so it is probable that more was said about homosexuality in these letters— both in the form of lovers' endearments and in the form of discussions of the subject per se—than we will ever know. Emmanuel Berl remarks in his preface to the letters that "Reynaldo no doubt destroyed those letters which would have moved us the most—and repulsed us the most."[85] Nevertheless, enough remains to give us a good idea of the special combination of gravity and humor with which Proust approached this, and all, subjects. In one of his first letters to Reynaldo Proust pensively recommends that Reynaldo read Plato's *Symposium*. "Don't read the whole volume of Plato, which will not interest you, but only the *Symposium*. . . . The bloom of the other dialogues is internal and—in spite of the fact that I don't remember which ones are included with the *Symposium* in that particular volume—a little austere for you."[86] But serious meditations on the *Symposium* do not deter Proust from laughing with Reynaldo at the ludicrous homosexual posturings of Robert de Montesquiou. After the death of Montesquiou's secretary and lover Gabriel d'Yturri, Montesquiou privately printed a memorial volume entitled *Le Chancelier des fleurs*, dedicated to Yturri's memory. Montesquiou did not invite Proust to the festive "inauguration" of the book, which took place at the Pavillon des Muses on 27 June 1908; but he did arrive later to present Proust with a copy in person. Proust wrote to Reynaldo:

Be advised that yesterday evening, after many exchanges of letters, the fatal Comte arrived in a pontifical yet urgent manner to read me and then give me the book about Yturri. . . . I wish you could have heard how, on the stroke of 2 a. m., with no pity for my neighbors the Gageys, he cried out, stamping the floor with his heel, "And now Scipio and Laelius, Orestes and Pylades, Hora and Posa, St. Mars and de Thou, Edmond and Jules de Goncourt, Flaubert and Bouilhet, Aristotle and Pythias, receive me, for I am worthy, into your august ranks."[87]

Philip Kolb in his notes to this letter suggests that Proust confused Aristotle with Damon and erred in writing "St. Mars" for Cinq-Mars. It is true that the Comte's transports of rhetoric, as Proust reports them, contain malapropisms and inconsistencies. But some of these apparent errors are probably deliberate distortions and embellishments of reality on Proust's part—jokes Proust has invented to satirize Montesquiou for Reynaldo's delectation. (Neither Proust nor Montesquiou would be likely to confuse Aristotle with Damon, or to include the Goncourt brothers in a list of famous male friends and lovers.) And yet Proust adds to the letter a serious postscript: "In Montesquiou's book there was a letter from the Prince de Radolin assuring him of his sympathy for the cruel loss [of Yturri]. He would have done better to keep a little of that sympathy for Eulenburg." Prince Hugo von Radolin was at that time the German ambassador to France, and Prince Philipp zu Eulenburg-Hertefeld was undergoing in Germany a trial for homosexuality which is, as we shall see, of considerable importance for understanding Proust's treatment of the theme in *A la recherche*. This letter is paradigmatic of a certain aspect of Proust's approach to homosexuality, for it shows how he could, and often did, move instantaneously from satire and mockery to sympathy and fellow feeling in his remarks on the subject.

Proust's relationship with Reynaldo Hahn had a significant impact on his creative writing. The year after they met at Madeleine Lemaire's, Proust and Reynaldo traveled together to Beg-Meil, a seacoast town in Brittany, where they took up residence in a small hotel in the country. They signed the register, not without a certain panache, as "Reynaldo Hahn, Musician" and "Marcel Proust, Man of Letters."[88] In this rustic, sylvan retreat Reynaldo worked on his music, while Proust began sketches for a new project, the unfinished, untitled, autobiographical novel we know as *Jean Santeuil*, a work which contains many glimpses of the themes and ideas of *A la recherche*. Later in Paris, after dropping by Reynaldo's for a visit and finding him not at home, Proust wrote to Reynaldo: "I had brought you some little things I've done and the beginning of a novel which [Léon] Yeatman himself . . . found very like the 'pony.' You'll have to help me correct everything that is too obviously so. I want you to be present in it always, but like a god in disguise that no mortal can recognize. Otherwise, you'll have to write 'tear up' over the whole book."[89] This statement underscores the strong autobiographical cast of *Jean Santeuil* and of Proust's writing in general. It is a statement totally in keeping with the epigraph Proust appended to *Jean Santeuil:* "Can I call this book a novel? It is less than that, perhaps, and more, the very essence of my life, gathered without any admixture. . . . This book was not composed, it was harvested."[90] In this work harvested from Proust's life Reynaldo Hahn is indeed, as Proust promised he would be, present in disguised form, but not so disguised as to be unrecognizable. Reynaldo's veiled appearances serve as a private tribute to his relationship with Proust and an acknowledgement of the inspiration he furnished Proust for this work. Reynaldo appears, for instance, in the form of Jean Santeuil's best friend Henri de Réveillon, whose initials are a reversal of Reynaldo Hahn's and whose name memorializes the château of Réveillon, where Proust and Reynaldo visited Madeleine Lemaire in the early days of their relationship. Reynaldo is also present in the portrait of the Marquis de Poitiers, a portrait in which the disguise becomes extremely thin and would have been, in fact, transparent to anyone who had heard Reynaldo perform:

As dinner came to an end and each one remained seated before his half-empty brandy glass and lit a cigarette, Poitiers took his glass and cigarette to the piano and started to sing to Jean everything Jean requested. Numerous accompaniments, sweet and sonorous, ran underneath his fingers; he sang with a charming voice, his cigarette dangling at the corner of his lip, while moving his head with a sort of half-nervous shudder, although he was usually a very calm young man. Each word of the song or of the air from an operetta could be distinctly heard. Without stopping, and keeping the accompaniment always in time, he sang the woman's part in a high falsetto and then came back to the choruses so strongly that everyone was transported. From time to time he sketched with stunning accuracy an impersonation of a well-known actor. Jean listened to him with prodigious admiration: all other singers and pianists would have seemed frigid and restricted when compared to this marvelous brilliance, to this charming voice, to these flashes of humor so well under control, so skillfully delivered that people admired Poitiers as much as if he had made them up on the spot, to this multiple accompaniment by means of which, looking at the notes with his indolent air and seeming to hesitate before striking the chords, he made it clear to everyone that here was a violin part, there some trombones, the delicateness and the violence of which he was able to reproduce simultaneously, unleashing all manner of sonorities, which he seemed to conduct with a distracted and weary air.[91]

There is also a bit of Reynaldo in the portrait of Daltozzi in *Jean San-teuil;* and there are no doubt echoes of Proust's spells of jealousy over Reynaldo in the scenes depicting Jean's jealousy over Françoise.

Throughout Proust's career Reynaldo remained a presiding ge-nius of his art, offering advice, criticism, and encouragement when Proust needed it most. Proust took Reynaldo's slightest reservations about his writing extremely seriously. Once Reynaldo remarked to Proust that he found his sentences a trifle long. Proust did not react right away, but he never forgot the remark. And a year later Reyn-aldo was astonished to hear Proust inject into a conversation the fol-lowing comment: "You, Reynaldo, you who don't care for my style. . . ."[92] When Proust was working on *Contre Sainte-Beuve*, he wrote to Georges de Lauris: "Georges, I am going to get down to work, because I read my beginning (200 pages) to Reynaldo, and his reac-tion greatly encouraged me."[93] Still later, during the period of Proust's early work on *A la recherche* in 1910, Reynaldo was still in his mind. He wrote to Reynaldo in August of that year, ecstatically describing the new throes of inspiration and creation: "Flaubert's soli-tary calls to Bouilhet—'Are you pleased with me?'—or those of a little girl to her doll are nothing compared to the words I shout all through the night: 'O my Bunibuls, don't you think that's rather nice?' "[94]

In Diotima's discussion of homosexual love in Plato's *Sym-posium*—the dialogue Proust recommended to Reynaldo soon after they met—she says: "So again a man with divinity in him . . . desires when he grows up to beget and procreate. . . . by attaching himself to a person of beauty, I think, and keeping company with him, he begets and procreates what he has long been pregnant with; present and absent he remembers him, and with him fosters what is begot-ten, so that as a result these people maintain a much closer commu-nion together and a firmer friendship than parents of children, be-cause they have shared between them children more beautiful and more immortal."[95] It would be difficult to find a better summation of the way Proust felt about his association with Reynaldo, and it is safe to say that *A la recherche* would not be quite the same book had Proust never met, and never loved, Reynaldo Hahn.[96]

Throughout his life Proust was fascinated by the French aris-tocracy. In *A la recherche* the demystification and remystification of the French nobility—principally in the form of the Guermantes family—is a major thematic movement, paralleling the narrator's initial disappointment with external reality and his eventual discovery of how reality can be transformed and redeemed in art. A large part of the inspiration for the aristocratic motif in *A la recherche* stems from the peculiar mixture of snobbery and eros with which, in life, Proust pursued the members of the *gratin*. For a time he was in love with the Comtesse de Chevigné, admiring her birdlike features from afar and finally receiving a rebuke. In *A la recherche* this experience is transformed into the narrator's impetuous and abortive courtship of the Duchesse de Guermantes.

But Proust also loved men of the French aristocracy. Around 1900 he began to hobnob with a group of young aristocrats who were to contribute, collectively, to the character in *A la recherche* known as Robert de Saint-Loup, the young nobleman who is for a time the narrator's best friend and who is discovered, late in the novel, to have homosexual tastes. In real life Proust's aristocratic friends included Gabriel de La Rochefoucauld, the Bibesco brothers Antoine and Emmanuel, Bertrand de Fénelon, and Georges de Lauris. There is no evidence that any members of the group were homosexually inclined. Certainly, among themselves, they claimed to be exclusively heterosexual and sometimes even denounced and mocked homosexuality. Proust played their game, at the same time harboring a secret love for the group, both individually and collectively.

The core of the group was a secret society originally formed by the Bibescos and Fénelon. It was a society bound together by code words and private languages, which bore some similarity to the linguistic games Proust was so fond of playing with Reynaldo. The friends called one another by anagrams or reversals of their real names: the Bibescos were the Ocsebibs, Fénelon was Nonelef, and Marcel was Lecram. The group's code word for "homosexual" was "Saturnian," perhaps a planetary echo of the term which was then current in European sexology: "Uranian." Proust remembers this word in the essay on homosexuality which opens *Sodome et Gomorrhe,* where he speaks of certain men who are attracted not only to other men but also to mannish traits in women and therefore "live perhaps less exclusively under the satellite of Saturn" (2: 622).

Proust—who had served, after all, in the army—was very profi-
cient at concealing his homosexual tastes and even in pretending to
hate anyone who was homosexually inclined. He found himself
frequently playing this bad-faith role when in the company of his
young aristocratic friends. Once Antoine Bibesco, who had been surprised to discover that Proust's handshake was weak and feeble, instructed him to grip the hand decisively and firmly. "But people
would take me for an invert!" Proust responded in horror, and with
typical reverse logic. On another occasion Proust told Emmanuel
Bibesco that he had been thinking a great deal about "Saturnism" and
had reached some conclusions that were "of the utmost severity." He
added that "almost the only things worth knowing about a fool are
that he's an anti-Dreyfusard or a Saturnian."[97] These remarks reveal
the self-contempt to which Proust often subjected himself by inter-
nalizing the social prejudice against homosexuality. They also
foreshadow the numerous passages in A la recherche that give, as we
shall see, wholesale endorsement to the most negative stereotypes
about homosexuality and thereby help to make Proust's novel the
knotty and self-contradictory document it is.

If one part of Proust denounced homosexuality to his aristocratic
friends, another part of Proust spoke to them in the voice of a lover.
When the others got together and Proust was unable to come along,
he felt, as he wrote to Antoine, "the jealousy of a masculine Andromeda chained to his rock."[98] In such remarks Proust trembled on
the brink of confessing his homosexual emotions. But his true confession—to himself, if not to the Ocsebibs and to Nonelef—came later in
his writing, where he compares the solitude imposed by homosexuality to that of "admirable Andromedas [who] reflect in their eyes
the pain they feel in longing for an impossible paradise"[99] and to that
of a "strange Andromeda whom no Argonaut will come to free"
(2: 626). When in A la recherche Proust endows the dashing and deb-
onair Saint-Loup with homosexual tastes, he is on one level perhaps
compensating, in the conscious fantasies and waking dreams of art, for
the erotic male devotion he sought, but never found, among his own
aristocratic friends.

Proust's experience of homosexual love was nothing if not far-
ranging. Not only did he pursue rich and handsome young aristocrats:

he also explored the homosexual underground in visits to male brothels. The stories about Proust's experiences in these brothels have
grown, by now, to such mythological proportions that it is probably
impossible ever to recover the grain of truth which lies at their center. They have become obligatory anecdotes for anyone who claims to
know something of the history of Paris low life, and they seem to take
a different form with every retelling. Gore Vidal recently transmitted
the legend in the following form:

> One evening, with Cocteau in the Palais Royal, I met an elderly man
> who had been, Cocteau assured me, Proust's closest friend. I have long since
> forgotten the best friend's name but he did tell me that Proust had bought a
> brothel for an Algerian boyfriend and both brothel and Algerian were still in
> business. On the back of a calling card, he wrote the address of the Hôtel
> Saumon and the name Said. . . .
>
> Though Eric and I had, separately, visited some of the more splendid
> Belle Epoque whorehouses neither of us had ever been to a male brothel.
> We wondered what it would be like. . . .
>
> . . . Just to the right of the front door, beaded curtains separated the
> dark hall from a small room where Said lay on a sagging divan. . . . He gave
> us a lecherous smile. . . .
>
> "*He* came here often?" I began.
>
> "Monsieur Marcel? Ah, very often. Yes. He would sit where you are sit-
> ting, in the corner, his back to the wall, wearing a fur coat, even in summer,
> he was always cold, always sick, poor Monsieur Marcel."
>
> But efforts to discover what Monsieur Marcel actually *did* were not di-
> rectly rewarded. In his way, Said protected the memory of his old patron,
> telling us no more than that Proust liked to watch others in the act of love
> through a hole in the wall. . . .[100]

Perhaps this information is accurate, and perhaps not. Many people
have claimed to have been Proust's "closest friend"; and no doubt
many proprietors of Paris brothels have attempted to burnish their
reputations by laying claim to firsthand knowledge of Monsieur Marcel's bizarre tastes and activities. All that can be said for certain is that
there is no mention of "Said" in any other biographical documents we
have concerning Proust.

It is indisputable, however, that Proust maintained a relationship
with a male-brothel keeper named Albert Le Cuziat—the famous Albert who is supposed to be one of the models for Albertine. Albert Le
Cuziat was having, when Proust knew him, an affair with a soldier

named André;[101] and Proust may have transposed this relationship into the novel as the suspected lesbian affair between Albertine and Andrée. Wolf von Harder claims that Proust was the third point of an amorous triangle in the Albert-André affair and that he was consumed with jealousy over the situation, as is the narrator over his suspicions about Andrée and Albertine.[102] It is doubtful, however, that Proust had any sexual feeling for Albert Le Cuziat; indeed, Céleste Albaret says that Proust at times expressed a positive antipathy for him.[103] But Albert served, nonetheless, a highly influential function as Proust's go-between, informant, and *metteur en scène*. And in this respect he contributed more to the portrait of Jupien in *A la recherche* than to the portrait of Albertine.

Proust met Albert Le Cuziat around 1911. Albert had begun his career as a footman to various members of the French aristocracy, serving such eminent aristocrats as Comte Orloff and Prince Radziwill. He was in the service of Orloff or Radziwill when Proust first made his acquaintance. Albert had two ruling passions: homosexuality and the nobility. He knew the most intimate details of aristocratic protocol and genealogy, and he no doubt provided Proust with a great deal of information on this subject that eventually passed into *A la recherche*.[104]

Very soon Albert left his post as a footman and went into business for himself. He opened a hotel near the Bourse and then a brothel *cum* bathhouse on the Rue Godot-de-Mauroy, a street which, in the words of Céleste Albaret, "has always had a reputation that's a book unto itself."[105] Finally, around 1915 or 1916, he opened his famous establishment on the Rue de l'Arcade. He was, according to Céleste, "a tall Breton, skinny as a rail, blond, vulgar, with blue eyes that were cold like those of a fish—the eyes of his soul—and he displayed the uneasiness of his profession in his gaze and on his face. He had a certain air of being hunted—and that's not surprising, since his place was always being raided by the police and he was constantly doing time in jail."[106] Albert's paranoia perhaps inspired the nervous, hunted demeanor the Baron de Charlus displays when on the prowl—a demeanor like that of a spy, says the narrator, or that of a crook (1: 751–52).

Around 1931 Maurice Sachs visited the brothel on the Rue de

l'Arcade, and later he left a description of the establishment that tallies in certain respects with Proust's picture of Jupien's male brothel in *Le Temps retrouvé*. Since Sachs visited the brothel about three years after the publication of *Le Temps retrouvé*, the question arises as to how much of what he saw, or thought he saw, was influenced by the portrayal of Jupien's brothel in Proust's novel. "I heard," Sachs writes, "about an establishment on the Rue . . . , which, under the guise of doing business as a public baths, carried on a covert trade in male prostitutes—rather soft boys, too lazy to look for regular work, who earned the money they took home to their *wives* by sleeping with men, for it is one of the most remarkable characteristics of this youth gone astray that it finds neither pleasure nor habit in its infamous corruptions."[107] Just so the boys in Jupien's brothel are putatively heterosexual lads who carry out their tasks in a bored and half-hearted manner. "Maurice," says the narrator of *A la recherche*, "apparently performed his terrible fustigations on the Baron simply out of mechanical habit, the effects of a neglected upbringing, the need for money, and a certain penchant for earning it in a way that was supposed to be less trouble than work but which was perhaps even more trouble" (3: 820–21). Moreover, Albert's baths struck Maurice Sachs as having a strangely religious atmosphere about them, with a courtyard that looked, he says, "like the courtyard of a parsonage."[108] This odd mixture of the sacred and the profane is also characteristic of Jupien's brothel, which Jupien wittily compares to a convent of Carmelites and in which he sometimes collects his fees by imitating a priest asking for donations (3: 830, 829). Is Sachs giving an objective report on reality? Or is he, consciously or subconsciously, writing an imitation of the brothel scene in *Le Temps retrouvé?*[109]

A story told about Proust and Albert by Wolf von Harder poses similar problems:

One day Proust wanted at all costs to see a butcher, to question him. Albert, who didn't have any butchers handy, asked a certain friend to come to see Proust and pretend he was a butcher. And this was done. Proust asked him, "Are you a butcher?" The visitor said yes. "Did you work today?" There came another yes. "Was there a killing?" Proust continued. The so-called butcher thought it wise to answer again in the affirmative. The writer became visibly excited. "Did you yourself kill an animal?" Again a yes. "What animal?" Embarrassed the young man answered, "A bull." Proust took more and more interest in the matter. "Did he bleed much?" he asked. "What do you mean?" answered the embarrassed young man. "You know! The bull, when it was slaughtered," said Proust. "Oh, yes," the visitor claimed, "very much." "Did you touch the blood with your hands?" . . . The so-called butcher came around. "Naturally," he observed, "I had to plunge them all the way into it." The writer was at the highest pitch of excitement; he felt fright, admiration, and a vague shiver. "Show me your hands!" he demanded. The young man did as he was told and suppressed the laugh that was welling up inside him. He had to remain serious. The writer, he knew, paid very well for these question-and-answer sessions, when he was satisfied with the results.[110]

In Jupien's brothel Charlus is aware that the boys who pretend to be monsters of sadism have been well rehearsed by Jupien beforehand and that they are performing a prearranged charade. Nevertheless, Charlus insists that they give a realistic performance and keep any underlying traces of altruism well concealed. Proust is telling us that the theater of sadism, the melodramatic pretense of cruelty, is just as important to the sadomasochist as the actual infliction of pain, if not more so. Do we conclude that Proust knew this truth because he himself gained sexual excitement from factitious scenarios of sadism? Or do we conclude that Proust has been cast retrospectively in this role by people who have read or heard about the brothel scene in Le Temps retrouvé and assumed that it must be based on similar events in Proust's own life?

We have also heard the Proust had rats brought to the brothel and pierced with hatpins in his presence[111] and that he enjoyed degrading with Albert's help pictures of respected women—including, some say, a picture of his own mother.[112] The story about the profaned pictures has an analogue in the scene in A la recherche where Mlle Vinteuil degrades her father's picture while making love to her female friend (1: 159–65). Is this scene a covert confession of similar conduct on Proust's part, the source of the rumors about Proust's similar conduct, or both? As for the rats, André Gide, Bernard Fay, and Boni de Castellane all reported that Proust confessed to them about his sadistic experiments with rats.[113] And George Painter talks of being able to meet, in Paris between the wars, "the very chauffeur who declared, with a proud and beaming smile: 'It was

I who used to take the rats to Monsieur Marcel.' "[114] Independent confirmations of the truth? Attempts on the part of Proust to give his friends a *frisson* of horror by pretending to be just as sadistic as his own sadistic characters? A greedy chauffeur trying to attract attention and tips from curious tourists and litterateurs?[115]

I am not suggesting that Proust was above committing the bizarre acts that have sometimes been attributed to him, as Céleste Albaret, for instance, thinks he was.[116] Proust certainly had a cruel side to his personality as well as a tender and affectionate side, as his letters show and as some of his friends have testified (a reminiscence by Antoine Bibesco, listed in the bibliography, is called "The Heartlessness of Marcel Proust"). Just how far Proust went in expressing the cruel side of his personality in sadistic sexual rituals is, however, a question we do not have sufficient evidence to answer. And since we cannot know the truth of this particular matter, the next best thing is to try to interpret the material we do have—the stories themselves, whether true or false. Why do these stories, with their lack of concrete foundation, continue to be told as literary gossip and to be accepted and publicized by some Proustian scholars? I suggest it is partly because they appeal to and help to perpetuate widespread and deep-seated fears and stereotypes about the "homosexual." As he appears in these stories, Proust is a familiar figure of sexual mythology: the "homosexual" as sexual blasphemer, the man whose sexuality is presumed to be itself so grotesque and distorted that it inevitably results in acts of sadism, brutality, and profanation. George Painter, in a chapter called "The Pit of Sodom," creates in its full regalia this image of Proust and, by extension, of homosexuality in general, offering the stabbed rats, the degraded pictures, and the homosexuality as three interrelated aspects of what he calls Proust's "moral abasement."[117]

As was mentioned in the first chapter, the epithet "Proustian" was for a long time fashionably applied to people thought to have a homosexual orientation. We can now see a bit more clearly what this epithet implies and something of what Proust represents as a cultural symbol. When Proust is the tenor of the metaphor and homosexuality is the vehicle, other metaphors are usually implied in which homosexuality is the tenor and rats, abattoirs, male brothels, sadism, and "moral abasement" are the vehicles. The legends feed upon these metaphors so that the metaphors can, in turn, feed upon the legends—a vicious cycle, which is, of course, helped along considerably by Proust's own homophobic texts.

Even if it could be shown beyond a doubt that some or all of the legends are true, that would simply raise the following, broader-ranging question: since homosexuality does not necessarily have anything to do with rats, profanation, or sadism (Painter and others to the contrary notwithstanding), why did Proust sometimes act as if it did? In answering such a question, we would still be dealing with the interpretation of cultural myth, because a satisfactory answer would require a thorough tracing of the particular sexual traditions and conventions that acted on Proust and helped to create his self-image. This is a realm of inquiry too large to be addressed in detail here but one to which we shall return in later chapters.

If Proust did degrade himself and his sexuality in the ways some people have claimed, he also made his novel an implicit *apologia pro vita sua*. One relevant passage is the scene where Françoise brutally slaughters a chicken for dinner:

When I came down Françoise was in the scullery which opened onto the barnyard killing a chicken which, in its desperate and totally natural resistance to a Françoise who was beside herself as she sought to split its neck at a point beneath the ear and uttered cries of "Filthy beast! Filthy beast!," placed the saintly goodness and unction of our servant in a less advantageous light than it would when it appeared at dinner tomorrow with its skin embroidered in gold like a chasuble and its precious juices dropping as if from a ciborium. When it was dead, Françoise cleaned up the blood, which ran freely but without drowning her rancor, had yet another impulse of rage, and, looking at the cadaver of her enemy, said one last time, "Filthy beast!" I went upstairs trembling all over. I would have liked to see Françoise fired on the spot. But then who would bring me hot water bottles scalding as only she could make them, coffee as fragrant, and even . . . these chickens? . . . (1: 121–22)

Françoise is an artist in her own right, and an unpleasant but undeniable aspect of her art is the sadism on which it is, in part, based. One day there is an impulse of madness and a bloody slaughter, and the next day there appears on the table a gorgeous work of culinary art. Like Françoise, Proust contained the ugly as well as the beautiful.

But if, like the narrator with Françoise, we are tempted to judge him, denounce him, and dismiss him on the spot, we are suddenly caught wondering who else could bring us the same insight into both sides of human nature, the same revelation of the diabolic within the divine, the same totality of vision. As the narrator says of Mlle Vinteuil, "A sadist such as she is an artist of evil, something a person who is entirely evil can never be, because in such a person evil is not an external trait, it seems altogether natural and is in no way distinguished from the person himself; and since such a person would have no regard in the first place for virtue, for the veneration of the dead, for filial affection, it follows that he would gain no sacrilegious pleasure from profaning these qualities" (1: 164). Perhaps in these passages, as so often in *A la recherche,* Proust is judging himself in order to forgive himself.

Céleste Albaret insists that Proust's interest in Albert and his brothels was the purely scientific interest of a student of human nature and its variations, and this was undoubtedly one of Proust's motives in cultivating Albert's friendship and frequenting his establishment. "The striking thing," says Céleste, "is that when [Proust returned from Albert's], he would talk with me about it in exactly the same tone as if he had just returned from a reception at the Comte de Beaumont's or the Comtesse Greffulhe's. It was the tableau of what he had seen that interested him. . . . When I pointed out to him, in my frank way, that I didn't understand how he could receive Albert in his home, much less go over there, he said to me: 'I know, Céleste. . . . But I can only write about things as they are, and for that I have to see them with my own eyes."[118]

During just such a quest for the realities of life Proust found the inspiration for one of the most important scenes of his novel: the flagellation of the Baron de Charlus. According to Céleste Albaret, this is a scene Proust never would have written had he not observed a version of it first with his own eyes. "I will always remember," Céleste writes:

that night he came back [from Albert's] after seeing the very spectacle to which he assigns such importance in his book. He arrived with his hat askew, as it always was when he was in a hurry. He rushed me into his room and, seated in the corner of the bed, told me the story.

Here is what had happened. In response to an inquiry, Albert had let him know that he could come and would see the thing about which Albert had been telling him.

"My dear Céleste, what I saw this evening is beyond imagining. I got to Le Cuziat's, as you know. He had informed me that there was a man who came to his place to have himself flagellated. I witnessed the whole scene from another room, through a little window in the wall. It's unbelievable, I tell you! I had my doubts; I wanted positive verification, and now I have it. It involves a rich manufacturer who makes a special trip for this purpose from the north of France. Imagine this: he is there, in a room, attached to the wall with padlocked chains, and some low-life character, picked up God knows where and who gets paid for what he does, is beating him with a whip until the blood spurts everywhere. And it's only then that the unfortunate soul attains the summit of his pleasure."

I was so overcome with horror that I said to him: "Monsieur, it's not possible. Things like that do not exist!"

"Oh, yes, Céleste. I did not make it up."

"But, Monsieur, how could you stand to look at it?"

"Precisely, Céleste, because it's not something one can invent."

And when I told him that Le Cuziat was a monster in my eyes, he answered: "Ah, Céleste . . . you are right; he's not a good boy. He disgusts me, even. But I learned something this evening."

"And you had to pay a lot to see it?"

"Yes, Céleste, but I had to do it." . . .

And so, that night, we talked about the horrible scene of flagellation for hours—I, horrified, as I said, and he repeating it over and over so as not to forget anything and no doubt already thinking out loud, in that way he had, about writing it down.[119]

In a tribute to Proust quoted in the first paragraph of this study, Ernst Robert Curtius states that "he surpasses Flaubert in intelligence as he surpasses Balzac in literary excellence and Stendhal in understanding of life and of beauty."[120] Though he may in some ways surpass them, Proust also retains close ties to the French realists who were his precursors. Like them, he strives first to understand life as it is lived before he begins to reinvent it as fiction. His topic is what Montaigne before him and Malraux after him called *la condition humaine*. The brothel was his laboratory. And when Proust entered that laboratory, he was, to echo his own images, a surgeon probing the condition of others and also, perhaps, a doctor trying out a dangerous drug by experimenting first on himself.

THE PERSON I LOVED THE MOST

Like Dante and Beatrice, Socrates and Alcibiades, Petrarch and Laura, and Shakespeare and his "master-mistress," Proust and Alfred Agostinelli have generated a wide range of critical controversy. Some critics claim that Agostinelli was the primary model for Albertine in *A la recherche;* others hold that Agostinelli had nothing to do with the portrait of Albertine; and still others steer a vague middle course by suggesting that Agostinelli probably contributed to Albertine in certain indefinable ways but was, after all, only one among several models both male and female.

It is surprising that such a degree of confusion exists on a subject for which the evidence is so clear. The reason for the confusion, perhaps, is that many people are not comfortable with the idea that great art can stem from homosexual inspiration, or that valid insight into the human condition can derive from homosexual experience. And so we hear from critics and biographers that "the long-standing notion that Albertine . . . was a fictional projection of the chauffeur Agostinelli, has been discredited."[121] Or, as Céleste Albaret phrases it:

People have constructed all sorts of fables concerning . . . the feelings [Monsieur Proust] had, or is supposed to have had, for Agostinelli. Several thinkers, whether great or small I don't know, have even discovered that he was, at least in part, the Albertine of the book, with whom the narrator is in love. For me, that's ridiculous. First, Albertine existed long before Agostinelli, in the brain and in the notebooks of Monsieur Proust. Second, I am convinced, from the way Monsieur Proust spoke to me about him, that . . . Monsieur Proust took an interest in him first because he was pleasant company as a chauffeur . . . and then because he had ambitions for rising above his station; since Agostinelli was far from stupid . . . Monsieur Proust's natural generosity moved him to help him achieve his ambition.[122]

There is a considerable gap between what Céleste knows from personal impressions and what scholars know from biographical and literary research. Recent studies of Proust's correspondence and notebooks have revealed that Proust was in love with Agostinelli, that his love for him probably led to the creation of Albertine, and that it had a cataclysmic impact on *A la recherche* as a whole. Some of this evidence has come to light only recently, and other parts of it have been (as in Céleste's statement above) blithely ignored. It is appropriate, then, to undertake a careful review of this episode in Proust's life, an episode which is in many ways responsible for imparting to *A la recherche* the form in which we know it.

Alfred Agostinelli was eighteen years old when he and Proust met in Cabourg in 1907. Proust hired Agostinelli to drive him around the surrounding countryside. In those days one needed special expertise to handle the intractable new invention known as the automobile. Indeed, the terms "chauffeur" and "mechanic" were used interchangeably. The skillful young chauffeur-mechanic from Monaco soon stepped from Proust's life into his art. In *Le Figaro* for 19 November 1907 Proust published a piece called "Impressions de route en automobile," in which he sketched with whimsical charm the technological wonders of the automobile and the skill of the young chauffeur he had met in Cabourg. Interestingly the article applies both male and female metaphors to Agostinelli, as if Proust were already experimenting with the sexual transpositions Agostinelli would undergo in *A la recherche*. Agostinelli is compared first to a pilgrim, then to a nun, then to Saint Cecilia—images inspired partly by the androgynous garb which was then required for motoring and partly by the Gothic churches Proust had been visiting with Agostinelli:

When we left Lisieux, it was pitch dark; my mechanic had put on a large rubber mantle and wore on his head a sort of wimple which, encasing the fullness of his young, beardless face, made him look, as we penetrated faster and faster into the night, like some pilgrim or rather some nun of speed. From time to time—Saint Cecilia improvising on some immaterial instrument—he touched the keyboard and pulled one of the stops of the organs concealed within the automobile, whose music, though it was continuous, we scarcely noticed, except during the changes in register which were the changings of the gears—a music which was, so to speak, abstract, all symbol and number, and which brought to mind the harmony the spheres are said to produce as they turn in the aether. But most of the time he simply held his wheel in his hand (the wheel which controls the direction of the automobile and which is known as the "steering wheel") and, as he held it, it recalled the consecration crosses held by the apostles which stand against the columns of the chancel in the Sainte-Chapelle in Paris . . . and in general suggested every stylization of the wheel in the art of the Middle Ages. He was so immobile that he seemed not so much to be using the wheel as to be symbolically grasping it, as if it were some emblem appropriate to him; in such a manner various saints, on the porches of cathedrals, hold an anchor, a wheel, a harp, a scythe, a grill, a hunting horn, or some paintbrushes. These attributes are usually meant to symbolize the craft in which the saints excelled during their lifetimes; but they are also sometimes images of the instruments by which they perished; may the steering wheel of my young chauffeur remain forever the symbol of his skill rather than the prefiguration of his martyrdom! [123]

The androgynous imagery is an artistic foreshadowing; the final sentence is a biographical prophecy. For several years later, after Proust had fallen deeply in love with him, Agostinelli perished at the controls of another of the new machines with which he was so fascinated. When Proust prepared "Impressions de route en automobile" for republication in 1919, he appended this footnote to the passage quoted above: "I scarcely foresaw when I wrote these lines that seven or eight years later this young man would ask me whether he could type one of my books, would learn aviation under the name of Marcel Swann—a name in which he had amicably combined my Christian name and the name of one of my characters—and would meet his death at the age of twenty-six, in an airplane accident, in the sea off Antibes." This remark, as Robert Vigneron has said, is but "a cold epitaph on an empty tomb." [124] It implies a great deal but reveals next to nothing about the complex relationship of Proust and Agostinelli from 1907 until Agostinelli's death in 1914. In order to fill in the gaps we shall have to return to 1907.

When "Impressions de route en automobile" appeared in *Le Figaro,* Proust received the usual congratulatory letters from his friends. And one of the letters which pleased him most was from the young man whose portrait he had included in the article. "Guess," he wrote to Mme Straus, "which among several other letters I received was the prettiest—Agostinelli's, to whom my valet sent a copy of the article." [125] Proust was, from the outset, impressed with Agostinelli's intelligence and skill with words. He later told André Gide that "I have letters from him which are those of a great writer." [126] And to Emile Straus he wrote that Agostinelli "was an extraordinary person and possessed perhaps the greatest intellectual gifts I have ever known." [127]

When Proust returned to Cabourg in 1908, he stayed close to the Grand Hotel and made only a few automobile excursions with Agostinelli. Then, in September of that year, Agostinelli drove Proust to Versailles. Proust fell ill soon after his arrival at the Hotel des Réservoirs and remained shut up in his room, playing dominoes with Agostinelli and with his valet and occasionally writing. But Proust's health worsened. He discharged Agostinelli and returned the rented car. And Agostinelli dropped out of sight.

Agostinelli reappeared in Paris in January of 1913 looking for a job. He called on Proust and asked to be reinstated in his old position as chauffeur. By that time Proust had hired another chauffeur, Odilon Albaret, soon to be Céleste's husband; so it was decided that Agostinelli would become Proust's secretary and help him type his book. Agostinelli moved in and brought with him a woman named Anna, who had previously been his mistress and who was now, Agostinelli claimed, his wife. (Proust later discovered that the two had never been legally married.) Anna was an extremely jealous woman, and Alfred was constantly unfaithful to her—"something she didn't know," Proust told Emile Straus, "or she would have killed him." He added that although Agostinelli regularly deceived Anna, "he loved her more than anything in the world."[128]

Whether Alfred was unfaithful to Anna with Proust, with other women, with other men, or with some combination of all these is not clear from the surviving documents. What is clear is that Proust fell in love with Agostinelli while living with him in Paris and that Agostinelli's roving eye caused Proust extreme unhappiness. The presence under one roof of Proust, the great scientist and practitioner of jealousy, Anna, the insanely jealous "wife," and Alfred, the habitually unfaithful man loved by both Anna and Proust made, no doubt, for a complicated emotional situation.

As the relationship with Agostinelli became more intense, Proust began, typically, to lay down a smoke screen of denials that the association was anything other than professional. To his friend Albert Nahmias (another possible model for Albertine) he wrote: "Avoid mentioning my secretary (the former mechanic). People are so stupid that they could see in this relationship (*as they saw in my friendship with you*) something homosexual. It wouldn't make any difference to me. But it would break my heart to wrong this boy." [129] At the same time Proust darkly alluded in other letters to the romantic difficulties which were plaguing his life. He wrote to Anna de Noailles around 15 February 1913, "I am at present oppressed by unhappiness, by problems of health, and also by the hardships imposed upon me by having contemporaries who are so harsh and so little obliging." [130] He wrote to Lucien Daudet: "My dear little fellow, you know I am very ill, very vexed, very unhappy. I hope you'll understand that it's on account of this that I am unable to respond adequately to many things you tell me, but writing causes me such fatigue." [131] And to Mme Straus he sent a veiled confession that his romantic problems were revolving around homosexuality: "I think all the pain I am enduring would be a little less cruel if I could tell you about it. Its character is sufficiently general, sufficiently human, that it would perhaps interest you." [132]

In August of 1913 Proust left for his customary visit to Cabourg. He traveled by automobile, with Agostinelli driving. But the sojourn was cut short when, on a drive with Agostinelli from Cabourg to Houlgate, a mysterious crisis occurred. Proust told the story to Georges de Lauris: "The other Monday I had told Nicolas [Nicolas Cottin, Proust's valet] that we would definitely stay in Cabourg for a few more days when, on a ride I took to Houlgate with my secretary, my secretary noticed that I was looking so sad that he told me I ought to cut short my indecision and take the train at Trouville without going back to the hotel. I sent a message to Nicolas telling him to pack the trunks, and my secretary sent a message to his wife telling her to leave with Nicolas as soon as he could. I returned to Paris without baggage, without a nightshirt, without having paid my bill at the hotel, without having told the people at the hotel I was leaving." The reason for this hasty departure was, Proust said, "when I went to Cabourg, I left behind me a woman I see only rarely in Paris, but at any rate I know she's there, whereas in Cabourg I felt too far away from her and therefore anxious and troubled." [133] This seems to be another reference to the mysterious "Girl of Cabourg," whom Proust once intended to marry. It seems likely, however, that even though the girl actually existed, she was not the real reason for Proust's return to Paris. Agostinelli was, at this time, the center of Proust's affections, and whatever precipitated the journey to Paris must have had something to do with him. It is probable that Proust simply wanted to be alone with Agostinelli and that he used the story of his concern over a woman as an excuse to leave Nicolas and Anna in Cabourg and go home alone with Alfred. In *A la recherche* the narrator does something similar with Albertine. When the narrator's jealousy is awakened by Albertine's revelation that she knows Mlle Vinteuil and her friend, he manufactures a fictional sorrow over a woman he has planned to marry and uses it as a stratagem to persuade Albertine to return to Paris with him. "At all costs I had to prevent her from being alone," he muses, "at least for a few days, to keep her near me so she could not see Mlle Vinteuil's friend" (2: 1,121).

It is therefore possible, as Painter suggests, that "Proust hurried Agostinelli to Paris . . . because he had detected him in a seaside flirtation."[134] Whatever the nature of Proust's jealousy, the return to Paris did not allay it. Sounding more and more like the narrator of *A la recherche*, Proust wrote to Albert Nahmias: "Excuse me for asking you a strange question, the answer to which, I suddenly find, would be of great service to me. Have you ever, for any reason, had anyone shadowed and, if so, did you keep the addresses of the detectives or maintain contact with them?"[135]

Perhaps the most significant thing about Proust's harried relationship with Agostinelli is that it seems to have inspired some last-minute changes in *Du côté de chez Swann*, which was published on 8 November 1913. After his return from Cabourg Proust busied himself correcting the proofs for the book; and he wrote to Lucien Daudet that he was adding to those proofs "some very important little details which tighten the knots of jealousy around poor Swann."[136] And so in the midst of his relationship with Agostinelli, Proust seems to have realized and consciously exploited the artistic and philosophical value of his jealous suffering. Interestingly the sections of *Du côté de chez Swann* which describe Swann's jealousy were, Proust thought, the most meaningful parts of the book. They were the sections he especially commended to friends and potential readers. To Mme de Noailles he wrote, "If you are able to read my book, that would make me very happy, especially the second part of the chapter called *Un Amour de Swann*."[137] And in May of 1914 he told René Blum: "I am delighted to hear that you are reading the entire ending of the second chapter, beginning with the time when Odette no longer loves Swann and even a little before. Excuse me for talking about myself, but it's one of those cases where, as Hugo says, 'I' and 'We' are the same. I believe in this fundamental unity of humanity."[138]

Though Proust seems thus to have found an artistic outlet for his unhappy love affair, he continued to undergo acute suffering. Just before the publication of *Du côté de chez Swann* he wrote to J.-L. Vaudoyer: "Thank you for thinking of my book. It's going to appear in two weeks, at precisely a time when I am so miserable that I cannot feel the joy I would perhaps have felt at another time, seeing it finished and seeing it read by those for whom it was intended."[139] And after *Swann* was published, he wrote to Robert de Montesquiou that "my health has gotten worse, and troubles which I could not imagine, an enormous sadness have for an entire year wrecked my life, with the result that the book appeared without giving me the least pleasure."[140]

Proust's greatest grief was yet to come. Agostinelli, who loved all things mechanical, began to take an interest in aviation—one of the most salient traits he shares with Albertine in the novel (3: 105–6). Proust immediately perceived this new interest as a threat to their relationship. Perhaps one aspect of Proust's jealousy is mirrored in *A la recherche* in the narrator's comment that "one day [Albertine] told me she had been to an airfield and was getting friendly with the aviator" (3: 612). Despite Proust's opposition Agostinelli talked him into paying for flying lessons, which Agostinelli took at the aerodrome at Buc, near Paris. Odilon Albaret drove him back and forth.[141] Proust feared an accident and redoubled his efforts to persuade Agostinelli to give up flying. In this he clashed with Anna, who was convinced that Alfred would make a fortune by learning the new art.[142] The situation soon became intolerable, and Agostinelli and Anna left Paris. In Antibes, using money he had saved from working for Proust, Agostinelli enrolled in the Garbero brothers' school of aviation under the evocative and emblematic name of Marcel Swann.[143] Proust and Agostinelli exchanged letters, and Proust tried unsuccessfully to persuade him to return to Paris. Trying to reach Alfred through Anna's cupidity, Proust wrote, "If ever ill fortune decrees that you have an airplane ac-

cident, you can make it clear to your wife that she will find in me neither a protector, nor a friend, nor a source of money."[144] Again, as
had also happened in 1907, Proust seems to have had a premonition
of Agostinelli's death.

The accident Proust feared took place on Saturday, 30 May 1914,
at around five o'clock in the afternoon, during Alfred's second solo
flight. He had been taking lessons for two months and had made
rapid progress. Apparently thinking that he was now ready for
grander adventures, he ignored a warning from Joseph Garbero and
flew out over the sea. There he attempted a low-altitude turn and
crashed into the water, a few hundred yards from shore. Ironically
and pathetically Agostinelli had never learned to swim. He slowly
sank, gesturing helplessly from the wreckage, and drowned before a
rescue could be organized. He was twenty-five years old.

Proust was, of course, inconsolable. In his grief he forgot his
threats to cut Anna off without a cent. Their sorrow brought them
back together, and she came to stay with Proust at 102 Boulevard
Haussmann. There the two tried vainly to console each other for the
loss of the young man they both had loved. Proust wrote to Robert de
Montesquiou, who had himself lost a beloved secretary and lover
some years before: "You were kind enough to write me a letter. . . .
If I have not thanked you for it before now, it is because there has
been added to the troubles that plague my life . . . the loss of my
secretary, who died in a terrible fashion. . . . everything that up till
then was fluid and bearable holds me now in a relentless grip. . . . I
have only enough strength to impart to the poor widow the courage I
lack."[145] On 11 June 1914 he informed André Gide, who was also in a
position to understand the nature of his grief, of "the death of a young
man I loved probably more than all my friends." And he added a brief
sketch of the relationship:

He was a boy of delightful intelligence; and, moreover, it was not on account
of that that I loved him. I went for a long time without perceiving this intelligence—not as long as he did, however. I discovered in him a merit
marvelously incompatible with his whole station in life, I discovered it with
stupefaction, but without its adding anything to the affection I already had for
him. After discovering it, I merely took a little extra joy in revealing it to
him. But he died before fully knowing what he was, and even before com-

pletely being what he was. The whole affair is shot through with such frightful circumstances that, already crushed as I am, I do not know how I can bear such grief.[146]

A year later the pain was still fresh. In April of 1915, in a letter to Clément de Maugny, Proust referred to the loss of a friend "who, with my mother and father, is the person I loved the most."[147] Still later, in a letter to René Blum written in 1916, he spoke again of Agostinelli as "the person I loved the most."[148]

When in *A la recherche* Albertine meets her death by falling from a horse, the incident may contain an allusion to Agostinelli's fall from the sky. But Alfred's death and Proust's grief are more clearly memorialized in another passage, a strange and beautiful interlude haunted with private symbolism. As the narrator of *A la recherche* is riding a horse around the hilly terrain near Balbec:

Suddenly my horse reared up; he had heard a strange noise, and it was only with difficulty that I got him back under control and avoided being thrown to the ground; I raised eyes filled with tears toward the point from which the noise seemed to come, and I saw, about fifty yards above me, in the sunlight, soaring between two great and shining wings of steel, a being whose indistinct face seemed to resemble that of a man. I was as overcome as an ancient Greek seeing for the first time a demigod. And I wept, for I was ready to weep from the moment I realized that the noise was coming from above my head—airplanes were still rare in those days—and at the thought that I was now going to see an airplane for the first time. As when, while reading, one senses the approach of a moving word, I was waiting only for the actual sight of the airplane before breaking into tears. But the aviator seemed to hesitate on his course. I felt opening before him—before me, if habit had not made me a prisoner—all the roads of space, all the roads of life; he flew on, glided for several seconds above the sea; then suddenly making up his mind, and seeming to yield to some force the opposite of gravity, as if he were returning to his native land, with a light movement of his golden wings, he rose into the sky. (2: 1,029)

Just as Reynaldo Hahn was the "god in disguise" in *Jean Santeuil*, so Alfred Agostinelli is the disguised god of *A la recherche*. The passage above is at once his memorial and his apotheosis as an inspiring spirit of Proust's novel. In life Icarus must fall; but in art he can fly on and on. In *A la recherche* Alfred Agostinelli soars, lives, and returns to his native land—the mind and imagination of Marcel Proust.

Critics who argue that Proust's relationship with Alfred Agostinelli had little or no effect on *A la recherche* usually assert that Albertine, for whom Agostinelli is presumably a model, existed in Proust's imagination and writing before he met Agostinelli; and they also sometimes point out that Proust's philosophy of love had crystallized by the time he wrote *Du côté de chez Swann* and that this book was completed before Agostinelli came to live with Proust in 1913.[149] The first assertion does not accord with the available evidence. A close study of Proust's notebooks suggests that he in fact created Albertine—or at least the Albertine that we know—during the period of his love for Agostinelli and grief over his death. The second assertion is an oversimplification. We have already seen that Proust's relationship with Agostinelli apparently moved him to add to *Du côté de chez Swann*, immediately before its publication, "some very important little details which tighten the knots of jealousy around poor Swann." Furthermore, after the departure and death of Agostinelli, Proust added to the later volumes of *A la recherche* a wealth of material which significantly deepened and broadened his analysis of love and death. Indeed, Proust's relationship with Agostinelli seems to have inspired two entire volumes of the novel, *La Prisonnière* and *La Fugitive*, volumes which, with their story of Albertine's sequestration, flight from Paris, and eventual death, follow the outline of Proust's own life from 1913 to 1914. The evidence is as follows.

When *Du côté de chez Swann* was published by Grasset in 1913, it contained an announcement that *A la recherche du temps perdu* would be a novel in three volumes, with two volumes yet to appear. It also contained a table of contents for the two future volumes. The table read:

To appear in 1914:
A la Recherche du Temps perdu—Le Côté de Guermantes:
At Mme Swann's—Place Names: The Place—First Sketches of the Baron de Charlus and of Robert de Saint-Loup—Character Names: The Duchesse de Guermantes—The Salon of Mme de Villeparisis.
A la Recherche du Temps perdu—Le Temps retrouvé:
In the Shadow of Flowering Young Girls—The Princesse de Guermantes—M. de Charlus and the Verdurins—Death of My Grandmother—The Heart's Intermissions—The Vices and Virtues of Padua and Combray—

Mme de Cambremer—Robert de Saint-Loup's Marriage—The Perpetual Adoration.[150]

The summary contains no mention of Albertine; and yet she is, in the present version of *A la recherche*, the central female character. Moreover, there was no reference to Albertine in the manuscript Proust submitted to Fasquelle and the *Nouvelle Revue Française* in 1912 or in the manuscript he submitted to Grasset in 1913.

Marcel Plantevignes, to whom Proust read large portions of his novel in its early stages, says that he was taken totally by surprise by the appearance of *La Prisonnière* and *La Fugitive*, since those volumes revolved around a character of whom, as far as he knew, there was no trace in Proust's early work on *A la recherche*. Plantevignes writes:

When after Proust's death *La Prisonnière* and [*La Fugitive*] appeared, many people who knew how well acquainted I had been with Proust asked me what I knew about these books and what I thought about them. I had to tell them that I knew absolutely nothing about them and that I didn't know what to think. My surprise, in fact, was very great, was total, and was naturally a good deal stronger than would have been the case for someone who hadn't known Proust. For neither in Cabourg nor in Paris did I ever hear Proust mention a beloved woman who would cause him grief, and no one by the name of Albertine ever appeared in his remarks.[151]

It is conceivable, of course, that Proust avoided mentioning Albertine to Plantevignes for the simple reason that Plantevignes and his friends in Cabourg seem to have served Proust as models for the little band. But the little band, as we shall see, probably came into being before Albertine herself. And, in any case, *A la recherche* in its present form is, quite simply, undiscussable without some mention of Albertine. If Albertine had been a part of Proust's first conception of his novel, it seems highly unlikely that he would have omitted her from his discussions of his work with Marcel Plantevignes.

In the present version of *A la recherche* Albertine makes her appearance in the second volume of the novel, *A l'ombre des jeunes filles en fleurs* (literally, *In the Shadow of Flowering Young Girls*). Originally, as we can see from the first table of contents reproduced above, the narrator's encounter with the young girls was to have taken place not in the second volume but at the beginning of the final, then the third, volume. Furthermore, Henri Bonnet's work on Proust's notebooks suggests that the girls to which this title refers did not at first include a girl named Albertine. In the notebook numbered 25 in the catalogue of the Bibliothèque Nationale the girls are called Maria, Solange, Anna, Septimie, Célia, and Arabelle; and in Notebook 29 there is mention of an Andrée and an Hélène. The name which recurs most often is Maria. But in the notebook numbered 13, in a summary of material to be developed, we find the name Maria stricken out and the name Albertine substituted for it. The summary reads, in part: "The girls. I make their acquaintance through the painter. I become enamored of Maria [stricken out; and written in: Albertine]."[152]

Bonnet dates this substitution—which seems to represent Albertine's first appearance in Proust's notebooks—as taking place in 1913 or 1914. "It is possible," he says, "that Proust utilized for new ends a name which already figured among those of the little band. It is also possible that he introduced the name into his book (substituting it for that of Maria) only in 1913 or 1914. In any case, it is only at that time that Albertine took on the importance with which we are familiar." Bonnet argues, in other words, that Proust created Albertine as we know her during the time of his relationship with Agostinelli. And he concludes, after discussing other evidence we shall review shortly, that "if there is . . . one incontestable 'key' in the *Recherche*, it is certainly Agostinelli for the character of Albertine."[153]

Maurice Bardèche has studied Albertine's entry into *A la recherche* even more closely. Bardèche demonstrates that when Albertine enters the work, the very nature of the narrator's infatuation with the little band begins to change. Previously the little band episodes, as described in the notebooks, were filled with witty flirtation, with persiflage, with *marivaudage*, as befits the rather precious names Proust assigned to the girls in the early drafts of this material. After the appearance of Albertine, however, the encounter with the *jeunes filles* begins to take on overtones of the characteristically Proustian equation of love, suffering, and jealousy. Apparently there was a point at which Proust changed his conception of the *jeunes filles* material and decided to use it as a foundation from which he would later extend the paradigm of love laid down in *Un Amour de Swann*. Proust writes, for instance:

Certainly my wound had not healed, certainly there was still a link between Albertine and my wound, and if I learned suddenly that Andrée had arrived in Balbec while Albertine was there and I was in Paris, it was as if the bandage had been torn from my wound; the flood of my sufferings started once again to flow. . . . I no longer thought of anything but going to Balbec or somehow causing Andrée to come back. Nothing else mattered to me. I ran around like a madman, here, there, finding out who was at Balbec, who could help me. I sent a telegram to the director of the hotel; I wrote the elevator boy, Elstir. . . .[154]

These remarks, as Bardèche says, represent "a closed bud, still folded up and fragile, holding within itself *La Prisonnière* and [*La Fugitive*]." Indeed, Proust realized on second reading that they were a too direct anticipation of things to come. He wrote in the margin of the manuscript, "This page which is essential and which contains the germ of others is not to remain here."[155] And, indeed, in the present version of *A la recherche* the narrator's jealousy reaches this level of intensity only gradually, as Albertine becomes more and more mysterious and more and more elusive.

Bardèche, like Bonnet, finds no mention of Albertine in Proust's work before 1913 and concludes that the character came into being in her present version as a result of Proust's relationship with Agostinelli in 1913 and 1914. He argues, with Bonnet, that Proust's jealousy over Agostinelli and grief after Agostinelli's death were directly responsible for the modification and expansion of the *jeunes filles* material and also for the core material of *La Prisonnière* and *La Fugitive*.[156] The work of Bardèche and Bonnet thus supports the conclusions of an earlier scholar, Robert Vigneron, who argued from evidence in Proust's correspondence that Agostinelli was the principal model for Albertine.[157] And it corrects George Painter's unsupported assumption that the story of Albertine's captivity, escape, and death and of the narrator's posthumous jealousy and forgetfulness existed in the version of *A la recherche* finished before Agostinelli's appearance in Paris in January of 1913—an assumption which has been widely adopted and transmitted as final authority.[158]

To be sure, Proust intended from the earliest conception of his novel to tell the story of how his narrator keeps a girl. In the memorandum book he began in February of 1908 we find the following notation: "In the second part of the novel the girl will be [financially] ruined. I will keep her without ever seeking to possess her through an incapacity for happiness." Philip Kolb comments that "the whole story of his affair with Albertine is already contained in this note."[159] But manifestly it is not. The 1908 notation is more instructive for what it omits than for what it forecasts. It says nothing about the sequestration in the Paris apartment (to keep is not the same thing as to sequester); nothing about the ravages of jealousy over Albertine's supposed infidelities; nothing about Albertine's flight from the apartment or the narrator's suffering after her death; nothing about the posthumous jealousy; nothing about the eventual forgetfulness. And Albertine's name, of course, does not appear anywhere in the memorandum book of 1908. It is obvious that something remotely resembling the Albertine story was present in a far corner of Proust's mind by that time. But the idea of a kept girl was, at best, a minor motif in Proust's conception of his novel from 1908 to 1913, so minor that he did not think it important enough to mention in the table of contents published in the Grasset edition of *Du côté de chez Swann*.

A year and a half after Agostinelli's death Proust had not only named the character and expanded her function in the novel but also drawn up a detailed plan for her role in the novel's later volumes. In November of 1915 he sent Mme Scheikévitch a copy of *Du côté de chez Swann* in which he had covered the blank pages with a long summary of the role Albertine would play in *A la recherche*. Mme Scheikévitch had just lost a brother in the war.[160] And Proust thought the story of how his narrator suffers over the loss of his mistress but eventually reaches a point of forgetfulness and surcease from suffering would help Mme Scheikévitch understand and bear up under her own bereavement. He wrote that the material he was sending her "is presently known to no one else. . . . So I will ask you not to show it to anyone until the rest of the work has been published. . . . The episode I have summarized for you . . . will naturally give you no idea of the unfolding of certain scenes which I did not think appropriate to tell you about just now, because they are happy and bright; nor will it give you any idea of *Le Temps retrouvé*. It will, however, be in direct communication with your inconsolable grief."[161] This attitude is typical of Proust's frequently stated conviction that the descriptions of suffering, separation, and loss in *A la recherche* are of universal application. It never seems to have occurred to him that the homosexual basis of some of those descriptions should detract in any way from their basic human meaning.

So after briefly answering Mme Scheikévitch's questions about what will happen to Odette, Proust continues to summarize *A la recherche* as follows: "But I would prefer to introduce you to the characters you do not yet know, especially one who plays the most important role in the novel and brings on the peripety—Albertine." He then proceeds to outline Albertine's appearance as a *jeune fille en fleurs;* the narrator's love for her; his eventual boredom with the idea of marrying her; the change in plans brought on by her revelation that she knows Mlle Vinteuil; the life together in the apartment in Paris and "the slavery to which my jealousy reduces it"; the flight of Albertine; his stratagems for trying to persuade her to return; the suffering which both repeats and surpasses Swann's suffering over Odette; the death of Albertine; and the eventual advent of forgetfulness and oblivion—all interspersed with lengthy quotations from *Sodome et Gomorrhe* and *La Fugitive*. Interestingly Proust makes no distinction in this summary between himself and his narrator but uses the pronoun "I" to refer to both. (At other times he insisted that he and his narrator were not to be confused.) And he concludes the long summary with this remark: "Alas, Madame, I'm running out of blank pages just as the suffering was becoming less acute."[162] The suffering of the narrator over Albertine? Or Proust's own suffering, which the act of writing helps him mitigate? There is a telling ambiguity in the remark, and also a moving statement of one of the relationships Proust establishes in *A la recherche* between suffering and artistic creation: as long as there are more blank pages to be filled with writing, with analysis, with self-confrontation, the grief can be controlled and the pain understood. The pages of writing are the suffering, but they are also the means of banishing the suffering. They are, to borrow a central paradox from Proust's descriptions of love, the sickness and the cure.

The radical change in Proust's plan for his novel brought on by the expanding role of Albertine shows, among other things, that we cannot take completely literally Proust's repeated claim that he knew from the beginning the form his work would take.[163] Proust made this claim principally to counter early criticism that his work seemed shapeless and chaotic. And it contains, of course, a good deal of truth, since Proust always intended to move from *temps perdu* to *temps retrouvé*. At the same time Proust did not allow himself to be restricted by the details of his original conception. Instead, he let his novel change and expand with the changing structure of his own life. The more he lived, the more he experienced, the more he was able—and compelled—to create. His life was his novel; his novel was his life; and writing, like living, was a process of constant exploration and discovery.

And so Proust did not follow the table of contents announced in the Grasset edition of *Du côté de chez Swann*. The plan for a novel of three volumes gradually became a plan for a novel of seven volumes. And the next volume to appear was not *Le Côté de Guermantes*, as originally announced, but *A l'ombre des jeunes filles en fleurs* (1918), a book for which Proust was awarded the Prix Goncourt in 1919 and which established his reputation as a major novelist. Then, before the eventual appearance of *Le Temps retrouvé*, came *Le Côté de Guermantes*, *Sodome et Gomorrhe*, *La Prisonnière*, and *La Fugitive*. In what order did Proust compose these works, and what was the effect of the relationship with Agostinelli on the order of composition?

Maurice Bardèche suggests that after the departure and death of Agostinelli Proust immediately drafted *La Fugitive;* that he then took up *A l'ombre des jeunes filles en fleurs*, fleshing out the character of Albertine and filling in the preparation for the crisis which occurs in *La Fugitive;* and that only then did he return to *Le Côté de Guermantes* and proceed with the other volumes of the novel. Bardèche reasons that Proust would naturally want to describe the narrator's grief over Albertine while his own grief over Agostinelli was still fresh in his mind. And he believes that the physical appearance of the first draft of *La Fugitive* bears out this conclusion. It is, says Bardèche, "perhaps the most moving of all the notebooks of Marcel Proust"; for in it Proust seems to be setting down rapidly and feverishly, "almost without erasure, as if in a hallucination, the transposition of his grief."[164]

It is not possible to know the precise sequence in which Proust worked. But it is possible to show that Proust transplanted many of the details of his relationship with Agostinelli directly from his life into his novel, sometimes changing little more than the names of the people involved. After Agostinelli left Paris, Proust sent Albert Nahmias, to whom he had written about hiring detectives, in pursuit of Agostinelli with instructions to try to work out conditions under which Agostinelli would return. In the same way the narrator of *A la recherche* sends Saint-Loup to Touraine to treat with Mme Bontemps and try to bring back Albertine (3: 436 ff.). Proust sent telegrams to Nahmias containing advice on how to deal with the Agostinellis. These telegrams are of remarkable length (Proust never let exigencies of cost affect his characteristic prose style); and they give a clear impression of Proust's agitated state of mind and of the importance he attached to having Agostinelli back in Paris as soon as possible. One of the telegrams reads:

I SPENT THE ENTIRE MORNING ON THE TELEPHONE AND I FINALLY GOT THE HOTEL ROYAL AT NOON BUT I COULDN'T HEAR ANYTHING AND FINALLY I HAD TO GIVE UP SO SEND ME AN URGENT TELEGRAM WITH ALL THE DETAILS BUT I CAN TELL YOU SOMETHING IN ADVANCE AND THAT IS THAT IT IS INSANE ABSURD IN A SPECULATION WHICH WAS TO HAVE REMAINED BETWEEN US TO HAVE ARRANGED A MEETING IN A HOTEL WHERE YOU ARE KNOWN—IN A MATTER OF SECONDS EVERYTHING WILL BE FOUND OUT—SO I ADVISE YOU TO RETURN IMMEDIATELY TO THE PLACE FROM WHICH YOU CAME AND DELIVER YOUR ANSWER THERE BY WORD OF MOUTH INSTEAD OF WAITING FOR HIS—SINCE I HAVE NOT YET RECEIVED YOUR TELEGRAM I CANNOT GIVE YOU PRECISE INSTRUCTIONS BUT BE AWARE THAT THEY WILL DOUBTLESS WANT TO BARGAIN WITH YOU AND ARRANGE BETTER CONDITIONS FOR THEMSELVES—SO YOU WOULD DO WELL TO KEEP THEM IN SUSPENSE AND AT LEAST WHEN YOU GET THERE TO SAY YOU ARE BRINGING A REFUSAL A NEGATIVE RESPONSE—PERHAPS THAT WILL HAVE THE EFFECT OF MAKING HIM GRAB THE OFFER AND GIVE IN—IF ON THE CONTRARY YOU SEE THAT THE BREAK IS DEFINITIVE PERHAPS YOU COULD ON THE OTHER HAND AFTER INSTANT OF HESITATION GIVE IN A BIT YOURSELF AND OFFER BETTER CONDITIONS—IT SEEMS TO ME THAT THESE ARE THE PRINCIPLES YOU SHOULD FOLLOW BUT I CAN SPEAK ONLY THEORETICALLY SINCE I DON'T KNOW WHAT'S HAPPENING BUT SUSPECT THAT THEY'LL TRY TO ESTABLISH THE MOST ADVANTAGEOUS CONDITIONS—DON'T SPARE THE TELEGRAMS—AS FOR THE TELEPHONE TRY IT BUT THIS MORNING WE COULDN'T HEAR A THING BEST MARCEL PROUST [165]

But Albert Nahmais was not successful in his attempts to bargain with Alfred and Anna.

Meanwhile, Agostinelli wrote Proust flattering letters in which he tried to persuade Proust to buy him an airplane, saying he would name it *Swann*. Ironically and tragically Proust received his last letter from Agostinelli after he had just received news of Agostinelli's death,[166] as also happens in *A la recherche* with two letters written to the narrator by Albertine (3: 477–78). To compound the irony Proust unknowingly posted a letter to Agostinelli on the very day Agostinelli was killed. The letter survives and reads in part as follows (a part of the letter is missing):

[Saturday, 30 May 1914]

My Dear Alfred,
    Thank you very much for your letter (one sentence was *ravishing:* "crepuscular," etc.) and for your preliminary telegram, which was an additional kindness. . . . Since your letter gave me pleasure, my letter was not completely useless. But with respect to everything else (you'll tell me again I don't know what I want) it *was* useless. Because I've decided it would be indelicate of me to accept this kind of service from you, and so I want to try on my own to succeed in getting what I ask. I won't explain why I consider it indelicate. I would risk making you angry again, and that's what I want most to avoid. I could have thought about it earlier, but the idea came to me after having written to you. Moreover, I don't have any doubt it will work itself out.
    For the airplane it's more difficult, for the same reason as with Grasset recently. You remember the day he wrote to me, "I release you from all agreements, do what you like." After that I could only do what he wanted me to. But I went back day before yesterday to see M. Collin, at night, in the rain, before going to the Ballets Russes. He was extremely nice and gave me my freedom after a fashion, but now I scarcely dare use it. In any case, I'll see. But don't think he has any interest at all in these sales. He doesn't get one cent of the 27,000 francs the machine costs. At all events, if I keep the airplane (which I don't think I'll do), since it will no doubt remain in the shed, I will have engraved on the (I don't know the name of the part and don't want to commit heresy before an aviator) the lines from Mallarmé you know:

> *Un cygne d'autrefois se souvient que c'est lui*
> *Magnifique mais qui sans espoir se délivre*
> *Pour n'avoir pas chanté la région où vivre*
> *Quand du stérile hiver a resplendi l'ennui.*
>
> *Tout son col secouera cette blanche agonie*
> *Par l'espace infligé à l'oiseau qui le nie,*
> *Mais non l'horreur du sol où le plumage est pris.*

Fantôme qu'à ce lieu son pur éclat assigne,
Il s'immobilise au songe froid de mépris
Que vêt parmi l'exil inutile le Cygne.

It's the poem you used to like, although you found it obscure, and which begins with the lines:

Le vierge, le vivace et le bel aujourd'hui
Va-t-il nous déchirer avec un coup d'aile ivre
Ce lac dur oublié que hante sous le givre
Le transparent glacier des vols qui n'ont pas fui! [167]

Alas, "today" is no longer "virginal," nor "long-lived," nor "beautiful."

But to get this matter of the airplane out of the way, I implore you to believe that my remarks on the subject contain no intention, however covert, of reproach. That would be idiotic. I have sufficient, and justifiable, reproaches to raise with you on other questions, and you know I'm not one to repress them. And, indeed, I would have to be really stupid to make you responsible (I mean morally) for the uselessness of a purchase of which you were not aware! . . .

I asked you to return my letter to me, but you didn't do it. And I also asked you to put a lot of seals on your envelope. You didn't do that either. As for the registered letter [. . . .
. . . .]
it don't [sic] straggle behind and you could return at the same time (with lots of seals) this one and the other. It's pointless to exhaust yourself writing to me since you're working a lot. All you have to do is put my letters in an envelope and return them. I send you a hearty handshake.

Marcel Proust

P. S. If you return the letters to me, you ought to put several large seals on them. Moreoever, you ought to put them in two different envelopes, because one won't hold them. [168]

Now for a third time, on the very day of Agostinelli's accident, Proust seems prophetically to have glimpsed, in his comparison of Agostinelli's airplane to Mallarmé's sterile, flightless swan, the death that was fast approaching in Antibes.

The prophetic dimension of the letter is hauntingly clear. But the literal level needs some explanation. Proust tells Agostinelli that he has ordered an airplane for him through an agent, M. Collin, who has now generously released him from his obligation. But Proust adds that since M. Collin was so kind and obliging in the matter, he now hesitates to cancel the purchase. In fact, Proust says, he may go ahead with the purchase and keep the airplane for himself, although once the airplane is in his possession, it will probably only sit idly in its hangar. In order to symbolize this eternal immobility Proust says he intends to engrave on the plane's fuselage the lines he quotes from Mallarmé's sonnet "Le vierge, le vivace et le bel aujourd'hui." Obviously Proust is leaving open for strategic reasons the possibility that if Agostinelli returns, the airplane might still be his. Indeed, when the lines from Mallarmé are engraved upon it, the airplane will be christened with a cleverly allusive modification of the name Agostinelli intended his airplane to have. Instead of *Swann*, after Charles Swann, it will be called *Le Cygne* (*The Swan*), after Mallarmé.

After Albertine's departure in *A la recherche* the narrator writes her a letter which is similar in many ways to this one from Proust to Agostinelli. The narrator tries to persuade Albertine to return by tempting her with an automobile and a yacht. "I had thought," the narrator writes to Albertine:

of organizing our existence in the most independent fashion possible and, to begin with, I had wished to give you that yacht in which you could have taken cruises while I, too sick to accompany you, would have waited for you in the port; I had written to Elstir to ask his advice, since you admire his taste. And for travel on land, I would have wanted you to have your own automobile, yours alone, in which you would go out and travel wherever your fancy took you. The yacht was already practically ready; it is called, after the desire you expressed at Balbec, *The Swan* [*Le Cygne*]. And, recalling that your favorite car was the Rolls, I had ordered one of those as well. But, now that we shall never see each other again, and since I have no hope of persuading you to accept the boat or the car, I find myself in possession of a boat and a car which are totally useless to me. So I had thought—since I had ordered them through an agent but in your name—that you could perhaps countermand them and thereby spare me the trouble of this useless yacht and car. But to do this and many other things we would have had to get together for a talk. But I find that as long as I am still capable of falling in love with you again, a state of affairs which will not last much longer, it would be mad, for the sake of a sailboat and a Rolls Royce, to see each other and thereby gamble with your happiness, since you have decided that that happiness consists in living far away from me. No, I would prefer to keep the Rolls and even the yacht; and, since I will never use them and they will probably always remain, one at its dock, at anchor, and dismantled, the other in its shed, I shall have engraved upon the . . . of the yacht (Heavens, I don't dare name the wrong part and commit a heresy that might shock you) those verses from Mallarmé you used to like. You remember, it's the poem that begins

with "Le vierge, le vivace et le bel aujourd'hui." Alas, today is no longer
virginal, nor beautiful. (3: 455–56)

Comparing the letters from life and from the novel, we find
many parallels of context, of motive, and of phraseology. In his letter
to Agostinelli Proust mentions a telegram he has recently received
from him; in the same way the narrator receives a telegram from Albertine just before her death (3: 452). Proust begins his letter to
Agostinelli with "Thank you very much for your letter (one sentence
was *ravishing:* 'crepuscular,' etc.)." Similarly, Albertine sends the
narrator a letter which contains a telling use of "crepuscular" (3: 468).
Furthermore, Proust's letter to Agostinelli seems to refer to a second
gift he and Agostinelli have discussed in addition to the airplane ("For
the airplane," Proust writes, "it's more difficult"). Perhaps this second gift was to have been, as is the case with Albertine in the novel,
an automobile, since Agostinelli was fond of driving as well as of flying. Proust also alludes to a service he has requested of Agostinelli
but has now decided to handle himself. And likewise, in his letter to
Albertine, the narrator tells her that he will need her help in can-
celing the order for the yacht and Rolls Royce but that he hesitates to
ask for this favor. In the novel, as in life, the order for the gifts is
made through an agent. There are similar references to Mallarmé and
to the name *The Swan.* And both letters pretend to accept a final separation while subtly trying to tempt the loved one to return. It is
clear that this part of the narrator's affair with Albertine is based so
closely on Proust's relationship with Agostinelli as to amount almost
to literal autobiography.[169]

The description of how the narrator gradually forgets Albertine
after her death is also, in part, a transcription of Proust's experience
with Agostinelli. A few months after Agostinelli's death Proust began
to undergo what he calls in *A la recherche* "the heart's intermissions"—periods in which suffering and grief seem to recede only to
return later in even more cruel onslaughts. Proust describes this particular instance of the heart's intermissions in one of his most brutally
honest letters. He wrote it not long after the outbreak of World War
I, after his return from Cabourg, where he had sought sanctuary from
a Paris threatened with invasion. And he wrote it, appropriately, to
Reynaldo Hahn:

[October, 1914]

Dear Reynaldo,

I thank you with all my heart for your letter, an imperishable monument to kindness and friendship. . . .

My dear little fellow, you are very kind to have worried that going to Cabourg must have caused me pain by reminding me of Agostinelli. I must confess, to my shame, that it was not as painful as I would have thought and that, on the contrary, the journey marked a first stage of detachment from my grief, a stage after which, once back in Paris, I started, fortunately, a backward movement toward the initial suffering. But in Cabourg, though I never ceased to be just as sad or to miss him as much, there were finally moments, perhaps even hours, when he disappeared from my mind. My dear little fellow, don't judge me too severely for this (not as severely as I judge myself!). And don't deduce from it a lack of fidelity in my affections. . . . I truly loved Alfred. No, to say that I loved him is not saying enough: I adored him. And I don't know why I write this in the past tense, because I love him still. But, in spite of everything, there is, in grief, an involuntary part and a dutiful part. . . . This dutiful part does not exist with respect to Alfred, who treated me very badly; so I accord him the grief which I cannot choose but accord him. . . . If, therefore, I experienced in Cabourg a few weeks of relative infidelity to Alfred's memory, don't judge me unfaithful. . . . Moreover, I was very happy when my suffering returned. But from time to time it is so acute that I find myself longing a little for the abatement I experienced about a [month] ago.

P. S. Don't let my letter, I beg you, give you the idea that I have forgotten Alfred. In spite of the distance I feel, alas, from time to time, I would not hesitate even then to cut off an arm or a leg if that would bring him back to life.[170]

Like Proust, the narrator longs for surcease from his grief but also strives to keep his grief alive as a final proof that Albertine existed and that he actually loved her. "Like the harm I did to my grandmother," he says, "the harm Albertine did to me was a final link between her and me which survived even memory. . . . [Yet] during long periods of time, [these sufferings] came to me so rarely that I started seeking on my own opportunities for grief, for a crisis of jealousy, trying to reattach myself to the past, trying to remember her better" (3: 526, 537). Proust's pessimism about love stems partly from his realization that the self is a perpetually changing entity, constantly unfaithful to its own past goals and aspirations. Eventually we forget those we loved. And this suggests that the love itself was less than real, was accident rather than substance.

Proust's pleas to Agostinelli to send back his letters suggest that he was thinking, even while he was suffering from jealousy and unrequited love, of how he was going to use these experiences and the letters which reflect them in *A la recherche*. Proust's friend Léon Daudet once remarked, "For while Proust, with part of his brain, admires and enjoys the sight of something, he criticizes it with another part, and with a third stands off watching indifferently what the other two are doing."[171] This powerful capacity for objectivity, for analyzing his own motives, for stepping back and seeing himself now as the clown in a comedy, now as the hero of a tragedy, was Proust's greatest blessing and his greatest curse. It afforded him the enormous consolation of being able to extract the larger meaning from his suffering and universalize it in art. "Ideas are substitutes for griefs," writes the narrator of *A la recherche*; "the moment these griefs change into ideas, they lose some of their noxious power over our heart" (3: 906). But the need for constantly channeling his life into his art also meant that Proust's personal relationships would always be mediated relationships, means rather than ends. Standing between Proust and those he loved was the omnivorous specter of his art, whose paradigms of human conduct seemed both to control and to feed upon his life. "And so I had to resign myself," the narrator says, "since nothing can endure without becoming general . . . to the idea that even those who were most beloved to the writer finally did nothing but pose for him, as models do for painters" (3: 905).

One of the most significant aspects of Proust's relationship with Agostinelli, and one seldom mentioned in criticism and biography, is that nowhere is there any evidence that Agostinelli loved Proust or regarded him as anything more than a source of money and presents and as a stepping stone to a better situation in life. The relationship, so far as we can tell, was emotionally one-sided. In this respect Agostinelli seems to have given Proust a harsh object lesson in the subjectivity of love. "He was," says Céleste Albaret, "an unstable boy who had ambitions for rising above his station. . . . He was haunted by a desire to be something other than what he was."[172] Plummeting through the darkness in his automobile, soaring over the sea in his airplane, remaining always just out of reach, Agostinelli is the quintessence of the Proustian *être de fuite*, the being who will not, either physically or psychologically, remain still long enough to be analyzed, understood, or loved. In Proust's first portrait of Agostinelli he portrayed him grasping a wheel which "in general suggested every stylization of the wheel in the art of the Middle Ages." Agostinelli's wheel proved to be, indeed, a medieval wheel of fortune. But as it rotates within *A la recherche*, it also becomes the mysterious, the endless spiral of human identity.

After Agostinelli, Proust had another male secretary, a Swiss named Henri Rochat. Rochat had a propensity for painting which may account in part for Albertine's flair for the art.[173] But, with the death of Agostinelli, Proust had lived his great passion; never again would he fall so deeply in love. As his life progressed, his attitude toward love and sexuality became more and more that of the detached, vaguely bemused scientist of human behavior. Jacques Porel, son of the actress Réjane, has left some revealing recollections of Proust's relationship with Henri Rochat. "When I met Proust," says Porel:

he seemed already to have withdrawn from the active life to devote himself to his fruitful form of contemplation. I mean there was no longer, I believe, any preoccupation in his life, any care, other than his health and the completion of his work. It is true that during the last years I saw him with a young male companion he had taken in; but I got the impression that he enjoyed giving himself the sight of a young creature for whom he was doing a service. Nothing more.

His own youth had caused many tongues to wag. But when he spoke of homosexuality during these years of 1917 and 1918, one got the impression that he was viewing it from afar, if not with indifference at least with impartiality. He took note of its continuous progress but in no way commended that progress and said as a kind of joke, "They are so numerous nowadays that one might say it is *they* who are normal." He added very easily: "Look here, So-and-So, well, he is normal. There's no doubt about it." Or he would say of a man who liked women, "But as for Mr. X., take my word for it, he is completely abnormal."

He knew I was "abnormal" and thought that was well and good.

I never felt in his presence that constraint so often manifested by "normal" men. He spoke of homosexuality in the easiest way in the world, as one who has withdrawn from everything, as one who sees everything, but from afar.[174]

Albertine had, of course, many models. And not all of those models were male. But without Alfred Agostinelli the story of Albertine would never have attained the imposing stature and meaning it finally achieves in *A la recherche*. Proust's relationship with Agostinelli brought him, if not a totally new character, certainly a new range, a new depth, and a new structural conception for the work to which he would devote the rest of his life.

There are many structures and many structures within structures in *A la recherche,* and there are many new departures in the history of its evolution. But Proust's relationship with Alfred Agostinelli shook the very foundations of his original conception and helped to impart to the novel both its tragedy and its universality. It played a major role in transforming what might have been simply a work into a great work, a *grand œuvre* in the moral sense, in the structural sense, and, I think Proust would agree, in the alchemical sense as well. (*Grand œuvre,* in addition to its other meanings, is the alchemical term for the transformation of base metal into gold.) Proust's love for Agostinelli was a cruel disappointment, not only because it seems to have been unrequited but also because it was cut short by the ultimate human tragedy: unexpected death. Without art Proust's experience would have ended in nothing, in less than nothing. With art it becomes meaningful not only to Proust but also to those of us who, like Mme Scheikévitch, at times find ourselves in need of proof that suffering will eventually pass and that even while it does its cruellest work it has the power of linking minds together in a community of human empathy and understanding. As the narrator says, his purpose is not only to describe and analyze the experience of suffering but also "to extract the general meaning from our grief" (3: 902). The suffering is the base metal; the general meaning is the gold.

It is not then surprising that Proust spent the rest of his life working out the implications of his relationship with Alfred Agostinelli. When Proust died in 1922, he was still revising and adding to *La Prisonnière* and *La Fugitive*.

CHAPTER THREE

A DREAM
OF ART

ROUST'S LIFE provides an important perspective on the meaning of his work, but there are other sources of meaning that are equally important.[1] There are special kinds of meaning that inhere in the text itself—its language, its structures, its theories, its myths. There is meaning that is generated by the interaction of the work with its time. And there is meaning that derives from the traditions of which the work is a part. In order to understand the role of sexuality in *A la recherche*, we must understand these additional contexts. The preceding chapter examined the importance of sexuality to Proust as a man and a practicing writer. The remainder of the study will examine its evolution as a theme in Proust's work.

In Proust's work before *A la recherche* homosexuality is rarely mentioned and, when it is, it is usually presented in a negative light. This immediately produces a paradox. We have seen that when Proust put together *Les Plaisirs et les jours* and when he wrote *Jean Santeuil,* he derived significant inspiration from his love for other men. He originally intended to dedicate *Les Plaisirs et les jours* to Edgar Aubert and Willie Heath, people whom he loved, as he told Robert de Billy, "with all my heart." And he intended *Jean Santeuil* to serve, among other things, as a tribute to his relationship with Reynaldo Hahn. Clearly one side of Proust celebrated homosexual emotion and cultivated it as an important source of inspiration. But another side of Proust—the side conditioned by cultural and societal prejudice—shunned homosexuality as unnatural, degrading, and shameful. These two aspects of Proust's personality quarrel and debate throughout his literary career. And in the early work, as in *A la recherche,* the conclusions about homosexuality are often negative.

In Proust's story "Violante ou la mondanité" (collected in *Les Plaisirs et les jours*), for instance, lesbianism is used as a symbol of all that is corrupt and depraved in human nature. When the Princesse de Misène makes a lesbian overture to Violante, Violante not only rebuffs the advance: "[she] ran away as fast as her legs could carry her." To get revenge for being thus rejected, the Princesse spreads false rumors about Violante's character and morals. "When Violante heard about this, she wept for herself and for the wickedness of women. She had made up her mind long ago about the wickedness of men."[2]

In *Jean Santeuil* there is an episode in which Jean, disgusted and horrified, forces his mistress Françoise to confess to lesbian desires and activities (a prototype of the similar interrogation scenes later enacted by Swann and Odette and the narrator and Albertine). Under relentless questioning by Jean, Françoise reveals that lesbianism is her "nature" and that she has made love to her girl friend Charlotte. Jean turns pale as he listens to these confessions and has Françoise swear that the experience with Charlotte is the only time she has succumbed to her lesbian tendencies.

Suddenly, however, the homophobic narrative gives way to a clear expression of empathy for the plight of people with homosexual tastes. Françoise concludes: "Oh, Jean, you don't know what it has been like for me. . . . I have been unhappy from the very day I discovered I was afflicted with this vice. . . . You will never know how much I have suffered. Some of my friends struck me; others refused to speak to me. . . . My confessor could find nothing to say to me, and my doctor told me I was insane."[3] There is genuine feeling in this speech, inspired no doubt by the ostracism Proust himself sometimes had to endure on account of his homosexuality. And there is also an implicit protest against the prejudice and injustice perpetrated by society on people like Françoise, especially through established religion ("My confessor could find nothing to say to me") and established medicine ("my doctor told me I was insane").

The note of protest, however, remains covert, and the only solution the young Proust offers for the suffering of his homosexual characters is suicide. This is the fate of an early version of M. de Charlus, the character in *Jean Santeuil* known as the Vicomte de Lomperolles. Lomperolles shares with Charlus an ostensible hatred for the current generation of young men; they are, in his estimation, weak, perfidious creatures—"nothing but women" (cf. 1: 762). One day this denouncer of young men is unexpectedly found dead, having shot himself twice in the head. And it is discovered, to everyone's surprise, that he has killed himself because he has been ruined by gifts and blackmail payments given to a series of male lovers, among them a Polish violinist and an ex-convict. "Then Jean understood the vehemence with which the Vicomte cursed young men; he was like an old man who has suffered over women all his life and who therefore consigns to hell a breed he has deeply loved but which has yielded him, after so many attempts, nothing but hard cases and sluts."[4]

"La Confession d'une jeune fille," another of the stories collected in *Les Plaisirs et les jours*, shows how a girl's sexual guilt leads her to attempt suicide. The girl's experiences are heterosexual; but critics generally assume that she is a projection of Proust himself and that her heterosexual experiences are transpositions of Proust's early homosexual affairs.[5] Several aspects of the story support this interpretation. For example, Proust describes heterosexuality—rather oddly— as if it were a dark secret which must at all costs be kept hidden. "No one," says the girl of her experiences with men, "suspected the secret crime of my life."[6] Then, too, the girl's chief concern is to keep her sexual adventures concealed from her mother, something which was also, presumably, of great importance to Proust. In the story's climactic moment, however, the mother discovers her daughter making love to a young man. The mother dies from shock, and the girl shoots herself out of guilt and remorse. It seems fairly obvious that this melodramatic ending reflects Proust's fear that if his own mother should discover the truth about his sexuality, the knowledge would be fatal to her. And the story as a whole seems to anticipate the message of the Lomperolles episode in *Jean Santeuil*—that is, that death is preferable to the revelation of one's homosexuality.

In "Avant la nuit," a story published in *La Revue Blanche* in December of 1893, suicide is again presented as the inevitable finale of homosexual experience. In spite of this, "Avant la nuit" contains the first explicit defense of homosexuality in Proust's work. In fact, this aspect of the story probably accounts for Proust's exclusion of it from *Les Plaisirs et les jours*. *Les Plaisirs et les jours* was published in 1896, only a year after the trial, conviction, and imprisonment of Oscar Wilde. The Wilde affair cast a pall of paranoia over the subject of homosexuality.[7] And though attitudes were slightly more tolerant in France than in England, 1896 was still a highly inopportune moment for an aspiring young writer to republish a story which contained a defense of homosexual love, even if the story's denouement almost completely vitiated that defense. Probably for this reason Proust laid aside "Avant la nuit" when he collected his early work for *Les Plaisirs et les jours*. As a result "Avant la nuit" remains to this day unknown to many readers.[8] It seems appropriate, then, to present the story here in a new translation, and it will be found in its entirety as an appendix at the end of the book.[9]

"Avant la nuit" is the only work by Proust in which homosexuality is the central and overriding theme. It is one of the first stories he ever wrote, and it is obviously the product of a young, unformed writer. The imagery is occasionally sophomoric, the syntax is sometimes clumsy, and the dialogue alternates between the precious and the bombastic. Nonetheless, "Avant la nuit" represents Proust's most sophisticated treatment of homosexuality before *A la recherche* itself. In fact, the story contains several ideas which later find their way into the novel. The speech in which Leslie says that homosexuality stems from a "nervous deterioration" and is therefore morally neutral foreshadows the theoretical, quasi-scientific tone of parts of *Sodome et Gomorrhe*. More importantly, the story suggests for the first time in Proust's work that there is an intimate connection between the sexual sense and the aesthetic sense, an idea which becomes pivotal in *A la recherche*. Leslie argues that it is possible to "[refine] erotic pleasure to the point of making it aesthetic," points out that "in the truly artistic nature physical attraction or repulsion is qualified by the contemplation of the beautiful," and insists that "physical dispositions, the pleasure of physical contact, the refinements of the palate, the joys of the senses stem from the place where our sense of the beautiful is rooted." Leslie's argument is that someone who is sensitive to beauty in all its forms can be just as easily attracted to a beautiful male as to a beautiful female and that, in either case, there is no cause for hysteria or for the passing of moral judgments.

And yet the overall view of homosexuality presented by "Avant la nuit" is far from the dispassionate, morally neutral approach Leslie advocates in this speech. Leslie's arguments have an unforeseen effect: they lead Françoise to experiment with lesbianism and then shoot herself in remorse. When this happens, Leslie finds that there is considerable distance between his liberal theories of homosexuality and his feelings when confronted with the phenomenon in reality. He listens with mounting horror as Françoise, in yet another version of the lesbian confession scene which recurs in Proust's work, tells of her fall from purity into sexual perversion. "Avant la nuit" issues a powerful plea for tolerance of homosexuality and at the same time suggests that such pleas are better left unsaid. It coils itself neatly into a paradox: "And never had we known so much ill, and so much good."

Leslie and Françoise, like Jean Santeuil and his mistress, and like Swann and Odette and the narrator and Albertine in their similar scenes, represent fundamental contradictions within Proust's own personality: the Proust who finds happiness and pleasure in homosexual love, and the Proust who is ravaged with guilt over it; the Proust who defends homosexual experience, and the Proust who denounces homosexuality. Throughout his life Proust composed versions of the sexual confession scene first sketched in "Avant la nuit." Throughout his life, in other words, he continued to torment and upbraid himself for something he knew, on another level of consciousness, to be in its essence morally neutral.

In *Les Plaisirs et les jours* and *Jean Santeuil* Proust's vision is severely hampered by this tendency to introject the conventional view of homosexuality. The image of Violante running away from another woman's advance "as fast as her legs could carry her" is a good summary of Proust's own attitude in this early work, which suggests that the best way to deal with homosexuality is to avoid it. Proust as yet has nothing original to say about the theme and so falls back on the literary tradition of using murder or suicide to resolve stories with a homosexual motif. But appeals to suicide as Proust uses them in the early work are not solutions: they are simply ways of evading a serious artistic confrontation with the subject. This approach to the theme has a long if not particularly venerable history in literature,[10] and Proust himself never completely outgrows it. Proust's characterization of Albertine, as is well known, is one of the most complex in all of literature. She is a symbol of the passage of time, of the flux of identity, and of the mutability of love. And yet when the narrator of *A la recherche* begins searching for ways to understand Albertine's life and death, all this richness of characterization, built up slowly and carefully throughout the middle volumes of the novel, is threatened and diminished by yet another flirtation with the deus ex machina of suicide: "[Albertine] hoped you would save her," Andrée tells the narrator, "that you would marry her. Deep down, she felt that [lesbianism] was a form of criminal lunacy, and I have often wondered whether it was not after an incident of this sort of thing, which had led to a suicide in a family, that she herself committed suicide" (3: 600).

WILDE, MACDONALD, KRUPP, MOLTKE, EULENBURG, AND CHARLUS

Proust had good reason to bow to conventional morality in his writing about homosexuality. The pressure to do so came from practically every direction and was extraordinarily intense. Homosexual relations were not against the law in France, since no provision had been made for their punishment in the Code Napoléon.[11] But Proust inherited a double dose of homophobia in the traditions transmitted to him by his Jewish mother and Catholic father. Homosexuality is forbidden in the Old Testament, where it is made punishable by death (Lev. 20:13) and in the New Testament, where it is mentioned as a trait which denies access to the kingdom of God (1 Cor. 6:9–10). And, of course, Sodom and Gomorrah are destroyed in Genesis for a sin traditionally interpreted as homosexuality (but which may have been, in reality, a violation of ancient rules of hospitality).[12] In France homosexuality was thought to be against the law of God and the law of Nature, if not strictly against the law of man. The following statement, published in the *Grande Revue* in 1910, gives a good indication of the official attitude: "If there is a vice or a malady which repulses the mentality of

France, the morality of France, the health of France it is, to call a spade a spade, homosexuality."[13] Small wonder that most of Proust's writing contains concessions to the conventional viewpoint and that for a long time homosexuality remained only a minor motif in his art.

Critics have often surmised that the death of Proust's mother in 1905 liberated him from the need to de-emphasize homosexuality in his writing. And it does seem likely that one reason homosexuality is so rarely mentioned in the early work is because, as Painter says, it was "not fit reading for [Proust's] mother in her lifetime."[14] But the pervasive importance Proust assigns to this theme in *A la recherche* cannot be explained simply by the end of his fear of offending or embarrassing his mother. There must have been other factors which influenced his attitude toward homosexuality and led to his decision to make it a fundamental concern of his novel. Those factors are to be found, I believe, partly in the notoriety homosexuality attained in Europe from 1895 to 1909 in a series of scandals beginning with the trial of Oscar Wilde.

In the fateful year of 1895 Oscar Wilde was a married man with two sons. But he had also been carrying on secret homosexual affairs, among them an affair with Lord Alfred Douglas. Douglas's father was the Marquess of Queensberry, a man who was, in the words of Noel I. Garde, "noted as a brawling whoremonger. . . . an ill-tempered and arrogant debauchee who treated his wife and children with . . . contempt [but who] nevertheless considered nothing else in the world as low as a homosexual."[15] Queensberry was infuriated by the rumors about Wilde and his son which began to circulate in London. He called at Wilde's club and left a card accusing Wilde of homosexuality.[16] Wilde sued Queensberry for criminal libel, but the trial produced so much support for Queensberry's allegations that Wilde found himself in an untenable position and withdrew the suit. His friends advised him to leave England at once, but Wilde refused. He was arrested on a charge of "gross indecency" and imprisoned without bail.[17]

Wilde's imprisonment caused national hysteria. His books, which up to that time had been among the most acclaimed in London, disappeared from the bookstores; his plays were closed; and he was constantly abused and maligned in the press. There was, as Frank

Harris says, "an orgy of Philistine rancor such as even London had never known before. The Puritan middle class, which had always regarded Wilde with dislike as an artist and an intellectual scoffer . . . now gave free scope to their disgust and contempt."[18] Wilde was forced to appear in another trial, this time as defendant. During the second trial he was read a poem by Lord Alfred Douglas which ended with the line "I am the Love that dare not speak its name." Wilde was asked to explain the kind of love to which the line referred. He responded:

"The love that dare not speak its name" in this century is such a great affection of an elder for a younger man as there was between David and Jonathan, such as Plato made the very basis of his philosophy, and such as you find in the sonnets of Michelangelo and Shakespeare. It is that deep, spiritual affection that is as pure as it is perfect. It dictates and pervades great works of art like those of Shakespeare and Michelangelo. . . . It is in this century misunderstood, so much misunderstood that it may be described as the "Love that dare not speak its name", and on account of it I am placed where I am now. It is beautiful, it is fine, it is the noblest form of affection. There is nothing unnatural about it. It is intellectual, and it repeatedly exists between an elder and a younger man, when the elder has intellect, and the younger man has all the joy, hope, and glamour of life before him. That it should be so, the world does not understand. The world mocks at it and sometimes puts one in the pillory for it.[19]

Wilde's eloquence produced applause in the courtroom. The jury, perhaps swayed by Wilde's speech, was unable to reach a decision and was dismissed. But the charges were not dropped. Wilde was brought to trial again on the same charge, and this time he was convicted. The judge pronounced the maximum sentence of two years at hard labor and accompanied it with a self-righteous tongue-lashing:

Oscar Wilde . . . the crime of which you have been convicted is so bad that one has to put stern restraint upon oneself to prevent oneself from describing, in language which I would rather not use, the sentiments which must rise to the breast of every man of honour who has heard the details of these two terrible trials. . . . I hope, at all events, that those who sometimes imagine that a judge is half-hearted in the cause of decency and morality, because he takes care no prejudice shall enter into the case, may see that that is consistent at least with the utmost sense of indignation at the horrible charges brought home to . . . you. . . . that you, Wilde, have been the centre of a circle of extensive corruption of the most hideous kind among young men, it is . . . impossible to doubt.[20]

The guilty verdict met with popular approval: there was dancing in the streets outside the Old Bailey when it was announced. But Seymour Hicks, an actor who had known Wilde when Wilde was at the height of his creative power, struck a different note. "I have seen many awful happenings at the Old Bailey," he remarked, "but to me no death sentence has ever seemed so terrible as the one which Mr Justice Wills delivered when his duty called upon him to destroy and take from the world the man who had given it so much."[21]

In his art and conversation Wilde had satirized English society and called its most fundamental values into question; and now society struck back by using the charge of homosexuality to silence him. "Wilde took the aggressive against the philistines," writes A. L. Rowse:

[he] contradicted their conventions, exposed their assumptions, made them look like fools—and so created enemies. One has only to scan his works for the epigrams to see how many groups, how many beloved illusions he offended, turned inside out or upside down, to realize how many enemies he had rallied against him when the day of judgment came. . . . 'We are not sent into the world to air our moral prejudices. I never take any notice of what common people say, and I never interfere with what charming people do.' . . . 'There is hardly a single person in the House of Commons worth painting; though many of them would be the better for a little whitewashing.'

Many of these arrows went home. One sees how many vested interests would be glad enough to get their own back, if the opportunity came.[22]

There was, as Arno Karlen points out, "only one social benefit in the whole catastrophe. Until now homosexuality, when spoken of at all, was 'the unspeakable vice,' a bizarre and mysterious bogey. Now it was daily fare in newspapers; the unmentionable was in everyone's conversation."[23] The affair attracted almost as much attention in France as in England. In 1896, the year following Wilde's conviction, Marc-André Raffalovich published a study of homosexuality called *Uranisme et unisexualité*. The book contained an account of the proceedings against Wilde, along with a history of homosexuality and a review of current scientific thinking on the subject. During the same year Georges Saint-Paul published, under the pseudonym "Dr. Laupts" and the ominous title *Tares et poisons*, another study of homosexuality. Like Raffalovich, Saint-Paul discussed the Wilde affair and summarized contemporary medical theory. Then, in Germany, two other important works on homosexuality appeared: *Sexual Inversion* by the British sexologist Havelock Ellis (first published in Germany and in German to avoid the repressive climate in England) and *Sappho und Sokrates* by the German sexologist Magnus Hirschfeld. The year 1896 also marked the appearance in Germany of the first homosexual periodical. It was called *Der Eigene* (*The Special*) and ran until 1929.[24] And it was, finally, in 1896 that Proust published his first book, excluding "Avant la nuit" and containing only one direct reference to homosexuality (in "Violante ou la mondanité"). But Proust's time would come.

Homosexuality returned to public attention a few years later in a scandal involving Sir Hector Archibald Macdonald (1852–1903), one of the most brilliant officers ever to serve in the British army. Macdonald fought in the Afghan War, the Boer War, in the Sudan, and in South Africa, winning several decorations and earning the nickname "Fighting Mac." In 1902 he was made commander of the British forces in Ceylon. Soon afterwards he was discovered in a compromising situation with four Singhalese boys. Macdonald's homosexual tastes were an open secret among the men with whom he served but had been willingly overlooked because of his great value to the army. Now, however, rumors began to spread throughout the British community about Macdonald's indiscretion, and the situation became embarrassing to the British authorities. Macdonald was summoned by the governor of Ceylon, Sir Joseph West Ridgeway, and asked to return to London and seek another appointment there. Sir Joseph hoped that Macdonald's return to London would close the matter. (Homosexual conduct was not illegal under Ceylon's civil law.) But Macdonald's superiors in London were not sympathetic. Field-Marshall Lord Roberts sent Macdonald to see King Edward, who suggested that Macdonald return to Ceylon for a military inquiry. The king went on to hint that suicide might be preferable to the official and personal embarrassment that would ensue. In the meantime the matter was brought up in parliament in Ceylon, where it was monitored by the international press. On his way back to Ceylon Macdonald stopped at the Hotel Regina in Paris, where he discovered a picture of himself and the story of his disgrace on the front page of the *New York Herald* for 25 March 1903. Realizing that his career was at an end, he went up to his room and shot himself.

Macdonald's case provides an interesting contrast to that of Oscar Wilde. Wilde was a gadfly and a mocker of society, whereas Macdonald was a patriot who was devoted to his country. Wilde was a dandy, an artist, and an intellectual, whereas Macdonald was a rough and hard-nosed fighting man. Macdonald did not, in short, fit the stereotype of the effeminate, artistically inclined, socially subversive "homosexual," which the press had been at such pains to establish in its treatment of Oscar Wilde. Consequently, there was some confusion over what the proper reaction to Macdonald should be. Ultimately Macdonald's reputation as a soldier and patriot won out, and, as Noel I. Garde writes, "a brief wave of sympathy for the plight of the homosexual swept England and Scotland, with some of the English and Scottish journals referring to [Macdonald] as the victim of unnecessary official scrutiny into 'personal affairs.' "[25] Wilde had been pilloried in the press and declared a pariah by society; but in 1907, only four years after his suicide, a monument was erected to Macdonald in Dingwall.

Macdonald's case throws into high relief the manner in which homophobia was used as a political weapon against Oscar Wilde. The brouhaha over Wilde's homosexuality was a personal and political vendetta. The "philistines" hated Wilde for a variety of reasons, and so they used public fear of and ignorance about homosexuality as a convenient means of eliminating him. But Macdonald, despite his homosexuality, was defended by the press and venerated as a hero after his death. The political consequences of someone's homosexuality often depend on the person's politics in general—and on the power of the person's friends and enemies.

Political motives also caused the downfall of Friedrich Alfred Krupp (1854–1902), whose case unfolded in Germany at about the same time as the Macdonald affair in England. Krupp was head of the armaments company upon which Germany's economy and military strength depended. Married but separated from his wife, Krupp was fond of vacationing in Italy. In a grotto above the sea on Capri he maintained, as Arno Karlen describes it, "a private pleasure palace where he brought the young fishermen, muleteers, barbers and beggars he wanted."[26] Rumors began to circulate about Krupp's "orgies" on Capri, but Krupp, who was a close friend of Kaiser Wilhelm II and who had apparently learned nothing from the case of Oscar Wilde, thought his wealth and influence would protect him.

Krupp was undone, however, by Italian and German politics. In Italy there was a local race for mayor underway in which a candidate from the clerical party was running against one of Krupp's friends. The clerical party got wind of the goings-on on Capri and passed the story to a newspaper in Naples, the *Mattino*. The clerics then denounced Krupp to the Vatican, which responded with an order that Krupp be expelled from Italy for corrupting the youth. Krupp returned to Germany, where the German newspapers picked up the story. It was lavishly advertised in papers hostile to the Kaiser, which tried to use it as a way of weakening Wilhelm II by humiliating and discrediting his friend. The socialist paper *Vorwärts*, which was opposed to Krupp's naval building program, was especially virulent in its attacks. The paper printed photographs supposedly documenting Krupp's immoral activities with Italian boys and editorialized as follows: "The [Krupp] case must now be discussed in public with due regard to seriousness . . . because it offers a picture of capitalist culture in the most garish colors. . . . The horrible picture of capitalist influence is not especially toned down by our discovery that this is a man of perverse orientation. The pity due the victim of a fateful error of nature must be denied when millions [of marks] have been placed at the service of that sickness' gratification."[27] Krupp brought a libel suit, but soon afterwards he was found dead. Like Macdonald, he had killed himself rather than risk a replay of the fate of Oscar Wilde. As with Wilde, homosexuality was the Achilles heel through which political and social enemies were able to destroy a man whose presence they found inconvenient.[28] The story of Friedrich Alfred Krupp was trumpeted throughout Europe and, as Magnus Hirschfeld wrote in 1903, once again "directed the attention of the broadest circles of the public to the homosexual question."[29]

The climax of this series of scandals also occurred in Germany and also involved people very close to the Kaiser. Again the affair was politically motivated. It revolved around Prince Philipp zu Eulenburg-Hertefeld, a distinguished diplomat who was an intimate friend

of and advisor to Kaiser Wilhelm II. The story of Eulenburg's fall is
one of Byzantine complexity, spanning as it does more than ten years
of German political intrigue. It nonetheless deserves our close attention, since Proust mentions it in A la recherche and since it contributed significantly to the cultural matrix from which A la recherche
took shape. Furthermore, the relevant facts of the Eulenburg case
have heretofore been available only in scattered sources. There has
never been a coherent narrative of the case emphasizing its relation
to the sexual and literary as well as the political climate of the time.

Eulenburg's fall was precipitated partly by his conflict with Friedrich von Holstein, a powerful figure in the German Foreign Office
who was jealous of Eulenburg's influence with the Kaiser.[30] In the
French-German confrontation over Morocco in 1905 and 1906, Holstein, who was counting on the support of England, persuaded the
Kaiser to take a belligerent stance toward France. But England unexpectedly aligned itself with France, and the Moroccan crisis ended in
humiliation for Germany. Holstein tendered a pro forma resignation
and, to his surprise, the Kaiser accepted it. Furious, Holstein concluded that Eulenburg had caused his ouster (Eulenburg was known
to a favor a pacifistic approach to foreign affairs).

Holstein decided that Eulenburg must be eliminated, and recent
history showed him an ideal way of bringing about his downfall. Holstein wrote Eulenburg a letter in which he mentioned that it would
be dangerous for a gentleman to be seen in the company of a man
with Eulenburg's reputation for homosexuality. This reputation had,
as a matter of fact, been fabricated principally by Holstein himself. In
1896 Holstein had placed on file in the Foreign Office a document
containing rumors that Eulenburg, when he was Ambassador to
Vienna, had been blackmailed by the superintendent of a bathhouse.
Holstein had then begun to spread gossip in the foreign service about
Eulenburg's supposed homosexuality. Holstein had also taken it upon
himself to pass Eulenburg's name to the Berlin police, who kept a
record of people suspected of homosexual inclinations. Eulenburg
was aware of some of these machinations, but there was little he
could do to prevent them. Upon receipt of Holstein's letter, however,
Eulenburg immediately issued the appropriate challenge: "Exchange
of pistol shots until disablement or death." Holstein demurred and,

when Eulenburg demanded a complete apology, Holstein sent a terse note which concluded, "I hereby withdraw the offensive remarks made upon [Prince Eulenburg] in my letter."[31] But the seeds of scandal had been sown and now needed only the customary tending by the newspapers and by public homophobia.

Soon a new figure entered the drama, a chauvinistic, right-wing journalist named Maximilian Harden. Harden was of Jewish and Polish descent. His real name was Isidor Wittkowski, an appellation of which he quickly divested himself, since it contradicted his public image as an anti-Semite, Christian moralist, and patriotic reformer. Brandishing his Teutonic pseudonym, Harden pursued a tawdry career of yellow journalism in which he combined conservative politics with scandalous revelations about people in high places. He idolized Bismarck and was a former enemy, but now a friend, of Holstein.

In October of 1906 Harden began to publish in his newspaper the *Zukunft* a series of articles in which he took certain rumors about Eulenburg and turned them into explicit accusations. Harden charged that Eulenburg and his close friend Count Kuno von Moltke were members of a "Round Table" of political figures which formed a camarilla around the Kaiser and gave him unpatriotic advice. He said that the members of this camarilla were closely connected with the French diplomat Raymond Lecomte, and he blamed this unholy alliance for the embarrassment of Germany in the Moroccan crisis. "The story goes," says Eulenburg's biographer Johannes Haller, "that the Prince had brought the Frenchman . . . into the Emperor's environment, in order to frustrate the Government policy in the Morocco question. . . . The Emperor was supposed to have been led by Lecomte to make certain asseverations which the French Ambassador was soon afterwards able to make use of against the Imperial Chancellor."[32] The allegation of treason was sensational enough; but the sting in Harden's charges was his claim that the members of the Kaiser's camarilla were indulging in homosexual vice at the same time that they were undermining the foreign interests of Germany.

The imputation of homosexuality was, as Haller points out, "drawn up with subtle skill."[33] Harden was careful to include in his attacks two persons whose reputations for homosexuality were well known—a certain General Count Hohenau and a certain Major Count

Lynar. Though Eulenburg had never associated with Hohenau or Lynar, the stories that were published in the newspapers created the impression that Germany was being destroyed from within by a closely knit conspiracy of degenerates, of which Eulenburg was supposedly a part. Fortunately for Harden homosexual practices were against the law in Germany, as in England. Under Paragraph 175 of the German penal code, "lewdness against nature, committed among persons of the masculine sex" was punishable by imprisonment and/or forfeiture of civil rights.

At first Harden's attacks focused more on Moltke than on Eulenburg. There were, Haller says:

good reasons for it. [Harden] had no tangible material against the Prince, all he had was Holstein's calumny—while he thought he knew a great many things about Moltke which could be made good use of in a court of justice. Count Moltke had for some years been most unhappily married to an extremely hysterical woman, who made his life such a hell that on the urgent advice of his friends he had set himself free by a painful divorce case. This lady . . . was Harden's source of information regarding Moltke and his relations with Eulenburg; he intended her to be his sensational crown-witness in the courts. By means of her depositions the Prince too could be exposed.[34]

After the first damaging articles appeared in the *Zukunft*, Moltke challenged Harden to a duel. But Harden was not interested in honor; he was interested only in selling newspapers and in advancing Holstein's vendetta against Eulenburg. A duel would put an end to the matter and to the publicity value of the scandal. Harden wanted a long, drawn-out battle in the courts which would produce daily headlines for a long time to come. So he refused Moltke's challenge.

Eulenburg and Moltke responded by bringing libel charges against Harden. But the Crown Prosecutor refused to prosecute, on the grounds that the matter did not involve "the general interest." And so Eulenburg adopted the strange tactic of lodging a complaint against himself in an attempt to prove his innocence. After a brief investigation Eulenburg was informed that no evidence of homosexuality could be found. Harden, who had been summoned as a witness in the inquiry, declared, moreover, that he had never accused Eulenburg of actual infractions of Paragraph 175 but had simply pointed out that Eulenburg, Moltke, and their friends seemed to entertain abnormally exaggerated sentiments of friendship for each other. Moltke, unsatisfied with this explanation and under official pressure to clear his name, brought his libel suit before a municipal court in Berlin, where proceedings began on 23 October 1907. But in his statements during the Eulenburg inquiry Harden had succeeded in redefining his case. In order to acquit himself of Moltke's libel charge Harden now had to prove only that Moltke had homosexual tendencies, not that he had actually committed homosexual acts.

The testimony of Harden's witnesses in this trial included some highly comical details. It was revealed that Eulenburg and Moltke called each other by pet names: Eulenburg was "Phili," and Moltke was "Tutu." Other witnesses claimed that Moltke kept about his person a handkerchief pilfered from Eulenburg, an article he would carry repeatedly to his lips while softly murmuring, "Oh, my beloved! . . . Oh, my dear Phili! . . . Oh, my love!"[35] Then Moltke's ex-wife was brought in to testify that Moltke was impotent; that he harbored a pathological aversion to women; and that after they were married, he locked himself in a separate room at night "for fear of being raped."[36] Other witnesses insisted that "Phili" and "Tutu" had been present at orgies of unnatural lust. The sexologist Magnus Hirschfeld testified that in light of this evidence Moltke could be declared homosexual in the eyes of science. Eulenburg, who had been summoned as a witness, did not appear. The court finally decided that Moltke's homosexual tendencies had been convincingly proved, and Harden was cleared of the libel charge on 29 October 1907.

No sooner had this trial ended than a new scandal emerged. Adolf Brand, an agitator for homosexual rights, published a tract called "Prince Bülow and the Repeal of Paragraph 175," in which he asserted that Bernhard von Bülow, Chancellor of Germany, was having an affair with his male secretary. (Brand thought this revelation would aid the cause of homosexual liberation.) Bülow responded with a libel suit, and the matter was brought to trial on 6 November 1907. Eulenburg was summoned as a witness, and this time he took the stand, denying everything of which he had been accused during Harden's trial and protesting against the persecution to which he was being subjected. Brand was found guilty of libel and condemned to eighteen months in prison.

Brand's case is important, because it reveals an additional layer
of complexity in the legal and social status of homosexuality at that
time. Though homosexual acts were against the law in Germany,
there was a homosexual rights movement underway which was actively working to repeal the German law against homosexuality.
Magnus Hirschfeld, the sexologist who testified in Harden's trial, was
himself a champion of homosexual rights and the leader of a group
called the Scientific-Humanitarian Committee, whose avowed purpose was the abolishment of Paragraph 175 (Hirschfeld antagonized
many of his supporters with his readiness to label Moltke publicly as
homosexual). Adolf Brand was a leader of another, more radical, ho-
mophile organization, the Community of the Special. Brand viciously
attacked the German law as "a real priest's paragraph . . . because it
allows the basest meddling in private lives, degrades the state to
being a jailer for morality snoopers, and is, especially since it does not
protect any legal rights . . . an utterly incredible invasion of the
freedom of the individual."[37] So at the same time that Harden was attempting to destroy Eulenburg and Moltke with charges of homosexuality, there were others arguing loudly and vehemently that there is
nothing wrong with homosexual love and that any law which makes it
possible to imprison people for it is ridiculous. Even Oscar Wilde had
protested at his first trial for homosexuality that "there is nothing unnatural about it." The forces of oppression were, of course, much
stronger than the forces working for enlightenment and liberation.
The point, however, is that attitudes were not monochromatic and
that not everyone took the official point of view for granted.

Meanwhile, a careful rereading of Harden's articles revealed
that, contrary to what Harden had been claiming, the articles accused
Eulenburg and Moltke of considerably more than exaggerated sentiments of friendship. On these grounds Moltke appealed the verdict
of the municipal court and a second trial was begun on 19 December
1907. During this second trial the testimony of the first witnesses was
discredited. Moltke's ex-wife was revealed to be a compulsive liar,
and her testimony was set aside. (Moltke had not contradicted her in
the first trial, because he thought it would be ungentlemanly to call a
lady a liar.) Magnus Hirschfeld recanted and averred that there
seemed to be, after all, no evidence to prove that Moltke had homo-

sexual tendencies. Eulenburg appeared, denied all imputations of homosexuality, and staunchly declared, "I have never practised any abominations."[38] It became quickly apparent that Harden's previous evidence amounted only to hearsay, gossip, and perhaps the suborna- tion of perjury. Harden was at a loss to produce any further evidence. On 3 January 1908 the court decided that Moltke was innocent of Harden's charges, and Harden was sentenced to four months in prison and ordered to pay the cost of the two trials. Three weeks later Hohenau and Lynar were tried before a court martial on charges of having homosexual relations with their subordinates. Hohenau— surprisingly—was acquitted. Lynar was given fifteen months in prison.

But this was not the end of the matter. The Kaiser, under pres- sure from Eulenburg's enemies, had declared that he expected Eu- lenburg to bring his own libel suit against Harden. Eulenburg had filed such a suit while the decision against Moltke was being ap- pealed, but the matter had been delayed pending resolution of Moltke's libel charges. Harden had, in the meantime, been carefully grooming witnesses who were prepared to charge Eulenburg with homosexuality, among them a fisherman named Ernst and a milkman named Riedl. Eulenburg perceived Harden's strategy very clearly. He wrote that "Harden's . . . ideal would be to have me arrested for perjury (as a witness in the last case. . . . They won't succeed in that, but they *will*, by means of witnesses like Riedl, raise the question of perjury, and that will be enough. . . . We must not forget, either, that this case is what Harden *was working for;* Moltke's was only the sauce for the dish."[39]

Suddenly a Munich paper printed the following item: "There is a queer story going the rounds among the populace, according to which Harden got a million from Prince Eulenburg to hold his tongue and make no disclosures."[40] Harden brought a libel suit against the editor of the paper, one Anton Städele. It is likely that Harden himself had manufactured and planted the story, for it gave him the perfect op- portunity to circumvent Eulenburg's libel suit and produce, as plain- tiff rather than as defendant, the evidence against Eulenburg he had been preparing.[41]

On 21 April 1908 Harden's libel suit against Anton Städele came before a Munich municipal court. From the first it was apparent that Eulenburg was the man who was really on trial. Riedl testified that more than twenty years before, in 1882, he had had improper relations with the Prince. Ernst was called in, browbeaten by Harden's attorney, threatened with imprisonment, and made to produce a similar confession. Eulenburg was not given an opportunity to testify or to confront his accusers. The court accepted the testimony of Ernst and Riedl as proof of Eulenburg's homosexuality and found against Städele—a finding which meant, of course, that Eulenburg must now be regarded as having perjured himself in his previous testimony. Städele was fined a hundred marks—barely a slap on the wrist. On 7 May 1908 Eulenburg was arrested, and the trial of Städele for libel metamorphosed into a trial of Eulenburg for perjury and homosexuality.

Eulenburg's health had always been poor, and the continual persecution to which he was being subjected in the courts had made it progressively worse. After his arrest it was necessary to transfer him quickly to the Charité hospital in Berlin. There Eulenburg spent five months under hospital arrest, while the investigation dragged on and on. He was indicted for perjury, and the matter came before a jury in the Moabit section of Berlin on 29 June 1908. Harden produced more witnesses, but nothing could be proved against the Prince. Eulenburg's health continued to degenerate. Finally he had to be carried into court on a stretcher. His doctors declared that he could not tolerate any more trips to Moabit, and it was suggested that the proceedings be postponed. But Eulenburg, who passionately desired to clear his name, objected. So on 14 July 1908 the court moved to the hospital, and the trial continued in the hospital committee room. Eulenburg was only half-conscious and was unable to concentrate on or respond to what was happening. His doctors declared him unfit to stand trial under any circumstances, and the court mercifully adjourned. The Crown Prosecutor began to press for Eulenburg's transferal to prison. But on 25 September 1908 Eulenburg was released on 100,000 marks bail and allowed to return to his Liebenberg estate.

But the persecution of Eulenburg was not yet at an end. In May of 1909 Eulenburg journeyed to Gastein for a cure; the press duly reported that he was attempting to flee to England. The Crown Prosecutor demanded that Eulenburg's bail be raised to half a million marks. Eulenburg had to return to Berlin and raise this exalted sum on a weekend, when his banks were closed. He narrowly avoided a second arrest.[42]

The trial recommenced on 7 July 1909. In less than an hour Eulenburg suffered heart convulsions and lost consciousness. A team of medical experts declared that he was no longer capable of defending himself, and the trial was adjourned *sine die*. Eulenburg continued to have periodic medical examinations, and the doctors repeatedly pronounced him unfit to stand trial. "So it went on," Haller relates, "even when the Prussian monarchy had fallen and the Revolutionary authorities occasionally thought of re-opening the case."[43] Finally the medical examinations were discontinued, and the case was closed. In the meantime, there had been an appeal and an annulment in the Moltke-Harden matter, and the case had been sent back to a lower court. Eventually Harden was fined six hundred marks plus court costs for libel of Moltke, and there Harden agreed to let the matter rest.

In a brief treatment of the Eulenburg affair in his biography of Proust, George Painter sets himself up as a latter-day judge and jury. "[Eulenburg] was guilty," Painter intones, "and his crime was homosexuality."[44] Perhaps; and perhaps not. The fact is that even after so many trials, so many witnesses, so many investigations, not a shred of legally viable evidence was ever produced to prove either homosexual tendencies or homosexual conduct on Eulenburg's part. "The Prince," says Haller, "never had justice done him in this life."[45]

In the first days of the scandal the Kaiser turned his back on Eulenburg, and he never made the slightest gesture to help his old friend in the travesty of justice to which Eulenburg was thenceforth subjected. With Eulenburg's departure to undergo legal harassment, the Kaiser was left, as Holstein and Harden intended, principally with militarist advisors. The militarists eventually had their way, and the Eulenburg affair was thus, as Noel I. Garde points out, "not without effect in the events leading to the catastrophic First World War."[46] Eulenburg died in blissful obscurity on 17 September 1921, having outlived by several years the government by which he had been so relentlessly persecuted.[47]

It should be clear from the foregoing that the Eulenburg affair was not so much a campaign to preserve German morality as a political maneuver aimed at destroying a particular man and putting an end to his influence on German foreign policy. Holstein and Harden wanted Eulenburg removed from his position of power—and what better way than to manufacture a homosexual scandal and set the Prince at its center? "The suit originated in politics," Haller points out, "and political, too, was the motive-power that kept it going—fear of so-called public opinion. That fear impelled the Government . . . to institute proceedings, and condone incidents which in their barbarian defiance of all fair-dealing would never have been tolerated towards an ordinary member of the community, and which [Germany tolerated only] because for many years it had been taught to see in the accused the source of public misfortunes." [48]

In other words, the charge of homosexuality is one of the few charges capable of unleashing the kind of hatred and venom which welled up around Eulenburg. Eulenburg's enemies knew, consciously or subconsciously, that they could count on the public to accept the unspoken assumption around which the entire affair revolved—that is, that there are mysterious but inevitable connections among homosexuality, unpatriotic conduct, and a general slackening of national power and influence. Harden depicted homosexuality as the vice of French sympathizers in the conflict between France and Germany, and he was careful to include a French diplomat in his portrayal of the network of perversion surrounding the Kaiser. Homosexuality thus became the sign of the turncoat and the traitor in Harden's algebra of prejudice.

Harden's strategy reached deep into the primordial superstitions of Western culture. One reason homosexuality was made a capital offense among the ancient Hebrews is because the Hebrews associated it with alien peoples and foreign religions and regarded it as a threat to their national unity. [49] Hebrew homophobia as recorded in the Old Testament heavily influenced the antihomosexual edicts of the Christian emperor Justinian, who again portrayed homosexuality as dangerous to the state and again made it punishable by death. (Justinian feared, among other things, that if homosexually oriented people were allowed to live, their presence would tempt God to reenact the fate of Sodom and Gomorrah.)[50] Justinian's laws, as such laws always do, created a climate of homophobia and allowed it to be exploited for personal and political ends. Edward Gibbon says that during Justinian's reign "a sentence of death and infamy was often founded on the slight and suspicious evidence of a child or a servant . . . and [homosexuality] became the crime of those to whom no crime could be imputed."[51] Justinian's code helped to shape both the secular and the ecclesiastical legislation of the Middle Ages and to bring about the long-lived practice of burning as heretics and witches people whose "crime" was the imputation of homosexuality.[52] It is from this tradition of law based on superstition that modern sodomy statutes, such as Paragraph 175 of the German penal code, derived.

The Western tradition is, in short, suffused with a superstitious equation of homosexuality, heresy, and treason.[53] The ruthless manipulation of this irrational and atavistic mode of thinking played a major role in the downfall of Wilde, Moltke, Eulenburg, and the other unfortunate people who were caught up in the whirlwind of homosexual scandal that swept through Europe at the dawn of the new century.

The Eulenburg affair attracted a great deal of attention in France and was reported in detail in the French press, where Proust was able to follow it closely (it was regularly discussed in *Le Figaro,* to which Proust had a subscription).[54] The French regarded the German convulsions over homosexuality with a feeling of aloof superiority. This did not preclude, however, an avid interest in all the latest gossip about Eulenburg and his circle. A book called *L'Homosexualité en Allemagne,* which purported to tell the inside story of the Eulenburg scandals, was hastily put together by Henri de Weindel and F.-P. Fischer and immediately became a French bestseller, going through twenty editions in the three months following its publication on 6 February 1908. "Homosexuality!" the book began. "It was a new word to French ears when, in October of 1907, launched from the very steps of the German throne, it began to reverberate through newspaper columns in a great tumult of scandal."[55] If in Germany homosexuality was the vice of French sympathizers, in France it became—naturally—*"le vice allemand."* The French referred to Ber-

lin as "Sodom-on-Spree" and gave Eulenburg the nickname "Eulen-
bougre." Meanwhile, in the French homosexual underground, people
began to ask each other, "Do you speak German?" An affirmative answer was a coded way of identifying oneself as homosexually inclined.[56]

It was natural that Proust should take an interest in these developments, for he had always been fascinated by homosexual scandal
and had always made a point of finding out which important or powerful people had homosexual tastes. Robert de Billy says that Proust
frequently knew the truth about someone's homosexuality long before
it became generally known and that on this subject "[Proust's] docu-
mentation was remarkable."[57]

Proust was acting true to form, then, when he wrote to Billy during the Eulenburg affair and asked, "What do you think about this
whole business of the homosexuality trial? I think they struck out
rather at random, although it's very true of some of the people involved, especially of the Prince."[58] In A la recherche Proust has
Charlus allude to the Eulenburg affair during one of his monologues
at the Verdurins'. In a discussion of the German connections of his
family and of the reign of Kaiser Wilhelm II, Charlus states that he
approves of most of the Kaiser's policies but finds that "as a man, he
is vile; he abandoned, betrayed, denied his best friends in circumstances where his silence was as contemptible as theirs was noble."
Charlus goes on to reveal that he is acquainted with one of the
highest-placed of the defendants in the Eulenburg trials and that the
man once told him: "Imagine how much confidence the Kaiser must
have had in our delicacy in order to have dared allow such a trial!
And, moreover, he was not mistaken in placing his faith in our discre-
tion. We would have gone to the scaffold with our lips sealed"
(2: 947).[59]

Proust, like most people of his day, assumed that Eulenburg was
guilty as charged: the treatment of Eulenburg in the French and German press hardly left room for any other conclusion. But, for our purposes, the question of Eulenburg's guilt or innocence under German
law is of secondary importance to the cultural and psychological patterns highlighted by the Eulenburg trials. The Eulenburg affair, like
the Wilde and Krupp scandals, is a paradigm of the use of homopho-

bia as a political weapon, a use so frequent and so influential in Proust's day that it amounts to a hallmark of the era.

In *A la recherche* Charlus suffers from the same kinds of politics, and it seems likely that this aspect of Charlus's story is directly related to Proust's observation of the homosexual scandals which made such big news around the turn of the century. (We know that Proust knew about Wilde, Eulenburg, and Moltke; and, given his curiosity about everything pertaining to homosexuality, he probably knew about Krupp and Macdonald as well.) Charlus has something in common with all these figures. Indeed, when he discourses on the Eulenburg affair at the Verdurins', he is unconsciously alluding to the nearest historical parallel to what will be his own fate.

That fate arrives, in classic tragic form, through a combination of *hamartia* and *hubris* on Charlus's part; scheming and plotting on the part of his enemies; and the action of a kind of historical inevitability which, like the *ananke* of Greek tragedy, gradually enfolds Charlus in the same net of scandal that closed in Proust's day around so many other influential people with homosexual tastes. Like Oscar Wilde, Charlus enjoys playing at social one-upmanship and as a result makes many enemies during his reign over high society. He regularly delivers himself of "the most cutting witticisms, in front of scandalized society people who had never dreamed he could go so far" (3: 317). In one celebrated diatribe Charlus tells Morel: "As for all the little gentlemen who call themselves the Marquis of Cambre*merde* or of Gofuckyourself [*Vatefairefiche*], there is no difference between them and the lowliest foot soldier in your regiment. Whether you pee at the Comtesse Poop's or poop at the Baroness Pee's, it's the same thing: you will have compromised your reputation and used a dirty rag instead of clean toilet paper" (2: 1,090). The subtle irony of the Wildean epigram is, of course, missing from this scatological vituperation, which is closer to the primitive satire of cursing and flyting.[60] Clearly Charlus sometimes goes even further than Wilde. But the result of the barbs and of the air of superiority with which they are delivered is the same: they leave in their wake many people anxious to get their own back from Charlus, should the opportunity present itself. Chief among these, as it turns out, is Mme Verdurin.

The clash between Charlus and Mme Verdurin is one of the most dramatic events in *A la recherche*. Mme Verdurin is one of the few characters whose ego and social pretensions rival those of the Baron. Throughout the novel Proust emphasizes the lust for totalitarian authority which characterizes her relationship to her "little clan." She insists that everyone who frequents her salon adhere to the belief that good times and meaningful culture are to be found only *chez* Verdurin (1: 188). And she especially abhors the formation of romantic attachments which lead people to pay more attention to each other than to her. As long as such relationships are carried on within the little clan and in full view of "the faithful," Mme Verdurin gives them her blessing; but as soon as a love affair seems on the verge of becoming too private, too special—as soon as it seems, in short, to threaten the dogma that outside the little clan there is no salvation—Mme Verdurin turns all her energy toward destroying it. In this way she intervenes in Swann's relationship with Odette, in Brichot's relationship with his laundress, and in Charlus's relationship with Morel.

She has an additional motive in her attack on Charlus's love life, for Charlus's social influence and condescending attitude toward the Verdurin circle pose a major threat to Mme Verdurin's own campaign of self-aggrandizement. So when, in *La Prisonnière*, Mme Verdurin receives a snub from Charlus, she mounts a devastating counterattack.

Charlus has arranged for Morel to participate in a performance of the Vinteuil Septet at the Verdurins', an event he has staged as a means of introducing Morel to the select members of high society he has invited for the occasion. Mme Verdurin, for her part, views the concert as an opportunity for establishing her own foothold among the aristocracy. During the reception Charlus and Mme Verdurin each make a bid for social dominance; and because of Mme Verdurin's clever manipulation of Charlus's reputation for homosexuality, Charlus emerges as the loser.

The reception unfolds in a crescendo of mounting tension between Charlus and Mme Verdurin. Charlus insults Mme Verdurin by banning from the concert certain people she would have liked to invite (3: 230 ff.). In addition, Morel has recently refused to perform for some friends of Mme Verdurin, simply because Charlus could not be present (3: 228–29). Furthermore, Charlus commits during the course of the reception the unpardonable sin of flaunting his private relationship with Morel. "M. de Charlus withdrew in the company of Morel, under the pretext of having Morel explain to him what he was going to play, but finding a special pleasure, while Charlie was showing him his music, in thus making a public display of their secret intimacy" (3: 243). The last straw for Mme Verdurin is the rude treatment she receives from the aristocratic guests Charlus has invited. They ignore her and act as if Charlus, and not Mme Verdurin, is to be credited with the social coup of the concert. "Having come both out of friendship for M. de Charlus and out of curiosity about such a milieu, each duchess went straight to the Baron as if it were he who were giving the reception and said . . . only a few steps from the Verdurins who could hear every word, 'Show me which one is Old Lady Verdurin; do you think it's really necessary that I be introduced to her?" (3: 245). Thus Charlus arouses in Mme Verdurin "that feeling of hatred which was, as manifested in her, only a special form—a social form—of jealousy" (3: 278).

Mme Verdurin smoulders with rage. She asks Brichot to take the Baron outside for a cigarette so that "my husband can take Charlus's Dulcinea aside . . . and enlighten him concerning the abyss into which he is falling" (3: 280). She hopes that Morel, who values above everything else his reputation as a musician and the manner in which good social connections can advance it, will react by publicly denouncing Charlus and breaking off their relationship. And the plan works exactly as she hopes.

The plan works because Mme Verdurin is able to wield with great dexterity the politics of homophobia. In order to turn the others against Charlus she invents all manner of falsehoods about him, falsehoods calculated to force him irretrievably into the stereotype of the criminally minded, socially subversive sexual pervert. "Let me tell you," she says to Brichot:

that I don't feel at all safe with that kind of person in my house. I happen to know that he's been involved in all sorts of filthy activities and that the police have him under surveillance. . . . It appears that he's done some time in prison. Yes, yes, I have it from very informed sources. I've also heard from someone who lives on his street that you couldn't imagine the kinds of criminals he has going and coming at his house. . . . Take my word for it. . . .

He'll be murdered one of these days, as people of his ilk always are. Or maybe it won't come to that, since he's in the clutches of this Jupien . . . who is—I have it, you know, on excellent authority—an ex-convict. It seems that he holds Charlus in his power by means of some frightful letters. I heard it from someone who has seen the letters; he told me, "You would be sick if you saw what they were about." (3: 280)

Mme Verdurin's remarks contain just enough truth to be verisimilar and just enough suggestive falsehood to trigger the construction of elaborate fantasies about Charlus. Charlus is, in fact, homosexually inclined; he is, in fact, being followed by blackmailers (3: 207). But he is not, of course, an ex-convict, and neither is Jupien. Like Harden in his attacks on Eulenburg, Mme Verdurin cleverly bases her assertions about Charlus on precisely the sorts of stereotypes that will make them credible and frightening to a homophobic mind.

So while Brichot distracts Charlus, M. Verdurin informs Morel that his relationship with Charlus poses a grave threat to his social and artistic career. And Mme Verdurin adds her own opinion that "you are the talk of the Conservatory. . . . another month of this life and your artistic future is ruined, whereas, without Charlus, you should earn more than a hundred thousand francs a year" (3: 310). Mme Verdurin goes on to embroider lavishly upon the theme of Charlus's association with blackmailers. "Even financially," she tells Morel, "[Charlus] can be of no use to you; he has been entirely ruined since he has fallen prey to blackmailers . . . everything he owns is mortgaged, his house, his château—everything" (3: 311). This is not, of course, the case. But for Morel it is the deciding factor, and when Charlus comes back into the room, Morel turns viciously against him. "Leave me alone, I forbid you to come near me," Morel shouts at the astonished Charlus. "It's obvious that this is not your first attempt, that I'm not the first young man you've tried to pervert!" (3: 316). Charlus, taken off guard, finds himself at a loss to respond. "Amid circumstances so cruelly unforeseen," the narrator comments, "this great rhetorician could do nothing more than stammer: 'What does this mean? What's going on here?' " (3: 317).

In the days following the fatal party the lies Mme Verdurin has concocted about Charlus grow, as such lies are wont to do, by geometrical progression. Soon it is whispered in society that M. de

Charlus was thrown out of the Verdurins' reception when he was caught trying to rape a young male musician (3: 319). Mme Verdurin has her revenge. And her machinations lay the groundwork for the assaults on Charlus's power and influence which continue throughout the rest of the novel. The attacks on Charlus in the Verdurin salon are on one level a powerful allegory of the unscrupulous methods that have always been used to exclude homosexually oriented people from the ranks of "the faithful."

In a later volume of *A la recherche* Proust raises the allegory from the world of the salon to the world of international politics. As the First World War approaches, the enmity between M. de Charlus and Mme Verdurin becomes more and more bitter. Mme Verdurin takes advantage of the new political climate to heap even more discredit and abuse on M. de Charlus. For several years she has depicted Charlus as socially outmoded; "now she summed up this condemnation and turned people generally against him by saying that he was 'pre-war' " (3: 764). Then, drawing upon the superstition which connects homosexuality with subversive foreign ideologies, she spreads the rumor that Charlus is not French but Prussian and that he is probably a German spy. "I don't like it at all," she declares:

the way this man insinuated himself into my house. There's something suspicious about it. We had a property that occupied very high ground and looked down over a bay. He was doubtless given orders by the Germans to reconnoiter there for a German submarine base. There were many things that surprised me then and which I now understand. For instance, he did not at first want to come to the house on the train with my other guests. I very graciously offered him a room in the house. But no, he preferred to live in Doncières, where there were a great many soldiers stationed. There was an unmistakable smell of espionage about the whole business. (3: 765–66) [61]

Mme Verdurin adds—looking prophetically ahead to the Nazi attitude toward Jews, people with a homosexual orientation, and all others who do not fit the conception of a pure and homogeneous national stock—"if we had a more energetic government, all those kinds of people would be in a concentration camp" (3: 765).

Mme Verdurin's slander is given national exposure by Morel, who is now working as a journalist and writing on the political situation. In a series of libelous articles highly reminiscent of Harden's at-

tacks on Eulenburg, Morel accuses Charlus simultaneously of homosexuality and sympathy for the enemy cause. "A little before the
war," says the narrator:

[Morel published] some short articles whose meaning was transparent to
those in the know [and which] had begun to do the greatest wrong to M. de
Charlus. Mme Verdurin had bought fifty copies of one of these—called "The
Misadventures of a Dowager Whose Name Ends in -us, or The Old Age of
the Baroness"—in order to lend them to her acquaintances, and M. Verdurin, declaring that Voltaire himself never wrote anything better, gave readings of the article aloud. Since the war the tone of the articles had changed.
Not only was the Baron's homosexuality denounced but also his supposed
Germanic nationality: "Frau Kraut" and "Frau van den Kraut" were M. de
Charlus's usual epithets. A piece in a poetic style had the following title, borrowed from certain dance tunes of Beethoven: "Une Allemande." Finally,
two short stories—"American Uncle and Frankfurt Auntie" and "Rear
Decks"—read in proof by the members of the little clan, had delighted Brichot himself, who had cried, "I only hope the all-high and all-powerful
goddess of Censorship doesn't blue-pencil us!" (3: 767)

The quarrel between Charlus and Mme Verdurin illustrates a
central idea of *A la recherche*, the idea that "just as there are collections of animals, collections of humans . . . in the same way there are
enormous organized accumulations of individuals which we call nations; their life only repeats on a larger scale the life of the cells which
compose them" (3: 771). The sexual politics within the little clan are a
microcosm of the sexual politics sometimes practiced by nations as a
whole. Mme Verdurin and Morel ride to social prominence partly on
a wave of antihomosexual and anti-German propaganda, a powerful
combination which allows them not only to bring down Charlus but
also to appear to be doing at the same time a favor for their country
and for humanity. As C. A. Tripp points out, "whole campaigns
against homosexuality have quite often originated as attempts to 'get
at' the power and influence of a single individual."[62] Proust shows
that this is just as true of snobbery and salon politics as it is of national
and international affairs. The difference between Holstein and
Harden on the one hand and Mme Verdurin and Morel on the other
is merely one of degree.

Proust does not explicitly protest against these strategies; rather,
he allows the cruelty and prejudice which underlie them to speak for

themselves and satirize themselves. In general, Proust sees very little possibility of and cares very little about social and moral reform. He compares society to a kaleidoscope, implying that the overall structures may shift and change but that the compositional elements—the fundamental traits of human nature—will always remain the same (3: 893–94).[63] The mature Proust almost never writes about heroes and villains. Instead, he writes about the good and the bad, the morality and the immorality that coexist in each human personality. He exposes the shabbiness of the Verdurins' treatment of Charlus, but he also exposes similar traits in Charlus's own personality. Earlier in the novel Saint-Loup tells the following story about Charlus:

One day a man who is currently, as Balzac would say, one of the people most in view in the Faubourg Saint-Germain but who in an earlier and rather unfortunate period manifested some rather bizarre tastes asked my uncle [Charlus] to accompany him to [my uncle's] garconnière. Scarcely had they arrived, however, when it was to my uncle Palamède, not to the women, that the man began to make his declaration. My uncle pretended he did not understand and found a pretext to summon his two friends. They came back, seized the guilty man, undressed him, beat him until he was bloody, and kicked him outside in weather which was ten degrees below zero, where he was later found half dead. The result was that the police began an inquiry, which the poor man had to go to enormous lengths to make them abandon. (1: 750)

Who is guilty in this complex tangle of victims and executioners? Everyone is guilty, because all the parties involved act at least partially in bad faith, pretending to have one set of motives when in reality they have another. And so no one is guilty, because the people who are punished in some respects deserve the bad treatment they get from others. The man whom Charlus beats up pretends to be interested in women in order to make a sexual advance to Charlus. Charlus beats him up because he wants to deny his homosexuality and project an image of heterosexuality. The Verdurins attack Charlus because they see how the homosexuality he tries so hard to conceal can be used to get him out of the way and facilitate their own social rise. The characterization of Charlus and of the people with whom he comes into conflict transcends the question of homosexuality to become, finally, a comment on the complexities and self-contradictions of human nature in general.

At the same time these scenes dramatize a synergistic relationship between character and culture. The characters do what they do partly because of the negative attitudes about sexuality and homosexuality inherent in their society and in the Judaeo-Christian tradition. Proust shows this very clearly. And yet, aside from a few murmurs of protest, he does not join the people of his generation who fought against these ingrained attitudes. His vision of society and of homosexuality within society is not utopian. On the contrary, it shows that as long as there are human beings, there will be sexual politics, Machiavellian intrigue, and ruthless attempts to crush others in order to gain personal influence and prestige. Proust uses the decline of Charlus as a model of how, in the conflict between tradition and individuality, conformity and originality, orthodoxy and heresy, the former forces have usually prevailed. But he also lays the groundwork from which strategies of social reform and even social revolution could well take shape. Few writers have analyzed the political dimensions of homophobia as well as Proust. And analysis is a necessary precondition for any attempt to eradicate the superstitions on which those dimensions depend.

LETTERS TO ROBERT DREYFUS AND LOUIS D'ALBUFERA

Proust's analysis of the clash between Charlus and the Verdurins is a measure of the intellectual distance he traversed between the early work and *A la recherche*. *Les Plaisirs et les jours* and *Jean Santeuil* have little to say about homosexuality other than to reiterate the literary cliché which associates it with suicide. And while it could be argued that such portrayals are justified—since people with homosexual inclinations do, in fact, sometimes kill themselves—it seems obvious that Proust adopts the suicide topos in the early work principally because he does not yet have a sure grip on the theme of homosexuality and is therefore content to say about it what others have said and what he thinks society wants to hear. In the story of Charlus and Mme Verdurin, however, Proust speaks with his own voice and with the sort of detached irony which characterizes his best writing on the theme. Unfortunately, Proust is not always able to maintain this perspective. *A la recherche*, like the early work, is often marred by a tendency to defend the accepted view at the expense of the original vision. In short, Proust never completely liberates himself from his own homophobia. But, paradoxically, this very trait helps him to achieve a keen insight into the recurring patterns of culture and the multiplicity of human motivation. There is something of Proust himself in both Charlus and Mme Verdurin, just as there is something of his age—and every age—in the story of their conflict.

There can be little doubt that the sexual scandals which occurred from 1895 to 1909 contributed to this broadening of Proust's field of artistic vision. Indeed, the French scholar Robert Vigneron suggested in 1937 that the Eulenburg affair was the single most important event in the genesis of *A la recherche*—the "point of departure for *Swann*." [64] This idea has not attracted a great deal of attention in Proustian criticism, no doubt because Proust's critics have never formulated a way of dealing with the suggestion that *A la recherche* is a work which owes its very existence to homosexual history and homosexual inspiration. Vigneron's thesis is, then, worthy of reexamination in light of what we have discovered about homosexuality and Proust's attitudes toward it. For although Vigneron's ideas need expansion, clarification, and qualification, they point the way to an understanding of some important additional aspects of Proust's vision of sexuality in *A la recherche*.

Vigneron shows that during the Eulenburg affair a great many works dealing with homosexuality and capitalizing upon its notoriety appeared in France, works which Proust could not help but notice. Many of these works were of a scientific or quasi-scientific nature and purported to reveal the causes of homosexuality and the psychology of people with homosexual tastes. For example, on 1 December 1907, five weeks after the opening of Harden's first trial for libel, Rémy de Gourmont published in the *Mercure de France* an article called "Dialogues des Amateurs, L: L'Amour à l'envers." The article featured an analysis of homosexuality based on the concepts of "tumescence" and "detumescence" expounded by the British sexologist Havelock Ellis. On 1 January 1908, two days before the verdict in Harden's second libel trial, Gourmont published in the same journal another article entitled "Dialogues des Amateurs, LII: Variétés." This second article proposed a distinction between homosexuality per se and so-called "Athenian friendship." "Dialogues des Amateurs" was the title of a regular column by Gourmont in which two interlocutors, M. Delarue (Mr. Man in the Street) and M. Desmaisons (Mr. Homebody) discussed current events and world affairs. Proust almost certainly read Gourmont's column, since he was, as his correspondence shows, a regular reader of the *Mercure de France*. Whether Proust read the columns dealing with homosexuality is not known, but the very fact that homosexuality appeared in "Dialogues des Amateurs" shows that it was a topic intellectual France was actively discussing and debating. Gourmont's treatment is typical, moreover, of the sources to which people were turning for explanations of homosexual emotion and behavior. They were turning principally to the sex research and pre-Freudian psychology of the nineteenth and early twentieth centuries, to such writers as Havelock Ellis in England; Ulrichs, Hirschfeld, and Krafft-Ebing in Germany; Tardieu, Brouardel, and Moreau in France; Mantegazza in Italy; and Tarnowsky in Russia. These were the inevitable sources, since homosexuality was generally regarded as a topic whose proper place was the physician's consulting room and the learned scientific tome. Whenever it appeared as a theme in imaginative literature, there were shocked protests that literature is not the place for discussions of such behavior. Yet at the same time there was widespread curiosity about homosexuality and about the implications of the Eulenburg affair.

People were, in short, interested in homosexuality but had for obvious reasons to avoid appearing too interested in it. It was fashionable to talk about the subject; but it was also *de rigueur* to approach it as did Rémy de Gourmont—as a curio of human nature which is admittedly repugnant but which is not without interest to a student of the vagaries of the human mind and heart. Consequently, nonscientific writers who attempted to analyze homosexuality—whether in newspapers, magazine articles, or fiction—usually excused their endeavor with appeals to scientific curiosity and allusions to contemporary medical theory. Proust's treatment of homosexuality in *Sodome I* and the later volumes of *A la recherche* is, at least on the surface, no exception to this trend.

To some readers and critics, however, homosexuality was unac-

ceptable even when presented as a scientific anomaly and mitigated
with medical terminology. The issue of the *Mercure de France* which
carried Gourmont's first article on homosexuality also contained a
review of a book by Schumann-Arndt called *Wir vom dritten Geschlecht (We of the Third Sex)*. The protagonist of this book is an
officer in love with a female impersonator. The plot is classic: blackmail, suicide, and, withal, supposed revelations of the inside facts
about homosexual life in Berlin. Henri Albert, the reviewer of German literature for the *Mercure de France,* commented on *Wir vom
dritten Geschlecht* as follows:

. . . one cannot pass over in silence the literary repercussions which the
Moltke-Harden affair is producing in Germany. For a long time now certain
German publicists, under the pretext of producing scientific studies, have
been unveiling for us the ravages of the "German Vice." Thus have the
lowest circles of Sodom-on-Spree been revealed to us. In order to protect
themselves from the police these writers generally appeal to a sense of
outraged morality, but, more often, their desire is simply to satisfy their
readers' avid and unhealthy appetite for novelty. The virtuous nation of Germany reproaches us for our pornography, but she herself cultivates, for her
own use, some of the most repugnant examples of this literary genre.

Here is the latest product of the genre, one which appeared only a few
days ago. The book is called *We of the Third Sex* and carries as a subtitle
Confessions of a Degenerate. [65]

The review concludes with a brief summary of the book's plot.

Albert's protest against *Wir vom dritten Geschlecht* did not stem
the tide of works dealing with homosexuality. In January of 1908 the
Paris publishing house of Rousset brought out, under the title *Les
Homosexuels de Berlin: Le Troisième Sexe,* a French version of
Magnus Hirschfeld's scholarly and influential study *Berlins drittes
Geschlecht*. In this work Hirschfeld demonstrated that the tastes attributed to Moltke and Eulenburg were not confined to the aristocracy but were to be found on all levels of society—an idea which is, of
course, central to *A la recherche* as well. Hirschfeld's book was followed by the previously mentioned *L'Homosexualité en Allemagne,*
which, in addition to telling the story of the Eulenburg scandals, offered an overview of current medical theories of homosexuality. *L'Homosexualité en Allemagne* gave special emphasis to Hirschfeld's idea
that homosexual people constitute a third sex which occupies a kind

of twilight zone between male and female—another key concept in *A la recherche*. The year 1908 also saw the publication of John Grand-Carteret's *Derrière "Lui": L'Homosexualité en Allemagne*, an anthology of political cartoons on the Eulenburg affair taken from German-language newspapers. (The *"Lui"* of the title referred to Wilhelm II.) Grand-Carteret's book had the salutary effect of showing the lighter side of the Eulenburg trials, though it included the usual sober allusions to the attitudes of contemporary medicine toward the "Uranian" personality.

Homosexuality also made inroads into French fiction in 1908. Proust's friend and erstwhile lover Lucien Daudet published during that year what Vigneron calls "a discreetly pederastic novel" entitled *Le Chemin mort*. In September of 1908 Proust wrote a favorable review of this book, though he cautiously avoided mentioning its homosexual implications.[66] About a year and a half later, on 22 June 1910, Jean-Gustave Binet-Valmer (1875–1940) published a novel called *Lucien*, which gave overt and even favorable treatment to homosexuality. *Lucien* flaunted an epigraph attributed to Oscar Wilde: "The most courageous man among us is terrified of himself." The novel's protagonist, the Lucien of the title, is torn between the impulse to kill himself because of his homosexual feelings and an underlying conviction that those feelings are, after all, natural, healthy, and non-criminal. At one point Lucien's father calls him "a wretched creature." And Lucien wonders: "Why 'wretched'? Because he did not make love like other people? Wretched? But what did *their* love amount to? . . . Only an admixture of dreaming ennobles human coupling. And who can prove that my dream of love is not higher than theirs?"[67] Lucien concludes that "I want to live. . . . They will not kill me as they killed the great Wilde, the wretched creatures! Yes, *they* are the wretched ones. Hypocrites! Executioners!" (pp. 94–95). For all that, Lucien is finally driven by family and social pressures to attempt suicide.

Lucien recovers, but by the end of the novel he is thinking once again that suicide is the only way out. He writes a letter to Costi Batchano, a man he has loved, confessing his feelings and outlining his new plans for ending it all. In the letter Lucien says that after the letter has been mailed, he will poison himself in the San Remo hotel where he is now staying with his homosexual friend Reginald. But when Costi attempts to verify Lucien's suicide, he receives the following unexpected report: "On 17 January Reginald Green and Lucien Ferney checked into the Riviera Palace Hotel in San Remo. The following day Green went to Nice, whence he returned on 22 January in the afternoon. The same day Lucien Ferney and Reginald Green departed, together, for Naples" (p. 329). These are the final words of the novel, and they bring the story to a surprise conclusion. They show that Lucien has changed his mind and decided that instead of killing himself over an impossible love for Costi he will go on living and continue his relationship with Reginald. *Lucien*, for perhaps the first time in modern literature, replaces the suicide topos with a vision of the continuity of homosexual life. The ending of the novel makes it plain that Lucien's only real crime was, as he writes to Costi, "trying to be something other than what I was" (p. 309).

To French literary pundits the sins of *Lucien* were twofold. First, it dared to bring homosexuality out from under the neat rubrics of medical treatises and dramatize it as a kind of behavior which partakes of all the complexity and nuance of other forms of human experience. Indeed, the novel derives a biting, satirical irony from the fact that not only Costi, the man Lucien secretly loves, but also Lucien's father, who sternly lectures the boy about homosexuality, and also Marie, the woman to whom Lucien becomes engaged in a futile attempt to "cure" his homosexual desires, are all respected psychiatrists. But their supposed learning and skill do them no good in their attempts to deal with Lucien. They try to understand him by fitting him into one of the pigeonholes of their discipline or into their individual moral preconceptions. But Lucien rebels, finds the courage to live life as he understands it, and thereby eludes psychiatric dogma. He is not "cured"; he passes beyond the need for cure. And he does this not because but in spite of the ostensible experts on homosexuality who surround him and belabor him with advice and prescriptions. Binet-Valmer consistently shows that the so-called science of the psychiatrists is simply a mask for moralism and homophobia. (One is reminded of Dr. Cottard's conduct in the scene of Charlus's sham duel.)

Second, *Lucien* sinned by suggesting that the unhappiness and failure which sometimes accompany homosexual love are due more to society's harassment of homosexuality than to the nature of homosexuality itself. Indeed, the final chapter of *Lucien* is a scathing indictment of the brutalization of homosexually oriented people by the medical establishment. In his letter to Costi Lucien comments meaningfully that "yesterday, I wanted to write you a confession covering my entire life. But you are a doctor, a psychiatrist, and I am afraid of being reduced in your eyes to nothing more than a case history" (p. 311). Immediately after reading these words Costi attends an autopsy, and, while waiting for the police to report on Lucien's supposed suicide, he watches a cadaver being dissected:

Before him, on the table, lay Lecamus, spread out flat on his stomach, offering up a spine whose vertebrae had been laid bare. . . . Joyfully Duprin wielded the chisel which would deliver to him the precious marrow. . . . [Batchano] had approached the table and was leaning over Lecamus. . . . But it was not Lecamus that Batchano was seeing. It was . . . Lucien. . . . Under Jacques Duprin's mallet and chisel Lecamus's vertebrae—the lumbar, the dorsal, the cervical—had yielded one by one. . . . The autopsy had scarcely begun, and it was expected that the microscope would produce some results. Batchano knew they would bend down once again before the mystery. Hundreds and hundreds of slides would pass under the lens. Their eyes would grow tired studying them. The soul would keep its secret. For centuries the soul has played hide and seek with ingenuous savants. And we still labor under the same ignorance we have always had. (pp. 317–21)

The symbolic equation of Lucien with the cadaver being "joyfully" dissected and scrutinized under the doctors' microscope is extremely powerful. The cadaver is a symbol of what Lucien might have become had he not decided to escape to Naples with Reginald—a dead personality, a case history, a medical exhibit to be probed, dismembered, and theorized about. Despite all these learned investigations, says Binet-Valmer, the soul keeps its secret, and the mysteries of identity remain inviolate.

Not surprisingly *Lucien* produced wails of outrage among reviewers. They regarded it as final evidence that homosexuality had been getting far too much exposure of late, and the novel provoked an explosion of the very attitudes it had so powerfully satirized. "Was it really necessary," said a reviewer in *Le Temps*, "to show us this unhappy boy falling step by step into the lowest regions of Sodom and

Gomorrah? There are things which should be left to treatises on pathology or to handbooks destined for the guidance of confessors in their exploration of the impurities of human nature."[68]

Lucien had broken some of the most sacrosanct of the unwritten rules governing public discussions of homosexuality. To be sure, the book was not entirely free of stereotype: Lucien is an artistic type (a playwright who writes only one play) and is presented as being rather effeminate. But *Lucien* struck, nonetheless, a new note in modern literature by contravening the obligatory suicide and by satirizing the official conception of homosexuality as a bizarre disease. The book actually suggested that it is possible to be homosexually oriented and to be at the same time reasonably happy and the master of one's own fate. So it paid the price in negative press. Despite, or perhaps because of, its denunciatory reviews, *Lucien* became something of a succès de scandale and ran very quickly through several editions. Robert Soupault says: "I remember the scandal provoked by the appearance, around 1910, of Binet-Valmer's novel *Lucien*. This was the first time in modern literature that the subject [of homosexuality] was openly broached. Schoolboys read the book on the sly."[69] Proust took due notice of the book's turbulent reception and mentioned it, as we saw in the first chapter, in a letter to Gaston Gallimard. In that letter Proust points out what should, by now, go almost without saying: that the optimistic vision of *Lucien* is not the vision of *A la recherche* and that, indeed, "nothing is more dissimilar."[70]

Some of the literature on homosexuality which appeared in France during and after the Eulenburg affair would no doubt have appeared had the Eulenburg affair never occurred. But it would not have attracted the same amount of attention and generated the same amount of interest. The Eulenburg scandals assured that what might have remained a minor tributary of French cultural life from 1907 to 1910 became instead a swelling tide of controversy which encompassed science, politics, literature, journalism, and social conversation. The issue was heated, and the debate was intense. It was a debate which, according to Robert Vigneron, Proust himself decided to enter in 1908 by writing and publishing a nonfiction article on homosexuality. Proust, of course, never published such an article. But Vigneron argues that his plans for doing so, though ultimately abandoned, brought him the inspiration for *A la recherche*. In Vigneron's view, Proust's desire to write an article on homosexuality gradually metamorphosed into his decision to undertake the monumental novel itself.

Did Proust in fact begin an essay on homosexuality during the Eulenburg affair? Until recently the evidence that he did so has rested primarily on a letter he wrote to Robert Dreyfus on 16 May 1908. The relevant portion of the letter reads as follows:

> I intended to ask you if you thought the forbidden article would be as inoffensive (I have such atrocious pens that, having labored for every word, I'll start using a pencil) in the *Mercure de France* or in another journal as in a volume. But, in the meantime, my plan has become more precise. It will be, rather, a short story, so there will be time to consult you again. But the same reason that makes me think that the importance and the suprasensible reality of art prevent certain anecdotal novels, however pleasant they may be, from altogether meriting, perhaps, the rank you seem to assign them (art being something too superior to life, as we judge it through the intelligence and depict it in conversation, to be content with counterfeiting it)—this same reason does not allow me to make the realization of a dream of art depend upon reasons which are themselves also anecdotal and too much drawn from life not to participate in its contingency and irreality—which, moreover, presented thusly, seems not false but banal and deserving of some sharp slap from irritated existence (like Oscar Wilde saying that the greatest grief he had known was the death of Lucien de Rubempré in Balzac, and learning a little afterwards, in his trial, that there are griefs more real). But you know that this banal aestheticism could never be my aesthetic philosophy. And if fatigue, the fear of being a bore, and especially the *pencil* prevent me from explaining this, give me credit not for its truth but for its seriousness.
>
> Marcel [71]

In the first sentence Proust speaks of an article he has planned to write and previously discussed with Dreyfus. And it would seem that Dreyfus has attempted to discourage Proust's plan because of the sensitive nature of the topic. Was it homosexuality? When Dreyfus first published Proust's letter he could not remember. "Why was I troubled by Proust's project?" he commented. "I no longer have the slightest memory." [72] But Dreyfus's memory seems to have been somewhat better when he published the letter again a few years later. At that time he appended to it the following footnote: "I believe I remember very vaguely that during the course of my recent visit

Proust had spoken to me of a plan for an article which I had not encouraged, doubtless wrongly. Perhaps it was related (I have sometimes wondered in rereading this letter) to his plan, still mysterious,
to explore the accursed regions upon which he was later to raise the
edifice of his great work."[73]

"Accursed regions" is, of course, a code for homosexuality (alluding to Proust's metaphor of the "race accursed"). And Dreyfus's "perhaps" forms the cornerstone of Vigneron's thesis about the genesis of
A la recherche. Vigneron argues that having taken note of the many
works dealing with homosexuality which were appearing during the
Eulenburg affair, Proust decided to write a nonfiction article on the
subject himself. But in Vigneron's view Proust soon changed his mind
and decided to use the planned article as the basis for a short story
("It will be, rather, a short story," Proust wrote to Dreyfus). Vigneron
further believes that this short story gradually took on the dimensions
of a novel in Proust's mind and that it eventually expanded to become
A la recherche du temps perdu.

To be sure, the letter to Dreyfus adumbrates A la recherche in
some very important ways. Proust says that what he really wants to
do is to transform his idea for a "forbidden article" into something superior to the sorts of anecdotal novels Dreyfus admires. I have,
Proust says, "a dream of art" which I will never realize if I try to
make it depend exclusively on material drawn directly from life. If
Proust is indeed talking about plans for writing on homosexuality, he
seems to be saying that although he originally intended to write an
anecdotal study tied directly to the Eulenburg trials—the kind of
study represented by, say, L'Homosexualité en Allemagne by Weindel
and Fischer, or by Rémy de Gourmont's columns in the Mercure de
France—he has now abandoned this conception. The sort of writing
produced by the topical, anecdotal approach is, Proust says, too
ephemeral, too contingent, tied too directly to everyday life. Art as
Proust understands it must deal in "suprasensible reality," in higher
truths than those discoverable by a simple reporting or "counter-
feiting" of existence. Otherwise the result will be both banal and, in
the highest sense, false to the very reality it has attempted to portray.
Proust says that art is superior to life, but not in the sense of the
"banal aestheticism" of Oscar Wilde, which sets up a barrier between

aesthetic truth and truth garnered from actual experience. Art is superior to life when it succeeds in accurately reflecting it and, at the
same time, transforming it into something more general, more lasting, and more universal.

Vigneron rightly perceives that this letter represents a crucial
stage in Proust's progress toward *A la recherche*. And it also seems
obvious that Proust's "dream of art" is revolving as he writes to
Dreyfus at least partly around the theme of homosexuality. The Eulenburg affair is being discussed all over Europe and is generating a
steady stream of articles and books on homosexual love. At the same
time Proust writes to a friend about his plan for a "forbidden article"
and wonders whether it might be appropriate to publish it in the
Mercure de France, a journal which, with its publication of Rémy de
Gourmont's columns and Albert's review of *Wir vom dritten Geschlecht,* has shown itself receptive to articles on homosexuality. Finally,
Proust concludes this meditation on his writing with an allusion to the
trial and misfortunes of Oscar Wilde.[74]

All this circumstantial evidence suggests that the subject of
Proust's article-short story could hardly be anything other than homosexuality. Recently, with the publication of a letter from Proust to
Louis d'Albufera, the evidence has become more than circumstantial.
The letter to Albufera was written in May of 1908, the same month
during which Proust wrote the letter to Dreyfus quoted above. In this
other letter Proust says that he has several projects in progress, and
he lists them as:

a study of the nobility
a Parisian novel
an essay on Sainte-Beuve and Flaubert
an essay on Women
an essay on Homosexuality (not easy to publish)
a study of stained-glass windows
a study of tombstones
a study of the novel[75]

It would seem, then, that the "forbidden article" of the letter to
Dreyfus is the "essay on Homosexuality" of the letter to Albufera.
Certainly an essay on homosexuality is the only project among those

Proust lists for Albufera which could reasonably be construed as "forbidden." Moreover, Proust frets in the letter to Albufera about the difficulty of publishing an article on homosexuality, and this recalls his worry in the letter to Dreyfus about whether "the forbidden article would be as inoffensive . . . in the *Mercure de France* or in another journal as in a volume." At any rate, the letter to Albufera conclusively proves what Vigneron long ago suspected—that Proust began an essay on homosexuality during the Eulenburg affair.

Before the letter to Albufera came to light, Henri Bonnet challenged the idea that Proust's "forbidden article" was to deal with homosexuality. Bonnet suggested that the reference was, instead, to Proust's plan for writing an attack on the criticism of Sainte-Beuve and that the "forbidden article" was ultimately realized as the chapter called "La Méthode de Sainte-Beuve" in *Contre Sainte-Beuve.* But Bonnet's thesis is untenable on several grounds.[76] To begin with, it is extremely doubtful that Proust would have viewed an attack on Sainte-Beuve as a "forbidden" enterprise. Indeed, when Proust wrote to Dreyfus in May of 1908, he had already published in *Le Figaro* some telling parodies of Sainte-Beuve and other respected literary figures, among them Balzac, Michelet, and Flaubert.[77] Proust was never shy about disagreeing with or making fun of the masters. But he was, as we have seen, extremely circumspect about associating himself publicly with homosexuality. Bonnet thinks that Proust harbored some "fear of causing displeasure" by disagreeing with Sainte-Beuve, "the idol of scholars and of professors of rhetoric."[78] But it is far more likely that Proust's fear stemmed from a quite understandable reluctance to speak out on homosexuality, a subject which had, after all, been branded as "the unspeakable vice" and "the love that dare not speak its name."

Bonnet further says that it is difficult to imagine how Proust could have considered writing an article on homosexuality in 1908 in the midst of the Eulenburg affair. But this is precisely when such an idea would most naturally have occurred to Proust. Proust had already written, some fifteen years previously, a short story about homosexuality which he withheld from *Les Plaisirs et les jours,* probably, as we have seen, because of the climate of panic which enveloped the subject immediately after the trial of Oscar Wilde. But things had changed considerably by 1908. There had been several other scandals drawing worldwide attention to homosexuality and stimulating open discussion of it. And by this time there were, as we have also seen, extremely vocal homosexual rights organizations in Germany working for the repeal of Paragraph 175 and disseminating throughout Europe information about homosexuality. So much, in fact, was being written about the subject that Proust probably felt, as Vigneron says, that he would have to make his own contribution very soon if he did not wish to be the last writer to speak out on it.[79] Bonnet's idea that 1908 was an inauspicious moment for writing an article on homosexuality is based on an incomplete grasp of the cultural situation at that time. There have been few moments before or since when general interest in the subject was so intense and public receptivity to discussions of it so widespread.

Finally, Bonnet believes that the "dream of art" Proust describes in his letter to Dreyfus "seems to go beyond the subject of homosexuality." Here Bonnet makes the common mistake of assuming that homosexuality plays only a minor aesthetic role in Proust's novel. On the contrary: homosexuality, as we have already seen, is directly related to the vision of art Proust outlines in his letter to Dreyfus, a vision which aims at achieving a delicate balance between the specific and the general, the historical and the universal.

And so Bonnet's thesis is seriously flawed. But Vigneron's thesis is not perfect either. Vigneron's argument that the Eulenburg affair brought Proust the inspiration for A la recherche as a whole has a glaring weakness: it does not take into account Proust's work on Jean Santeuil and Contre Sainte-Beuve, works in which Proust had previously experimented with some of the most important of the themes and ideas he later developed in the novel. When Vigneron published his article in 1937, Jean Santeuil and Contre Sainte-Beuve had not yet been discovered among Proust's papers. And Vigneron was also unaware that Proust began work on a novel in January of 1908[80] and thus several months before he wrote to Dreyfus about his plans for a "forbidden article." It therefore seemed to Vigneron that some cataclysmic event—which was, he thought, the Eulenburg affair— must have occurred in order to transform the superficial author of Les Plaisirs et les jours into the titanic literary genius of A la recherche.

The truth, of course, is that Proust served a long literary appren-
ticeship between the time of *Les Plaisirs et les jours* and the time of *A
la recherche*.

So things are not as simple as they seemed to Vigneron. Proust's
novel has many sources, including Proust's own life; his readings in
other writers; his translation and study of Ruskin; his parodies; his society columns for French newspapers; his experiments with fiction
and criticism in *Jean Santeuil*, in *Contre Sainte-Beuve*, and in the
novel begun in January of 1908; his plans for writing articles on
women, on stained-glass windows, on tombstones, on the aristocracy—and on and on. From the perspective of *A la recherche* we can
see that everything Proust previously wrote or planned to write was,
consciously or subconsciously, a finger exercise for the great novel to
come. To argue that any single event or theme brought Proust the inspiration for *A la recherche* is to oversimplify the complex evolution of
his genius.

It is nonetheless true that Vigneron discovered, even if he then
misinterpreted, an important factor in the genesis of *A la recherche*.
Vigneron's facts were incomplete but, as Maurice Bardèche says, "his
intuition was correct."[81] The Eulenburg affair did not bring Proust
the idea for the novel as a whole. It did, however, give him one of the
final and most important pieces to the vast artistic puzzle he was trying to solve. Among the scattered ideas for a novel in Proust's memorandum book of 1908 the name "Eulenburg" occurs along with a few
theoretical jottings on the nature of homosexuality (these we shall
discuss in the next chapter).[82] Maurice Bardèche's study of Proust's
notebooks shows, moreover, that the theme of homosexuality remained at the center of Proust's work from 1908 on. "The two currents which were feeding Proust's thought," Bardèche writes, "the
novel of 1908 and the narrative essay dealing with Sainte-Beuve,
were proceeding . . . along the same line."

But suddenly we encounter, in the middle of Notebook 6 and the middle of
Notebook 7 . . . two series of developments foreign at once to the novel of
1908 and to the essay on Sainte-Beuve: the diverse fragments whose union
will form the chapter entitled "La Race maudite" . . . and the first pieces
devoted to the "little nucleus" of the Verdurins. Finally, as a decisive indication, in the middle of Notebook 7, we read about the entrance of the Baron

de Charlus, presented here under the name of M. de Guercy; and at the same moment we rediscover the anonymous beach, which Proust will henceforth call throughout this preparatory phase of his work "Querqueville."

On convincing evidence Bardèche dates the entry of this material into Proust's work as occurring in March or April of 1909, a time when the Eulenburg affair was still making news in France and Germany. Bardèche argues that these experiments with homosexuality as a literary theme gave Proust's work a "new orientation." And he concludes that it was at about this time that Proust "realized that he could produce a book from his fragments."[83]

Bardèche's research shows, then, that homosexuality was among the first topics to which Proust turned when he began to compose, during the Eulenburg affair, some of the sketches which distinguish A la recherche from the work which preceded it. Another of those topics was, as Bardèche demonstrates, the "little nucleus" of the Verdurins, a motif which eventually becomes, as we have seen, itself extremely important in Proust's analysis of the cultural and social implications of homosexuality. Bardèche's research thus supports Vigneron's idea that the Eulenburg affair brought Proust important inspiration for A la recherche, and it allows us to continue to entertain, with the qualifications mentioned, Vigneron's thesis.

Curiously neither Bardèche nor Vigneron speculates on precisely what Proust learned from the Eulenburg affair that made it such a crucial event in his artistic development. Both critics gather a great deal of evidence to show that it influenced Proust's plans for writing on homosexuality, but they offer no ideas as to how, if at all, that influence extends into the art of A la recherche. I have already made one suggestion: Proust's analysis of the political dimensions of homophobia seems directly related to his observation of the Eulenburg trials and similar scandals. But Proust could have profited from the Eulenburg affair in another important way. Harden's attacks on Eulenburg and Moltke, destructive and politically motivated as they were, had, like the trial of Oscar Wilde and the misfortunes of Macdonald and Krupp, at least one beneficial side effect. They posed once again, and this time with great intensity, questions which had been before the public mind since Wilde was sentenced to two years at hard labor in 1895. What, exactly, is homosexuality? Where does it come from? Can it be "cured"? Is it a perversion? Or is it perhaps a basic component of human nature, a trait which exists in everyone in varying degrees? How widespread is it? Is it more prevalent on one social level than on others? Does it have any good effects? Should it be treated as a crime, as an illness—or should it be simply left alone? The Eulenburg affair moved many European thinkers and writers to attempt new answers to these questions and at the same time to rediscover some of the old answers which had been formulated in previous literature and sexology. This renewed interest in the social and psychological aspects of human sexuality is an important part of the cultural matrix of *A la recherche* and is, as we shall see, echoed implicitly and explicitly throughout the novel.

CHAPTER FOUR

THE GOOD FAITH
OF A CHEMIST

*G*EORGE PAINTER suggests that Proust's desire to write an article on homosexuality was eventually realized as "the preliminary sketch for the first and second chapters of *Sodome et Gomorrhe* which forms Chapter Twelve, 'La Race Maudite,' of [the 1954 edition of] *Contre Sainte-Beuve*."[1] And there are, indeed, traces of essayistic writing in "La Race maudite" and in *Sodome et Gomorrhe* (especially in *Sodome I*), which suggest that Proust is here recasting material originally intended for publication as a nonfiction essay. Ultimately, however, *A la recherche* itself is a greatly expanded realization of Proust's early plan to write an article on homosexuality: after the discovery of Charlus's true nature in *Sodome I* the novel adopts as one of its primary purposes an extended analysis of this theme.

Proust's narrator advances many ideas about homosexuality in *A la recherche*. Whether Proust himself would have agreed with all the narrator's ideas is a moot point. Sometimes Proust deliberately allows the narrator to express opinions which subsequent experience will cause him to modify or discard. Proust wrote to Jacques Rivière that "I have not tried to analyze abstractly [the] evolution of thought but rather to recreate that evolution and bring it to life. I am therefore obliged to depict errors without believing I must say I regard them as errors. So much the worse for me if the reader thinks I hold these errors to be the truth."[2]

It is clear, however, that Proust thought his novel taken as a whole reflected the truth about human nature. When Mme Schiff voiced concern that the later volumes of *A la recherche* might bring her "a great deal of grief," Proust interpreted the remark to mean that "you have been disappointed to see Swann becoming less sympathetic and even ridiculous." But he explained that "I am not free to go against the truth and violate the laws of the characters. 'Amicus Swann, sed magis amica Veritas.'[3] The nicest people sometimes go through hateful periods. I promise you that in the following volume, when he becomes a Dreyfusard, Swann will begin once more to be sympathetic. Unfortunately—and this causes me a great deal of grief—he dies as early as the fourth volume. Moreover, he is not the principal character of the book. I would have liked him to be. But art is a perpetual sacrifice of sentiment to truth."[4]

Proust made similar remarks about his treatment of homosexuality. He was aware that some of the things his narrator was saying about homosexuality were extremely unpleasant. But he was convinced these things had to be said, because they were, he thought, true. He wrote to Louis de Robert:

If without ever mentioning homosexuality at all I portrayed vigorous adolescents and tender, serious friendships, never implying that this sort of thing goes further, then I would have all the homosexuals on my side, because I would be showing them the very thing they love to see. But it is precisely by dissecting their vice (I use the word "vice" with no intention of reproach) that I reveal their sickness, that I say precisely the thing that causes them the greatest horror—that is, that this dream of masculine beauty is the result of a nervous disorder [une tare nerveuse]. The best proof is that a homosexual adores men but hates other homosexuals.[5]

These are some of the ideas Proust regarded as true and in need of exposition. In another letter to Robert on the same subject he commented that "I cannot . . . modify the results of moral experiments that I am obliged to report with the good faith of a chemist."[6]

In this comparison of the novelist to a scientist, Proust reveals, among other things, the extent to which he was influenced by Naturalism, particularly Zola's attempts to make literature scientifically precise. But this Naturalistic strain is complicated by several factors: by the irony resulting from the disjunction that is sometimes present between what Proust thinks and what the narrator says, by the attempt to "recreate" rather than "analyze abstractly" the evolution of thought, and perhaps most importantly by the lack in both Proust's

correspondence and in the novel itself of a clear and unified conception of what constitutes homosexuality. Self-contradictions proliferate
in Proust's letters and statements to his friends, just as they proliferate in the narrator's theories. In both the novel and the letter quoted
above the self-contradictory tone is established by the choice of the
word "vice" to refer to homosexuality followed by the assertion that
this word contains "no intention of reproach" (cf. 2: 613, 618, 625). It
seems pointless, then, to try to determine everything Proust thought
about homosexuality and then try to decide in every instance how
Proust's ideas are different from or similar to the narrator's. A more
profitable endeavor is to analyze the text of the novel itself in an attempt to describe and interpret the extremely complex vision that
emerges there. For Proust insists that in the novel, in spite of all the
deliberately planted false trails, lies *veritas*.

Many critics have agreed that Proust's novel tells the truth about
homosexuality. Colette, for instance, speaks of "the thundering truth"
with which Proust discusses the theme. André Maurois comments
that Proust's treatment of homosexuality "is accurate and . . . helps
to illuminate for the uninitiated this phenomenon 'so misunderstood,
so uselessly condemned.' " And Milton Hindus says that "Proust has
done . . . an enormous amount of good in bringing about a greater
understanding [of homosexuality] and consequently a greater forg-
iveness."[7]

But others have expressed a different opinion. André Gide read
an extract from *Sodome et Gomorrhe* with, he says, "an impulse of indignation." And he explains:

Knowing what [Proust] thinks, what he is, it is difficult for me to see [in these
pages] anything but a dissimulation, a desire to protect himself, a camouflage
of the cleverest sort, because denouncing him can be to no one's advantage.
Moreover, this offence to truth is likely to please everyone: the heterosexuals, whose prejudices it justifies and whose repugnances it flatters; and the
[homosexuals], who will take advantage of the alibi provided by their lack of
resemblance to the [homosexuals] he depicts. In short, considering the general cowardice which will help it along, I know of no other piece of writing
which has a greater potential for implanting erroneous opinion than Proust's
Sodome.[8]

Similarly, J. Z. Eglinton complains of the "distorted image [which]
has been built up—influencing literary people and psychiatrists alike

. . . —of the 'typical' homosexual as more or less resembling Baron de Charlus."[9]

Which critics are right? It is important to try to decide, not only because a decision will help us to understand *A la recherche* but also because *A la recherche,* as Eglinton points out, has exerted considerable influence on later images of homosexuality. To ask whether the novel's portrayal is accurate and whether its influence has been for good or ill is to ask fundamental questions about the sexual conventions and assumptions of modern society.

Throughout *A la recherche* we are offered various theories of homosexuality, and theories can be evaluated only by empirical testing. It is not sufficient simply to declare (as most previous critics have done) that this statement about homosexuality is true and this other statement false. Fortunately, most of the theories of homosexuality advanced in *A la recherche* have, under different names and for different purposes, been subjected to extensive empirical testing by contemporary sex researchers. Such testing does not conclusively prove the truth or falsehood of any of the theories in question, but it does give us a firmer basis for understanding the narrator's ideas and placing them within their proper cultural context. This chapter will undertake a systematic review of the narrator's generalizations about homosexuality (both implicit and explicit), indicate how those generalizations cohere and how they fail to cohere, and at the same time show where they stand in relation to present-day research on human sexuality. As we proceed, we should bear in mind that the "general laws of love" (3: 820) formulated in *A la recherche,* whatever else they may be, are parts of a work of creative art and, as such, usually have special functions within their particular aesthetic world in addition to their function as statements about the nature of the world in general. Our ultimate purpose is to discover how the epistemological function of Proust's writing relates to the creative function both in the "general laws of love" and in the novel as a whole.

THE MEDICAL BACKGROUND

We may begin by asking how much of the view of homosexual psychology delineated in *A la recherche* is original with Proust. Critics have frequently asserted that Proust's treatment of this topic was revolutionary for its time and that it illuminated the question by bringing to it "new points of view."[10] The opposite is, in fact, very often the case. Most of the theories of homosexuality found in *A la recherche* were commonplace long before Proust wrote, and many of them were adopted directly from the standard medical theories of Proust's day.

It is not difficult to understand why Proust drew so extensively on contemporary medical theory. He wanted to tell the truth about homosexuality, and at that time it was generally assumed that homosexuality was an illness and that the truth about it therefore reposed in medical writing. Furthermore, Proust had a habit of doing scholarly research on subjects which interested him. He told Lucien Daudet that while writing *A la recherche* he sought advice from "horticulturists, couturiers, astronomers, heraldists, pharmacists, and so on."[11] When Proust wanted to know something, he usually went directly to the recognized experts. And for homosexuality the recognized experts were the physicians and sexologists who had written on the subject. Then, too, the theories of these writers gained new recognition in France during the Eulenburg affair and were popularized in the works dealing with the German scandals. The medical theories were well known, readily accessible, and widely accepted. They represented the official point of view, and for Proust to contradict them in his novel might have reduced the chances of winning a wide audience for *A la recherche*.

There was, then, considerable cultural pressure on Proust to adopt the medical view of homosexuality. There was also indirect if not direct family pressure. Proust was brought up in a family where medical opinion was highly respected. His father and brother were well-known physicians, and his father was a colleague and friend of two of the leading French authorities on homosexuality: Dr. Ambroise Tardieu (1818–79) and Dr. Paul Brouardel (1837–1906). The theories of Tardieu and Brouardel were homophobic in the extreme. Nonetheless, they were cited all over Europe as the apex of French research on this subject.[12] If the question of homosexuality ever arose around the Proust household, it is likely that the theories of Tardieu and Brouardel would have been those advocated by Proust's father and instilled into the young Marcel. In any case, it is clear that when Proust decided to make homosexuality one of his major themes, he turned for guidance partly to the views of writers such as Tardieu and Broudardel.

Now Proust, as we have seen, sometimes satirizes the medical approach to homosexuality, as when he has Dr. Cottard make a fool of himself by assuming that Charlus, since he belongs to "the category of 'abnormals,' " is out to rape him. But in this, as in many other matters, Proust was of two minds. He recognized the limitations of the medical approach; but at the same time he was profoundly influenced by that approach in his own attempt to understand homosexuality and depict it truthfully in his art. Milton L. Miller points out that Proust mentions reading the work of Krafft-Ebing, the German physician whose book *Psychopathia Sexualis* had such far-reaching impact on sexual attitudes of the time. And Miller also points out that Proust mentions reading the work of the British sexual theorist Havelock Ellis.[13] Miller does not pursue the implications of this information, which take us, as we shall see, very deeply into Proust's treatment of sexuality. *A la recherche* is, among other things, a sort of summa of the sexual theory of Proust's day, and Proust's reading in that theory obviously did not stop with Krafft-Ebing and Havelock Ellis.

ORIGINS AND CAUSES

In its consideration of the origins and causes of homosexuality *A la recherche* mirrors the general uncertainty of contemporary medicine as to whether it is an inborn or an acquired trait. The German physician Casper (in 1852 and again in 1863) was the first to draw a distinction between inborn and acquired homosexuality, and many theorists after Casper accepted this distinction.[14] Sometimes, however, it was urged that some sort of hereditary "taint" was necessary to produce even cases of apparently acquired homosexuality. Paul Moreau in *Des aberrations du sens génésique* and Krafft-Ebing in *Psychopathia Sexulis* argued that homosexuality arises when an individual predisposed by heredity is placed in a situation which favors the development of the morbid predisposition.[15] This is very like the way Proust's narrator accounts for the lesbianism of Mlle Vinteuil. Mlle Vinteuil's relationship with her female friend is "one of those situations wrongly believed to be the exclusive appanage of bohemian life: such situations are produced each time a vice which Nature herself causes to appear in a child (sometimes only by mixing the virtues of the father and the mother, as She might mix the colors of their eyes) needs to reserve for itself the situation and security which are necessary for its development" (1: 148).

Throughout *A la recherche* the narrator emphasizes the role of heredity in the etiology of homosexuality. The meeting of Charlus and Jupien is predestined "not only by their own temperament, but by that of their ancestors, by their most remote heredity" (2: 627). Homosexually oriented people constitute a "race"; their attraction to their own sex is the result of "an innate disposition. . . . [a] special taste, inherited without their knowledge, like a disposition toward drawing, toward music, toward blindness" (2: 614, 617–18). The Guermantes clan is "a perverted family," so suffused with homosexuality that the heterosexually inclined Duc de Guermantes, who happens to have been spared the "hereditary illness," must be regarded as exceptional because of his normality (3: 687). The Prince de Foix, who has homosexual tastes, tries in vain to protect his son from homosexuality: "For the Prince de Foix had been able to protect his son from bad outside company but not from heredity" (3: 828). For Proust's narrator, as for Dr. Moreau and many other medical theorists of the day,[16] homosexuality is sometimes passed down from generation to generation.

The narrator also allows for conditioning and imitation in the development of homosexual tastes. Like most writers of the time, however, he never clearly delineates the relationship between hereditary and acquired homosexuality or between internal and external causes. At times he speaks of homosexuality as if it can be contracted by force of habit—"By virtue of thinking affectionately about men, one becomes a woman" (2: 908–9)—or as the result of seduction by a person of the same sex (3: 351, 678). He also alludes to the idea, widespread in nineteenth-century sexology, that men sometimes seek homosexual experiences because they have become sated or jaded with ordinary pleasures. In his lectures on legal medicine Brouardel singled out idleness and boredom as primary causes of "immoral acts committed by old men."[17] Similarly, Charlus's conduct in Jupien's

brothel and his general libertinage in later life are attributed partly to
"his satiety with social pleasures, his caprices easily transformed into
passions for men" (3: 832). In a like manner we encounter in Jupien's
brothel "an old man all of whose curiosities had doubtless been sated
[who] was urgently asking if it would be possible for him to meet a
man who had been maimed" (3: 823). Charlus's peculiar brand of
homosexual masochism was also well known to contemporary sexologists. Havelock Ellis observed that the desire to be chained and
fettered "not infrequently coexists with a tendency to inversion."[18]
And Krafft-Ebing pointed out that "it is a common proceeding for
blasés and impotents to have themselves whipped" and described the
case of a man who "visited brothels to have himself flogged by prostitutes."[19]

Charlus in old age displays symptoms of what French physicians
called *la pédérastie des ramollis,* a condition in which homosexual
tendencies either appear or become more pronounced with the onset
of senility.[20] When the narrator meets Charlus in *Le Temps retrouvé,*
the Baron is in something of a second childhood and appears to have
lost control over most of his actions and gestures. Jupien has constantly to watch over his "big baby," as he calls him, to ensure that he
does not run off with the next boy who passes by (3: 865). Furthermore, Jupien tells how Charlus took up to his room a boy not more
than ten years old (3: 864). To be sure, Jupien attributes this conduct
to Charlus's being misled, in his blindness, by the child's unusually
deep voice. But it was thought that the tastes of aged *ramollis* ran
especially to young boys,[21] and Charlus's actions are perhaps intended to exemplify this common belief. Or perhaps they stem from
the taste for boys which, earlier in the narrative, Charlus is said to
have acquired *faute de mieux,* on an occasion when there were no
men available to him (3: 769); or from the incipient interest in boys
he displays as early as *Combray,* where he stares at the young narrator with "eyes that were popping out of his head" (1: 141). At all
events, it is clear that Charlus's homosexuality becomes more exaggerated and less subject to control as he grows older and that this process corresponds to theories of homosexuality widely accepted in
Proust's day.[22]

In *Sodome I* Proust's narrator speaks of homosexually oriented men who, in their youth, cover their walls and mirrors with pictures of women and write love poetry to them. And he asks, "Must we for that reason assign to the beginning of these lives a taste which will never recur, like those blond curls of childhood which are destined to turn the darkest brown?" (2: 623–24). Here the narrator anticipates an important discovery of recent sex research, which has shown, as we have seen, that a person can be heterosexually oriented at one stage of life and homosexually oriented at another, and the converse. But the narrator never explicitly affirms that such evolution is possible: he simply asks the question and leaves it hanging. Like the medical theorists of the day he vacillates between the idea that homosexuality is an innate condition and the idea that it can be acquired through various external causes—though he gives, perhaps, a slight edge to the idea that homosexual tendencies are innate and hereditary.

This emphasis on heredity in the etiology of homosexuality serves to make Proust's work scientifically respectable by the standards of his time. But it also has an aesthetic and philosophical purpose. For Proust heredity is an important force in the shaping of anyone's character and not just the character of someone who is homosexually inclined. Throughout the novel the narrator argues that we are who we are partly because of the traits we have inherited from our parents and our ancestors (e.g., 1: 34, 564–66; 3: 78–79), an argument which, as Margaret Mein points out, "owes a great deal to a long deterministic tradition that goes back perhaps as far as Montesquieu and passes by Buffon, Balzac, Taine, and Zola."[23] The concept of hereditary homosexuality fits very neatly into this overall vision of hereditary determinism and thereby helps to unify the novel.

But it produces at the same time an oversimplification. Homosexuality is not hereditary; or, if it is, it is hereditary only in the sense that, like heterosexuality, it is a recurring trait of human nature. Both responses are natural components of mammalian sexuality, and they have existed as long as humans and animals have existed.[24] To argue that homosexuality is a "hereditary illness" is to miss the point. Such an argument assumes that extraordinary conditions must prevail before homosexuality can arise, and this, as we have seen, is not the case.

Indeed, the whole process of seeking causes for homosexuality without, at the same time, seeking causes for heterosexuality erroneously assumes that homosexuality requires a kind of explanation which heterosexuality does not require. Proust's narrator writes at great length about the ways people fall in love, heterosexually and homosexually, and he affirms that in both cases the basic patterns of illusion, suffering, and jealousy are the same. But he never suggests that heterosexual feelings in and of themselves are due to conditioning, to heredity, or to any of the other causes he offers for homosexuality. Such an approach postulates that heterosexuality is natural and self-explanatory, while homosexuality is unnatural and therefore in need of an explanation. This is, of course, the assumption which dominated sex research in Proust's era and which continued to dominate it until only recently. Recent studies, however, have redefined the kinds of questions we must ask about human sexuality, and they have done so partly by challenging the old belief in a heterosexual instinct. Kinsey and his associates pointed out that:

Biologists and psychologists who have accepted the doctrine that the only natural function of sex is reproduction, have simply ignored the existence of sexual activity which is not reproductive. They have assumed that heterosexual responses are a part of an animal's innate, "instinctive" equipment, and that all other types of sexual activity represent "perversions" of the "normal instincts." Such interpretations are, however, mystical. They do not originate in our knowledge of the physiology of sexual response . . . and can be maintained only if one assumes that sexual function is in some fashion divorced from the physiologic processes which control other functions of the animal body. . . .

In actuality, sexual contacts between individuals of the same sex are known to occur in practically every species of mammal which has been extensively studied.[25]

In place of the old pattern of a heterosexual instinct set over against various sexual perversions, many sex researchers now believe that all sexual preferences—heterosexual as well as homosexual—are caused by outside conditioning of an originally undifferentiated sexual urge. According to this now widely accepted view, homosexuality and het-

erosexuality arise in the same way, and no one is exclusively homosexual or exclusively heterosexual unless that person has been in
some way conditioned to be. Mark Freedman writes:

the ultimate choice of sexual outlets does appear to be determined by social-
learning experiences: that is, sexual behavior is dependent on the individual's
past . . . experiences with various sexual stimuli. For example, a man would
be sexually responsive toward other men if he had positive, rewarding sexual
experiences with his peers during adolescence. However, if these experiences were aversive to him or if he had been deeply imbued with societal
taboos against homosexual behavior, then men would not be sexually stimulating to him, or homosexuality a likely sexual outlet. . . .
    It must be emphasized here that this sexual-behavior pattern is not es-
tablished through one unique experience; it is multidetermined.[26]

The implications of this new approach to human sexuality are far-
reaching. "From the moment it is realized that there are no instincts
to guide human sexuality," says C. A. Tripp, "the whole problem of
the origins of heterosexuality looms as a major puzzle. . . . Most people see their heterosexual responses as innate and automatic, but
trained observers understand that people are specifically heterosexual
because they have been geared by their upbringing to expect and to
want to be."[27] Tripp then proceeds, quite rightly, to consider the
etiology of heterosexuality and the etiology of homosexuality as interdependent questions. In his theoretical statements about homosexuality Proust's narrator does not consider the matter in this way but,
like most other people who have written on the subject, assumes that
homosexuality requires an explanation which heterosexuality does not
require. This approach imparts, at the outset, a subtly negative coloration to the whole concept and ensures that even when the narrator
speaks favorably about homosexuality, as he occasionally does, his
words will have a paradoxical and ambivalent ring.

HOMOSEXUALITY AND PERSONALITY

From the origins and causes of homosexuality we now turn to the
relationship between homosexuality and personality depicted in
Proust's novel. Here again the narrator's presentation is firmly
grounded in the sexual theory of the day. For example, it was often

suggested in medical writing (and in its popularizations) that "homosexuals" as a type are subject to rapid and extreme changes of mood. In 1908 Edward Carpenter, describing what he called "the more normal type of the Uranian man," wrote that "emotionally they are extremely complex. . . . 'full of storm and stress, of ferment and fluctuation' of the heart."[28] Benjamin Tarnowsky went further, declaring that "good alternates with evil in [the homosexual man]. At times he is gentle, then cruel without reason. He is either benevolent or irritable and vindictive. The dissoluteness of his morals gives way to remorse. Humility and manifestations of morbid self-love, justness and brutality succeed one another."[29] Carpenter and Tarnowsky could easily have been describing the Baron de Charlus or Morel, for these two characters, in addition to having homosexual inclinations, are also the most volatile, explosive, and self-contradictory in *A la recherche*. In the episode of the narrator's visit to Charlus toward the end of *Le Côté de Guermantes*, Charlus displays remarkable fluctuations of mood, going in an instant "from haughty rage to an affection so suffused with sadness that I thought he was going to start weeping" (2: 557). It is, moreover, during this visit that Charlus makes a sexual advance to the narrator, disguised as an offer that the narrator become his protégé (2: 562 ff.). Morel, of course, carries on relationships with both sexes. But he too displays the schizophrenic oscillation of character which was then regarded as a distinguishing trait of the "homosexual." In one memorable scene Morel heaps vilification on Jupien's niece only to break down a few hours later and weep with remorse (3: 164, 194). And throughout the novel Morel, like Charlus, alternates between cruelty and kindness, anger and affection, "humility and manifestations of morbid self-love."[30]

But to say this is, after all, to say something which is true of Proust's characters in general. Most of the characters in *A la recherche* reveal new, surprising, and mutually contradictory selves as the novel progresses; and most of them (the exceptions are the saintly mother and grandmother) are paradoxical mixtures of cruelty and kindness, sadism and altruism. As a person with homosexual tastes Proust was continually instructed by the medical science of his era that he belonged to group characterized by just this sort of schizophrenia. What becomes in *A la recherche* a characteristic of human identity in general may therefore have been encouraged by and to some extent dependent on the self-image held out to Proust by the medical science of his day.[31]

One reason homosexually oriented people were regarded as emotionally unstable was that homosexuality itself was thought to be a form of mental illness. Scientists in Proust's era believed there was such a thing as "moral insanity," a concept devised in 1835 by the English psychologist Pritchard, who defined it as a " 'morbid perversion' of the feelings and impulses without delusion or loss of intellect."[32] In France Paul Moreau applied this theory to homosexuality, asserting that it occupies an intermediate stage between reason and madness.[33] Similarly, Brouardel advised his class in legal medicine to deal with homosexually inclined men in the same way they would deal with madmen.[34] Even people with homosexual tastes sometimes acquiesced in this image of homosexuality. Oscar Wilde stated in a letter of petition written from prison that "the terrible offences of which [I] was rightly found guilty . . . are forms of sexual madness . . . diseases to be cured by a physician rather than crimes to be punished by a judge."[35]

In *A la recherche* homosexuality is presented in the same way. Charlus's preference for men is a "mania" (3: 205) and a sign of a "nature [which is] slightly deranged" (2: 610). And in *La Prisonnière* the narrator imagines that Mlle Vinteuil might be able to exculpate herself for her lesbian conduct by using a version of the self-justification used by Wilde: "It was not I . . . I was mad" (3: 262). Running parallel to the imagery of insanity is a complementary imagery of disease. As Charlus grows older and his homosexuality more noticeable, he becomes "a sick man ravaged now by the illness which, a few years ago, was only a faint blemish which he was easily able to conceal" (3: 204). And when he has himself whipped in Jupien's brothel, his actions represent "a new stage in [his] illness . . . which . . . had pursued its evolution with greater and greater speed" (3: 838).

It is important to understand that not everyone in Proust's era accepted the notion that homosexuality is an illness. Several of Proust's contemporaries argued forcefully and convincingly against this idea. Benedict Friedländer, a leader of one of the homosexual rights organizations in Germany, wrote in 1907:

Taken by itself, the very fact that the general public never sees anyone but doctors in the movement's leadership must further the erroneous notion that the movement is concerned with disease or at least some kind of sickness. Certainly sickness can be pitied, the sick can be treated "humanely," and a "cure" can even be attempted; but equality will never be accorded to those who are held to be physically inferior.

The more progressive doctors have now expressly dropped the dogma that same-sex love is a sickness; they had to, of course, or their clients would have left them.[36]

The date of these remarks needs emphasis: 1907, a time when Proust had not yet conceived, or was only just conceiving, his novel. Friedländer's opinion was echoed by other advocates of homosexual rights, and attacks on the sickness theory often figured in the debates about homosexuality which accompanied the Eulenburg affair. Later, in 1910, Binet-Valmer's *Lucien* further undermined the idea that homosexuality is a disease. And still later, in *Corydon*, André Gide declared that there is such a thing as "healthy homosexuality" (Gide loaned this book to Proust on 13 May 1921, shortly after the publication of *Sodome I*).[37] The idea of a guilt-free, nonpathological homosexuality was available to Proust, had he chosen to take advantage of it.

But he did not so choose, no doubt because the concept of homosexuality as an illness was attractive to Proust for reasons other than the status of this view as the officially accepted one. Proust's health was poor for most of his life, and he also suffered from acute hypochondria. Antoine Bibesco called him "the chilliest of professional invalids."[38] And Jacques Porel, who conversed with Proust at Proust's bedside, observed that "there are certain people we can only imagine standing up. Proust is [to be imagined] lying down, an eternal convalescent."[39] When we recall Proust's recurring complaints in his letters about continually failing health and forever flagging energy, the aptness of Porel's observation becomes apparent. Being sick was an essential part of Proust's self-image, and his threshold of resistance to the idea that homosexuality is a disease was correspondingly low. Indeed, it probably seemed inevitable to Proust that this other affliction should come to take its place beside his asthma, his allergies, his hypersensitivity to noise and odor, and so on. Proust simply did not have the constitutional and emotional base from which to endorse Friedländer's or Gide's belief in a healthy homosexuality.

When the narrator calls homosexuality an illness, he is expressing an idea that is patently false as long as it is applied exclusively to homosexuality and used as a generalization about it.[40] But to the extent that love itself can be a form of illness and madness, the narrator's image tells a fundamental truth about homosexuality—and heterosexuality. A la recherche presents all forms of love, not just homosexuality, as types of disease, and in this it draws upon a long literary tradition dating back at least as far as Catullus' lyrics to Lesbia. Swann's love for Odette reaches a stage where it becomes "inoperable"; and, conversely, the grandmother's illness is compared to the relationship of men and their mistresses (1: 308; 2: 317; cf. 1: 297, 300). Because of the pervasive presence in A la recherche of this traditional love-as-illness figure, we need a tolerance for paradox in approaching the disease imagery the narrator applies to homosexuality. On one level he is wrong; on another level he is right. We also need to bear in mind that Proust might have been particularly susceptible to the love-as-illness figure because of the cultural pressure on him and on all other people with homosexual tastes to view their lives as governed by an emotional malady. In this case as in most others there would seem to be an intricate combination of cultural conventions and private, personal motives acting on Proust's images of sexuality, love, and art. The point is not that Proust saw the world the way he did because he was "a homosexual." The point is that Proust, because of his complex sexuality, because of the particular kind of man he was, because of the time and place in which he lived, and because of the special kind of novel he wanted to write, responded to certain trends and pressures in certain unique ways.

There is an interesting qualification to the narrator's equation of homosexuality with disease. According to the narrator, the homosexuality of the classical era, of the Greece of Socrates or the Rome of Augustus, was a "conventional homosexuality" and therefore practiced by "men who were absolutely normal" (3: 205; 2: 954). But since homosexuality is no longer socially acceptable, the variety that survives today must be considered an illness. It cannot be affected by changes in social custom and is generally not susceptible to cure.[41] It is "the involuntary variety, the nervous variety, that which one hides from others and misrepresents to oneself" (3: 205; cf. 2: 616–17). This idea contradicts a passage in Proust's early story "Avant la nuit." In that story the cause of homosexuality is said to lie in "a nervous deterioration"; but the homosexuality of Socrates and that of the modern era are viewed as the same phenomenon, and Leslie's argument for tolerance uses the former to justify the latter. A la recherche, however, draws a distinction between modern and classical, "nervous" and "conventional" homosexuality, a distinction that was commonly drawn in Proust's time. It was made by Rémy de Gourmont in one of his columns for the Mercure de France[42] and also by Dr. Moreau in Des aberrations du sens génésique, which contrasted the homosexuality "of our countries" to that "of other countries where homosexuality is, on the contrary, permitted and accepted."[43] Like Proust's narrator, Moreau claimed that the homosexuality "of our countries" is pathological because it is unaccepted and that the homosexuality of countries where it is "permitted and accepted" is nonpathological by virtue of being permitted and accepted. John Addington Symonds pointed out the obvious weakness in this position in a discussion of the work of Moreau: "The bare fact that ancient Greece tolerated, and that modern Europe refuses to tolerate sexual inversion," Symonds wrote, "can have nothing to do with the etiology, the pathology, the psychological definition of the phenomenon in its essence. . . . The passion has not altered; but the way of regarding it morally and legally is changed. A scientific investigator ought not to take changes of public opinion into account when he is analysing a psychological peculiarity."[44]

The narrator's distinction between classical and modern homosexuality[45] is perhaps best illustrated by comparing the history of a typical boy with homosexual tastes as given in Sodome I with the history given by Aristophanes in Plato's Symposium, a work with which, as we have seen, Proust was familiar. Whether intentionally or not, the narrator's scheme reverses Aristophanes' at practically every point. In the two characterizations, such youths:

Aristophanes	Proust's narrator
Are fond of men while young and take joy in lying with and embracing them	Mistake the first stirrings of desire when pressing against a comrade for the mutual desire for a woman

Are the best of boys, the bravest, the most manly	Are shy, withdrawn, effeminate
Are open about their desires, often to the point of being called shameless	Are forced to conceal their desires, meet in the dark
Grow up to be men of public affairs	Often lead solitary, lonely lives
Tend to reject the idea of marriage to women in favor of living unmarried together	Live hypocritical lives and pretend they are attracted to women; if lucky enough to find a partner, they are likely to lose him when the partner marries a woman
Delight in the company of those that are like them	Often shun each other's company out of shame and self-hatred[46]

And so on. In the narrator's presentation modern homosexuality, as a psychological illness, is for its victims as ineluctable, as inescapable, as cruel in its onsets and false remissions as the grandmother's dreadful physical ailment—whose pattern, moreover, it follows (withdrawal, loneliness, suffering, attempts at concealment, rejection by those who should be the most concerned, gradual degeneration of the personality). The outlook is dark, to be sure, but is brightened somewhat in ways we shall consider presently.

Homosexuality in A la recherche is a sociological as well as a psychological phenomenon. Proust works into the novel the idea, widespread at the time and much talked about during the Eulenburg affair, that people with homosexual tastes comprise a special subclass of society—"a freemasonry," as the narrator phrases it, "much more widespread, more efficacious and less suspected than that of the lodges . . . within which the members . . . recognize each other by signs which are natural or conventional, voluntary or involuntary" (2: 617). It is a society which extends across all the earth, "having adherents everywhere, among the common people, in the army, in the temple, in prison, on the throne," a society whose members can be found "in London, in Berlin, in Rome, in Petrograd, or in Paris" (2: 617, 632). Here it is easy to see how the ideas, the imagery, even the enumerative, distributive style derive from writing on homosexuality contemporary with Proust. Both style and substance were commonplace, whether the writer was interested in denouncing homosexuality, defending it, or giving an objective, scientific evaluation. John Addington Symonds wrote in 1891 that homosexuality "confronts us on the steppes of Asia . . . in the bivouac of Keltish warriors . . . upon the sands of Arabia. . . . among the palm groves of the South Sea Islands . . . under Eskimos' snow-huts; beneath the sultry vegetation of Peru. . . . It throbs in our huge cities. The pulse of it can be felt in London, Paris, Berlin, Vienna, no less than in Constantinople, Naples, Teheran, and Moscow."[47] Similarly, the German physician Casper reported that homosexuality is to be found "on the Rigi, at Palermo, in the Louvre, in the Highlands of Scotland, in Petersburg, at the port of Barcelona."[48] Casper, Tarnowsky, and the Italian sexologist Mantegazza mentioned the arcane signs and signals people with homosexual preferences supposedly use to recognize each other.[49] And well before Proust, Richard Burton, Edward Carpenter, and Maximilian Harden compared the subsociety of homosexuality to freemasonry.[50] Harden wrote that men with homosexual inclinations form "a comradeship which is stronger than that of . . . freemasonry, which . . . unites the most remote, the most foreign, in a fraternal league of offence and defence. Men of this breed are to be found everywhere, at Courts, in high positions in armies and navies, in the editorial offices of great newspapers, at tradesmen's and teachers' desks, even on the Bench. All rally together against the common enemy."[51]

Harden's idea that homosexually oriented people are united in a worldwide conspiracy having evil designs on the rest of humanity is echoed in A la recherche. The narrator also envisions a homosexual conspiracy, equating it metaphorically with the Jewish or Zionist conspiracy about which so much had been heard during the Dreyfus affair. He avers that people with homosexual tastes proselytize for their cause with a zeal comparable to that of Zionists, draft-dodgers, Saint-Simonians, vegetarians, and anarchists (2: 620; cf. 632). He says that such people live "in an endearing and dangerous intimacy with men of the other race, provoking them . . . until the day of scandal when these subduers are themselves devoured" (2: 617). In La Prisonnière the narrator describes two women who go out, with one of them dressed as a man, for the purpose of picking up children and "initiating" them into the homosexual way of life (3: 351). And later in the novel Andrée says that Morel had a special arrangement with Albertine whereby he used his attractiveness to women to lure young girls into lesbian adventures with her. "Once he had the audacity," Andrée continues, "to take Albertine and one of these girls into a house of ill repute at Couliville, where four or five of the women had her together or in succession. That was his passion, as it was also Albertine's" (3: 600). Thus do male and female adherents of homosexuality join forces to corrupt the youth of France.

The idea that "homosexuals" conspire against and attempt to seduce the people "of the other race" is one of the hoariest myths surrounding homosexuality. It is, as we have seen, a myth Proust exposes and satirizes in the conflict between Charlus and Mme Verdurin and in the encounter between Charlus and Cottard in the scene of the sham duel. And yet in other sections of the novel Proust allows his narrator to advance this bit of prejudice as if it were the general truth, to write, indeed, as if he were taking his inspiration directly from Maximilian Harden. The narrator decides that Albertine hid her lesbianism from him "like a woman who might have hidden from me that she was a spy from an enemy nation, and more treacherously even than a spy, because a spy deceives only with respect to her nationality, whereas with Albertine the deception had to do with her most profound humanity" (3: 527). Although the primary purpose of this image is to emphasize the mystery of Albertine's identity, it depends upon and endorses the traditional equation of homosexuality with treason and conspiracy. And in other sections of the novel the narrator pushes the idea as far as it will go by suggesting that people with homosexual inclinations, when given a chance, will aggressively seduce other people, whether children or adults, into the homosexual way of life.

Sex researchers tell us, however, that the seduction of children is extremely rare among homosexually oriented people and is, in fact, principally a heterosexual practice.[52] And there are, of course, no more grounds for believing in a homosexual conspiracy than there are for believing in a Jewish conspiracy. In 1927 Magnus Hirschfeld perceptively wrote: "It is untrue that homosexuals form a sort of 'secret society' among themselves with all sorts of code signals and mutual defense arrangements. Aside from a few minor cliques, homosexuals are in reality almost totally lacking in feelings of solidarity; in fact, it would be difficult to find another class of mankind which has proved so incapable of organizing to secure its basic legal and human rights."[53] Recently, of course, the homosexual liberation movement has made significant gains in securing civil rights for people with a homosexual orientation. But the point, which should be obvious to anyone who reflects for a moment, is that homosexually oriented people do not organize or communicate with each other any more regularly or any more skillfully than other classes of people. True, they have an argot referring to various sexual attitudes and practices. But so do heterosexually oriented people, and in many instances the argot is the same. Proust's narrator's assertion that people with homosexual tastes form a worldwide confederacy and communicate by means of an esoteric code unknown to people with heterosexual tastes is simply a piece of sexual mythology.

It is, however, a piece of mythology which fits very well into the overall aesthetic philosophy of *A la recherche,* and this is no doubt one reason Proust preserves it. Gilles Deleuze has spoken incisively on the general pattern to which this idea relates:

The word "sign" is one of the most frequent words in *A la recherche.* . . . The work is presented as the exploration of different worlds of signs, which. . . . are specific and which constitute the substance of this or that world. We can see this immediately in the secondary characters: Norpois and the diplomatic code, Saint-Loup and the military signs, Cottard and the medical symptoms. A man can be adept at deciphering the signs of one realm but remain an idiot in every other case: thus Cottard, the great clinician. Moreover, in a shared realm, the worlds are sectioned off: the signs of the Verdurins have no currency among the Guermantes. . . . The unity of these worlds derives from the fact that they form systems of signs emitted by persons, objects, substances: we discover no truth, we learn nothing, unless we decipher and interpret. But the plurality of the worlds derives from the fact that these signs are not of the same sort, do not have the same way of appearing, are not subject to the same processes of decipherment, do not have an identical relation to their meaning.[54]

The signs and signals of Proust's homosexual freemasonry serve the same function as the encoded signs and signals emitted by other social groups, by individual characters, by works of art—by all the modes of reality in *A la recherche*. Grappling with the codes of these private universes is one way of approaching truth in Proust's novel. And so we can say that the narrator's delineation of a worldwide homosexual brotherhood with its own secret language is artistically "true," since it corresponds to a pervasive aesthetic and epistemological pattern in *A la recherche*. But by any criterion other than the novel's own web of self-referential metaphor it is false.

Although writers such as Casper, Symonds, Harden, and Proust himself emphasized the universality of homosexuality, it was usual in Proust's day to give very low estimates of the actual number of homosexually oriented people. It was generally thought, as Weindel and Fischer pointed out in *L'Homosexualité en Allemagne* (1908), that the number of "homosexuals" in the population was somewhere around 2 percent—a figure based on some rather haphazard statistics gathered by Magnus Hirschfeld.[55] This is the figure which would have been available to Proust, if and when he investigated contemporary scientific thinking on the incidence of homosexuality.

Several decades later, in findings which have since become famous, Kinsey and his associates revolutionized both this figure and the philosophy of homosexuality which underlay it. As we saw in Chapter 2, Kinsey demonstrated that it is pointless to try to determine the number of "homosexuals." All one can safely do is chart the number of people who have had homosexual feelings or experiences and rate these people on a scale indicating duration and exclusivity of homosexuality. The Kinsey researchers found that: (a) 8 percent of the males in the American population were exclusively homosexual over a period of at least three years; (b) 13 percent reacted "**erotically to other males without having overt** homosexual contacts"; (c) 30 percent had "**at least incidental homosexual experience** or reactions . . . over at least a three-year period"; (d) 37 percent had "**at least some overt homosexual experience** to the point of orgasm."[56] When the 13 percent and the 37 percent groups are combined, Kinsey's study shows, as Wainwright Churchill points out, that "approximately 50 percent of the male population become directly involved emotionally and/or physically with homosexuality to some extent after sexual maturity."[57] This does not mean that 50 percent of American men are "homosexuals." It simply means that approximately this many American men have, after puberty, some experience of homosexual feeling and/or behavior. Furthermore, the Kinsey researchers regarded 50 percent as a conservative estimate, stating that although "there can be no question that the actual incidence of the homosexual is at least 37 and 50 percent," the tests suggest that "the actual figures may be as much as 5 percent higher, or still higher."[58]

One of the most remarkable things about Kinsey's figures is that they come from a country with an extremely repressive attitude toward homosexuality. Moreover, Kinsey's study was carried out before the so-called sexual revolution. Had the study been done in a country with less repressive social traditions, the percentages of homosexuality could well have been higher. If the study were to be repeated in the America or the Europe of the 1980s, the percentages would almost certainly be higher—not because there are more "homosexuals" now but because the stigma on homosexuality has become less severe and the potential for homosexual experience correspondingly greater. Since there has never been another study of the scope and precision of Kinsey's, however, sex researchers continue to accept his figures as the most accurate index currently available of the incidence of homosexuality in Western culture.[59] "When Kinsey's pioneering work appeared in the forties," says Arno Karlen, "his figures on the prevalence of homosexual behavior shocked laymen and scientists alike. The shock subsided, and now they are generally accepted." And Fritz Fluckiger recently termed Kinsey's material on homosexuality "to this day . . . the single most comprehensive set of empirical data" we possess.[60]

The estimates of the incidence of homosexuality given in A la recherche vary at different points in the novel. It is clear, however, that the narrator wishes to convey the impression that the number of people susceptible to homosexual experience is legion. First of all, the novel eventually gives us cause to suspect almost every character we meet of homosexual desires, activities, or both—even Swann does not escape innuendo (3: 299–300). Then, too, the narrator explicitly declares that the number of homosexually oriented people is astronomical. At the beginning of Sodome I he is impressed with the seemingly miraculous circumstances that have brought Charlus and

Jupien together: what he has taken to be the extreme rarity of men of this type would seem to have put insurmountable obstacles in the way of one man's ever finding the other (2: 607, 627). But at the end of *Sodome I* he tells how later experience corrected this first impression: "these exceptional beings whom we pity are a multitude, as we shall see during the course of this work. . . so numerous that one could apply to them the other verse of Genesis: 'If one could number the sands of the earth, one could also number this posterity' " (2: 631).

Charlus echoes this idea. In a discussion of people who have reputations for homosexuality, he tells Brichot: "you probably believe like everyone else the things people say about this or that famous man who is the incarnation of these tastes in the eyes of the masses, when there's not 2 sous' worth of truth in the idea. I say 2 sous, because if we raised the ante to 500 gold francs, we would see the number of tinhorn saints dwindle down to zero. Otherwise the tally of saints, if you see any sanctity in that sort of thing, holds as a general rule between 3 or 4 out of 10" (3: 297). By "saints" Charlus could mean two things: (1) those who have never felt homosexual desire or had homosexual experience, or (2) those whose reputations have remained unblemished, regardless of what their actual experience has been. In either case he is asserting that homosexuality is much more prevalent than people generally think, for he also says that he has known, personally, only "two reputations [for homosexuality] that were undeserved" (3: 297). It is likewise difficult to tell precisely what Charlus means by "if we raised the ante to 500 gold francs, we would see the number of tinhorn saints dwindle down to zero." He may mean that any man, if the financial inducement were great enough, could be lured into homosexuality. Or he may simply mean that any reputation could be ruined, if enough money were offered to those in a position to ruin it. Or he may mean both things at the same time. Charlus's phraseology is ambiguous, and it reflects the ambivalence of his motives. He wants to suggest that homosexuality is prevalent but at the same time show that those who are not initiated into its mysteries—in this case, Brichot—have no conception of exactly how that prevalence is manifested. He also wants to conceal his own homosexuality and at the same time present himself as an expert on the subject. His meanings, here as elsewhere, tend to devour themselves.

Brichot understands Charlus to mean that heterosexually oriented people are the "saints" and that they account for only 30 to 40 percent of the population, with people who have homosexual inclinations making up the other 60 to 70 percent. "Even if I reversed the proportion," Brichot says, "I would still have to multiply the number of the guilty by a hundred" (3: 298). The narrator also understands Charlus to mean that from 60 to 70 percent of the population is "guilty." To be sure, he points out that Charlus is indulging in wishful thinking and scandelmongering when he delivers these statistics and that Charlus probably inflates them accordingly (3: 298). And yet the narrator cannot help but take the figures seriously with another part of his mind and is shocked at the support they give his suspicions about Albertine's lesbianism when transferred to the female sex (3: 297–98). Furthermore, there is a direct correlation between Charlus's statements, tendentious though they are, and the narrator's own statement in *Sodome I* that men with homosexual tastes are as numerous as "the sands of the earth."

The narrator's remark in *Sodome I* and its later echo in Charlus's speech are striking contradictions of the opinion generally held in Proust's day. Even later, in the era of the Kinsey Report, there were still, as Kinsey pointed out, "many persons who believe the homosexual to be a rare phenomenon, a clinical curiosity, and something which one may never meet among the sorts of persons with whom he would associate."[61] That such is not in fact the case is also one of the points of *A la recherche*.

Not that we should view Charlus as a prophet of the Kinsey Report. His utterances are too ambiguous and too privately motivated to admit of that interpretation. That the figures mentioned in Charlus's speech accord with Kinsey's later statistics simply adds a historical irony to the ironies already present in the passage.[62] As is often the case with Proust's characters and their analyses of the world, Charlus is both right and wrong at the same time. He is right because homosexuality is in fact more prevalent than people generally imagine, and one of the purposes of Proust's novel is to show that this is the case.

He is wrong because his motives and his vision are those of a man who does not really believe that homosexuality is as prevalent as he says but nonetheless wants to convince himself and others that it is. The fundamental irony of the passage is that the truth Charlus feels compelled to exaggerate needs very little exaggeration, as the novel as a whole repeatedly suggests.

How does the narrator's statement that homosexually oriented people are as numerous as "the sands of the earth" accord with his position that they are sick, mentally deranged, suffering from a hereditary affliction, and, in general, physically and psychologically different from the rest of the population—"[belonging] not to common humanity but to a strange race which mixes with it, hides within it, but never merges with it" (3: 527)? These ideas do not, of course, accord at all. When the narrator says people with homosexual tastes are found everywhere, in great numbers, and in all walks of life, he seems to forget that elsewhere he says they are grotesque anomalies who are radically, ontologically different from the general run of humanity. It may be that Proust uses the former idea because he knows from personal experience it is true and the latter idea because it is the expected and the socially acceptable thing to say. In any case, the extremely high incidence of homosexuality depicted in A la recherche is one of the most original aspects of Proust's treatment of the theme, owing very little to—in fact, directly contradicting—both the scientific and the popular thinking of his era.

If in its estimates of the number of people with homosexual tastes A la recherche departs from the conception of homosexuality current at the time, it rejoins the mainstream of contemporary thought in its treatment of another aspect of the social significance of homosexuality. It was generally thought, as Havelock Ellis pointed out in Sexual Inversion, that "inverts are less prone than normal persons to regard caste and social position."[63] And Edward Carpenter described homosexuality as "a sentiment which easily passes the bounds of class and caste, and unites in the closest affection the most estranged ranks of society." Carpenter went on to observe that "it is noticeable how often Uranians of good position and breeding are drawn to rougher types, as of manual workers," and he asserted that the resulting alliances "have a decided influence on social institutions."[64] Timothy d'Arch Smith has called this idea as it appears in literature the "Prince and the Pauper" theme—a "longing for an attachment to a boy either of a far higher or, more often, of a far lower social rank."[65] Smith analyzes the theme in British "Uranian" literature from 1889 to 1930. But it is also a part of the French tradition. In Verlaine's *Hombres,* a work on which Proust comments in his article on Baudelaire,[66] the poet declares that "My male lovers do not belong to the wealthy classes / They are workers from the suburbs or from the country"—and so on.[67]

In *A la recherche* Proust makes extensive use of the Prince and the Pauper theme. Practically all the homosexual liaisons in the novel are between members of different social classes. The Baron de Charlus has affairs with Jupien, a tailor, and with Morel, the son of a valet de chambre; manifests a keen interest in a streetcar conductor and in the merchants near the Hôtel de Guermantes; and in Jupien's brothel has himself whipped by young men from the working class. The Marquis de Saint-Loup has an affair with Morel and is suspected of a liaison with the elevator boy at Balbec. The son of the Prince de Foix attracts a man of inferior social standing, and the Duc de Châtellerault has an encounter with Mme de Guermantes's usher. In homosexual society, the narrator remarks, "the ambassador is the convict's friend," and the beggar recognizes one of his confreres "in the great lord for whom he closes a car door" (2: 617).

Sometimes, as Smith points out, the Prince and the Pauper theme takes the form of "the myth . . . of the boy who, thanks to a man's intervention in his life, overrides and supersedes his lower-class birthright and becomes a boy of great beauty and intellect."[68] In *A la recherche* the Baron de Charlus tries to create precisely this sort of relationship with young men who are his social inferiors. At one point he tries to make the narrator his protégé, emphasizing that they are from different social classes but commenting that "I have more sympathy for an intelligent worker than for many dukes" (2: 557, cf. 563). And when later in the novel Charlus becomes Morel's protector, he seizes every opportunity to deflect to himself the credit for Morel's musical gifts and social rise (3: 275 ff.). As manifested in the Baron de Charlus, however, the desire to elevate is commingled with the desire to degrade, and in making Morel a Prince he never lets him forget his origins as a Pauper. At the Verdurins' reception in *La Prisonnière* Charlus cannot help but let the secret of Morel's social origins slip out. He comments that "we are not of the same class, say that he is my dependent, my protégé" (3: 314)—an obvious strategy for keeping Morel under control and ensuring his own continuing superiority in the relationship.

These affairs between men from different social classes have a parallel in Proust's own life. I am not speaking of the rumors about Proust's fascination for butcher boys and working-class types, though if these rumors are true they are certainly germane. I am speaking of Proust's well-documented love for Alfred Agostinelli, a man who was clearly his social inferior. Proust regarded his relationship with Agostinelli partly as one of teacher and pupil. He told André Gide that Agostinelli was "of the most humble 'condition' and [had] no education" but went on to describe, in a letter quoted earlier, the pleasure he found in cultivating Agostinelli's intelligence and revealing it to Agostinelli himself.[69] Similarly, in *A la recherche* Albertine tells the narrator: "I am horrified when I think that, without you, I would have remained ignorant. Don't deny it. You have opened to me a world of ideas whose existence I never suspected, and the little I have become I owe only to you" (3: 64). Perhaps Albertine's words echo words actually spoken by Agostinelli to Proust; or perhaps they are Proust's fantasy of what he would have liked Agostinelli to feel and to say. In any case, it is clear that Proust's emphasis on how homosexual love breaks down barriers of social class has a biographical as well as a sexological and a literary resonance.[70]

We should recall, however, that heterosexual love also cuts across social caste in *A la recherche*. Odette is a cocotte, vastly below Swann's social standing; the Marquis de Saint-Loup has an affair with the actress Rachel; and the narrator's head is constantly being turned by girls from the servant and working class. Here again what seems at first to be a trait peculiar to homosexuality gradually emerges as part of a general truth about society. Proust's society is constantly changing, and love, both heterosexual and homosexual, is one of the most important of the forces which cause it to change. Love elevates some and topples others from their pinnacles of social power—as when Mme Verdurin becomes Princesse de Guermantes by marrying the

Prince, while the Duc de Guermantes's social position is undermined by his love for Odette (3: 955, 1,015–19).

The homosexual version of the Prince and the Pauper theme reaches its logical conclusion when at the reception given in *Le Temps retrouvé* by the Princesse de Guermantes (the former Mme Verdurin), Morel symbolically changes places with Charlus in a manner which recalls the exchange of identities in Mark Twain's *The Prince and the Pauper*. Because of his love for Morel, which puts him at the mercy of the Verdurins, and because of his encroaching senility, Charlus has now lost most of his social power and prestige. Morel, on the other hand, has become "an important man," before whom there is "a movement of curiosity, when he entered, and of deference" (3: 1,018–19, 956).

Love which crosses social boundaries and causes upheavals in the stratification of society is one of the oldest literary themes. It is likely, however, that Proust's personal experience of this process in his love for Agostinelli, coupled with the general visibility of the Prince and the Pauper theme in the sexology and literature of the period, contributed to his decision to assign to all varieties of love such an important role in society's perpetually changing structure. "Society is like sexual taste," the narrator concludes, "because one never knows what perversions it is likely to attain" (3: 235).

THE RACE OF AUNTS

That homosexually oriented men are especially inclined toward art and literature is a prepossession with which most everyone is familiar, and we might naturally expect it to appear in a work where art and homosexuality are concurrent themes. It is a very old notion and goes back at least as far as Dante. In the *Inferno* (15: 106–8) Brunetto Latini says of his companions: "In sum, know that all were scholars / And great and famous men of letters, / In the world defiled by one same sin." The "one same sin" is homosexuality. In Proust's era, when Oscar Wilde was asked to define "the Love that dare not speak its name," his reply included, as we have seen, the observation that "[this love] dictates and pervades great works of art like those of Shakespeare and Michelangelo." On another occasion, arguing that homosexuality should be treated as a psychological illness rather than punished as a crime, Wilde referred to the work of researchers such as Lombroso and Nordau, where "this [idea] is specially insisted on with reference to the intimate connection between madness and the literary and artistic temperament." Similarly, the Danish writer Herman Bang (1857–1912) believed that "homosexuality is notably and unexplainably related to artistic inclination." And in many of the case histories of homosexuality published by Krafft-Ebing, Havelock Ellis, and other sexologists artistic interests figured prominently in the subject's background.[71] The idea of a connection between homosexuality and creativity was very much in the air when Proust was composing *A la recherche*, and it is not surprising that he made it a part of the book's general philosophy of homosexual love.

Homosexuality, according to *A la recherche*, is an illness and a madness, true; but, as for Wilde, there is a great compensation: those whom it afflicts find that a whole world of artistic sensitivity and talent which is closed to other men becomes accessible to them. Charlus's homosexuality is the result of a "slight, purely physical displacement of taste," of a "slight disorder of a sense," traits which also mean that "the universe of poets and musicians, so closed to the [heterosexual] Duc de Guermantes, opens partially for M. de Charlus" (3: 206). Let us be precise. The narrator does not say in this passage that because Charlus is homosexually inclined, he is endowed with artistic sensitivity. He says, rather, that the same neurotic defects which give Charlus a homosexual orientation also contribute to making him "a delightful pianist, an amateur painter not without taste, an eloquent speaker" (2: 953). The relationship between homosexuality and creativity here established is a variation on the idea, common in fin de siècle literature, of an intimate connection between disease in general, madness in general, and the sensitive, artist's nature.

The idea depends, nonetheless, on stereotype. Since homosexuality is not an illness, there can be no connection between the sickness of homosexually oriented people and their supposed artistic sensitivity. Nor are they, as Bang asserted, "unexplainably" inclined to artistic pursuits. George Domino recently helped to dispel this notion in a long-overdue empirical study. He gave a battery of tests intended to measure creativity to four groups of people with a homosexual orientation and to four groups of people with a heterosexual orientation. "In all cases," Domino writes, "homosexuals scored lower. There is thus no support [for] the contention that homosexuals are more creative." Domino's tests do not mean that homosexuality automatically means less creative ability; they simply show that there is no necessary connection between the two. As we might logically expect, subjects of both orientations who were creative to begin with scored higher on the tests than subjects who had previously shown no special creative ability.[72]

How did the association of homosexuality with creativity arise? It arose partly from the belief that an interest in the "finer" things of life—art, music, poetry, fashion, and so on—is a feminine characteristic, and from the corresponding belief that "homosexuals" are more feminine than "heterosexuals." Both beliefs are relatively recent in Western society but were firmly established by Proust's time. Sources contemporary with Proust regularly assert that men with a homosexual orientation can be immediately identified by their effeminate characteristics and unmanly ways. Tardieu was especially famous for his list of the signs by which the typical "aunt" can be recognized: "Coiffed hair, a made-up face, the neck décolleté, the waist compressed so as to make the figure stand out, the fingers, the ears, and the chest laden with jewels, the entire person giving off a most penetrating smell of perfume, and in the hand a handkerchief, flowers, or needlework: such is the strange, repugnant, and . . . suspicious physiognomy presented by homosexuals." Or to quote Edward Carpenter: "In the male of this kind we have a distinctly effeminate type, sentimental . . . mincing in gait and manners, something of a chatterbox, skillful in woman's work, sometimes taking pleasure in dressing in woman's clothes; his figure not unfrequently betraying a tendency towards the feminine, large at the hips, supple, not muscular, the face wanting in hair, the voice inclining to be high-pitched." For Krafft-Ebing too there was a type of homosexual man in whom the bone structure, the form of the face, and the pattern of musculature were all noticeably feminine; and Krafft-Ebing also reported that homosexual men like to wear women's clothes (or, failing this, clothes featuring a "bosom-like prominence of the upper garments"), make feminine gestures, speak to each other in the feminine, and so on. Tarnowsky echoed this tradition (for it was a tradition passed from writer to writer rather than a description of scientific fact) by declaring that the typical homosexual youth "shows a propensity for giving himself a feminine air, he likes to don women's attire, to curl his hair, to go about with his throat exposed and waist drawn in, to perfume himself, to apply powder and rouge, to paint his eyebrows, etc."[73]

Again most of these traits are to be found in Proust's homosexually oriented characters. In "La Race maudite" Proust describes men with homosexual tastes as follows: "Their breasts stick out, they seek occasions to dress as women in order to show their breasts off, like young girls they enjoy dancing, fine clothes, rouge, and in the most serious gatherings they are seized with the mad desire to laugh and sing."[74] In *A la recherche*, of course, Charlus is notorious for his self-conscious attempt to banish any trace of the flamboyant or feminine from his outfits. But in our first glimpse of Robert de Saint-Loup we see that, unlike his uncle, he dares to wear clothes which could be interpreted as effeminate (1: 729). As for the feminine gestures and postures of men who are homosexually inclined, Jupien, in his attempt to attract Charlus, "placed with grotesque impertinence his fist on his hip, stuck out his derrière, struck poses with the same coquettishness the orchid could have displayed to the bee" (2: 604). And throughout *A la recherche* the narrator attributes a feminine physiognomy to his homosexually oriented characters (2: 603–4; 3: 824, 991). Indeed, in the case of Charlus, he delineates a process of "purely physical ferments" which seem to change the Baron's body gradually into that of a woman, complete with pendulous breasts (2: 908; 3: 207). Charlus also displays the feminine pitch of voice Edward Carpenter singled out as characteristically homosexual (1: 764); and both M. de Charlus and M. de Vaugoubert have the fondess for referring to men in the feminine mentioned by Krafft-Ebing (2: 610–11; 3: 46, 207; cf. 212). These feminine traits, according to *A la recherche*, make homosexually oriented men immediately recognizable. Both Charlus and the narrator claim they can identify such men on sight; and Morel says he can spot at a glance both men and women who have homosexual tastes (2: 664–66, 1,007–8; 3: 297).[75] "First appearance of the men-women," says the first epigraph to *Sodome et Gomorrhe*, and throughout the novel the narrator suggests that to be homosexually inclined is to be a kind of physical and psychological hermaphrodite.

This view seems to derive in part from the work of the German jurist, Latinist, and pioneering sexologist Karl Heinrich Ulrichs (1825–95), now little known but one of the most significant influences on the theories of sexuality formulated in the late nineteenth and early twentieth centuries.[76] Ulrichs's most important work was *Memnon* (1868), in which he defined the homosexually oriented man in the Latin formula *anima muliebris virili corpore inclusa* ("the soul of a woman enclosed in the body of a man"). He applied the converse of this formula to the homosexually oriented woman: *anima virilis muliebri corpore inclusa*. Ulrichs's theories were influenced by contemporary speculation about a lack of gender identification in the early stages of the human embryo. He thought a man with homosexual preferences was one in which "nature developed the male germ . . . physically but the female spiritually." He coined the term *Uranier* or *Urning* (*Uranian* in English, *uraniste* in French), to denote the kind of psychic hermaphrodite he described.[77]

The imagery with which Proust portrays the blending of masculine and feminine qualities in his homosexually oriented characters shows that he was familiar with Ulrichs's ideas, whether directly, by reading the texts themselves, or indirectly, through their mention in Hirschfeld, Krafft-Ebing, and practically every other important sexologist who came after Ulrichs. The psychology of Mlle Vinteuil, an inner conflict between a "shy and suppliant maiden" and "a rough and conquering old soldier," recalls Ulrichs's theories, as does the narrator's comment that Mlle Vinteuil "had the look of a boy" (1: 161, 113). Similarly, Morel is said to have "the suggestion of a young girl in the midst of his male beauty" (2: 1,007). Often the echoes of Ulrichs's Latin formulas are direct and explicit. The narrator speaks of "the woman an error of nature had placed within the body of M. de Charlus" (2: 908). He attributes the effeminacy of homosexually oriented men to the fact that "for a long time a certain number of angelic women have been enclosed by mistake within the masculine sex" (2: 967). And he states that in practically every aging man with homosexual tastes one can discern under "the thick layers of grease paint and rice powder a few fragments of a beautiful woman in her eternal youth" (3: 991).

In such images the theme of multiple personality is once again clearly present. There is an alien identity—the soul of a woman— enclosed within the body of Charlus. He tries to keep that identity hidden, just as Jekyll tries to suppress the appearances of Hyde. But the hidden self gradually grows stronger and more inexorable, until finally it envelops, overcomes, and all but destroys the outer personality. As Charlus grows older, he begins involuntarily to make the womanly gestures he can no longer control (3: 212). He enters the Verdurin salon; and "although he had asked his body to manifest . . . all the courtesy of a great lord, this body . . . deployed, to the extent that the Baron would have merited the epithet 'lady-like,' all the seductions of a great lady" (2: 908). The physical dysfunction is accompanied by moral decline. When late in life the Baron tries to put on a devout expression, he succeeds only in looking like "a Grand Inquisitor painted by El Greco," or like "a priest who was under an interdict," since "the necessity for indulging his [homosexual tastes] and for keeping that indulgence hidden [had] had the effect of bringing to the surface of his face precisely what the Baron had sought to conceal: a life of debauchery manifested in moral degeneration" (3: 207).

These aspects of Proust's vision are extremely grim. But, as Proust wrote to André Gide, the homosexually oriented man as depicted in A la recherche is "in some respects worse, in many other respects infinitely better" than other men.[78] And, indeed, the mixture of masculine and feminine qualities in such characters has an important redeeming quality. Proust's Uranian men, like those of the sexology of his era, derive from their inner, feminine selves a host of talents and abilities which are usually held to be the exclusive province of women. Tarnowsky wrote that men who are homosexually inclined possess "an amazing memory for the most complicated women's apparel and can describe them in all their details."[79] The Baron de Charlus has precisely this connoisseur's appreciation of feminine attire and, in general, an uncanny ability to see the world from the masculine and the feminine perspectives simultaneously (3: 208–9). In one sense this dual vision makes Charlus a freak; but in another sense it sets him apart from and above the general run of men.

There are, then, two sources of Charlus's aesthetic sensitivity and creative ability: his deranged personality, which accounts at once for his artistic talent and his homosexuality; and his homosexuality itself, which endows him with both male and female modes of vision. Again these ideas were commonplace in Proust's era. Edward Carpenter remarked that the Uranian man, "while possessing thoroughly masculine powers of mind and body, combines with them the tenderer and more emotional soul-nature of the woman," a combination which produces, according to Carpenter, "the artistic nature, with the artist's sensibility and perception." And in *The Alternate Sex* (1904) C. G. Leland attributed creativity in males—Shakespeare, Goethe—to the high degree of development of their female egos and creativity in women—George Sand, George Eliot—to the high degree of development of their male egos.[80] Most of the characters in *A la recherche* are artists in one way or another: Françoise is an artist in the kitchen, the Duchesse de Guermantes and Odette are artists in fashion, Mlle Vinteuil is an "artist of evil" (1: 164), and the narrator himself eventually becomes a novelist. Presenting the homosexually oriented characters as aesthetically sensitive "men-women" allows them to function as a part of and as a commentary on this overarching theme of artistic creativity.

Proust also finds the "man-woman" idea useful because of its comical and satirical potential. He comments in one of his notebooks that the images of the "aunt" and the "third sex" are particularly appropriate for his work, since the characters to which these terms apply are "almost all old, almost all members of high society . . . where they prattle and chatter, magnificently dressed and ridiculed." He then goes on to rhapsodize on this idea: "The aunts! The word alone conjures up their ceremoniousness and their whole manner of dress; this word-in-skirts calls forth visions of a society reception and of the plumage and chirping of a different kind of bird."[81] The primness and prissiness contained in the concept of the "aunt" are extremely useful to a novelist who is fond of satirizing social pretense in all its forms. Indeed, Proust was so taken with this image of homosexuality that he gave to one of the drafts of "La Race maudite" the title "La Race des Tantes" ("The Race of Aunts").[82]

Proust's peregrinations through the concept of the "man-woman" are, then, ingenious and elaborate. But what of the *veritas* of the matter? Unfortunately, the novel loses in *veritas* what it gains in comedy, satire, and aesthetic coherence. By speaking of the "aunt," the "third sex," and the "man-woman" as if these concepts embodied general truths about homosexuality, Proust presents a seriously distorted picture. The distortions are summarized and concentrated in the term the narrator most often uses to refer to homosexual men: *inverti* or "invert." Kinsey demonstrated that "the characterization of the homosexual as a third sex fails to describe any actuality,"[83] and sex researchers after Kinsey have repeatedly affirmed that effeminacy and the inversion of traditional gender roles have no necessary connection to homosexual feeling and behavior. C. A. Tripp, who has pursued the question in some detail, writes:

Only in popular thinking are homosexuality and inversion synonymous. For several decades biologists and experimental psychologists have recognized that these are distinctly different phenomena, though they may or may not occur together. Homosexuality refers to any sexual activity between members of the same sex. Inversion, on the other hand, implies nothing about the sex of the partner; it refers to a reversal of the commonly expected gender-role of the individual. . . .

In the past, homosexuality and inversion were universally thought of as identical. The main image seems to have been that when two men have any sexual contact, at least one of them (or both if they interchange roles during sex) would have to be sexually submissive, thus inverting his expected male role. In addition, the stereotyped notions of homosexual men being effeminate and lesbians being masculine have reinforced the idea that inverted gender-roles and homosexuality go together.

But . . . there are several homosexual practices . . . in which both partners are equally active and neither demonstrates any role-inversion. Then, too, many effeminate men and aggressive women are primarily, if not entirely, heterosexual. Moreover, there are many entirely homosexual men and women who never invert their expected gender-roles in either their social or their sexual behavior. Thus, it eventually became necessary to recognize inversion as a behavioral entity in its own right—a behavior found throughout the mammalian species and one which is almost as frequent in heterosexual as in homosexual relations. . . .

In sexuality, inversion varies all the way from a momentary reversal of a person's expected role to the more or less continuous reversals seen in effeminacy and transsexuality.

"Ordinarily," Tripp continues, "homosexuality neither generates nor springs from anything approaching an outright effeminacy," for homosexually oriented people are "a behavioral category of individuals who are about as diffusely allied with each other as the world's smokers or coffee drinkers, and who are defined more by social opinion than by any fundamental consistency among themselves."[84]

In A la recherche, however, things are a good deal simpler. There, when a man displays feminine traits, it is a sure sign of homosexuality. "When we admire in a man's expression a delicacy which moves us, a gracefulness, a natural amiability such as men do not ordinarily possess, why are we then dismayed to learn that this young man has a desire for boxers? These are different aspects of the same reality" (2: 622). Later we are given to understand that exceptions to the effeminacy-equals-homosexuality rule are so rare that, for all practical purposes, they do not exist (2: 966–67).[85]

It seems obvious that the narrator's characterization of homosexually oriented people as "men-women" was heavily influenced by sexological topoi such as Tardieu's description of the typical "aunt." But Tardieu's ideas, like most theories of homosexuality in Proust's day, contained huge doses of fantasy. What passed for research on homosexuality around the turn of the century was often only a restatement, dressed up in scientific language, of the biblical abhorrence of men who lie with other men "as with a woman" (Lev. 20: 13). The careful inductive methods of Kinsey and later researchers were unknown to Tardieu and his colleagues, and so, as John Addington Symonds says, "imagination . . . acted powerfully in the formation of [their] theories."[86] Tardieu, especially, singled out as typical of all homosexually oriented men traits which occur only rarely in homosexuality if at all. His theories of homosexuality are, consequently, as wide of the mark as offering the rapist or the wife-beater as characteristic examples of heterosexuality. Nowadays the theories of Tardieu, Ulrichs, Krafft-Ebing, and their followers are as outmoded as the phlogiston theory. We have not yet, of course, discovered the whole truth about human sexuality, and perhaps we

never will. Thanks to Kinsey and other inductive researchers we are
gradually ceasing to think in stereotypes and coming to see that there
are as many different kinds of homosexuality as there are of heterosexuality. But such is the power of stereotypes, once they have taken
hold, that many otherwise intelligent people naively continue to view
the distortions enshrined in A la recherche as profound insights into
homosexual psychology. An awareness of the social climate in which
A la recherche took shape and of the particular body of theory on
which it drew helps to correct this imbalance and place A la recherche
in its proper cultural and intellectual perspective.

One reason the stereotype of the "man-woman" has seemed verisimilar to literary critics is that it is supported by Freudian psychology. Freud pretended to break with nineteenth-century sexual attitudes but very often he simply recast them in different forms. In the
Freudian view of homosexuality illness becomes "arrested development" (a distinction that is really no distinction at all)[87] and the soul
of a woman in the body of a man becomes overidentification with the
mother figure. These Freudian ideas, as we have seen, ignore the
complexities and nuances of real life when they do not utterly falsify
it. They are, nonetheless, still widely credited, because they support
the traditional view that the only "natural" sex is that which occurs
between a man and a woman and has reproduction as its goal. "It
takes a fair amount of sophistication," says Tripp, "to realize that intimate expressions of sex and affection can . . . occur between
partners who are alike in their gender and in their general behavior.
Thus, when people who are not familiar with homosexual relationships try to picture one, they almost invariably resort to a heterosexual frame of reference, raising questions of which partner is 'the
man' and which 'the woman.' . . . But . . . neither partner in the
great majority of homosexual relationships shifts [or inverts] gender-
behavior."[88]

A further reason for the persistence of the "sexual invert" stereotype is that it serves as a convenient prop for stereotyped notions of
heterosexual identity. "Being a man," says D. A. Begelman, "to a
great extent depends upon possessing a certain self-image, fortified as
it is contrasted with fictionalized identities thought to differ from it."
Hence the multitude of "contrived beliefs about homosexuals which

have nourished ancient conceptions of the difference between 'normals' and 'queers.' "[89] On the one hand the Marquess of Queensberry, heterosexual, chest thrown out, fists at the ready; on the other hand Oscar Wilde, homosexual, dandyish, intellectually and artistically inclined: these are among the myths by which we have lived. And Proust, greatly to his discredit, has done much to propagate those myths. One of the fundamental ideas of *Sodome et Gomorrhe* is that there are profound physical and psychosexual differences between men with homosexual tastes and what the narrator calls "real men" (2: 615). But Kinsey demonstrated and Wainwright Churchill later emphasized that "homosexual males do not present a picture of feminine psychosexuality. Their sexual pattern, except for the choice of partner, is typical of all other males. Similarly, homosexual females display a typically feminine pattern of erotic responsiveness in all respects other than choice of partner."[90] *A la recherche* has probably done more than any other work of literature or of science to spread what George Weinberg calls "the misconception that because a man feels sexual desire for men he must fancy himself a woman."[91]

I am not asserting that homosexual preferences never coincide with the stereotype of effeminacy, because of course they sometimes do. I am, however, emphasizing that there is no evidence of any correlation between the stereotype and any particular sexual inclination.[92] There would no doubt be even fewer cases in which effeminacy accompanies homosexuality if the "sexual invert" idea were not so firmly ingrained in Western culture. Weinberg and Williams perceptively observe that "in searching for an identity, many homosexuals acquire the same stereotypes of homosexuals that many heterosexuals hold, or they are influenced by what in the past have been the most visible types of homosexuals. The result can be their 'acting out' being homosexual in an effeminate manner."[93]

This may have been what happened to Proust. Many of the people who knew him perceived him as effeminate,[94] and, as we saw in the first chapter, critics often assume that Proust's so-called feminine traits are an inevitable part of the syndrome of homosexuality. In reality, Proust's effeminacy may have been inculcated by the medical and social opinion of his age. Proust's guilt and insecurity about his homosexuality could easily have led him to imitate in life as well as in art

the officially recognized characteristics of the "third sex." The idea of
being a sexual mutation offers an unattractive identity, to be sure.
But at least it offers an identity, and it was one many homosexually
oriented men of Proust's time embraced. Baron Hermann von
Teschenberg, for instance, gave Magnus Hirschfeld a picture of himself dressed as a woman for publication in Hirschfeld's *Jahrbuch für
sexuelle Zwischenstufen* (*Yearbook for Sexual Intermediate Types*) and
accompanied it with the following note: "Being thoroughly convinced
of the justice and importance of your endeavors, not out of vanity or
other self-centered motives, I send you this picture, which reveals
my true nature, gladly putting it at your disposal for publication along
with my name in the Yearbook."[95] Proust may have been equally
convinced that by portraying homosexually oriented people as "men-
women" he was depicting their—and his own—true nature.

There are, of course, gestures made in *A la recherche* toward a
sophisticated awareness of the many types of homosexuality. In *Sodome I* the narrator says that men with homosexual tastes fall into
several types: those who form cliques, and those who withdraw from
society to lead solitary, lonely lives (2: 618–19); those who love men
of their own age, and those who are attracted only to older men
(2: 628); and so on.[96] Furthermore, Proust says in a letter to Gide
that in his portrait of Charlus he "tried to portray the homosexual in
love with virility because he is a Woman without realizing it." He
goes on to mention that "I by no means claim this is the only type of
homosexual. But it is a very interesting kind and one which, I believe, has never been described."[97] But this awareness that not all
homosexually oriented men are cast ·in the mold of the Baron de
Charlus receives very little emphasis in *A la recherche*. Indeed, the
novel frequently suggests precisely the opposite. The narrator often
uses such phrases as "*un Charlus*," "*les Charlus*," or "*[les] messieurs
de Charlus*" as synonyms for "homosexual" and "homosexuals"
(3: 217, 212; 2: 613). Even more to the point, he once mistakes
Charlus for another man who also has homosexual preferences, because when he first looks at Charlus he sees, he says, not M. de
Charlus but the prototype of all such men—"that look which was
common to them all" (3: 764).

Even if Proust had insisted in *A la recherche* that Charlus is not a typical example of homosexuality, the overwhelming importance of Charlus's character and of homosexuality within it would have implicitly contradicted this idea. As Louie Crew and Rictor Norton have written: "Because we live in a homophobic society, any critical statement about a particular homosexual character in a particular work will automatically be understood by the readers of such criticism to mean that all homosexuals resemble that character. One can point out an anal fixation in one of Chaucer's fabliaux, and readers will let it go at that because Chaucer is heterosexual; if a critic points out an anal fixation in a homosexual work, however, readers will say that all homosexuals tend to have an anal fixation."[98] And readers of Proust have, indeed, assumed that all homosexually oriented men are like the Baron de Charlus, partly because of the homophobic cultural context in which A la recherche was written and is read and partly because Proust explicitly and implicitly encourages this assumption throughout the novel.

Proust said in the letter to Gide quoted above that as far as he knew the "man-woman" character exemplified by Charlus had never been described before. Proust here gives himself a bit too much credit for originality. This type of character had been described before, both in literature and in contemporary theories of sexuality, and Proust probably knew this was the case. In Théophile Gautier's Mademoiselle de Maupin (1835) the protagonist says: "In reality, I belong to neither of the two sexes . . . I belong to a separate, third sex which does not yet have a name . . . I have the body and soul of a woman, the mind and strength of a man." And in La Science de l'amour (1911) by the Sâr Péladan there is a discussion of a "third sex" composed of people whose souls and bodies are of different genders. Both authors were known to Proust.[99] In Germany Magnus Hirschfeld's Scientific-Humanitarian Committee used the idea of the "third sex" as an argument against homosexual oppression, claiming that people should not be penalized for a condition over which they have no control. At the same time other advocates of homosexual rights rejected the "third sex" theory and argued persuasively against it. In 1900—a good two decades before the publication of Sodome I—Elisàr von Kupffer wrote: "It has now become fashionable in humane-scientific and related circles to talk about a 'third' sex whose soul and body are supposedly mismatched. . . . [This concept] has spread like a menacing epidemic. The matter has been investigated, criticized, categorized, medico-hypnotized, popularized, and God knows what all." Benedict Friedländer attacked the "third sex" theory even more vehemently. He called it "degrading and a beggarly . . . pleading for sympathy." Rejecting the notion of "a poor womanly soul languishing away in a man's body," Friedländer called for a cross-cultural and historical approach to homosexuality. He asserted that "a glance at the cultures of countries before and outside of Christianity suffices to show the complete untenability of the [third sex] theory. Especially in ancient Greece, most of the military leaders, artists, and thinkers would have had to be 'psychic hermaphrodites.' " In *Corydon* André Gide echoed these sentiments and anticipated Kinsey's 7-point scale by pointing out that "every intermediary exists between exclusive homosexuality and exclusive heterosexuality."[100] It is clear that Proust did not use the "third sex" theory because he invented it or because it was the only theory available to him; he used it, typically, for a complex variety of aesthetic, cultural, and personal reasons.

HOMOSEXUALITY, TRANSSEXUALISM, AND BEYOND

Current sex research has not abandoned the idea of the soul of a woman in the body of a man. For the most part, however, it has ceased to apply the formula to homosexuality and begun to apply it to "transsexualism." "Transsexuals" are those who feel that their true identity is contradicted by their sexual anatomy. A "transsexual" male has an unshakable conviction that he is, in reality, a woman, and a "transsexual" female feels equally strongly that she is a man. Consequently, such people sometimes seek corrective surgery to make the outside match the inside. These patients and the doctors who treat them emphatically assert that their feeling of being sexually inverted is quite different from homosexual feeling. They say that a "transsexual" male believes he is a woman and is attracted to men as a woman, whereas a "homosexual" man knows he is a man and is attracted to men as another man. People with a homosexual orientation, therefore, do not wish to change their sex. Milton Edgerton, founder of the Gender Identity Clinic at the University of Virginia, has pointed out that "homosexuals don't wish operations . . . if one of them were operated on, it would be a tragic mistake." [101]

A good deal of what the narrator says about homosexuality would now be understood as a description not of homosexuality but of "transsexualism." When Charlus's desire for men is revealed in *So-dome I*, the revelation is presented as the emergence of the "woman" inside the man and, concomitantly, of the "reality" of Charlus's character (2: 614, 607). The narrator comments that "I now understood why . . . M. de Charlus had the look of a woman: he *was* one" (2: 614). This belief that there can be a second self of a different gender that represents someone's true sexual nature is the hallmark of "transsexual" psychology. In reading Jan Morris's story of her sex-change surgery and its motivations, one is reminded of the narrator's theory of the "man-woman" on practically every page. "I was born with the wrong body," Morris writes, "being feminine by gender but male by sex." And at another point: "I was in masquerade, my female reality, which I had no words to define, clothed in a male pretense." Morris concludes that "my conundrum . . . concerned not my [sexual] apparatus, but my *self*." [102] Desire for sexual contact with someone of the same anatomical sex is for the narrator, as it is for Jan Morris and other "transsexuals," a mode of identity proceeding from a mistake of nature rather than a particular form of sexual stimulation.

In his memorandum book of 1908 Proust wrote: "The homosexual . . . would like to have a non-aunt. . . . He would like to find non-aunts and believes he finds them, because . . . he thinks he has a natural desire that can be satisfied outside homosexuality." And Proust commented in one of his notebooks that "a homosexual is not a man who loves homosexuals but a man who, when he sees an African hunter, would like to make friends with him." [103] Proust seems to have believed, in other words, that a homosexually oriented man will never be satisfied with another homosexually oriented man, that what such a man wants, but by definition can never have, is a heterosexually oriented man—a "real man," a "non-aunt." Throughout *A la recherche* the narrator reiterates this idea. He says, for instance, that men who have homosexual tastes are "lovers to whom is almost totally closed any possibility of finding that love the hope for which gives them the strength to endure so many risks and so much solitude, since they are, precisely, looking for a man who has nothing of a woman, a man who is not an invert and who, therefore, cannot return their love" (2: 615, cf. 631; 3: 820). These ideas also survive in current theories of sexuality but are now usually applied to "transsexualism" rather than to homosexuality. A "transsexual" supposedly has no interest in other "transsexuals" or in people with a homosexual orientation but longs instead for heterosexual love, although the "transsexual" feels that he/she must change his/her sex in order to achieve it. A "transsexual" male wishes to be a woman in order to love men as a woman loves men, and a "transsexual" female wishes to be a man in order to love women as a man loves women.[104] Without surgery such people perceive themselves as caught in precisely the problem the narrator attributes to "homosexuals"—they are really women but they appear to be men and therefore men will not love them (or the converse in the case of female "transsexuals"). This may be the "transsexual" quandary, but it has little to do with homosexuality. George Weinberg, among others, has shown that the guiding ambition in the life of a homosexually oriented person is often precisely what Proust's narrator says it never is: the establishment of an enduring relationship with another homosexually oriented person of the same sex. And such enduring relationships are, of course, successfully established more often than society likes to admit.[105] The narrator's notion that homosexuality is always doomed to failure because it involves "men-women" longing for the impossible love of a "real man" is based on a totally erroneous conception.

At the same time, of course, this idea echoes Proust's larger vision of love, in which multiple selves and constant mutations of the personality make genuine contact between the lover and the beloved impossible. It has often been suggested, as we saw in the first chapter, that this general pessimism about love stems from Proust's homosexuality, the assumption here being precisely the one Proust encourages in *Sodome I*, i.e., that "homosexuals" cannot love and that homosexuality is always doomed to failure. A more complex view of the situation might surmise that Proust's pessimism about love springs in part from cultural conditioning: Proust was, at least at certain points in his life, homosexually inclined, the medical establishment told him he was therefore a member of a "third sex," he believed it, concluded that true love could never be his, and from this conclusion extrapolated the pessimistic view of homosexuality and of heterosexuality we find in *A la recherche*. A still more complex view would realize that Proust is by no means the only writer who takes a pessimistic view of love and that his vision has many possible sources and many analogues. Racine's *Phèdre*, for instance, to which Proust constantly alludes, is also pessimistic about the power of love to solve the ultimate human problems and militate against the human tragedy, and in this it echoes a great deal of literature that has appeared throughout the ages. Always in Proust we must deal with multiple traditions.

How unfortunate, then, since the "third sex" theory fits so well into the novel's overall perspective on love, that from a scientific point of view the idea as applied to homosexuality is false. But wait: so is the theory of humors and their effect on the personality, yet this knowledge does not lessen our appreciation of, say, Chaucer, who takes the theory of humors seriously and draws on it extensively. Here as well we must bring to Proust a sense of paradox, recognizing that on one level the novel offers us an explanation of human behavior that is now recognized to be erroneous and that on another level it uses that explanation as an effective metaphor for enduring human problems. But before we can approach the novel in this way, we must first abandon stereotyped modes of thinking. For if we do not, we will never get past the errors that lie on the surface of the novel and of our own minds and into the complexities that lie below. We must avoid the pitfall of saying that Proust's writing on homosexuality can be ignored because it is wrong; and we must also avoid the pitfall of saying it must be accepted because it is right. The narrator's theories of sexuality send out tendrils to all the corners of the novel and, in so doing, tap sources of special, poetic strength, which they lack when presented in isolation and solely as theories. And yet the novel does at times present them as theories to be entertained in their own right and thus occasionally militates against its own most complex meanings.

It is not, then, sufficient to read Proust from the perspective of his own time, his own place, and his own life. We must simultaneously read him from the perspective of our own times, our own places, and our own lives. Like Einstein's time and space, culture and knowledge are relative. We do not know what Proust means until we have plotted not only the coordinates joining him to his own culture but also those joining him to the culture that came after him and that is fashioned partly in his image.

This is why it is useful, for instance, to understand the relationship between what the narrator calls "homosexuality" and what is now called "transsexualism," for "transsexualism" is a concept that works such as *A la recherche*, with its argument for the existence of a "third sex" composed of "men-women," have helped to create. It is striking that people who study "transsexualism" have taken many of the old, discredited stereotypes about homosexuality and attempted to derive from them explanations of this other phenomenon. We now hear not only that "transsexuals" are men trapped in women's bodies and that they long for the love of a "heterosexual": we have also begun to hear that "transsexualism" is caused by the influence of a dominant mother and that "transsexual" patients sometimes display a remarkable degree of artistic creativity, a gift that is, we are asked to believe, somehow connected to their inversion of gender identity.[106] Amid this reshuffling of stereotypes, one is compelled to wonder just how much clinical validity the concept of "transsexualism" has. The notion of "a transsexual" seems in many ways as suspicious as the notion of "a homosexual." Furthermore, as Milton Edgerton once emphasized to me in conversation, "transsexual" surgery is simply a variety of cosmetic surgery. It does not take men and change them into women, and the converse. That sort of change is impossible. It takes men and makes them look and to a certain extent feel like women, and the converse. It is an elaborate, surgical disguise, used to recognize and thereby mitigate the patient's inability to accept his/her anatomical gender.

What is called "transsexualism" may be nothing more than a pathological flight from homosexuality. As Robert Stoller has suggested, it is possible that "the transsexual avoids the accusation of being homosexual by telling himself that he is in fact a woman and that it is normal for him to desire men."[107] If this is true, then "the transsexual," like "the homosexual," is a creation not of nature but of homophobia. This is a frightening possibility, considering that physicians have been willing to change anatomical men into approximations of anatomical women because these people seem to fit the symptoms of "transsexualism." Western society and medicine have never felt comfortable with the coexistence in a single personality of traits traditionally regarded as masculine and traits traditionally regarded as feminine. Whenever such coexistence has occurred, pathological labels have been invented to explain it and, by implication, isolate it from the rest of society. "The homosexual" used to be the scapegoat; now, it seems, it is "the transsexual."[108]

Sexual inversion exists, and homosexuality exists. They are not, however, the same thing, nor even necessarily connected. Some people, however, continue to equate them and to insist, à la Proust, that they are a category of identity, a mode of selfhood, rather than a form of sexual activity. But all attempts to define and describe sexual identities of any sort—to delineate with precision and verifiability the distinguishing characteristics of "a homosexual," "a heterosexual," or "a transsexual"—have been mystical, arbitrary, and self-contradictory. Our conclusion should not be, then, that Charlus is "a transsexual" rather than "a homosexual." Our conclusion should be that in *Sodome I* and elsewhere Proust's narrator deals in sexual stereotypes that are still with us, though they have now modulated to a different category and are generally viewed as evidence of "transsexualism" rather than homosexuality.

Proust's narrator seems dimly aware that the word "homosexuality," which properly denotes an attraction of like for like, does not apply very comfortably to the phenemenon he attempts to portray in his book. In *Sodome I* he calls Charlus's condition an example of "what people sometimes wrongly call 'homosexuality'" (2: 607)—without, however, explaining just why it is wrong to call it "homosexuality." He prefers to speak of "inversion" and thus seems to be groping briefly toward some sort of distinction between "homosexuality" and "inversion." But the glimmer of a distinction, if that is what it is, is soon lost, submerged in the complexities and paradoxes of the idea that all men who love other men are really women in disguise.

One of Proust's major purposes in *A la recherche* is to find a way of dealing with the overlapping of gender traits and roles that is often observable in real life. Having his narrator equate homosexuality with sexual inversion, as did the medical theory of the time, is one way of dramatizing and attempting to analyze this phenomenon. Proust seems to adopt the "third sex" theory not only for the reasons that have been suggested but also because, as we shall see in detail in the next chapter, one of the overarching themes of A la recherche is, in fact, sexual inversion—not sexual inversion understood solely and erroneously as homosexuality but as any crossing or blurring of the traditional boundaries separating male from female. The equation of homosexuality with sexual inversion reflects and to some extent reinforces this larger androgynous vision. From a strictly theoretical point of view, however, the idea leads to a dead end, because it confuses two phenomena that must be carefully distinguished before an understanding of the realities of sex can occur.

The narrator's failure to distinguish between homosexuality and sexual inversion may account in part for his insistence that the homosexuality of classical times is something altogether different from the homosexuality of the modern era. Homosexuality as practiced in Greece, and especially as described in Plato's Symposium and manifested in Dorian boy-love, had little to do with effeminacy or sexual inversion. For the Greeks sex between males was an attempt to arrive at the pinnacle of manhood; it was not an attempt to create a parody of a heterosexual relationship with one partner playing "the man" and the other "the woman." The aim of Greek love, as Thorkil Vanggaard says, was "to make of the boy a man with strength, a sense of duty, eloquence, cleverness, generosity, courage, and all the other noble virtues."[109] This conception of homosexuality is obviously a far cry from the diseased, guilt-ridden compulsion of Proust's "men-women." But Proust's narrator does not stop at pointing out that the view of homosexuality delineated in A la recherche is not the Greek view. He goes on to insist that Greek love—sexual passion and emotional attachment between men who are, to use the narrator's language, "real men"—is a dead concept and is no longer observable in modern times.

No wonder that André Gide, who felt very close to the Greek ideals of homosexuality, was such an outspoken critic of the narrator's equation of homosexuality with sexual inversion. In a discussion of A *la recherche* in a footnote to *Corydon,* Gide comments: "The theory of the man-woman . . . is perhaps not false; but it explains and concerns only certain cases of homosexuality, precisely those with which I am not concerned in this book—cases of inversion, of effeminacy. . . . This theory of the 'third sex' can in no way explain what we customarily call 'Greek love' . . . which does not involve effeminacy on either side."[110] Gide agreed with Proust's narrator to the extent of asserting that the concept of sexual inversion "explains and concerns . . . certain cases of homosexuality." But at the same time he insisted that there are other kinds of homosexuality that have nothing to do with inversion. In this passage Gide is searching for a vocabulary that will allow him to describe the complexities and nuances of real life, where both homosexuality and sexual inversion exist but do not necessarily overlap. Proust's narrator worries briefly about terminology but is finally content to use "homosexual" and "invert" interchangeably, with a marked preference for the latter term. This aspect of Proust's novel both oversimplifies and distorts reality.

And yet in this respect as well *A la recherche* ultimately transcends its own theoretical limitations. Consider, for instance, a letter from Léa to Morel, which accidentally falls into the hands of the Baron de Charlus:

the Baron was plunged into grief and stupefaction by a letter which he opened by accident, addressed to Morel. This letter . . . was written by the actress Léa, famous for her exclusive taste for women. But her letter to Morel . . . was written in the most passionate tone. Its obscenity prevents its being reproduced here, but it can be mentioned that Léa spoke to Morel exclusively in the feminine, saying, "Dirty lady, go on," "My beautiful, darling woman," "As for you, at least you're one," and so on. . . . The Baron was especially troubled by the words "you're one." Having once been unaware of it, he had long ago discovered that he himself "was one." But now this notion he had acquired was called back into question. When he had discovered he "was one," he thought he had thereby learned that his tastes, as Saint-Simon says, were not directed toward women. But now it happened that, in the case of Morel, the expression "to be one" took on an extended meaning which was unfamiliar to M. de Charlus, for Morel proved, by this letter, that he "was one" because he had the same taste for women that women themselves had. From that moment on M. de Charlus's jealousy no longer had any reason to limit itself to the men Morel knew but was going to include the women as well. For the people who "were one" were not only those he had previously thought but the entirety of an immense part of the globe, composed of women as well as men, of men who loved not only men but also women, and the Baron, faced with this new definition of a phrase which was so familiar to him, was put to the torture by an anxiety which was as much of the mind as of the heart, faced as he was with this double mystery, composed simultaneously of the enlargement of his field of jealousy and the sudden inadequacy of a definition. (3: 214–15)

Here the "sudden inadequacy of a definition" pertains as much to the image of homosexuality found in earlier parts of *A la recherche* as to the jealousy of M. de Charlus. As Charlus reads the letter from Léa, he has to grapple with what appears to be an endless chain of sexual roles. He thought he understood that men who "are one" are men who direct their sexuality toward other men. But it now appears that Morel has been able to invert his own inversion and become, in effect, a kind of male lesbian, loving women as homosexually oriented women love them and being loved by such women in the same way in return (cf. 2: 622–23). This situation is further complicated by the fact that Morel, as we learn in other sections of the novel, is also attractive to women on purely heterosexual grounds, because of his masculine qualities (e.g., 3: 218). And these same masculine qualities also, of course, make him attractive to men such as M. de Charlus on purely homosexual grounds. Or so we, and so M. de Charlus, thought. The passage quoted above, however, makes it impossible to speak of "purely homosexual" or "purely heterosexual" grounds, for it shows that Morel, with his "suggestion of a young girl in the midst of his male beauty," can be all things to all people. He is, the narrator says, "sufficiently fond of women and of men to give pleasure to one sex with the help of things he had tried out upon the other" (2: 910). Like Curio's Caesar, Morel is the wife of every husband and the husband of every wife, and even more: he can be a man to men, a man to women, a woman to women, and a woman to men. In the character of Morel Proust's permutations of love are complete.

What Proust is really doing in this passage is turning the idea of the "man-woman" into a metaphor for human sexuality in general. For who can say whether someone who loves Morel loves the male or the female in him? Different people see different things, and any definition we attempt to apply falls short of the ambiguous network of desires and feelings which constitutes sexual reality. Just as Proust himself seems by turns homosexual, heterosexual, bisexual, or transsexual, so his characters ultimately escape from all labels and expand into the infinite.

Or sometimes their actions simply contradict the stereotypes of homosexuality other sections of the novel ask us to accept. Saint-Loup, for instance, turns out to be homosexually inclined but also a war hero. And far from impairing his effectiveness as a soldier, his homosexual feelings provide him with strength and inspiration during his life in the army. He thinks of himself as belonging to "a purely masculine order of chivalry, remote from women, where he could risk his life to save his orderly and die a death which would inspire a fanatical love in the hearts of his men" (3: 746). To be sure, the narrator says that Saint-Loup is not fully aware of the homosexual basis of these sentiments and tells himself that he is serving an ideal of pure and elevated friendship (3: 746). But this passage nonetheless presents Saint-Loup's homosexuality as a totally male feeling and thereby contradicts the mincing, prancing, painted and powdered image of homosexual "disease" found in other parts of the novel. Saint-Loup's heroism is, in fact, very much in the Greek tradition. In particular, it recalls the story of the Sacred Band of Thebes, the supposedly invincible army composed of male lovers.[111] Earlier volumes of the novel have declared that Greek love no longer exists. But here, it seems, is Greek love redivivus, at least in one of its aspects.

Furthermore, Proust makes a point of revealing Saint-Loup's homosexuality before telling of his heroic conduct and gallant death in battle (3: 662, 678, 841, 846–47). It is as if, at this point in the novel, he is deliberately forcing his readers to reevaluate all the prejudices and stereotypes the preceding narrative has implanted. If homosexuality is a degrading illness, a moral monstrosity, a manifestation of effeminacy, how can it at the same time inspire a man to acts of courage, patriotism, and self-sacrifice? When Saint-Loup loses his *croix de guerre* in Jupien's brothel—the same place where Charlus degrades himself before fantasies of machismo—the knot of paradox could hardly be more firmly tied. Saint-Loup, like Charlus, sometimes has relations with male prostitutes. But, unlike Charlus, he finds in his life as a soldier a socially valuable and personally redeeming outlet for his homosexual desires. "I have," the narrator says, "infinitely more admiration for Saint-Loup's request to be assigned to the most dangerous post of battle than for Charlus's avoidance of light-colored neckties" (3: 746). Proust remembers, after all, that homosexuality is a trait that leads different people to different ends.

And yet the story of Saint-Loup's heroism by no means gives a wholly positive image of homosexuality, for it implies, first, that homosexuality requires special acts of redemption and sublimation before it becomes acceptable and, second, that Saint-Loup can redeem his homosexuality only by a suicide mission to the front. The passage is one of Proust's most optimistic; but it is at the same time haunted by echoes of the suicide motif so common in the early work.

Roger Shattuck has commented that "because Proust was too canny to have stayed very long with any schematic description of the human mind, one can demonstrate almost anything by quoting from [A la recherche]."[112] This is especially true when it is a question of the novel's image of homosexuality. One could read Sodome I and decide that the national security of any nation depends on the exclusion of homosexually oriented men—those hermaphroditic sexual mutations—from the armed services. Or one could read the story of Saint-Loup's heroism and come to an entirely different conclusion.

Such self-contradiction may be an essential part of Proust's canniness. Sometimes Proust seems to create homosexual stereotypes only so that he can knock them over, like so many straw men, later in the novel—pretending, as it were, to be a member of the sexual establishment in order to gain the protective coloration necessary for attacking the establishment on its own terrain. There may be in A la recherche something of the strategy employed by Richard Burton in the famous "Terminal Essay" to his translation of the Arabian Nights (1885–86), a translation and an essay with which Proust could well have been familiar, given his passionate interest in this work. John Lauritsen and David Thorstad point out that in the "Terminal Essay" Burton "referred to homosexuality as 'vice,' 'Le Vice,' 'pathologic love,' etc. . . . It is pretty clear, however, that he was writing tongue in cheek, for he also described pederasty with the warmest enthusiasm. . . . the 'Terminal Essay' was double-edged. The enlightened could read a powerful, well-documented defense of homosexual love, written with pride, relish, and even arrogance; while the pious could cluck their tongues disapprovingly over the 'terrible vice.' "[113] It would, however, be a mistake to argue that this sort of irony is always present in *A la recherche*. What may appear to the "enlightened" to be sly double meaning is often simply the result of guilt and ambivalence on Proust's part. It is clear from Proust's correspondence and notebooks that he actually believed, at least at certain junctures of his life, that homosexually oriented people are sick, that they are a "third sex," and so on. And it is equally clear that Proust was never able fully to accept the homosexual side of his personality and that he rarely, if ever, thought about the subject without concomitant feelings of guilt and self-recrimination.

We should bear in mind too that Proust wrote a revised *A la recherche* over a period of some fourteen years and that in the process he could have changed his mind—perhaps several times—about the nature of homosexuality. The novel as we have it is a complicated palimpsest in which ideas formulated in 1908 coexist with ideas formulated in 1922 and in all the years in between. We should also remember that *Sodome I* may have begun as a nonfiction essay on homosexuality and that this may account in part for the fact that its ideas sometimes clash with events and characterizations found elsewhere in the novel. It is possible that when Proust incorporated the essay into the novel he inadvertently left some of the seams showing and never fully succeeded in reconciling the preexistent theory with the developing fictional practice. Whatever the reasons—and they seem to be partly biographical, partly historical, partly aesthetic—*A la recherche* is the product of a continually evolving consciousness, and it dramatizes its own evolution in the changing opinions and perspectives of its narrator. It is a Penelope's web of the imagination, in which what is woven in one part is constantly unraveled, reorganized, and rewoven in another.

The theme of homosexuality is, then, no different from Proust's other themes for being founded on paradox and self-contradiction. As Leo Bersani has noticed, it is not unusual to find in *A la recherche* discrepancies "between dramatizations of certain kinds of behavior and the narrator's theoretical analyses" of that behavior.[114] What the narrator says about homosexuality in *Sodome I* gives us only a rudimentary outline of the intellectual and aesthetic apparatus we need to understand the variations on this theme in *La Prisonnière, La Fugitive,* and *Le Temps retrouvé. A la recherche* is a great novel partly because its characters consistently turn out to be more complex than the theories which are supposed to account for them, even though those theories are often extremely complex in their own right.

Caution is therefore called for in any attempt to apply to the outside world Proust's writing on homosexuality. That writing teems with distortions, half-truths, outmoded ideas, and constant eruptions of Proust's internalized homophobia. But it also occasionally combines great structural and expressive beauty with unprecedented insights into human nature. Given such strengths and such weaknesses, the best summation of Proust's treatment of this theme is perhaps what Proust himself once said, in a different context, about the work of John Ruskin: it is "often stupid, cranky, jarring, false, irritating, but . . . always worthy of esteem and always great."[115] The cranky, jarring, false, and irritating qualities have been, I hope, sufficiently analyzed. But proper homage to the greatness will require another chapter.

CHAPTER FIVE

MONSTERS OF
TIME

. . . . it suddenly seemed to me that my humble
life and the realms of truth were not as separate
as I had thought, that they even coincided at
certain points. . . .

(1: 96)

*T*HERE ARE two conflicting desires in *A la recherche*, as in most art: the desire to describe the world as it is, and the desire to create a new world of the imagination. Proust struggles to bring his private vision into accord with reality; and he also struggles to transform reality to make it accord with his private vision. The points at which these struggles coincide—the points at which they cease to be private and become universal—are the subjects of this chapter.

In order to discuss this topic we must reexamine the question of the narrator's sexuality and its relationship to his art. The narrator describes himself as "the exact contrary, the antipode" of M. de Charlus (3: 208) and asserts throughout the novel that his orientation is heterosexual. But some critics have insisted that it is, in reality, homosexual. Maurice Samuel says, "Marcel is and wants us to know that he is a homosexual." And Melvin Seiden says, "Marcel is and Proust wants us to know Marcel is a homosexual." Marcel Muller, in a more thoroughgoing examination of the evidence, shows that *A la recherche* tends in many ways to identify the "I" (and by implication Proust himself) with the homosexually oriented characters of the novel. But Muller does not conclude that the "I" is "a homosexual." Rather, he argues for a sophisticated appreciation of the multiple narrative "voices" which coexist in the novel and which simultaneously suggest, among other things, that the "I" is and is not Proust and is and is not homosexually oriented.[1]

Muller's insights are very much to the point and can stand some elaboration. We might begin by examining some previously overlooked evidence for the narrator's homosexuality. The information we

207

are given about the psychology and conduct of the narrator—
especially the young narrator—accords very well with the image of
homosexuality current around the turn of the century. The narrator is
sickly and neurasthenic, and such a person was thought to be especially prone to homosexuality.[2] Moreover, he uses his various illnesses and neuroses to justify conduct which otherwise might seem
blameworthy. In the episode of the good-night kiss he succeeds in establishing a situation in which his need for his mother is no longer
considered "as a punishable fault but as an involuntary illness which
had just been officially recognized . . . a nervous condition for which
I was not responsible" (1: 38). In Proust's era arguments of this sort
were often advanced in favor of tolerance for homosexuality, on the
grounds that sick people cannot help the way they are and therefore
should not be denigrated or punished. (Krafft-Ebing was one de-
fender of this idea.) Later in the novel the narrator himself voices a
version of the familiar argument. Comparing Andrée's supposed lesbianism to that of Albertine, he says that "if [Andrée] were afflicted
with the same vice, [it] seemed to me more pardonable, because she
was sick and neurasthenic" (2: 805). That the narrator has these same
characteristics does not, of course, mean that he is homosexually
inclined, though it does give us grounds for suspecting (in Proustian
terms) that he might or could be. At the very least these passages
show that the narrator shares with his homosexually oriented characters a knowledge of what it is like to suffer from physical and psychological conditions over which he has no control.

A similar effect is produced by the repeated emphasis on the narrator's lack of will power. This is, of course, a trait the narrator overcomes when he undertakes the composition of his novel. Nonetheless, a weak will was thought to be another distinguishing
characteristic of homosexuality,[3] and the narrator clearly aligns his
own personality with that of homosexually oriented men when he says
that such men seek each other's company because of "a certain vice,
the greatest vice of all, the lack of will power" (3: 836). Furthermore,
the narrator has the kind of heredity which, in the thinking of
Proust's time, would mark him as "tainted" and predisposed to a variety of illnesses and psychological aberrations, among them homosexuality. Krafft-Ebing, Moreau, Tarnowsky, and other theorists be-

lieved that any physical or mental disorder manifested in one
generation could assume the form of sexual perversion in succeeding
generations. Tarnowsky wrote that "a father, who is epileptic, or
afflicted with some form or other of cerebral ailment; a mother subject to hysteria, or possessing a pathologic predisposition . . . a nervous illness of the grandfather or grandmother, or other parent, these
are the causes which, together with other possible hereditary tendencies, are the principal factors in the predisposition to perversion of
the sexual instinct."[4] The characterization of Tante Léonie in *Combray* shows that the narrator's family has just such a tendency to
neurasthenia. Léonie is a hypochondriac and recluse, and she is certainly psychologically unbalanced if not as physically ill as she pretends to be. In *Le Côté de Guermantes* Dr. du Boulbon draws a connection between the grandmother's illness (which he takes to be
psychosomatic) and the fact that she had a first cousin, Léonie, who
was a pathological recluse (2: 304)—a diagnosis typical of that branch
of contemporary medicine which held that nervous as well as physical
disorders could run in a family. If the narrator or another member of
his family had been subsequently brought to Boulbon as a victim of
homosexuality, the doctor would no doubt have pointed once again to
the family tendency to neurasthenia as manifested in Léonie.

Léonie's influence also causes the narrator to become a case of
anima muliebris virili corpore inclusa. During the affair with Albertine he reaches a point where he seldom gets out of bed or goes out,
not even in order to verify his suspicions about Albertine's lesbianism. And the person who causes him to act in this way "was a
person who was not Albertine, who was not a person with whom I
was in love, but a person with more power over me than a beloved
person—it was, transmigrated into me, despotic . . . my Tante
Léonie" (3: 78–79). The narrator is saying, figuratively, that heredity
is catching up with him and causing him to imitate Léonie's reclusive
habits. But the metaphor of transmigration may contain a message of
its own, since it combines the idea of a morbid heredity with the idea
of a female soul trapped in a male body. Ulrichs's formula of homosexuality is not specifically mentioned. But earlier in the novel the
narrator observes that the effeminacy of certain homosexually
oriented men stems from the presence within them of "the soul of a

relative of the feminine sex, watchful like a goddess or incarnated like a double," and he illustrates this idea with another aunt-nephew combination: the soul of Mme Cottard seems to inhabit the body of her homosexually inclined nephew and control his movements (2: 907).

Another point at which the narrator's psychology intersects with the image of homosexuality current at the time is in his childhood masturbation. After Kinsey we are prone to accept masturbation as a normal facet of human sexuality,[5] and a present-day reader would probably regard this aspect of the narrator's story as no more than a realistic detail in a portrait of a boy's growing up. The first readers of *A la recherche* would probably not have reacted to it in this way but would have regarded it as evidence of something exceptional and abnormal in the narrator's character. In medical theory and popular opinion alike masturbation was condemned as morally abhorrent and physically and psychologically debilitating. It was said to destroy virility, weaken the will, and lead perhaps ultimately to homosexuality. Krafft-Ebing was especially famous for his opinion that where a hereditary predisposition to homosexuality exists, it can be definitively crystallized by onanism.[6]

There was such a horror of masturbation in Proust's day that Proust's translator C. K. Scott Moncrieff felt compelled to bowdlerize the novel's second reference to it. More explicit than the first (which speaks only of "solitude" and "pleasure" [1: 12]), the second reference describes the actual process of orgasm: "I carved out within myself an unknown trail that I believed to be deadly ("que je croyais mortelle"), until a natural mark, like the track of a snail, was added to the leaves of the wild currant which sloped above me" (1: 158).[7] There is a familiar ambivalence in the imagery. The narrator depicts the seminal fluid that results from masturbation as something eminently natural, like the track of a snail on a leaf. But at the same time he associates the act with the fear of "deadly" consequences. The function of "mortelle" in this sentence is ambiguous. The narrator may be saying that when he was young, he considered masturbation a mortal sin. Or he may be saying that he believed the act might actually kill him and found out that it would not only when he did not die as a result. But even if masturbation is not, finally, depicted as being "deadly" in the religious or the physical sense, there seem to be evocations of other

harmful results that were supposed to accrue from it. Within two
pages in the Pléiade edition we learn that the young narrator has a
delicate constitution, flagging energy, a weak will—and is given to
masturbating in the little upstairs room at Combray (1: 11–12). No
direct relationship is drawn between the act and its supposed consequences, but the familiar syndrome is nonetheless present. Given
these personality traits and this history of masturbation, almost any
physician of the era would have diagnosed the narrator as headed for
homosexuality, if not already afflicted with it.

Furthermore, the novel seems to invite us in several indirect
ways to view the narrator's heterosexual experiences as artistically
disguised homosexual experiences. We learn in *Combray* that when
the narrator masturbates, he can see from his upstairs room the tower
of the old dungeon in Roussainville-le-Pin. He personifies the
dungeon as "the only confidant I had for my early desires" and asks it
to send him a Roussainville peasant woman to satisfy his lust (1: 158).
A few pages earlier there is a description of Roussainville in a rain-
storm, where it appears to be "punished like a village in the Bible by
all the lances of the storm which were obliquely flagellating the
houses of its inhabitants" (1: 152). The narrator's fantasies ostensibly
revolve around a Roussainville peasant woman, but Roussainville itself reminds him of a biblical city punished by heaven. It is not explicitly compared to Sodom, but there is an unmistakable prefiguration of the imagery to be developed later in *Sodome I.* And the
reference to flagellation may look even further forward in the novel's
development of the homosexual theme, to Charlus's experience in
that miniature Sodom which is Jupien's brothel.

Krafft-Ebing published a letter from a homosexually oriented
man, who pointed out that society is so constructed that a person who
has homosexual tastes often suffers under the illusion that "he alone
of all the world has such abnormal feelings."[8] Similarly, the narrator
surmises that if he had actually met on one of his walks the Roussainville woman of his fantasies and declared his desires to her, "she
would have thought me mad; [so] I ceased to think that the desires
which I formed during these walks and which were never fulfilled
were shared by other people and had any validity outside myself.
They no longer appeared to me as anything but the purely subjective

creations—impotent, illusory—of my own temperament" (1: 158–59).
The feelings the narrator here describes on one level allude to the
solipsism which constantly threatens his experience. But on another
level they anticipate and reflect the emotions he later attributes to
homosexually oriented men who think "their vice to be more exceptional than it is" (2: 623).

The narrator's affair with Albertine also seems at times deliberately constructed to appear suspiciously homosexual. Again the effect
is produced partly through echoes and juxtapositions of images.
When the narrator puts around himself the arms of the sleeping Albertine, he compares her to "a climbing plant, a convolvulus whose
branches continue to grow on whatever support is provided for them"
(3: 113). This description recalls a passage in *Sodome I*, where men
with homosexual preferences are said to seek other men "just as the
convolvulus casts its tendrils wherever it can find a pick or a rake"
(2: 622). Justin O'Brien takes note of these sorts of parallels and concludes that Albertine should be understood as a transposed homosexual lover. To support his point O'Brien claims that only once in the
story of the narrator's cohabitation with Albertine is Albertine given
"an incontrovertibly female body."[9] The passage to which O'Brien
refers describes how the narrator undresses Albertine and gazes at
her nude form before taking her to bed. "Her two little upstanding
breasts," the narrator says, "were so round that they seemed not so
much to be an integral part of her body as to have ripened there like
two pieces of fruit; and her belly (concealing the place which in the
man is disfigured as by a hook which remains attached to a statue removed from its setting) closed at the junction of her thighs upon two
valves of a curvature as soft, as restful, as claustral as that of the horizon after the sun has set" (3: 79). But is this, in fact, a description of
"an incontrovertibly female body"? The breasts are made to seem
somehow out of place, rather than "an integral part of the body." And
when the narrator looks at the curve of Albertine's belly, the first
thing he notices is that there is no penis in the place where, in the
body of a man, we would normally expect to find one. Furthermore,
Albertine's belly is not simply said to be lacking a penis; it is said to
be *concealing* (*dissimulant*) the place where the penis would appear
in the body of a man. The narrator then proceeds to describe the

male body as "disfigured" by the presence of a penis, thus seeming to affirm his exclusively heterosexual tastes. But if his inclinations and his experiences are heterosexual, why does he think of a penis in the first place when he looks at a nude female body? And why does he take such pains to convince us that he finds the female body attractive and the male body repellent? The whole description has a distinct flavor of protesting too much.

If the purpose of this passage is to describe "an incontrovertibly female body" and an incontrovertibly heterosexual experience, we must judge it a failure. But this does not seem to be the purpose. The purpose seems to be to create yet another case in which the narrator's heterosexual experiences, when viewed from a slightly tilted angle, take on a distinctly homosexual coloration.

Later in the novel there is a passage where the narrator comes very close to making a confession of homosexual desires:

The poet is to be pitied who, with no Virgil to guide him, has to traverse the circles of an inferno of sulfur and pitch, throwing himself into the fire which falls from heaven in order to rescue a few inhabitants of Sodom. . . . Where is the psychiatrist who has not had an attack of madness as a result of keeping company with madmen? Still more fortunate is the one who can affirm that it was not some latent, anterior madness which moved him to devote himself to them. In the case of a psychiatrist, the subject of his study often reacts upon the man himself. But, before this happens, what obscure inclination, what fascinated terror, caused him to choose this subject in the first place? (3: 206–7)

Only the use of the third person and of the rhetorical questions keeps this from being an admission that the narrator is aware of homosexual tendencies within his own personality.

We should notice, however, that the evidence for the narrator's homosexuality is circumstantial and nothing more. And we should also bear in mind the distinction between a required interpretation and a possible one. It is possible to view the narrator as homosexually inclined. But nothing in the novel requires us to do so.

And yet Proust has obviously taken pains to ensure that the question will arise and that the homosexual interpretation will represent a strong temptation. The subtlest and at the same time most pervasive example of this technique may lie in the narrator's propensity for inverted modes of conduct and perception. One reason for the view that people with homosexual preferences were "inverts" was that they were thought to have a psychological makeup which literally reverses that of ordinary people. In their 1908 book on the Eulenburg affair Weindel and Fischer quoted Krafft-Ebing's opinion that in homosexual psychology "more often than not it happens that the feelings, the thought, in short the entire character is modified to the point of becoming absolutely the opposite of the character, the thought, and the feelings which pertain to the natural sex of the homosexuals."[10] In myth and legend too we find the suggestion that people with homosexual tastes are inversely oriented not only in their sexual conduct but in all the affairs of life. In his "Terminal Essay" to the *Arabian Nights* Richard Burton pointed out that the story of Sodom and Gomorrah "has been amply embroidered by the Rabbis who make the Sodomites do everything *à l'envers:* e.g., if a man were wounded he was fined for bloodshed." Burton also mentioned that in the Koran Lot's city is destroyed by being turned upside down—presumably a fitting punishment for those who have insisted on living against the grain of nature.[11]

The portrayal of homosexuality in *A la recherche* echoes these theories and legends. Charlus's sexual feelings and attitudes, for instance, are presented as the opposites of those of ordinary men. Suppose Charlus should one day experience the urge to sleep with a woman. This would not mean that he was at last becoming normal. It would mean, rather, that he had experienced a desire comparable to the sort of stray impulse which might tempt a man with heterosexual tastes to sleep with a boy—"through a curiosity which is similar, inverse, and in both cases equally unhealthy" (3: 211). Similarly, when Charlus admires the beauty of Mme de Surgis and her sons, he does so in a manner which reverses the practice of his heterosexually oriented counterparts: "For if each man took pleasure in admiring in the sons the queenly bearing and the eyes of Mme de Surgis, the Baron could take an inverse but equally acute pleasure in finding these charms gathered up and reunited in their mother" (2: 695). There are even allusions to the idea that people who have homosexual preferences cast a general aura of "everything *à l'envers.*" In the little train which takes "the faithful" to La Raspelière, Ski comments that if

Charlus continues to stare at the conductor, the train will start going backwards (2: 1,041). Likewise, Jupien's brothel is presented as a latter-day version of the Rabbinical Sodom where everything was done in reverse. Some of the introductions made in the brothel are mirror images of introductions made in certain other social milieux. Elsewhere someone might say, "I am going to present to you M. Lebrun" and then whisper that the man who goes by the name of M. Lebrun is really the Grand Duke of Russia. "Inversely," says the narrator, "Jupien felt that it was not yet enough to introduce a milkboy to M. de Charlus. He whispered to him with a wink of his eye, 'He is a milkboy, but basically, and especially, he is one of the most dangerous thugs of Belleville' " (3: 816–17). And after explaining that the financial exigencies of his brothel are such that it must rent some of its rooms to respectable lodgers, Jupien wittily comments: "Here it's the opposite of the Carmelites; it's thanks to vice that virtue is able to live" (3: 830).

But the person with the most inverted perspective on the world is not Charlus, nor Jupien, nor any of the other homosexually oriented characters. It is the narrator himself. The narrator regularly interprets life in terms of inverse relationships, and the word "inversion" and its variants are among the most frequently recurring words in his vocabulary. "People say that beauty is a promise of happiness. Inversely the possibility of pleasure can mark the beginning of beauty" (3: 140). "The nature we display in the second part of our life is not always . . . a developed or faded, magnified or attenuated form of our first nature; it is sometimes an inverse nature, a garment veritably turned inside out" (1: 434). "My mother, by a movement of heart which was the inverse of that of the scoundrels who derive pleasure from the idea that people they do not like have suffered more than they think, was unwilling, in her affection for my grandmother, to admit that any sadness, any impairment, could befall her" (3: 660). "Doubtless all the efforts which the maître d'hôtel's son and Françoise's nephew had made to avoid military service had been made by Saint-Loup in the inverse direction, and successfully, in order to be in constant danger" (3: 841). "Like a traveler who returns on the same road to the point from which he set out, I had, before attaining my initial feeling of indifference [for Albertine], to traverse in

the inverse direction all the feelings through which I had passed
before arriving at my great love" (3: 558).

Inversion is not simply a characteristic of the narrator's vocabulary. The impressionistic narrative which pervades the novel depends
upon a radical inversion of traditional aesthetics. Proustian impres-
sionism shows us first the effects and then the possible causes; it
thereby echoes what the narrator calls "the Dostoevsky side of Mme
de Sévigné." Both these writers, according to the narrator, "instead
of presenting things in the logical order, that is to say by beginning
with the cause, [show] us first the effect, the illusion which strikes us"
(3: 378). In composing his novel the narrator emulates the impres-
sionism of Dostoevsky and Mme de Sévigné and also that of the
painter Elstir. This means, among other things, that "supposing that
war is scientific, it would still be necessary to depict it as Elstir
painted the sea, by coming at it from the other direction, by beginning with illusions, beliefs which would be rectified little by little, as
Dostoevsky would tell the story of a life" (3: 982–83). A charming example of this technique is the narrator's discovery that his article has
finally been published by Le Figaro: "I opened Le Figaro. What a
nuisance! The first article had exactly the same title as the one I had
submitted and which had not appeared. And not only the same title,
there were a few words which were exactly the same. That was going
too far. I would send a letter of protest. And not only a few words,
but the whole thing, and my signature as well. . . . It was my article,
which had at last been published!" (3: 567–68).

The technique of creating an impression and then inverting it
also has important structural implications. The entire novel is built
around the narrator's passage from a state to its inversion, from *temps
perdu* to *temps retrouvé*. Indeed, as Jean Milly points out, the movement through time in *A la recherche* is a sort of simultaneous forward
and backward movement, with the two directions converging at the
end of the work: in composing his novel Proust "has . . . gone back
in time to his childhood; then he has gone down through time once
more, backwards, in the company of his character, revealing to the
latter little by little the different facets of reality."[12] Roger Shattuck
describes the same dimension of *A la recherche* by commenting that
the end of the novel, when it folds back upon the beginning, "leads

us firmly out of [*A la recherche*] as Marcel's story and across into a symmetrical mirror-novel, consisting of all the same words and incidents," but told now from the reverse perspective of the mature artist-narrator.[13] There can be little doubt that Proust intended this overall inversion of the narrator's perspective to serve as a reflection of his general impressionistic aesthetics. Speaking of the end of *Du côté de chez Swann*, which concludes on a note of despair over lost time ("the houses, the streets, the avenues are as fugitive—alas!—as the years" [1: 427]), Proust wrote to Jacques Rivière: "It is only at the end of the book, and once the lessons of life have been understood, that my thought will be unveiled. The idea I express at the end of the first volume . . . is the *opposite* of my conclusion."[14]

This inversion of the whole is anticipated by and reflected in various inversions of individual episodes. After Albertine's death the narrator receives a telegram which seems to indicate that she is still alive. But he has by this time become indifferent to Albertine, and the news causes him no joy. His experience here thus inverts his experience with the heart's intermissions after his grandmother's death. "Then there occurred, in inverse fashion, the same thing that had happened with my grandmother: when I had learned that my grandmother was, in fact, dead, I felt no grief at first. Indeed, I did not suffer over her death until involuntary memories had brought her back to life for me. Now that Albertine was no longer alive in my mind, the news that she was actually alive did not cause me the joy I would have thought" (3: 641). Similarly, at the beginning of his love for Gilberte, the narrator describes a day when spring seems to appear in the midst of winter (1: 405). Later, when his love for Gilberte is dying, he describes an unseasonable penetration of winter into spring (1: 634). This complex interplay of inverse emotion and symbolic seasonal change produces what H. Kopman, who has analyzed the two scenes, calls "Proustian contrast-equilibrium."[15]

Appropriately *Sodome et Gomorrhe*, the volume of the novel where sexual inversion becomes a theme of major importance, is a volume where the techniques of structural inversion and contrast-equilibrium are starkly and dramatically visible. As we have already seen, the conclusion of *Sodome I* reverses an idea advanced at its beginning: the narrator at first thinks that the world contains very few "inverts" but finally decides they are as numerous as the sands of the earth. Moreover, the discovery of Charlus's true nature is depicted as a total "revolution" in everything the narrator has thought about Charlus up to this point (2: 613). In this way the exposure of Charlus's sexual inversion is underscored by and reflected in various intellectual and emotional inversions on the part of the narrator.

The narrator's love for Albertine is accompanied by similar inversions of sentiment and opinion, many of which revolve around Albertine's supposed lesbianism. At the end of the final chapter of *Sodome et Gomorrhe II* (Chapter 4) the narrator becomes jealous of Mlle Vinteuil and her friend and decides to marry Albertine at all costs. This decision reverses the conclusion of Chapter 3, which ends with the narrator's seemingly irrevocable resolution to break with Albertine ("The idea of marrying Albertine seemed to me a folly"). But this statement is itself an inversion of the developing need for Albertine as portrayed in Chapters 1, 2, and 3 of *Sodome et Gomorrhe II*. These are typical Proustian coups de théâtre. But it is noteworthy that they allow the affair with Albertine as told in *Sodome et Gomorrhe II* to reflect on an extended scale the same sorts of reversals of perception which punctuate the first extended discussion of sexual inversion in *Sodome I*.

There is a passage in *Le Temps retrouvé* which is especially rich in similar examples. The narrator is trying to find out from Gilberte whether Albertine was a lover of women. Gilberte has previously commented that Albertine was once prone to act in "bad form" ("mauvais genre"). At the time the remark seemed to refer to lesbianism. But now Gilberte says she does not remember making this statement and claims, moreover, that if she did make it, "I was speaking on the contrary about flirtations with young men" (3: 707). This reversal in Gilberte's position itself reverses Albertine's conduct with respect to the same subject: "Gilberte's remarks, from the 'bad form' of previous times to the certificate of good conduct and morals of today, followed a course which was the inverse of Albertine's affirmations, for Albertine had finally almost confessed to a semirelationship with Gilberte" (3: 707). Furthermore, the narrator realizes that his own thinking about Albertine's lesbianism reversed itself twice during the course of his relationship with her. When he first saw Albertine among the little band of young girls at Balbec, he attributed to her a perverse nature; then, as he got to know her better, he decided he was wrong; then, "I had traveled the road in the opposite direction, considering once again that my initial suspicions were true" (3: 707–8). Finally, the narrator remembers that there was once a time when Albertine seemed willing to respond to his questions about lesbianism but that this willingness lasted only "until the day when she had understood that [my questions] were motivated by jealousy and had reversed her position" (3: 708). "Inverse fashion," "on the contrary," "the inverse of Albertine's affirmations," "opposite direction," "reversed her position"—structurally and stylistically the affair with Albertine is furiously inverted.

These inversions perhaps have as much to do with Proust's well-known desire to imitate musical composition as with the theme of homosexuality. The articulation of a musical theme and then of the inversion of that theme (sometimes including retrogrades and retrogrades of the inversion) is one of the most common devices of musical scoring, one which can be traced from Bach to Bartok and even further. But one wonders all the same whether the narrator's virtuoso manipulation of so many kinds of inversion—sexual, philosophical, aesthetic, psychological, structural—might not also be intended to associate the narrator (and by extension Proust himself) with a fundamental trait of homosexual psychology as it is depicted in *A la recherche*. As Roland Barthes has noticed, "the reversal of appearances . . . always provides the narrator with a delightful astonishment . . . [a] veritable jubilation, so entire, so pure, so triumphant . . . that this mode of inversion can obviously stem only from an eroticism (of discourse), as if the describing of the reversal is the very moment when Proust revels in writing."[16] We need only qualify the statement that the reversal of appearances always causes the narrator "delightful astonishment" and "jubilation." Sometimes (as in the jealousy over Albertine) it produces the opposite reactions. But in both cases the relationship between stylistic eroticism and triumphant sexuality per se may be closer than Barthes suspects. At times we can almost hear the narrator saying: "I am he who sees and feels things the opposite of the way they are usually seen and felt. I am he who lives his life backwards in order to make it meaningful, he who organizes his experience by approaching it *à l'envers.* I am he who has understood more and practiced more inversion than anyone else in my book. In short, I am a Sodomite, and my struggle with the agony and inspiration of that destiny is a fundamental basis of my art." When the narrator speaks of himself as "the exact contrary, the antipode" of M. de Charlus, he is ostensibly asserting his heterosexuality. But at the same time he is paradoxically reminding us that he shares with Charlus and with the other homosexually oriented characters in the novel a tendency to view the world as a concatenation of various modes of inversion.

Is Proust then writing a novel in which he consciously tries to present as much material as possible from a homosexual, "inverted" point of view and thereby embody in the totality of his vision a truth society forbids him to reveal more directly? Or is he using inversion as one of many metaphors for a preexistent vision of the reversals of fate and expectation to which humanity has always been prey? Proust has combined these two aspects of the novel so thoroughly that it seems impossible to separate them.

Finally, then, we must answer both yes and no to the question of the narrator's homosexuality. The narrator's sexual identity is deliberately left ambiguous in order to show that traits which are usually regarded as the private property of "homosexuals" are, in reality, characteristics of human nature in general. In certain parts of *A la recherche* (such as *Sodome I*) Proust suggests that only homosexually oriented people know the fluctuations of an inverted destiny and identity. But in other parts of the novel he demonstrates that everyone is an invert in one way or another. The inversions of *A la recherche* range from the most obvious dramatic peripeties to the subtlest shades of irony and paradox. Charlus the man turns into Charlus the woman; Bergotte the "sweet Singer" becomes a ridiculous little man with a goatee; members of the lower classes rise to positions of influence while members of the aristocracy tumble from their positions of power; people fall in love only when it is apparent that the loved one is unattainable; they attain the loved one only when they have ceased to desire such attainment; they tell lies which eventually become truths and truths which eventually become lies; they gain paradise by losing it and, by losing it, find it. Proust depicts a Heraclitean world, in which reality is constantly in flux and "the way up" is also "the way down." And he dramatizes this view by making the narrator the supreme invert of the novel, an invert in every sense except the specifically sexual sense exemplified by M. de Charlus and perhaps, we are sometimes led to believe, in that sense as well. He allows all manner of ontological possibilities—sexual and otherwise— to hover around and within the central consciousness of the novel, so that we gradually come to think of the narrator as someone who has the potential for becoming all the paradoxes he describes. And this makes the "I" of A la recherche, in the largest sense, a "We."

THE HOMOSEXUAL DIASPORA

The story of the narrator's development as an artist could be described as the story of his search for a meeting ground between scientific truth and mythic truth. In the narrator's life as retold in his art there is no science without myth and no myth without science. Science becomes visionary and fantastic; myth becomes analytical and precise. And nowhere is this relationship more evident than in the treatment of homosexuality.

Consider, for instance, the overlapping scientific and mythic perspectives in *Sodome I*. On one level the narrator describes his observation of Charlus and Jupien as objectively as if he were a naturalist reporting on the pollination of plants or the mating habits of animals. Indeed, he is waiting to see whether a bee will arrive to pollinate an orchid belonging to the Duchesse de Guermantes when the drama of homosexuality begins to unfold before him. Having reflected that "the laws of the vegetable kingdom are themselves governed by higher and higher laws," he decides that Charlus and Jupien are also conducting themselves according to a particular set of natural laws and rituals. He realizes that the devices Jupien uses to signal and attract the Baron are like the special adaptations by which orchids attract bees. And then, in a famous *morceau de bravoure,* he metaphorically transforms Jupien into the beckoning, coquettish flower and Charlus—noticing, approaching, happily whistling—into the curious and questing bee (2: 603–7). He presents himself, in short, as a scientist as well as an artist of human behavior. "Lacking the perspective of the geologist," he comments, "I at least had that of the botanist" (2: 601). And he concludes that Jupien, with his taste for older men, represents a subvariety of human flora which "every human botanizer, every moral botanist will be able to observe, in spite of their rarity" (2: 628).

But side by side with this scientific language we find the suggestion that we are reading not science but myth. We find it, for example, in the mythological allusions which recur throughout *Sodome I*. When an "invert" is in bed in the morning, the female spirit within him suggests "Galatea, who is scarcely awake in the unconscious of this man's body where she is imprisoned" (2: 620–21). A solitary "invert" before going "home to dream in his tower like Griselda . . . lingers on the beach like a strange Andromeda whom no Argonaut will come to free" (2: 626). And Charlus and Jupien recognize each other as men of similar orientation because "gods are immediately recognizable to other gods . . . and so was M. de Charlus to Jupien" (2: 613).

The narrator does not stop with allusions to myth but goes on to create his own whimsical mythology of homosexual love. According to *Sodome I* present-day men who have homosexual tastes are descendants of the inhabitants of Sodom who escaped the destruction of their city (2: 601). So far there is nothing particularly new or original in the idea. It was, of course, common practice to refer to homosexually oriented men as Sodomites, and in 1864 an article on homosexuality had appeared in *La Petite Revue* under the title "Les Echappés de Sodome."[17] But the narrator derives a full-blown etiological myth from what had previously been a common figure of speech. In the account given in *Sodome I* the Sodomites escaped their doom by telling clever lies to the two angels who were set at the gates of Sodom as interrogators. This was God's great mistake: to send angels who were not themselves homosexual to judge the inhabitants of Sodom. In their innocence and naiveté the angels were deceived by what would otherwise be transparent alibis: "Father of six children, I have two mistresses, etc." (2: 631). In this way the Sodomites made their escape. If they happened to turn their heads to look back at a boy, they were not, like Lot's wife, turned into pillars of salt. On the contrary, they now have numerous descendants, who cover the face of the earth and who have inherited this involuntary glance of desire together with the talent for deceit which enabled their forebears to elude the fiery judgment. It is conceivable, the narrator says, that the descendants of these Sodomites will one day try to recolonize the biblical city. But this would be a mistake, because "scarcely having arrived, the Sodomites would leave the city in order to make it appear that they were not a part of it" (2: 632). They would take a wife, keep mistresses, and establish residence in other cities where they could find all the distractions they require. They would go to Sodom only on "days of supreme necessity, when their own city was empty, in times when hunger forces the wolf to come out of the woods." That is to say, things would continue to happen just as they presently happen all over the world (2: 632).

Homosexual love continues despite the necessity for secrecy and concealment, because homosexually oriented men have, according to the narrator, a racial memory which enables them immediately to recognize certain other men as having the same ancestral homeland and therefore the same sexual tastes. Charlus and Jupien, as they exchange glances of mutual recognition, remind the narrator of two people from Zurich who have met by chance in some other corner of the world; but "in the eyes of both men it was not the sky of Zurich but the sky of some Oriental city whose name I had not yet divined which had just materialized" (2: 605–6). Later in the novel the same powers of recognition are attributed to homosexually oriented women, whose mythical homeland, according to A la recherche, is Gomorrah.[18] At Balbec a young woman directs at Albertine "looks laden with memory, as if she were. afraid . . . my mistress did not remember" (2: 851). Through these memories of the mythical homeland "Gomorrah, though dispersed, tends in each city, in each village to rejoin its separate members, to reform the biblical city, while, everywhere, the same efforts are pursued, even though they may lead only to an intermittent reconstruction, by the nostalgic, the hypocritical, the sometimes courageous exiles of Sodom" (2: 852; cf. 3: 23).

This presentation is based on one of the oldest and most universal mythic patterns, that of primal unity, painful separation, and the ensuing quest for reintegration of the primal whole.[19] The same pattern underlies, for instance, the story Aristophanes tells in Plato's

Symposium to account for heterosexual and homosexual love. The
first humanity, according to Aristophanes, was composed of three
sexes. Each sex was circular in form and had two faces, four arms,
four legs, four ears, and two sets of sexual organs. Some of these two-
fold beings were male-male, some female-female, and some male-
female. They were creatures of prodigious· strength and great pride,
and they challenged the sovereignty of the gods, causing Zeus to
weaken them by splitting them down the middle. Ever since then,
says Aristophanes, the descendants of these two-fold creatures have
been trying to regain their original shape and "heal the natural structure of man." Men formed from a cutting of the male-male creature
fall in love with other men; women formed from a cutting of the
female-female creature fall in love with other women; and men and
women formed from a cutting of the original androgyne fall in love
with members of the opposite sex.[20] Since Proust was acquainted
with the *Symposium,* it seems likely that his myth of the dispersal and
reintegration of the inhabitants of Sodom and Gomorrah was inspired
at least in part by Aristophanes' myth. Sodom corresponds to Aristophanes' divided and dispersed male body and Gomorrah to Aristophanes' divided and dispersed female body. And love, in both accounts, is an attempt to reunify what once was whole.

The narrator thickens this mythic plot by superimposing upon it
a congruent historical pattern. He compares the diaspora of the Sodomites to the Diaspora of the Jews and the rebuilding of Sodom to the
Zionist efforts (much in the news when Proust was working on *A la
recherche*) to rebuild a Jewish nation in Palestine. Just as there is a
"Zionist movement," the narrator fancifully suggests, there could one
day be a "Sodomite movement" with similar goals (2: 632). Once
again the "chosen race" and the "race accursed" become metaphors
for each other in Proust's work. One of the results is to lend homosexuality some of the same power of survival, some of the same sense of
a paradoxical interweaving of cursedness and election which have
characterized Jewish history. "Our brethren will be scattered over
the earth from the good land, and Jerusalem will be desolate. The
house of God in it will be burned down and will be in ruins for a
time. But God will again have mercy on them, and bring them back
into their land; and they . . . will return from the places of their cap-

tivity, and will rebuild Jerusalem in splendor." This statement of the perennial hope of Judaism comes from the book of Tobit (14:4–5). And it is perhaps no accident that the Baron de Charlus knows that book well and is fond of applying it to his own life (2: 1,073–74; 3: 324).[21]

In telling the story of the homosexual diaspora the narrator has angels guard the gates of Sodom with a flaming sword after the Sodomites have made their escape (2: 631). There is, of course, no angel with a flaming sword in the biblical account of the destruction of Sodom. But there is such an angel in another section of Genesis: the angel who guards the tree of life after Adam and Eve have been banished from the garden of Eden. Very subtly and allusively Sodom is equated not only with the old and new Jerusalem but also with the old and new Eden, and the homosexual diaspora and reintegration become emblems of that movement from paradise lost to paradise regained which is all important in a novel where "the true paradises are the paradises we have lost" (3: 870).[22]

By thus conflating the myth of Sodom with the myths of Eden and of Jerusalem, the narrator effects a transvaluation of one of the primary sources of the Western prejudice against homosexuality. He cleverly turns the biblical story of Sodom from a fantasy of homosexual genocide into an affirmation that homosexuality can never be destroyed. In A la recherche the Sodomites live on, love on, and elude their enemies and oppressors just as they did when they originally escaped the fire from heaven. And Sodom itself rises from its ashes to be continually reborn in different forms. "For the two angels who had been placed at the gates of Sodom to find out if all the inhabitants . . . had done the things about which the cry had risen to the Eternal had been, *and one can only rejoice at this fact*, very badly chosen by the Lord, who should have assigned this task only to one of the Sodomites" (2: 631, italics mine). Proust allows himself and his narrator to express joy and triumph at the divine blunder which allowed the Sodomites to go free. The expression of rejoicing is very clearly heard (though rarely mentioned in discussions of A la recherche), and it contrasts strongly to what Edmund Wilson calls the "[sepulchral] groans and wails over the hard lot of the homosexuals"[23] found elsewhere in *Sodome I*.

The narrator's myth of Sodom is, then, partly an assault on re-pressive and oppressive attitudes toward homosexuality. But it is also a commentary on the themes and goals of *A la recherche* as a whole. When Sodom and Gomorrah are rebuilt in the love affairs of homo-sexually oriented people, the solution is found to "a puzzle composed of pieces which come from places where one would least expect to find them" (3: 90). To reconstruct Sodom and Gomorrah is to recon-struct both an individual and a collective identity from the scattered pieces of human history and human experience; and a similar recon-struction of individual and collective identity is one of the things the narrator sets out to achieve in writing his novel, where by putting together the fragments of his own life he will attempt to make sense of the human condition in general. As the narrator articulates and at-tempts to solve the puzzle of the cities of the plain, he gradually transforms it into the puzzle of recognition, the puzzle of memory, the puzzle of heredity. And these, taken together, represent the greatest puzzle of all—the puzzle of the past.

There is a dinner at Rivebelle attended by ten women with les-bian tastes, "as dissimilar as possible, and yet perfectly reunited, so that I never witnessed a dinner which was at once so homogeneous and yet so composite" (3: 90). And there is an embassy staffed by homosexually oriented men, a group of the most disparate sorts of people, who have, however, one thing in common, something which unites them, after all, into "a perfect . . . whole," a "little diplomatic Sodom," a recreation of the biblical city which lasts for more than ten years before the introduction of attachés with different tastes brings about the inevitable destruction and dispersal (2: 675).[24] Establishing, if only fleetingly, the similarity of dissimilars—this is the classic defi-nition of the artist's use of metaphor. And in this sense the new Sodoms and Gomorrahs which coalesce, break up, and recoalesce throughout *A la recherche* serve as metaphors of the process of meta-phor itself, paradigms of the working of that famous linguistic and ar-tistic tool which, more than any other, allows the narrator to unify his book and, through it, his life. In a celebrated passage in *Le Temps re-trouvé* the narrator observes that "truth will begin only when the writer takes two different objects, establishes their relationship . . . [and] reveals their common essence by uniting them one with the other in order to remove them from the contingencies of time, in a metaphor" (3: 889). What is involuntary memory, if not the creation of a temporal metaphor linking the past and the present? And what is metaphor, if not a discovery of similarity where only difference was thought to exist, an "inversion" of the usual way of seeing, and therefore an eroticism, as Barthes would say, of discourse? Like the dinner at Rivebelle, like the "little diplomatic Sodom," like the encounter of Charlus and Jupien, the narrator's book is about the momentary union, across great geographical, chronological, and social distances, of "like" with "like" (2: 613). It shares with the cities of the plain and with the stream of time itself a continual coming into and passing out of being: "Everything which strikes us as imperishable tends toward destruction [but] reconstructs itself every moment through a sort of perpetually continued creation. . . . The creation of the world did not take place in the beginning; it takes place every day" (3: 669).

THE ANDROGYNOUS VISION

As for your patron saint, my good Eulalie, Sancta Eulalia, *do you know what's happened to her in Burgundy? She's become a male saint known simply as Saint Eloi. So you see, Eulalie, after you die, they'll turn you into a man.* (1: 105)

"Monsieur le Curé will always have his little joke," Eulalie responds, when the Curé tells her that saints sometimes undergo sexual metamorphosis and that, in the afterlife, the same thing could happen to her. The little joke goes by very fleetingly in *Combray* but provides, nonetheless, one of our first glimpses of a recurrent motif in Proust's novel.

Since the publication of Carolyn Heilbrun's *Toward a Recognition of Androgyny* (1973) there has been a great deal of talk about "androgynous literature" and "the androgynous vision." Now that these labels have become fashionable, we often find them attached to works which offer very little explicit justification for them, works as unlikely and diverse as *The Odyssey* and *The Brothers Karamazov.* But in all this discussion of androgyny Proust, who wrote one of the most clearly and unmistakably androgynous of all novels, has been strangely ignored. Heilbrun says his work is "marvelously androgynous," but this is, quite literally, all she says about it.[25] To be sure,

Gilles Deleuze and Lisa Appignanesi have commented on the androgynous implications of *A la recherche*.[26] But a great deal remains to be said, especially with respect to Proust's concept of the "man-woman."

We have seen that Proust probably had many reasons for describing homosexually oriented men as "men-women," not the least of these being the high esteem in which this view was held in the medical science of Proust's day. But we have also seen that Proust eventually used the idea of the "man-woman" to suggest the androgynous nature of humanity in general. In this Proust was also a man of his time. A. J. L. Busst has shown that the art and literature of the nineteenth and early twentieth centuries were suffused with the image of an androgynous humanity, an image which occurred, according to Busst, more often in France than in the other European countries.[27] The psychology and natural science of the period also frequently revolved around concepts of androgyny. In *The Descent of Man* (1871) Darwin advanced the thesis that since among the vertebrates one sex appears to possess rudimentary sexual organs of the other and since "at a very early embryonic period both sexes possess true male and female glands . . . some remote progenitor of the whole vertebrate kingdom appears to have been hermaphrodite or androgynous."[28] These ideas, coupled with the "third sex" theory of the early sexologists, had a profound impact on Freud's view of sexuality. Arguing from the supposed androgyny of the first vertebrates and the apparent androgyny of the early stages of the human fetus, Freud asserted that humanity was fundamentally bisexual. He also thought, however, that a failure to overcome this fundamental bisexuality was evidence of psychopathology. Jung too emphasized the underlying androgyny of the human personality but was not as quick as Freud to label its manifestations pathological. He viewed the androgyne as an archetype of the collective unconscious and the human psyche as itself androgynous: men possessed an *anima*, or feminine aspect of the psyche, and women an *animus*, or masculine aspect of the psyche.[29] These beliefs led Jung to a liberal if somewhat mystical view of homosexuality. He said that homosexuality should probably not be considered an illness, because "the psychological findings show that it is rather a matter of incomplete detachment from the

hermaphroditic archetype, coupled with a distinct resistance to identify with the role of a one-sided sexual being. Such a disposition
should not be adjudged negative in all circumstances, in so far as it
preserves the archetype of the Original Man, which a one-sided sexual being has, up to a point, lost."[30]

And so it was frequently argued in the early modern period that
androgyny is a common human heritage. But at the same time it was
often urged that homosexually oriented men and women are the only
androgynous people and that andrognyny—whether its manifestations
are physical or purely mental and spiritual—is abnormal. Proust
stands somewhere near the center of this conflict of ideas and is
pulled in both directions by it. Like Freud he presents the "sexual invert" as a case of perversion. But he also tends, like Jung, to use the
"sexual invert" as a symbol of the fully integrated human personality,
the personality which resists identity as a one-sided sexual being and
becomes something more complete: the "man-woman."

This possibility of discovering a transcendent unity within the
duality of sex fascinated Proust throughout his life. He was, as he
reveals in a letter, fond of visualizing how male acquaintances would
look if suddenly transformed into women, and the converse. When he
was asked as a teenager to name his favorite heroines in fiction, he
said, "Those who are more than women without taking leave of their
sex." And on the questionnaire to which he responded around the age
of twenty ("Marcel Proust par lui-même") he made even more revealing comments. Asked to name "The quality I look for in a man," he
answered, "Feminine charms." And for "The quality I prefer in a
woman," he wrote, "Manly virtues and sincerity in camaraderie."[31]

In *A la recherche* this desire to break down the barriers between
the sexes is a fundamental part of the narrator's personality, for in
order to become an artist the narrator has to become androgynous
like his homosexual characters. This he does in part by recapturing,
through art, the feminine side of his personality. I say "recapturing,"
because the division of the narrator's personality into symbolic male
and female halves is one of the first examples of the fragmentation of
the self we witness in the novel. On the fourth and fifth pages of the
Pléiade edition, in the description of the narrator's half-waking, half-
sleeping state, we read:

Sometimes, just as Eve was born from Adam's rib, a woman was born during my sleep from a strained position in my thigh. She was formed from the pleasure I was about to experience, and I imagined that it was she who offered me that pleasure. My body, which sensed in hers its own warmth, tried to rejoin itself to her, and I awoke. The rest of humanity appeared very remote in comparison to this woman I had left only a few moments ago; my cheek was still warm with her kiss, my body was still bent beneath the weight of her form. If, as sometimes happened, she had the features of a woman I had known in life, I would give myself over entirely to one goal: finding her again. . . . (1: 4–5)

In a certain sense this is a prefiguration of all the love affairs to follow, in which the narrator thinks he is loving outside himself but is loving mainly projections of his own imagination and fantasy. In other words, throughout most of the novel the narrator looks outside and beyond himself for the feminine complement to his personality, when actually it has been within all along.

His love for Albertine is, among other things, a desperate and disappointing attempt to reconstruct in life a version of the mythic unity which obtained before Adam and Eve were divided, before man and woman became separate beings and separate concepts. There is a Rabbinical tradition with which Proust may have been familiar which holds that Adam was at first a hermaphroditic creature, half man and half woman, and that God created woman by simply dividing his original hermaphroditic creation. It was even thought by one ancient writer that Plato had read Genesis and had gotten from it the idea for the myth of the dual beings he assigns to Aristophanes in the *Symposium*.[32] Though there is no direct reference to the concept of a hermaphroditic Adam in *A la recherche*, something like this idea is clearly implied in the narrator's continuing fascination with Adam and Eve as symbols of the male and female modalities of a single personality. His desire for Albertine "made me dream . . . of mingling with my flesh a substance which was different and warm, of attaching at some point to my outstretched body a body which was divergent, just as Eve's body barely held by the feet to Adam's hip, to which she lies almost perpendicular, in the Romanesque bas-reliefs of the cathedral in Balbec" (2: 354). Sex with Albertine finally takes on a metaphysical dimension: it is nothing less than an attempt to undo the work of the Creator by rejoining the Male to the Female: "O lofty attitudes of

Man and Woman where, in the innocence of the first days and with the humility of clay, that which Creation has put asunder seeks to come together again" (3: 79).

This attempt to compete with God as a creator is, for Proust, one of the traits of the successful artist. Elstir's studio strikes the narrator as "the laboratory of a sort of new creation of the world"; and he says of Elstir's use of visual metaphor that "if God the Father had created things by naming them, it was by taking away their names, or by giving them another, that Elstir created them anew" (1: 834, 835). It is therefore appropriate that after being exposed to the visual metaphor which abounds in Elstir's painting the narrator should discover a portrait, *Miss Sacripant*, depicting a model of ambiguous sex dressed partly as a man and partly as a woman.[33] In this portrait, moreover, Elstir "had . . . seized upon these [sexually] ambiguous traits as upon an aesthetic principle which deserved to be thrown into relief and which he had done everything in his power to emphasize" (1: 849). The sexual ambiguity of *Miss Sacripant* is archetypal metaphor. We could almost say it is *the* archetypal metaphor. It is as if the narrator, in looking first at paintings which blur the distinction between land and sea and then at *Miss Sacripant*, has made his way back to the very origin of the metaphorical impulse. God separates the land from the water; Elstir puts them back together. God separates man from woman; Elstir puts them back together. The clear implication is that if Elstir were not able to do the one he would not be able to do the other. The demiurgic power of Elstir's painting has a profoundly erotic and a profoundly androgynous basis. As Proust elsewhere says of Gustave Moreau (one of the possible models for Elstir): "Gustave Moreau has often . . . attempted to create an abstract representation of The Poet. Dominating on a horse harnessed with gems . . . a kneeling crowd composed of the diverse castes of the Orient . . . enveloped in white muslin . . . inhaling with passionate solemnity the odor of the mystical flower he holds in his hand, his face imprinted with a celestial sweetness, one wonders, upon looking more closely, whether this poet might not be a woman. Perhaps Gustave Moreau wished to signify that the poet contains within himself the whole of humanity and that he must possess the tenderness of a woman." [34]

The androgyny of *Miss Sacripant* alludes to something people have felt throughout the ages about the source of the artist's godlike power to combine and recombine diverse realities. Transvestism as a kind of symbolic androgyny has often accompanied artistic and religious celebrations of human totality. Marie Delcourt points out that transvestism frequently figures in the lives of the gods and heroes of Greek mythology, for the Greeks believed it had the "power to promote health, youth, strength, longevity, perhaps even to confer a kind of immortality." Cross-dressing was also linked in the Greek tradition to the origin and practice of the creative arts. The Dionysian revels from which Greek tragedy and comedy developed featured an exchange of dress between the sexes, and Dionysus himself, the god of the theater, was often depicted as androgynous. In Aristophanes' *Frogs* Dionysus descends into Hades in search of a "fecund poet," one who incarnates the spirit of true artistic creativity. The costume Aristophanes thinks appropriate to such a quest is a mixture of masculine and feminine garb: he has Dionysus appear wearing the lion skin of Heracles over a saffron gown.[35]

In *A la recherche* the relationship between androgyny and creativity is made still more explicit in the conduct of the heavily made-up, effeminate dancer who rehearses backstage in the theater to which the narrator goes with Rachel and Saint-Loup: "in a cap of black velvet, in a hydrangea-colored skirt, his cheeks painted with rouge . . . a smile on his lips and his eyes turned toward heaven, tracing graceful signs with the palms of his hands and bounding lightly, [the young man] seemed . . . to belong to another species than the proper folk in jackets and frock coats, in the midst of whom he pursued like a madman his ecstatic dream" (2: 177). The appearance and the gestures of this dancer are pure theater, recalling at once the origins and the highest achievements of the art. Simultaneously Apollonian and Dionysian, they are ecstasy and madness carefully structured and controlled. The dancer seems at once to transcend the laws of nature and to combine the natural and the artificial in "natural arabesques," in "winged, capricious, painted frolics" (2: 177). Rachel comments: "it's really amazing what he can do with his hands. Even I, who am a woman, couldn't do what he's doing there" (2: 179).

The sexual ambiguity of the dancer reminds us that the god of the theater was himself androgynous: he was the "man-womanish" one, the "many-formed" one.[36] It reminds us too that those other "men-women" of A la recherche, Proust's homosexually oriented characters, are nothing if not themselves actors. Like the dancer, whose eyes and mouth, as they silently respond to Rachel's compliments, reveal the presence of another personality underneath the thick layers of makeup (2: 178), these characters display a constant, theatrical interpenetration of various modes of identity: half-hidden selves (the woman inside, the man who desires other men) and selves which are projected in order to survive (the "real man," the man who pretends to desire women). "Men-women" such as Charlus cannot choose but make their lives a form of theater, a form of art. As Weinberg and Williams point out, the feeling of being constantly "on stage"—of "being unable to present themselves authentically"—is a feeling known to most homosexually oriented people in the West.[37]

Consider, for example, the scene where Charlus attempts to attract the young narrator's attention in front of the casino in Balbec:

He hurled at me a supreme leer, which was at once bold, prudent, rapid, and profound, as one might fire one last shot just as one decides to beat a retreat, and, having glanced all around, suddenly adopted a distracted and haughty air; with an abrupt revolution of his entire person he turned toward a poster and absorbed himself in the reading of it, humming a tune and arranging the moss rose he wore in his buttonhole. He took a notebook out of his pocket and seemed to be jotting down the title of the performance which the poster announced, pulled out his watch two or three times, lowered over his eyes a black straw hat and extended its brim by placing his hand upon it like a visor, as if to see whether someone was finally arriving, made that gesture of annoyance which people use to indicate they have waited long enough but which they never make when they are really waiting, then, pushing back his hat to reveal closely cropped hair, which, however, gave way at each temple to two rather long, undulating "pigeon wings," he emitted that loud sigh people employ when they are not, in reality, too hot but would like people to think they are. I thought he was probably a hotel swindler who had been watching my grandmother and me for several days, preparatory to taking us in, and who had just noticed that I had noticed him while he was spying on me. . . .
(1: 751–52)

Charlus's pantomime is a concentration of procedures which are basic to the theater, to art in general, and to Proust's art in particular. We notice the "abrupt revolution of his entire person," a gesture which anticipates the sexual peripety of *Sodome I* and which also alludes, perhaps, to Proust's fondness for theatrical inversions of every variety, in which one aspect of reality is eclipsed in order that another may be revealed. Eric Bentley writes:

Nothing seems more clearly written into the lawbook of dramatic art . . . than that its first principle is concealment, its first implement (as well as symbol) the mask. True, this concealment can be regarded as a paradox. Just as one can *reculer pour mieux sauter*, so to conceal can be preparatory to revealing. . . . But here again we are in the realm of metaphor. Nothing physical is uncovered at the end of a comedy, or, if it is, as for instance by the removal of a disguise, there are other clothes underneath. . . . Pirandello called his plays "naked masks," not "naked faces," to express, among other things, his sense that the mask is itself an ultimate in the theater.[38]

—as it usually is, of course, in *A la recherche*.

In Charlus's pantomime we see masks behind and within masks. The severely cropped hair is the conventional mask of masculinity. But this mask is framed, softened, and feminized by the flowing "pigeon wings" (*ailes de pigeon*) Charlus has allowed to sprout at his temples. Here and elsewhere the characterization of Charlus is haunted by the androgyny of the god of the theater and is, in fact, a commentary on what that androgyny signifies. Discussing Dionysus the "man-woman" and cross-dressing in the theater in general, Jean Gillibert states: "the actor . . . at the beginning of Attic tragedy, became . . . a priest, an initiator, an interpreter. Magic [and] demiurgic creation would be his lot . . . and the basis for his future persecution. . . . The idea of what we call in the West 'an actor' implies . . . this register of totality. If one 'plays a role,' then one is capable of playing everything: man, woman, life, death. One needs only to find the guide marks, the reference points, the conventional signs."[39]

The narrator seems to have similar ideas in mind when he comments that "the young [sexually inverted] man we have just tried to depict was so obviously a woman that women who looked at him with desire were doomed . . . to the same disappointment as the women who, in Shakespeare's comedies, are deceived by a girl in disguise who passes herself off as a boy. The illusion is the same, the invert himself knows it, he divines the disillusionment the woman will experience once the disguise is removed, and he feels the extent to which this error about sex is a source of fanciful poetry" (2: 621). The narrator compares his art to the art of Shakespeare's comedies and his homosexually oriented characters to the girls in those comedies who disguise themselves as boys. The comparison is apt, since in Shakespeare these sexually ambiguous characters—Northrop Frye calls them "Eros figures"—are, as are the "men-women" in Proust, harbingers of inspiration, embodiments of ways of understanding which go beyond those of ordinary reality. In *Twelfth Night*, as Frye points out, "Orsino and Olivia are languishing in melancholy until out of the sea comes an ambiguous figure 'that can sing both high and low,' who eventually becomes male to Olivia and female to Orsino and so crystallizes the comic society."[40] And in *As You Like It* Rosalind, in her disguise as a boy, tells Orlando: "Believe, then, if you please, that I can do strange things. I have, since I was three year old, conversed with a magician, most profound in his art. . . . I say I am a magician" (v.ii. 59–61, 71). Proust's fondness for having Charlus appear in thicker and thicker makeup as he grows older may be, in part, a pandering to stereotype (3: 207). On another level, however, it reminds us that Charlus is constantly on stage, that he always has something to hide, and that in a work filled with actors, directors, and theaters of various kinds he is the quintessence of all these things (cf. 3: 232). In the scene before the casino the narrator fails to understand that Charlus is making a sexual advance to him. But in taking Charlus for a swindler he glimpses something much more basic to Charlus's conduct: it is an allegory of the metaphysical swindling of art itself.

The performance of the effeminate dancer has something else in common with Proust's "men-women": it recaptures lost time by evoking the idea of something "anterior to the practices of . . . civilization" (2: 177). The narrator here emphasizes that he wishes to associate androgyny not only with totality but with primal totality. Dreams in *A la recherche* serve as a means of contacting the history of the race. And dreams, appropriately, are inhabited by a "race which . . . like the first race of humans, is androgynous. [In dreams] a man, after a moment, takes on the appearance of a woman" (2: 981). We see an example of this oneiric androgyny when, in Swann's dream toward the end of *Un Amour de Swann*, Mme Verdurin suddenly sprouts a mustache (1: 379). Similarly, speaking of homosexually oriented men who attempt to trace their ancestry to the ancient Orient or to classical Greece, the narrator comments that "inverts . . . could go back further still, to those experimental epochs when neither dioecious plants nor unisexual animals existed, to that initial hermaphroditism of which a few rudiments of male organs in the anatomy of the female and female organs in the anatomy of the male seem to preserve the trace" (2: 629).

The narrator has now modulated from myth back to science. He is alluding to the Darwinian theory of primal hermaphroditism and to the many attempts which were made after Darwin to explain homosexuality with reference to this idea. The immediate source may be the following passage from Krafft-Ebing:

> Later researchers . . . proceeding on embryological (onto- and phylogenetic) and anthropological lines seem to promise good results.
> Emanating from *Frank Lydston* ("Philadelphia Med. and Surg. Recorder," September, 1888) and *Kiernan* ("Medical Standard," November, 1888), they are based (1) on the fact that bisexual organization is still found in the lower animal kingdom, and (2) on the supposition that mono-sexuality gradually developed from bisexuality. *Kiernan* assumes in trying to subordinate sexual inversion to the category of hermaphroditism that in individuals thus affected retrogression into the earlier hermaphrodisic [*sic*] forms of the animal kingdom may take place at least functionally. These are his own words: "The original bisexuality of the ancestors of the race, shown in the rudimentary female organs of the male, could not fail to occasion functional, if not organic reversions, when mental or physical manifestations were interfered with by disease or congenital defect."[41]

So in order to recapture lost time in art, in order to make his book a history of the race as well as a history of an individual life, the narrator must rediscover and exploit in his novel something of, on the mythic level, the androgyny of primal humanity and, on the scientific level, the hermaphroditism of the first plants and animals; and then he must show how the two relate. This he does in *Sodome I* in the comparisons of the courtship of Charlus and Jupien—those androgynous inhabitants of the mythical city of Sodom—to various processes of mating and fertilization which occur in nature. Jupien has been placed on earth for the specific purpose of serving the sexual needs of older men, just as certain hermaphroditic flowers exist for the purpose of fertilizing other hermaphroditic flowers which otherwise would remain sterile; he is "indifferent to the advances of other young men, just as the short-styled, hermaphroditic flowers of the *Primula veris* remain sterile so long as they are fertilized only by another short-styled *Primula veris*, whereas they welcome with joy the pollen of the long-styled *Primula veris*" (2: 628).

Biologically, of course, the union of Charlus and Jupien is sterile. But according to the narrator a special kind of fertilization can occur in homosexual love, a spiritual fecundity comparable (though he does not draw the comparison directly) to the intellectual and artistic inspiration homosexuality provides in Plato's *Symposium:* "here the word 'fecundation' must be understood in the moral sense, since in the physical sense the union of male with male is sterile, but it is not unimportant that an individual may encounter the only pleasure he is able to enjoy, and that 'here below every creature' can impart to another 'its music, its flame, or its fragrance' " (2: 627). The quotations in this passage are from Victor Hugo's poem "Puisqu'ici-bas toute âme." In this poem the poet first enumerates various processes of giving and then enumerates the things which, in like manner, he is able to give his beloved:

> Puisqu'ici-bas toute âme
>   Donne à quelqu'un
> Sa musique, sa flamme,
>   Ou son parfum;
>
> Puisqu'ici toute chose
>   Donne toujours
> Son épine ou sa rose
>   A ses amours;
>
> Puisqu'avril donne aux chênes
>   Un bruit charmant;
> Que la nuit donne aux peines
>   L'oubli dormant;
>
>   .   .   .
>
> Je te donne, à cette heure,
>   Penché sur toi,
> La chose la meilleure
>   Que j'aie en moi!

Reçois donc ma pensée,
 Triste d'ailleurs,
Qui, comme une rosée,
 T'arrive en pleurs!

.   .   .

Mes transports pleins d'ivresses,
 Purs de soupçons,
Et toutes les caresses
 De mes chansons![42]

The allusion to Hugo underscores a point the text itself makes abundantly clear. The homosexually oriented characters in *A la recherche* may not produce mortal children. But, like Plato's homosexual lovers, they can produce "children more beautiful and more immortal":[43] thought, spirit, intellect, art. Mlle Vinteuil's relationship with her female friend brings her father so much pain that it probably hastens his death, causing him to leave his Septet incomplete. But this same relationship later assures Vinteuil of "the compensation of an immortal glory," when Mlle Vinteuil's friend deciphers the composer's notes and reconstructs his masterpiece after his death (3: 262). Similarly, it is partly because of the relationship of Charlus and Morel that the Vinteuil Septet is performed at the Verdurins' reception, where the narrator hears it and is inspired by it (3: 264). "From relationships not consecrated by the laws," the narrator says, "issue ties of kinship as manifold, as complex, and even as solid as those which are born from marriage" (3: 262). This passage on the Vinteuil Septet is, in part, a celebration of the often ignored fact that homosexual relationships can be just as meaningful, just as productive, and just as influential on later generations as heterosexual relationships.

In Plato's *Symposium* Diotima says that "those who are pregnant in body . . turn rather to women . . . and thus, by begetting children, secure for themselves, so they think, immortality and memory and happiness . . . but those who are pregnant in soul . . . conceive in soul still more than in body . . . [and] to this class belong all creative poets, and those artists and craftsmen who are said to be inventive."[44] The *Symposium* thus elevates homosexual love over heterosexual love as a source of artistic inspiration, and sometimes *A la recherche* does this as well, as in the theoretical passages which suggest that homosexually oriented people are more aesthetically sensitive than heterosexually oriented people. In its dramatizations of human relationships, however, the novel tells a different story. The course of history, the shape of society, the personalities of the major characters, the creation, transmission, and interpretation of art are influenced in A la recherche by both kinds of love, sometimes directly, sometimes only indirectly. Heterosexuality impinges on the fate of Charlus just as surely as homosexuality impinges on the fate of Swann. For Proust life is a complex network of crisscrossing destinies in which no human relationship and no individual identity is without the potential for profoundly altering the world.

The special fecundity the narrator sometimes attributes to homosexual love arises partly from the ability of his homosexually oriented characters to function as complementary selves: one partner supplies what the other lacks and thereby, in the words of Aristophanes' myth, "heal[s] the natural structure of man." From the social perspective the beggar unites with the aristocrat, the ambassador with the convict, the priest with the male prostitute, the young man with the old man—and society becomes an organic whole. From the aesthetic perspective Morel's technical skill on the violin finds its perfect complement in Charlus's ability as an accompanist: "I felt that [Charlus] would give to Morel, who was marvelously gifted with respect to virtuosity and tone, exactly those traits he lacked: culture and style" (2: 953). From the erotic perspective the fair and the somber, the brilliant and the brooding, unite in the love affair of Saint-Loup and Morel: "It is possible that Morel, who was extremely dark, was as necessary to [the blond] Saint-Loup as shadow is to the sunbeam" (3: 705).

This complementariness is strengthened by the androgyny the narrator associates with homosexuality. In the conjunction of two Proustian "men-women" there is a simultaneous conjunction of male with male, female with female, and male with female. "Real man" unites with "real man," anima unites with anima, and anima unites transversally with "real man." On both the mythic and the scientific levels this union should be extraordinarily fecund and powerful. It reverses the flow of time by recovering the hermaphroditism of the first plants and animals, and it simultaneously restores body and mind to the androgynous perfection of the mythic dream. It returns to Adam, Eve, and Adam-Eve; to Sodom, Gomorrah, and Sodom-Gomorrah; to the male-male, female-female, and male-female of Aristophanes' myth.

Throughout *Sodome I* the narrator emphasizes that the cross-fertilization of hermaphrodites is not simply a product of the mythological imagination but is something which can actually be observed in nature, in "what happens with so many hermaphroditic flowers and even with certain hermaphroditic animals, such as the snail, which cannot fertilize themselves but can be fertilized by other hermaphrodites" (2: 629). The process by which Jupien finds himself attracted to older men is, the narrator says, "a phenomenon of correspondence and of harmony comparable to that which regulates the fertilization of heterostyle trimorphous flowers such as the [hermaphroditic] *Lythrum salicaria*" (2: 628). The source of this image and of the reference to the *Primula veris* on the same page is probably Darwin's treatise *The Different Forms of Flowers on Plants of the Same Species* (translated into French in 1878).[45] Describing in that work the manner in which the three forms of the hermaphroditic *Lythrum salicaria* pollinate each other, Darwin gives a similar emphasis to the complexity of the sexual patterns:

Two of the three hermaphrodites must coexist, and pollen must be carried by insects reciprocally from one to the other, in order that either of the two should be fully fertile; but unless all three forms coexist, two sets of stamens will be wasted, and the organisation of the species, as a whole, will be incomplete. On the other hand, when all three hermaphrodites coexist, and pollen is carried from one to the other, the scheme is perfect; there is no waste of pollen and no false co-adaptation. In short, nature has ordained a most complex marriage-arrangement, namely a triple union between three hermaphrodites. . . .[46]

Sodome I uses words such as "miracle," "marvelous," "correspondence," "harmony" (2: 628) and thereby invites its readers to appreciate the wonders of another kind of "marriage-arrangement," one from which they might ordinarily turn away in disgust.

The narrator is writing, then, within the best traditions of nineteenth-century natural history when he makes this appeal to the artistry and formal beauty of nature. For another parallel we could turn to a contemporary description of the courtship ritual of snails (the hermaphroditic animals to whose mating the narrator alludes in the passage quoted at the beginning of the preceding paragraph). The description is from Havelock Ellis's *Analysis of the Sexual Impulse* (1903):

It begins toward midnight on sultry summer nights, one slug slowly following another, resting its mouth on what may be called the tail of the first, and following its every movement. Finally they stop and begin crawling around each other, emitting large quantities of mucus. When this has constituted a mass of sufficient size and consistence they suspend themselves from it by a cord of mucus from nine to fifteen inches in length, continuing to turn round each other till their bodies form a cone. Then the organs of generation are protruded from their orifice near the mouth and, hanging down a short distance, touch each other. They also then begin again the same spiral motion, twisting around each other, like a two-strand cord, assuming various and beautiful forms, sometimes like an inverted agaric, or a foliated murex, or a leaf of curled parsley, the light falling on the ever-varying surface of the generative organs sometimes producing iridescence. It is not until after a considerable time that the organs untwist and are withdrawn and the bodies separate, to crawl up the suspending cord and depart.[47]

The naturalist makes us see beauty in the mating of snails, and the narrator makes us see beauty in a homosexual encounter. The reader's reaction to *Sodome I* is meant to follow the same course as the narrator's changing reaction to the jellyfish. When he first saw this animal at Balbec, the narrator says, he was repelled by it; but when he looked at it as did Michelet, "from the point of view of aesthetics and natural history," it suddenly became "a delightful girandole of azure" (2: 626). Just so the narrator says of the encounter of Charlus and Jupien that "this scene was, moreover, not positively comical; it was stamped with a strangeness, or, if you will, a naturalness whose beauty continually increased" (2: 605). The beauty is natural; the beauty is strange. The narrator is here fulfilling one of the most basic duties of the artist: to reveal beauty where little has been thought to exist and in places where people have been previously ill inclined to look for it. Later, in a discussion of the homosexuality of M. de Vaugoubert and M. de Charlus, he makes this aspect of his goal explicit:

the author wishes to emphasize how disappointed he would be if the reader took offense at such strange portrayals. . . . To say that this sort of thing is alien to us and that poetry should be derived from truths which are familiar

to us would be a serious . . . objection if it were justified. There is, indeed, a
type of art based on the most familiar reality, and its domain is perhaps the
largest. But it is also true that great interest, and sometimes beauty, can issue
from actions which stem from a turn of mind so remote from everything we
feel, from everything we believe, that we are not even able to bring ourselves
to understand them, that they unfold before us like a spectacle without a
cause. (3: 46–47)

The narrator insists, then, on preserving the "strangeness" as well as
the "naturalness" and the "beauty." His comparison of homosexual
love to various processes of fertilization in nature is not aimed, as
some have thought, at showing that homosexuality is natural and good
rather than unnatural and evil. It is aimed, rather, at transcending
and redefining conventional notions of what is good or evil, natural or
unnatural. *Sodome I* undermines our complacent conceptions of what
nature is and replaces them with a vision of the awesome things nature tends to be. The "man-woman" is the nexus—gracefully grotesque, harmoniously hideous—of all the unnamed and dimly
imagined potentialities of nature. "The multiplicity of these comparisons," the narrator says, "is itself all the more natural in that the same
man, if we study him for a few minutes, seems successively a man, a
man-bird, a man-fish, a man-insect" (2: 606). In the same spirit the
narrator later compares the homosexually oriented man to a centaur
(2: 614). This comparison is particularly appropriate, since in *A la
recherche* these men embody the intellectual power and aesthetic
sensitivity of that very special centaur Chiron and the grotesquerie,
brutishness, and ugliness of the other centaurs, those who represent
the negative modality of the horse-man concept—mutation, freak,
lusus naturae.

   Once we follow Proust to this level of meaning, the traditional
complaint that Albertine, Gilberte, and certain other female characters in *A la recherche* are unconvincing because they have too many
masculine characteristics dwindles to insignificance. Critics tell us
that the episode where the young narrator wrestles with the young
Gilberte and has an orgasm from the contact of their bodies
(1: 493–94) should be read as "really" a homosexual experience between two boys, because, as Jocelyn Brooke puts it, "it was surely
rather unusual for young girls so *bien élevées* as Gilberte to wrestle

with boys in the park; and it seems pretty certain that Marcel's partner was, in reality, of his own sex." Or they tell us that when Albertine moves into the narrator's apartment, we are to understand that the arrangement is "really" a homosexual liaison, because, in the words of André Maurois, it would be "absolutely inconceivable" for a young man and a young woman to live unmarried together "before the war of 1914," when the episode is supposed to take place.[48] And then there is the first description of Albertine among the little band of girls at Balbec. Does she not seem in that description more like a boy than a girl, as she appears "pushing a bicycle with an ungainly rolling of her hips and . . . using slang which was so vulgar and so loudly uttered . . . that . . . I concluded . . . that all these girls belonged to the crowd which frequented the cycle tracks" (1: 793)?

It is easily granted that these scenes attribute traits to Gilberte and Albertine which are more often associated with boys than with girls. But it does not follow that the girls Proust describes are "really" boys. It only follows that Proust describes girls who do things girls do not ordinarily do, just as he describes men who seem at times to turn into women. Proust never shows us a female doing something a female could never do. Critics who think he does probably have, as Maurice Bardèche says, "a mistaken idea of what the girls of 1909 were like"[49]—or a mistaken idea of what girls and women in general are like. In A la recherche there are many scenes in which women usurp traditionally masculine roles. But in all the novel—even in the sections of La Prisonnière and La Fugitive directly inspired by Proust's love for Alfred Agostinelli—there is not a single scene in which we are required to read "boy" for "girl," "man" for "woman" or "he" for "she" before the novel makes sense.

To accept the literal level of the narrative does not mean that we must then close our minds to the figurative and symbolic level, where we find, after all, an "Albert" within "Albertine," a "Gilbert" within "Gilberte," and an "André" within "Andrée." We must, however, leave the "Albert" within "Albertine" rather than taking it out and displaying it as a revelation of what the author "really" means. If we transpose and retranspose the sexes in an attempt to force Proust's work to make sense in conventional sexual terms, we miss the point. Proust did not play the pronoun game of so many homosexually oriented novelists and poets. In his manuscripts and notebooks there are no examples of "he's" changed to "she's" or male names changed to female names for the purpose of disguising the actual sex of the beloved.[50] Proust did not play the pronoun game because he had no need to play it. The famous sexual transpositions, when they take place, take place in Proust's mind and spirit, before he puts pen to paper. They are not attempts to conceal the truth about the author's sexual experience; they are attempts to reveal the truth about that experience.

It is justifiable, then, to criticize Proust for sometimes distorting the truth about homosexuality. But it is not justifiable to criticize Proust for portraying girls and women in roles generally considered to be more masculine than feminine. In the former case Proust submits to prejudice; in the latter case he rebels against it. The truth about A la recherche is the converse of what critics generally take it to be. The parts of the novel which "groan and wail" over the tragedy of being a homosexual "man-woman" and of suffering from homosexual "disease" have little to do with reality as it was then or as it is now. They are endorsements of stereotype. The parts of the novel which depict girls and women in rebellion against traditional female roles, on the other hand, shatter stereotype and challenge some of the most fundamental assumptions of Western culture. That is why these sections have been denounced and rejected as unconvincing, while the sections which preserve the conventional view of homosexuality have been applauded as faithful representations of reality. The miracle of the novel is that, ultimately, the two visions are made to intermesh, so that what begins as homosexual stereotype ends by becoming itself a challenge to traditional conceptions of sexuality and gender. Proust constructs the novel in such a way that no matter which aspect of the vision we at first accept—the challenge to stereotype or the inculcation of stereotype—we end by revising our views of what it is to be a man and what it is to be a woman.

The view of the sexes at which the narrator finally arrives contradicts the view Alfred de Vigny develops in "La Colère de Samson," the poem which gave Proust the second epigraph for Sodome et Gomorhe ("Woman will have Gomorrah and Man will have Sodom"). In Vigny's poem the full context of the epigraph is as follows:

Soon, withdrawing into a hideous realm,
Woman will have Gomorrah and Man will have Sodom,
And, directing at each other remote, angry glances,
The two sexes will die, each on its own side.[51]

As he writes his novel, the narrator reverses this conception and dramatizes the fact that the demarcation between masculine and feminine is, as with so many other modes of Proustian ontology, often only a question of shifting perspective. This is the case in the portrait *Miss Sacripant*, where, before the narrator's fascinated gaze, "the sex seemed about to declare that it was that of a slightly boyish girl, vanished, then reappeared again further on, suggesting instead the idea of an effeminate, vicious, and dreamy young man, then fled once more, remained elusive" (1: 849). The bisexual visual perspectives of this symbolic portrait are reflected in the constantly shifting erotic perspectives of the novel's love affairs. Saint-Loup seems to fall in love with Morel partly because he notices a resemblance between Morel and Rachel (3: 682–83, 686). And it is suggested that Albertine loves the narrator partly because of a resemblance between the narrator and Andrée. Once, when the narrator and Albertine are in bed together, Albertine, half-awake, addresses him as "Andrée" (3: 114). And later, when he is questioning Andrée about Albertine's supposed lesbianism, he glances into a mirror and realizes that he does, in fact, bear a resemblance to Andrée, to this girl with whom Albertine perhaps had a concurrent lesbian affair while she was his mistress (3: 549). The characters in *A la recherche* often function as erotic anagrams of each other, a fact Proust seems to underscore by sometimes making them, as Serge Gaubert has shown, linguistic anagrams of each other as well. Robert de Saint-Loup loves both Charles Morel and the actress Rachel, and "Charles" is a near anagram of "Rachel." Charlus also loves Charles Morel, known as Charlie, and "Charlus," "Charles," and "Charlie" are almost the same word. Charlie Morel is also loved by the narrator's friend Robert de Saint-Loup, and "Robert de Saint-Loup" contains all the letters necessary to spell "Albertine." (The letters which are left over—ignoring the "de"—are the letters we need to spell "Proust.") The narrator loves both Albertine and Gilberte, and Gilberte signs her name in such a way that it can easily be mistaken for "Albertine" (1: 502; 3: 656). At one point Charlus tries to persuade Morel to adopt the stage name "Charmel"—a name which seems to combine the names "Charlus" and "Charles" with the name "Marcel" (2: 1,062). And so on.[52] The apparent system of anagrams does not, of course, involve every character and does not apply flawlessly even to the characters it seems to involve. But the principle seems pervasive enough and suggestive enough to represent a deliberate artistic strategy. As Leo Bersani has noticed, "there are important psychological parallels between Marcel and the people he is supposedly remembering from his past, parallels which make us feel that the objective report on reality is actually a self-dramatization by means of novelistic character and incident."[53] Not the least of these parallels is the manner in which the narrator exemplifies in so many ways his own analysis of homosexual psychology. There are, of course, important differences between the narrator and his homosexually oriented characters as well as striking similarities. But Proust nonetheless constantly suggests that the kaleidoscopic interrelationships among the people in A la recherche can, from one point of view, be understood as projections of desires and conflicts which are basic not only to the personality of his imaginary novelist but to the personality of Marcel Proust as well.

Lisa Appignanesi has argued that Proust views creativity as a special province of the feminine and that the narrator's art springs from the feminine characteristics he adopts from the women he knows.[54] This is an oversimplification. Proust's vision is not feminine: it is androgynous. If we assert, along with Appignanesi, that the narrator becomes an artist by imitating the women in his life, what do we then do with his declaration that "in sum, if I reflected upon the question, [I realized that] the material of my experience, which would be the material of my book, came to me from Swann" (3: 915). And what do we do with the fact that Bergotte, Elstir, and Vinteuil— the writer, the painter, and the composer who furnish the narrator with a significant part of his inspiration—are male? Proust's recurrent message is that to be an artist is to be able to comprehend and draw upon a multitude of different experiences and perspectives. That the narrator has been able to create both men and women in art implies that he has identified with and understood both men and women in life.

The point is that for Proust there are no easy solutions to the mysteries of identity and of inspiration. Proust occasionally writes as if there were, as when he has the narrator declare melodramatically that Charlus is really a woman. Statements such as this reveal that one side of Proust was sorely tempted by the simple answer. But the rest of the novel reveals how another side of Proust scrutinized and qualified the simple answers which sometimes tempted him the most. Even androgyny, with all its complexities, is not the final answer in Proust. It is a trapdoor through which we enter realms of even greater ontological complexity: man-bird, man-insect, man-fish, man-horse, man-flower, and so on through the whole range of cosmic possibility.

These greater complexities are clearly visible in the narrator's re-action to a letter about Albertine written by Aimé. The narrator has sent Aimé to Touraine to investigate Albertine's activities there, and Aimé's letter brings apparent confirmation of the narrator's worst fears. According to Aimé, Albertine had a lesbian affair with a young laundress in Touraine. The laundress, he says, would meet Albertine in a wooded spot by the water early in the morning, where, in the company of some of the laundress's girl friends, they would go swimming and then lie around in the grass exchanging caresses. Albertine would undress, and the laundress would lick her naked body, even the soles of her feet, causing Albertine to exclaim: "Ah! You send me to heaven!" Then the laundress would undress as well, and she and Albertine would play at pushing each other into the water (3: 524–25).

This letter plunges the narrator into a paroxysm of jealousy and creates a suggestive interplay of memory and fantasy:

I had as a matter of fact seen two paintings by Elstir depicting two nude women against a leafy landscape. In one of them, one of the girls is raising her foot as Albertine must have done when she held it out to the laundress. With the other foot she is pushing the other girl into the water, and this girl is merrily resisting, raising her thigh and barely dipping her foot into the blue water. I now recalled that this elevation of the thigh created, with the angle of the knee, the same swan's-neck curve as the fall of Albertine's thigh when she lay beside me on the bed, and I had often wanted to tell her she reminded me of these paintings. But I had not done so, in order to avoid awakening in her the image of nude female bodies. Now I saw her, with the

laundress and her girl friends, recomposing the group I had loved so much
when I was seated in the midst of Albertine's girl friends in Balbec. And if I
had been a connoisseur sensitive to beauty alone, I would have seen that Albertine recomposed this group a thousand times more beautifully, now that
its elements were nude statues of goddesses like those the great sculptors
scattered under the thickets at Versailles or gave to the fountains to be
washed and polished by the caresses of the billows. And now, by the side of
the laundress, I saw her as a girl by the seashore, more so than she had been
for me in Balbec: in their double nudity of feminine marbles, in the midst of
the bushes and the vegetation, and soaking in the water like nautical bas-
reliefs. Remembering what she looked like as she lay upon my bed, I thought
I saw her curved thigh, I saw it, it was a swan's neck, it was seeking the
mouth of the other girl. Then I no longer saw even the thigh but the bold
neck of a swan, like that which, in a throbbing picture, seeks the mouth of a
Leda depicted in all the specific palpitation of feminine pleasure, because
there is only a swan, because she seems all the more alone. . . . In this picture the pleasure, instead of going toward the woman who inspires it, who is
absent and replaced by an inert swan, is concentrated in the woman who
feels it. (3: 527–28)

This passage describes nothing less than a mystical experience, a
glimpse of the hidden harmony of the natural, the unnatural, and the
supernatural. The narrator remembers Albertine as she lay in bed beside him with her thigh curved like a swan's neck; and he remembers
her as she appeared among the little band of young girls in Balbec.
These memories meld into Aimé's description of the lesbian activities
in Touraine, and the resulting vision is superimposed upon two other
memories: that of a painting by Elstir depicting female nudes and that
of a picture depicting Leda and the swan. The result is not a memory,
not a fantasy, not a work of art: it is all these things at the same time,
a complex imaginative reticulation in which Apollonian clarity and
grace are shot through at every point with Dionysian grotesquerie
and abandon. Albertine seems at once heterosexual (the girl who
slept with the narrator), lesbian (the girl who extends her foot to the
mouth of the laundress), inanimate (the girl who freezes into a bas-
relief), human (the playful nude in the woods), animal (the girl whose
leg suddenly becomes the neck of a swan), and divine (the girl who is
both Leda and the swan and who is a part of a group which suggests
statues of nude goddesses). She is a figment of the imagination; an
emblem of transcendent fecundity, impregnation, and metamor-

phosis; a point at which life intersects suggestively with various modes of artistic creation; and the center of a symbolic, mythic drama which generates both suffering and beauty. It would be difficult to find a better summation of her role and of the role of sexuality in general in Proust's art.

It may be that Albertine does not "live" as convincingly as some of Proust's other characters. But this is partly because Proust uses Albertine to redefine conventional conceptions of literary character. Etymologically the word "character" denotes an impress, a distinctive mark, a well-defined outline. This is what it meant to Theophrastus in his *Characters*, and this is what it has traditionally meant in literature. Proust dismisses this concept and shows that except on the most superficial levels of understanding there is no well-defined outline for human identity. Proust depicts the unlimited, the limitless personality. We are never given indisputable proof of any of the claims made about Albertine in the novel. We never even get incontrovertible evidence of her supposed lesbianism. She may be, or she may not be. Albertine is ambiguity, and ambiguity is Albertine. Proust leaves her free, along with the narrator, to imply and become anything in human experience. And yet critics complain that Proust has failed to give us an Albertine who is convincing in everyday terms. This criticizes Proust for not doing something he never intended to do. If we could close the novel and declare that now, at last, we have captured Albertine, then, and only then, could we say the portrait of Albertine is a failure. Jocelyn Brooke, who thinks Albertine is nothing more than a failed sexual transposition, says she is "the flattest of flat characters."[55] Quite the contrary. She is, to borrow an image from *Combray*, like "that game in which the Japanese play at dipping into a porcelain bowl filled with water little pieces of paper which until then are indistinct but which, once plunged into the water, stretch out, take on contours, colorations, nuances, become flowers, houses, people" (1: 47). Any facet of Albertine's character, when bathed in the fluid medium of Proust's art, expands to produce not just a character but a world.

On the final page of *A la recherche* the narrator says he wishes to depict people as they exist in time, "even if this should make them resemble monstrous creatures" (3: 1,048). The homosexually oriented characters in *A la recherche* are precisely this, monsters of time, and monsters not only in the usual sense (a combination of ontologically disparate elements) but also, and especially, in one of the possible etymological senses (Latin *monstrum:* a portent, an omen). In their androgyny, in their plurality of being, both the evolutionary and the mythic history of the race remain strikingly visible and accessible. They have that comprehensive reach across the chain of being and the span of time which the novel as a whole describes and imitates. Through them the narrator is able to achieve a goal of characterization he enunciates as early as *Un Amour de Swann*—the goal of "extracting from the simple forms [of man] a richness so varied that it seems to be borrowed from the entirety of living nature" (1: 324).

To love a homosexually oriented person is, the narrator says, "to desire Protogonos 'with the dual sex, with the bellow of a bull, with the numerous orgies, the memorable one, the indescribable one, who goes down joyously to the sacrifices of the Orgiophants' " (2: 840). This passage—borrowed from Leconte de Lisle's translation of the Orphic hymns[56]—is a microcosm of one aspect of the sexual symbolism in *A la recherche*. In the Orphic cosmogony Protogonos ("Firstborn") was the name given to Eros, the first god to come into existence and the creator of all things. According to the Orphic myths Protogonos-Eros was hatched from the cosmic egg fashioned by Chronos ("Time"). Not only was he male and female but he also had, in Robert Graves's description, "four heads [and] sometimes roared like a bull or a lion, sometimes hissed like a serpent or bleated like a ram."[57] He was both a symbol and a seed of the pluralistic universe he proceeded to create. His androgyny and monstrosity were affirmations of his totality and of his power to mediate between Chronos and Creation. In *A la recherche* Charlus the "man-woman"—also called "this powerful monster" (3: 204)—is the equivalent of the Orphic Protogonos. And so is the Albertine of the narrator's lesbian fantasies, the Albertine who is a swan-girl, an animal-goddess, a lover of men and a lover of women, an "orgiastic Muse" (1: 873), "a sorceress holding out to me a mirror of Time" (2: 351), "a great goddess of Time" (3: 387). These characters symbolize both the fragmenting and distorting effect of time on the personality and the multifaceted ontology the narrator must acquire in order to defeat time through artistic creation.

The homosexually oriented characters in *A la recherche* know what it is like to be a creature of dual sex; the narrator spends a great deal of time and effort trying to find this out. "Moreover," he says, "the idea that a woman had perhaps had relations with Albertine no longer caused me anything but a desire to have relations myself with this woman. I told this to Andrée, while I caressed her. Then . . . Andrée said to me with a secret smile: 'Ah, yes, but you are a man. And so we can't do quite the same things together that I used to do with Albertine' " (3: 599). The narrator's jealousy of lesbian love amounts, ultimately, to ontological and metaphysical jealousy. What drives him to the brink of madness is the realization that, in order to understand Albertine fully, he would have to become a woman himself, while remaining at the same time a man.[58] In the literal sense this is impossible. But in the aesthetic sense it can be achieved. Although the narrator cannot actually transform himself into Albertine or take Albertine's place with another woman, he can do the next best thing: he can write a novel in which he searches for and analyzes the aspects of his personality which led him to desire Albertine in the first place. After all, as the narrator points out early in the novel, the women we love are only "an image, a projection in reverse, a 'negative' of our own sensibility" (1: 894). When the narrator attempts to merge so closely with Albertine that the boundaries of male and female are effectively erased, he is striving for more than androgyny. He wishes to incorporate Albertine into his own personality; but Albertine herself has already incorporated whole worlds and universes, at least in the narrator's imagination. Love, according to *A la recherche*, has as its object "the extension of [the beloved being] to all the points in space and time that this being has occupied and will occupy" (3: 100). Or, to put it another way, "it was within me that Albertine's possible actions took place" (3: 252).

The ultimate monster of time in *A la recherche* and the ultimate harbinger of the narrator's creative work is Mlle de Saint-Loup, the daughter of Gilberte Swann and Robert de Saint-Loup. At the reception given by the Princesse de Guermantes in *Le Temps retrouvé* the narrator asks Gilberte whether she can introduce him to some very young girls (he is looking for a replacement for Albertine). To the narrator's surprise Gilberte offers to introduce him to her own daughter—"a girl around sixteen years old whose tall form was a measure of [the temporal] distance I had tried not to see. Time, colorless and elusive, had materialized in her so that, so to speak, I could see it and touch it; it had molded her like a masterpiece. . . . I found her very beautiful: cheerful, still full of hope, formed from the very years I had lost, she resembled my Youth" (3: 1,031–32).

But Mlle de Saint-Loup resembles more than the narrator's youth; she contains and symbolizes the entirety of his past experience:

Like the majority of human beings, moreover, was she not like those star-shaped intersections in a forest where roads converge which have come, as they also do in our lives, from the most different directions? The roads which led to Mlle de Saint-Loup and radiated around her were numerous for me. First, the two great "ways," where I had taken so many walks and dreamed so many dreams, led to her—through her father Robert de Saint-Loup the Guermantes Way, through her mother Gilberte the Méséglise Way, which was also Swann's Way. One of them led me by way of the girl's mother and the Champs-Elysées to Swann, to my evenings in Combray, to the Méséglise Way; the other led me by way of her father to my afternoons in Balbec, where once again I saw him against the sunlit sea. And then transversals were established between these two ways. I had met Saint-Loup in the real Balbec largely because what Swann had told me about the churches and especially about the Persian church had given me such a desire to go there; on the other hand, through Robert de Saint-Loup, the nephew of the Duchesse de Guermantes, I came back to Combray and to the Guermantes Way. And Mlle de Saint-Loup led to many other points in my life, to the Lady in Pink, who was her grandmother and whom I had seen at my great-uncle's. And here another transversal was established, because my great-uncle's valet de chambre, who had let me in that day and who had later allowed me, through the gift of a photograph, to identify the Lady in Pink, was the father of the young man whom not only M. de Charlus but also the father of Mlle de Saint-Loup had loved and on whose account her father had caused her mother to suffer. And was it not Mlle de Saint-Loup's grandfather, Swann, who had first mentioned Vinteuil's music to me, just as Gilberte had first mentioned Albertine to me? Yet it was in discussing Vinteuil's music with Albertine that I had learned about the girl who was Albertine's great friend and had begun living with Albertine the existence which had led to her death and which had caused me so much grief. And it was also Mlle de Saint-Loup's father who had gone to try to make Albertine return. And I had arrived in a similar fashion at my entire social life, whether in Paris at the Swanns' or the Guermanteses' or, at the opposite pole, the Verdurins', thus bringing into alignment, beside the two ways of Combray and the Champs-Elysées, the beautiful terrace of La Raspelière. Do we, in fact, know anyone whom we would not have to place successively in all the different sites of our lives, if we were to tell the story of our friendship with that person? . . . [Life] is forever weaving threads which connect people and events, crisscrossing and redoubling them to thicken the fabric, so that between the least point in our past and all the others a rich network of memories leaves only the choice of this or that communicating path. (3: 1,029-30)

This essay on Mlle de Saint-Loup is both a summary of the narrator's life and a foreshadowing of the novel he is about to write. Mlle de Saint-Loup is the narrator's past existence and his future art incarnated "so that, so to speak, I could see it and touch it." In her literal and symbolic heredity she contains Swann and Odette, Gilberte and Saint-Loup, the narrator and Albertine, Charlus and Morel, Saint-Loup and Morel, Albertine and Mlle Vinteuil's friend. She is the husband and the wife, the male and the female, the lover and the beloved, the parent and the child. And when the narrator looks at her and finds her beautiful, he is seeing at once himself and all his characters. The meeting of the two ways in Mlle de Saint-Loup has a deeply androgynous significance. It is the final embrace of art and eros.

When the narrator realizes that the characters who exist in Mlle de Saint-Loup exist also in him, he renounces the outward pursuit of others which has occupied so much of his life and begins, instead, to pursue those people inwardly, in a voyage through the mind and the spirit. "I would have the courage to tell the people who came to see me or who sent for me," he writes, "that I had . . . a capital, an urgent appointment with myself" (3: 986). In order to keep this appointment he will need the combined powers of man, woman, and god. In writing his book he will have to "bear it like a fatigue, accept it like a rule of life, construct it like a church, follow it like a regimen, vanquish it like an obstacle, conquer it like a friendship, feed it like a child, create it like a world" (3: 1,032). He feels himself "grown big" (accru) with "this work I was carrying within me" (3: 1,036). And, as Leo Bersani has pointed out, "there is, in fact, a process suggesting the stages of pregnancy: the joyful conception of the idea [for the book] at the Guermantes matinée, the weakness and dizziness on the staircase some time later, and a painful delivery."[59]

According to certain mystical traditions Adam was not only androgynous in the garden of Eden, before the creation of Eve; he will
regain his androgyny at the end of time, when all things are restored
to their original perfection. This is the doctrine, as Marie Delcourt
explains, of "androgyny both initial and final," the idea that "in the
perfection of Eden, man had the two powers; he will regain them in
his supreme ascension."[60] This pattern is one of the most important
of the several mythic structures attached to the narrator's development as an artist, moving as it does from the initial division of his personality into a symbolic Adam and Eve, through the long quest to
"[find] her again," to the recovery of the androgynous feeling and
vision in *Le Temps retrouvé*. In *Le Temps retrouvé* the narrator is like
those androgynous creator gods—Protogonos in the Orphic cosmogony, Elohim in certain interpretations of the Bible—who create
the universe at the beginning of time.[61] And he is simultaneously like
the Adam of the mystical tradition, who regains his androgyny in Paradise at the end of time. In the cyclical Proustian myth the end is the
beginning, and the ripening of experience is the inception of creation.

When the two ways meet, when Adam and Eve reunite in Mlle
de Saint-Loup and in the narrator himself, he is able to begin dividing himself once again, this time in order to create the characters of
the novel—for, as he points out in a discussion of Swann's dream,
"certain novelists" are prone to distribute their own personality
among the various personalities they create (1: 379). From the perspective of *Le Temps retrouvé* the narrator presides over his work in
the same role the poet Valerius Soranus ascribed to Zeus: *Progenitor
genetrixque*.[62] And in this way he is able to realize something of what
he calls early in the work "that possible multiplication of oneself,
which is happiness" (1: 794).

The thought brings us back to 1908, to the time of Proust's first
work on *A la recherche*, and to a haunting line he jotted in the memorandum book he kept during that year: "When the rain was beating
down, I could have given birth to worlds."[63]

CHAPTER SIX

EPILOGUE

*T*HERE IS," writes Jonathan Katz, "no such thing as homosexuality in general, [there are] only particular historical forms of homosexuality." And he continues:

There is no evidence for the assumption that certain traits have universally characterized homosexual (or heterosexual) relations throughout history. The problem of the historical researcher is thus to study and establish the character and meaning of each varied manifestation of same-sex relations within a specific time and society. The term "situational homosexuality" has been applied to same-sex relations within prison and other particular institutional settings. The term is fallacious if it implies that there is some "true" homosexuality which is *not* situated. All homosexuality is situational, influenced and given meaning and character by its location in time and social space. Future research and analysis must focus as much on this conditioning situation as on the same-sex relations occurring within it.[1]

Katz is speaking about historical research, but his observation applies equally well to literary research. The time when it was possible to assert that the many manifestations of human sexuality conform to a priori, eternally valid psychological stereotypes has long since passed. We now know that homosexuality, like heterosexuality, varies with the individual who experiences it, with the historical time during which it is experienced, and with the different traditions and conventions that impart to the experience their special meanings and nuances. Attempts to generalize about Proust as the "typical homosexual" get us nowhere. Proust no more conforms to the stereotype of the "typical homosexual" than the "typical homosexual" conforms to the life and mind that produced *A la recherche du temps perdu*.

255

Proust's homosexuality obviously colors his experience and his out-look, but it does so in combination with many other factors in his per-sonality and culture—and these include his heterosexuality. Proust's novel is what it is because Proust was what he was as a man and an artist, not because he was "a homosexual." To understand Proust's sexuality and its impact on his writing we have to understand the kind of individual he was; we have to understand the era in which he lived; we have to understand the religious, literary, social, and scientific traditions that influenced his homoeroticism and his homophobia; and we have to understand his conception of himself as an artist who strives both for a faithful representation and an imaginative recon-struction of life.

In his book *The Performing Self* Richard Poirier takes as his cen-tral metaphor the following description of an unfinished statue by Michelangelo:

The body is emerging from stone, the right leg, thick and powerful, is strain-ing up as from the elements that imprison it; the left arm is raised, the elbow forward, and the hand and forearm push at what would be the back of the head. Except there is no head. Where it would be is instead a heavy block of stone. So that it is as if the arm and hand . . . were trying to push off the im-posing weight which imprisons the head. The communicated effect is not of aspiration but of some more elemental will toward the attainment of human shape and human recognition. . . . [but] the imagined head cannot be con-ceived except as part of the material that will not willingly yield itself to the head's existence.[2]

Proust's vision of sex and of the self, in Poirier's metaphor, "cannot be conceived except as part of the material that will not willingly" allow the vision to exist. As he creates his novel, Proust is implicitly warned, reprimanded, or encouraged to proceed by various voices within his culture. These are not just the voices of tradition and con-vention but also those of innovation and revolution, all of which im-pinge on his claim to artistic originality. There is no way for Proust to escape these voices: without them he would have nothing to write about, nothing to perform against. He needs them, just as Pro-metheus needs his vulture. And so he pays tribute to them even as he struggles against them. Sometimes he breaks free, but when he does, he leaves a part of himself behind.

A *la recherche* dramatizes, among other things, a conflict between the character of the author and the culture in which that character took shape. This conflict is intensified by Proust's homosexuality, but it is by no means unique to Proust or to homosexuality. Every original artist must find a way of dealing with the potential antagonism between tradition and the individual talent. "One cannot say," Leslie says in "Avant la nuit," "that because most people see objects said to be red as actually being red those who see them as being purple are mistaken." The story of Proust's artistic career is in large measure the story of his search for a way of relating what most people see to what he alone can see—a search for a way of seeing, and allowing his readers to see, red and purple at the same time.

Proust's novel retains strong ties to the old while striving toward the new, advocating outworn stereotypes on one page and questioning and discarding them on another. It is kinetic literature, overflowing with what Poirier calls "energy which cannot arrange itself within the existing order of things" and which, consequently, "makes literature not a source of comfort and order but rather, of . . . dislocating, disturbing impulses."[3] "I have not tried to analyze abstractly [the] evolution of thought," Proust wrote to Jacques Rivière in a letter quoted in Chapter 4, "but rather to recreate that evolution and bring it to life." When thought is brought to life, it takes on all the absurdities, self-contradictions, successes, and failures of life. A *la recherche* has these things in abundance, and has them partly because it recreates not only the evolution of a single consciousness but that of an entire era of intellectual history.

Like Proust within his time and within his art, we are constantly in a state of transition, constantly moving from the old to the new, from a world of stasis and stereotype to a world that surprises us yet again with its richness and complexity. Proust shows us that we must not mistake the act of going for the act of arriving. We must go farther and farther still—"for truth lies always beyond."

CHRONOLOGY OF SIGNIFICANT DATES

1871. 10 July: Marcel Proust is born in Paris.

1881. 30 May: Albert Le Cuziat is born.

1882–89. Proust studies at the Lycée Condorcet.

1885. 16 March: Robert de Montesquiou meets Gabriel d'Yturri (probable date).

1886. Proust answers questions about personal tastes and preferences in an album belonging to Antoinette Faure (latest probable date).

1887. July: Proust plays on the Champs-Elysées with Marie de Benardaky.

1888. Proust writes love letters to his schoolmates Jacques Bizet and Daniel Halévy.
11 October: Alfred Agostinelli is born in Monaco.
December: Proust meets Laure Hayman.

1889–90. Proust serves a year in the army.

1891. January: Oscar Wilde meets Lord Alfred Douglas (probable date).
1 May: Proust meets André Gide (probable date).
Summer: Proust pays court to Jeanne Pouquet at afternoon tennis parties in Neuilly.
November–December: Proust meets Oscar Wilde in Paris.
Winter: Proust meets Edgar Aubert.

1892. Spring: Proust makes friends with Robert de Flers.
August: Proust courts Marie Finaly.

1 September: Proust writes "Violante ou la mondanité."

18 September: Edgar Aubert dies.

1892 or 1893. Proust answers questions about himself in an album under the title "Marcel Proust par lui-même."

1893. 11 April: Gaston Arman de Caillavet marries Jeanne Pouquet.

13 April: Proust meets Robert de Montesquiou at Mme Lemaire's.

3 October: Willie Heath dies.

December: "Avant la nuit" is published in *La Revue Blanche*.

1894. 15 March: Proust introduces Léon Delafosse to Robert de Montesquiou.

April: Oscar Wilde again visits Paris and again sees Proust socially.

22 May: Proust meets Reynaldo Hahn at Mme Lemaire's (probable date).

18 August: Proust leaves for a visit to Réveillon, Mme Lemaire's château.

20 August: Reynaldo Hahn joins Proust at Réveillon.

1895. Oscar Wilde is tried for homosexuality, convicted, and imprisoned.

6 September: Proust and Reynaldo Hahn go to Beg-Meil, where Proust begins work on *Jean Santeuil*.

1895–99. Proust works on *Jean Santeuil*.

1896. March: Léon Yeatman reads the beginning of *Jean Santeuil*.

12 June: *Les Plaisirs et les jours* is published.

1 July: Jean Lorrain alludes to Proust's homosexuality in a review of Robert de Montesquiou's *Les Hortensias bleus*.

Uranisme et unisexualité by Marc-André Raffalovich is published.

Tares et poisons by Georges Saint-Paul is published.

Sexual Inversion by Havelock Ellis is published.

Sappho und Sokrates by Magnus Hirschfeld is published.

The first homosexual periodical, *Der Eigene*, begins publication in Germany.

1897. 3 February: Jean Lorrain publishes a review of *Les Plaisirs et les jours* and alludes to Proust's relationship with Lucien Daudet.

6 February: Proust fights a duel with Jean Lorrain.

1898–1900. Oscar Wilde lives intermittently in Paris; is perhaps visited by Proust while Proust is writing *Jean Santeuil*.

1899. June: Proust meets Antoine Bibesco (probable date).
October: Proust abandons work on *Jean Santeuil* in favor of studying Ruskin.
December: Proust begins to translate Ruskin.

1900. 30 November: Oscar Wilde dies in Paris.

1902. Friedrich Alfred Krupp commits suicide during a scandal over his homosexuality.

1903. 25 March: Sir Hector Archibald Macdonald shoots himself in a Paris hotel room during a scandal over his homosexuality.
26 November: Proust's father dies.

1904. Proust publishes his first Ruskin translation (*La Bible d'Amiens*).

1905. 6 July: Gabriel d'Yturri dies.
26 September: Proust's mother dies.

1906. 12 May: Proust publishes his second Ruskin translation (*Sésame et les lys*).
October: The German journalist Maximilian Harden begins a series of articles in which he accuses Prince Philipp zu Eulenburg-Hertefeld and Count Kuno von Moltke of homosexuality and of treason.

1907. Summer: Proust visits Cabourg and drives through the countryside with his chauffeur Alfred Agostinelli.
23 October: Kuno von Moltke's libel suit against Maximilian Harden opens in a Berlin municipal court.
29 October: Harden is acquitted of Moltke's libel charge.
6 November: Bernhard von Bülow, Chancellor of Germany, brings a libel suit against Adolf Brand, who has accused him of homosexuality.
19 November: Proust's article "Impressions de route en automobile" is published in *Le Figaro*.
1 December: "Dialogues des Amateurs, L: L'Amour à l'envers" by Rémy de Gourmont is published in the *Mercure de France*. The same issue contains Henri Albert's review of Schumann-Arndt's *Wir vom dritten Geschlecht*.

19 December: Proceedings open in Moltke's appeal of Harden's acquittal.

1908. *Derrière "Lui": L'Homosexualité en Allemagne* by John Grand-Carteret is published.

January: Proust begins a novel, an early version of *A la recherche du temps perdu*. *Les Homosexuels de Berlin: Le Troisième Sexe* by Magnus Hirschfeld is published.

1 January: "Dialogues des Amateurs, LII: Variétés" by Rémy de Gourmont is published in the *Mercure de France*.

3 January: Harden is found guilty of libel and sentenced to four months in prison.

3 February: Proust begins a memorandum book in which he will make scattered notes for his novel and for his work on Sainte-Beuve.

6 February: *L'Homosexualité en Allemagne* by Henri de Weindel and F.-P. Fischer is published.

22 February, 14 March, and 21 March: Proust publishes in *Le Figaro* parodies of Balzac, Faguet, Michelet, the Goncourt brothers, Flaubert, Sainte-Beuve, and Renan.

21 April: Harden brings a libel suit against the newspaper editor Anton Städele for implying that he has accepted a bribe from Eulenburg.

7 May: Prince Eulenburg is arrested. Proust informs Louis d'Albufera that he is writing "an essay on Homosexuality."

16 May: Proust writes to Robert Dreyfus about his plans for a "forbidden article."

Summer: Proust completes the draft of *A la recherche* begun in January of 1908. In Cabourg he meets a young woman he later thinks of marrying.

27 June: Montesquiou presides over the "inauguration" of *Le Chancelier des fleurs*, a memorial volume about Gabriel d'Yturri.

29 June: Eulenburg's trial opens in Berlin.

July: *Le Chemin mort* by Lucien Daudet is published.

14 July: Eulenburg's trial moves to the committee room of the Charité hospital.

August: Proust meets Marcel Plantevignes in Cabourg. Shortly thereafter he breaks with Plantevignes on the grounds that Plantevignes has countenanced rumors about his homosexuality. Proust threatens a duel, then allows himself to be dissuaded.

September: Agostinelli drives Proust from Cabourg to Versailles, where Proust remains from September to November.

8 September: Proust's review of *Le Chemin mort* by Lucien Daudet is published in *L'Intransigeant*.

25 September: Prince Eulenburg is released on bail.

November: Proust begins work on the narrative essay *Contre Sainte-Beuve* (probable date).

1909. March–June: Proust's work on *Contre Sainte-Beuve* and his work on *A la recherche* begin to overlap. Gradually the narrative essay will be abandoned as a separate project and the novel will take precedence.

7 July: Eulenburg's trial recommences but is adjourned *sine die* when it becomes apparent that Eulenburg is physically unfit to stand trial.

1910. 22 June: *Lucien* by Binet-Valmer is published.

1911. Proust meets Albert Le Cuziat (approximate date). The first edition of Gide's *Corydon* is published (limited to twelve copies). This edition is not circulated.

1912. August: Proust meets Mme Scheikévitch.

November: Proust writes to Gaston Gallimard about "the shocking things in the second volume" of *A la recherche* and mentions that he has created a character who exemplifies "the virile pederast."

1913. January or February: Proust hires Alfred Agostinelli as his secretary. Agostinelli and his mistress move in with Proust.

27 March: Céleste Gineste marries Odilon Albaret.

August: Proust goes to Cabourg but suddenly returns to Paris with Agostinelli. He says that his longing for a woman in Paris is the reason for the sudden return.

Late August or early September: Proust adds to the proofs of *Du côté de chez Swann* "some very important little details which tighten the knots of jealousy around poor Swann."

Late October or early November: Céleste Albaret begins to work for Proust.

November: Agostinelli goes to Antibes to study aviation (probable date).

8 November: *Du côté de chez Swann* is published by Grasset.

December: Proust sends Albert Nahmias to Antibes to try to persuade Agostinelli to return to Paris.

1914. Late March or early April: Agostinelli enrolls in the Garbero brothers' school of aviation, using the name Marcel Swann.

30 May: Agostinelli dies in an airplane accident in the sea off Antibes. On the same day Proust writes Agostinelli a letter about his purchase of an airplane as a gift for Agostinelli.

7 June: Agostinelli's body is recovered from the sea near Cagnes.

1913–14. Period during which Proust seems to have conceived and created the present version of Albertine.

1915. November: Proust sends Mme Scheikévitch a detailed outline of Albertine's role in *A la recherche*.

1918. 30 November: *A l'ombre des jeunes filles en fleurs* is published.

1918–21. Proust maintains a relationship with Henri Rochat, who serves as his secretary.

1919. 25 March: *Pastiches et mélanges* is published.

14 June: A new edition of *Du côté de chez Swann* is published.

10 November: Proust receives the Prix Goncourt for *A l'ombre des jeunes filles en fleurs*.

1920. The second edition of Gide's *Corydon* is published (limited to twenty-one copies).

7 August: *Le Côté de Guermantes I* is published.

4 November: Paul Souday publishes a review of *Le Côté de Guermantes I* and attributes to Proust a "feminine" sensibility.

1921. 30 April: *Le Côté de Guermantes II* and *Sodome et Gomorrhe I* are published in a single volume.

13 May: André Gide pays a visit to Proust and lends Proust a

copy of *Corydon*. The next day Gide records in his *Journal* Proust's statement that he "has never known love except with men."

June: Proust's article "A propos de Baudelaire" is published in *the Nouvelle Revue Française*.

17 September: Prince Eulenburg dies.

11 December: Robert de Montesquiou dies.

1922. 3 April: *Sodome et Gomorrhe II* is published.
18 November: Marcel Proust dies.

1923. 14 November: *La Prisonnière* is published.

1925. 30 November: *Albertine disparue* is published (later called *La Fugitive*).

1927. 22 September: *Le Temps retrouvé* is published.

1931. Maurice Sachs pays his first visit to Albert Le Cuziat's male brothel (approximate date).

1952. *Jean Santeuil* is published.

1954. *Contre Sainte-Beuve* is published (coupled with *Nouveaux mélanges*). The three-volume Pléiade edition of *A la recherche du temps perdu* is published.

1971. The Pléiade editions of *Les Plaisirs et les jours, Jean Santeuil, Contre Sainte-Beuve, Pastiches et mélanges,* and *Essais et articles* are published in two volumes.

BEFORE NIGHTFALL
("AVANT LA NUIT")
By Marcel Proust (1893)

"ALTHOUGH I am still strong enough, you know," she said to me with a more intimate tenderness, as one attenuates with inflections of the voice the harsh things one must say to those one loves, "you know that I could die any day now—just as it is possible that I could still live several months longer. So I can no longer hold back from you something which is weighing on my conscience; afterwards, you will understand how painful it has been for me to tell you." Her eyes, symbolic blue flowers, lost their color, as if they were wilting. I thought she was going to cry, but she did nothing of the sort. "It makes me very sad to destroy voluntarily my hope for being well thought of after my death by my best friend, to tarnish, to shatter the memory he would have kept of me, a memory through which I often visualize my own life to make it appear more beautiful and more harmonious. But my desire for an aesthetic arrangement (she smiled as she uttered the adjective with the slight ironic exaggeration she always gave words of this type, which were extremely rare in her conversation) cannot restrain the pressing need for truth which forces me to speak. Listen, Leslie, I have to tell you about it. But, before I do, give me my coat. It's a little cold on this terrace, and my doctor has forbidden me to get up when it's not necessary." I gave her her coat. The sun had gone down, and the sea, which was visible through the apple trees, was mauve. As delicate as pale, withered wreaths and as persistent as regrets, little blue and`pink clouds were floating on the horizon. A melancholy row of poplars plunged into the darkness, their heads submerged in a stained-glass pink. Without touching the trunks the last rays of sunlight colored the branches and hung upon those shadowy balustrades garlands of light. The breeze intermingled the three smells of the sea, of damp leaves, and of milk. Never had the Norman countryside sweetened more voluptuously the melancholy of evening, but I scarcely savored it, so disturbed was I by the mysterious words of my friend.

"I have loved you very much but given you little, my poor friend," she said.

"Excuse me, Françoise, if I disregard the rules of this literary genre and interrupt a 'confession' I should have listened to in silence," I exclaimed, trying to make a joke in order to calm her, but in reality fatally dejected. "What do you mean, you've given me little? The less I asked for, the more you gave me, and, in truth, you gave me a great deal more than would have been the case had there been a sensual dimension to our affection. You have been divine as a madonna, gentle as a nurse. I have adored you, and you have soothed my spirit. I have loved you with an affection whose sensitive circumspection was untroubled by any desire for carnal pleasure. And you brought me in return an incomparable friendship, exquisite tea, naturally ornate conversation—and how many bunches of fresh roses? You alone were able to soothe my burning, fevered brow with your maternal and expressive hands, pour honey between my withered lips, fill my life with noble images. Dear friend, I do not want to listen to this absurd confession. Give me your hands and let me kiss them; it's cold; let's go inside and talk about other things."

"My poor little Leslie, you must hear me out. It is necessary. Have you ever wondered whether, since I have been a widow from my twentieth year, I have always remained . . ."

"I am sure of it, but it is none of my business. You are a creature so superior to all others that a failing on your part would have the noble and beautiful character which is missing from the good actions of others. You have acted as you thought right, and I am sure you have never done anything that was not delicate and pure."

"Pure! Leslie, your confidence pains me like a reproach before the fact. Listen . . . I don't know how to tell you. It's a lot worse than if I had loved you, for example, or even another man, yes, really, any other man at all." I went white as a sheet, as white, alas, as she was, and, trembling with fear lest she notice it, I tried to joke and murmured without really knowing what I was saying: "Ha! Any other man at all! How strange you are."

"I said it was *worse* than that, Leslie. I'm not seeing too clearly, even though the moment is luminous. In the evening one sees things more calmly, but I don't see *this* thing clearly, and there are enormous shadows over my life. But if, deep within my conscience, I think it was not worse, why should I be ashamed to tell you about it? Was it worse?"

I did not understand; but, prey to a horrible uneasiness impossible to conceal, I began trembling with fear as in a nightmare. I did not dare look at the walkway, filled now with darkness and terror, which opened before us, neither did I dare close my eyes. Her voice, which had lowered as it broke with a sadness more and more profound, suddenly rose again, and in a clear, natural tone, she said to me: "Do you remember when my poor friend Dorothy was discovered with a female singer whose name I've forgotten" (I was gladdened by this digression, which, I hoped, would steer us definitively away from the story of her sufferings) "how you explained to me then that we could not hold her in contempt? I remember your very words: 'How can we be shocked by practices of which Socrates (it was a question of men, but it's the same thing, isn't it?), who drank the hemlock rather than commit an injustice, heartily approved among his favorite friends? If fruitful love, which is destined to perpetuate the race, and which is esteemed as a familial, social, and human duty, is superior to purely voluptuous love, by the same token there is no hierarchy among sterile loves and it is no less moral—or, rather, no more immoral—for a woman to seek pleasure with another woman than with someone of the other sex. The cause of this love lies in a nervous deterioration which is so exclusively a nervous condition that it admits of no moral content. One cannot say that because most people see objects said to be red as actually being red those who see them as being purple are mistaken. Moreover,' you added, 'if one refines erotic pleasure to the point of making it aesthetic—for masculine and feminine bodies can be equally beautiful—there is no reason why a truly artistic woman should not fall in love with another woman. In the truly artistic nature physical attraction or repulsion is qualified by the contemplation of the beautiful. Most people turn away from the jellyfish with disgust. Michelet, who appreciated the delicacy of their colors, collected them with pleasure. In spite of my distaste for oysters, after I had reflected,' you continued, 'on their journeys through the ocean—journeys which their taste would suggest to me now—they became for me, especially when I was away from the sea, a richly evocative pleasure. In such a way do physical dispositions, the pleasure of physical contact, the refinements of the palate, the joys of the senses stem from the place where our sense of the beautiful is rooted.' Don't you think that such arguments could lead a woman physically predisposed to this kind of love to become conscious of her vague curiosity, especially if certain statuettes by Rodin, for example, had already triumphed, artistically, over her repugnance; that such arguments could excuse her in her own eyes, reassure her conscience—and that this could lead to great misfortune?"

I do not know how, at that point, I kept from crying out. In a flash the meaning of her confession and an awareness of my dreadful responsibility became simultaneously clear to me. But I gave myself up to one of those higher inspirations which, when we are not up to our usual self and are incapable of playing our usual role in life, will suddenly take hold of the mask we wear and offhandedly play our role for us; and I said calmly, "I assure you that in that case I would feel no remorse, because, in truth, I have no feeling either of contempt or of pity for such women."

Mysteriously, and with infinite sweetness and gratitude, she said to me, "You are generous." She added, a little lower and faster, and with an air of being bored—as one expresses contempt for mundane details at the same time that one utters them—"You know, I realized very clearly, in spite of the air of secrecy you adopted in front of everyone, that you are dying to know who fired this bullet which could not be extracted and which is responsible for my illness. I always hoped the bullet would not be discovered. Well, since the doctor now seems certain of the outcome and you might begin to suspect innocent people, I will confess. But I prefer to tell you the truth." And she added, with that tenderness she adopted when broaching the subject of her imminent death, in order to ease by the way she said them the pain her words would cause, "I, in one of those moments of despair which are entirely natural for those who *live*, shot myself." I wanted to go to her and embrace her; I tried to contain myself, but in vain; for, as I drew near her, an irresistible force took hold of my throat, my eyes filled with tears, and I began to sob. At first she wiped my eyes, laughed a little, gently consoled me with a thousand kindnesses, just as she used to do. But deep inside her an immense pity for herself and for me welled up, sprang to her eyes—and fell down in burning tears. We wept together, in an understanding of great and melancholy harmony. Our mutual pity was now directed toward something which was larger than ourselves and for which we wept voluntarily, freely. I tried to drink her poor tears as they fell upon her hands. But others always followed, and they brought a chill over her body. Her hands became icy, like the pale leaves floating in the basins of the fountains. And never had we known so much ill, and so much good.

French text: *Les Plaisirs et les jours*, "Appendice," pp. 167–71.
Translated by J.E. Rivers.

NOTES

1. PROBLEMS AND PERSPECTIVES

1. *Hommage à Marcel Proust*, pp. 228, 285, 269.

2. Prior to O'Brien's article Robert Vigneron, in "Genèse de *Swann*" (1937), emphasized the impact on *A la recherche* of Proust's homosexual experience and of his probable reading in contemporary works on homosexuality.

3. Justin O'Brien, "Albertine the Ambiguous," p. 952.

4. For a summary of the long history of these ideas in literary criticism—and a critique of the ideas themselves—see Benjamin De Mott, "But He's a Homosexual . . . ," in Irving Buchen, ed., *The Perverse Imagination*, pp. 147–64.

5. Arno Karlen, *Sexuality and Homosexuality*, p. 512.

6. For an overview of recent thinking on homosexuality see Wainwright Churchill, *Homosexual Behavior Among Males;* Mark Freedman, *Homosexuality and Psychological Functioning;* Alfred C. Kinsey, Wardell B. Pomeroy, and Clyde E. Martin, *Sexual Behavior in the Human Male;* C. A. Tripp, *The Homosexual Matrix;* George Weinberg, *Society and the Healthy Homosexual;* Martin S. Weinberg and Colin J. Williams, *Male Homosexuals.*

7. Milton Hindus, "The Pattern of Proustian Love," p. 398.

8. Hindus, "Pattern," p. 395.

9. D. G. MacDonald Allen, *The Janus Sex*, p. 93.

10. Vladimir Nabokov, *Pale Fire*, p. 162.

11. Vladimir Nabokov, *Ada or Ardor*, pp. 168–69. Nabokov alludes to the laundress of Touraine, with whom the narrator suspects Albertine of having a lesbian affair.

12. Harry Levin and Justin O'Brien, "Proust, Gide, and the Sexes," pp. 648–52.

13. Levin and O'Brien, p. 653.

14. Maurice Sachs, *Le Sabbat*, p. 282.

15. "An Interview With Eric Bentley," p. 296.

16. See Churchill, Freedman, and Tripp.

273

17. For a summary of Freud's theories of sexuality and their influence see J. A. C. Brown, *Freud and the Post-Freudians.*

18. Tripp, pp. 78–79.

19. Irving Bieber et al., *Homosexuality.*

20. Churchill, pp. 95–96; see also Fritz A. Fluckiger, "Research Through a Glass, Darkly: An Evaluation of the Bieber Study on Homosexuality."

21. Tripp, p. 251.

22. Churchill, pp. 60–61; cf. Tripp, p. 26, n.

23. Tripp, p. 252.

24. George Weinberg, p. 69.

25. Tripp, p. 250.

26. For further thoughts see Tripp, pp. 243–67.

27. See "Homosexuality Shift Upheld," *Washington Post,* 9 April 1974, p. A 9, cols. 1–3.

28. *Essais et articles,* p. 335.

29. Milton L. Miller, *Nostalgia,* pp. 163–64, 172, 183.

30. Milton Miller, *Psychanalyse de Proust,* tr. Marie Tadié (Paris: Fayard, 1977).

31. George D. Painter, *Proust: The Early Years,* p. 7.

32. George D. Painter, *Proust: The Later Years,* p. 269.

33. Ernest Jones, *Essays in Applied Psychoanalysis,* 1: 326.

34. J.-B. Boulanger, "Un Cas d'inversion coupable," p. 483.

35. Edmund Bergler, "Proust and the 'Torture-Theory' of Love," pp. 271–73.

36. Miller, pp. 164–65.

37. Lisa Appignanesi, *Femininity and the Creative Imagination,* p. 202.

38. Tripp, p. 98.

39. Appignanesi, p. 158.

40. Miller, p. 168.

41. Gilles Deleuze, *Proust et les signes,* p. 7.

42. Serge Doubrovsky, *La Place de la madeleine,* p. 21.

43. A. L. Rowse, *Homosexuals in History,* pp. 182–83.

44. Jocelyn Brooke, "Proust and Joyce," p. 7.

45. *Francis Jammes-Arthur Fontaine: Correspondance,* p. 175.

46. *Choix de lettres,* p. 250.

47. *Lettres à la N. R. F.,* pp. 102–4. In the final version of the novel, of course, M. de Charlus picks up not a concierge but the tailor Jupien and keeps not a pianist but the violinist Morel.

48. *Essais et articles,* pp. 630–32.

49. In the definitive French edition *La Prisonnière* bears the subtitle *Première partie de "Sodome et Gomorrhe III"* and *La Fugitive* the subtitle *Deuxième partie de "Sodome et Gomorrhe."* In addition, the title *A l'ombre*

des jeunes filles en fleurs may allude to Baudelaire's poem "Lesbos" and to the lines "Car Lesbos entre tous m'a choisi sur la terre / Pour chanter le secret de ses vierges en fleurs" ("For Lesbos has chosen me among all men on earth / To sing the secret of her flowering maidens"). See Painter, *The Later Years*, p. 323; and *Essais et articles*, p. 633.

50. According to André Gide, Proust thought Baudelaire "was homosexual." Gide visited Proust in May of 1921, a month before the Baudelaire article appeared in the *Nouvelle Revue Française*. The talk was of homosexuality, and Gide's record of the conversation runs in part as follows:

> [Proust] tells me he is convinced Baudelaire was homosexual. "The way he talks about Lesbos, and the simple fact that he needs to talk about it, would be enough to convince me." And when I protest, "In any case, if he were homosexual, it was almost without realizing it himself; and surely you don't imagine he ever practiced. . . ."
>
> "What!" [Proust] exclaims. "I am convinced of the contrary; how can you doubt that he practiced, he, Baudelaire!"
>
> And the tone of his voice implies that by doubting I am insulting Baudelaire. But I am willing to believe he is right. (André Gide, *Journal, 1889–1939*, p. 692).

2 . THE PRIVATE LIFE OF A GENIUS

1. Quoted and translated in Painter, *The Later Years*, pp. 306–7.

2. On this see Painter, *The Early Years*, p. xii.

3. For a statement of this idea see *"Contre Sainte-Beuve" précédé de "Pastiches et mélanges" et suivi de "Essais et articles,"* pp. 221–22.

4. For examples see Maurice Bardèche, *Marcel Proust, romancier,* 1: 10.

5. Bardèche, 1: 15.

6. Gide, *Journal, 1889–1939*, p. 692.

7. Céleste Albaret, *Monsieur Proust*, pp. 359–61. For a similar point of view see Robert Soupault, *Marcel Proust du côté de la médecine*, p. 195.

8. *Correspondance générale*, 3: 86; and Paul Souday, *Marcel Proust*, p. 31.

9. For a fuller account of Proust's duel see Painter, *The Early Years*, pp. 257–58.

10. Henri Bonnet, *Marcel Proust de 1907 à 1914*, p. 197.

11. All quotations in the Plantevignes anecdote are translated from the report of the incident in Marcel Plantevignes, *Avec Marcel Proust*, pp. 98–114.

12. Bonnet, pp. 74–75.

13. *"Contre Sainte-Beuve" suivi de "Nouveaux mélanges,"* pp. 255–56.

14. Roger Shattuck, *Marcel Proust*, p. 72.
15. D. A. Begelman, rev. of *Beyond Sexual Freedom*, by Charles W. Socarides, p. 323.
16. Cf. Churchill, pp. 36–59.
17. Soupault, pp. 195–96.
18. *A un ami*, p. 214.
19. *Correspondance générale*, 5: 180.
20. *A un ami*, pp. 138–39.
21. *Correspondance générale*, 4: 119; Albaret, p. 223.
22. On the Proustian motif in *Lolita* see David L. Jones, "Dolorès Disparue."
23. Quoted and translated in Painter, *The Early Years*, p. 55.
24. "I love the green light of your long eyes." A line from Baudelaire's "Chant d'automne." Albaret, p. 214.
25. Albaret, pp. 214–15.
26. *Correspondance générale*, 4: 119.
27. Albaret, p. 222.
28. Ibid., pp. 218–19.
29. Painter, *The Early Years*, p. 109.
30. Albaret, pp. 219–21.
31. The full text of Proust's inscription can be found in André Maurois, *A la recherche de Marcel Proust*, p. 107; the translation quoted above is from Painter, *The Later Years*, p. 12.
32. The popular hostess and still-life painter, said by Dumas to have "created more roses than anyone after God." She illustrated Proust's first book *Les Plaisirs et les jours*, perhaps the very book over which Proust here imagines Louisa to be nodding.
33. *Correspondance générale*, 5: 152–53.
34. Ibid., 5: 174.
35. Ibid., 5: 170.
36. Quoted and translated in Painter, *The Later Years*, pp. 12–13.
37. Ibid., p. 77.
38. *A un ami*, p. 151.
39. Ibid., p. 168.
40. Antoine Bibesco, "The Heartlessness of Marcel Proust," p. 424.
41. Albaret, pp. 215–17.
42. For a discussion of these relationships see Painter, *The Early Years*, pp. 135–40 and 110–16.
43. Irving Bieber et al., "Playboy Panel: Homosexuality," pp. 63–67.
44. Brooke, p. 17.
45. Antoine Bibesco, p. 424.
46. Painter, *The Early Years*, p. xii.
47. Ibid., pp. 62–63; cf. Maurois, p. 107.
48. Bieber et al., *Homosexuality*, p. 220.

49. Bieber et al., "Playboy Panel: Homosexuality," pp. 67–68; Lawrence J. Hatterer, *Changing Homosexuality in the Male*, p. 394.

50. Kinsey, Pomeroy, and Martin, *Male*, p. 639.

51. Ibid., p. 647.

52. Ibid., pp. 610–66.

53. William G. Cochran et al., *Statistical Problems of the Kinsey Report on Sexual Behavior in the Human Male*, pp. 142–45. See also Wardell B. Pomeroy, *Dr. Kinsey and the Institute for Sex Research*, pp. 272, 369–72; and Tripp, pp. 232–40.

54. Kinsey, Pomeroy, and Martin, *Male*, p. 659.

55. Churchill, pp. 38–39.

56. Freedman, pp. 15–16.

57. Bardèche, 2: 63, n. 2.

58. André Ferré, *Les Années de collège de Marcel Proust*, p. 201, n. 1.

59. *Correspondance de Marcel Proust, 1880–1895*, 1: 103–4.

60. Perhaps a reference to masturbation.

61. *Correspondance, 1880–1895*, 1: 123–24.

62. Painter, *The Early Years*, p. 141.

63. *Great Dialogues of Plato*, p. 152.

64. *Correspondance, 1880–1895*, 1: 107.

65. Ibid., 1: 114–15.

66. Quoted and translated in Painter, *The Early Years*, p. 93; and see Anthony Powell, "Proust as a Soldier," in *Marcel Proust*, ed. Peter Quennell, pp. 149–64.

67. *Les Plaisirs et les jours*, p. 6.

68. Robert de Billy, *Marcel Proust*, p. 52.

69. Billy, p. 103.

70. Painter, *The Early Years*, pp. 148–49; cf. Soupault, pp. 198–99.

71. Ibid., p. 166.

72. Albaret, p. 310.

73. Fernand Gregh, *Mon amitié avec Marcel Proust*, pp. 35–36.

74. Albaret, p. 303.

75. Painter, *The Early Years*, pp. 127–28.

76. Philippe Jullian, *Prince of Aesthetes*, p. 161; cf. Billy, p. 89.

77. Quoted in Maurois, p. 133.

78. As pointed out in Léon Guichard, *Introduction à la lecture de Proust*, pp. 164–67.

79. Guichard, p. 167; on Diaghilev and Nijinsky see Noel I. Garde, *Jonathan to Gide*, pp. 683–93.

80. Albaret, p. 229.

81. William Sansom, *Proust and His World*, p. 57.

82. *Lettres à Reynaldo Hahn*, pp. 54–55.

83. Albaret, p. 431.

84. Sachs, p. 286.

85. *Lettres à Reynaldo Hahn*, p. 10.

86. Ibid., p. 27.

87. Ibid., p. 153.

88. Philip Kolb, "Historique du premier roman de Proust," p. 225.

89. *Lettres à Reynaldo Hahn*, p. 53.

90. *Jean Santeuil*, p. 181.

91. Ibid., pp. 564–65.

92. Gregh, pp. 149–50.

93. *A un ami*, p. 169.

94. *Lettres à Reynaldo Hahn*, p. 188.

95. *Great Dialogues of Plato*, p. 150. It is possible that Proust is remembering this passage from the *Symposium* when in *A la recherche* he shows how Swann's daughter effaces her father's memory and concludes that the hope of surviving through mortal children is a vain and empty one. On the other hand, Bergotte's books—which the narrator at one point calls his "daughters" (2: 326)—assure him of lasting fame.

96. See also Painter, *The Early Years*, pp. 210–33 and passim.

97. Quoted and translated in Painter, *The Early Years*, p. 379.

98. Ibid., p. 365.

99. *"Contre Sainte-Beuve" suivi de "Nouveaux mélanges,"* p. 260.

100. Gore Vidal, *Two Sisters*, pp. 191–93.

101. Sachs, p. 282; Albaret, p. 238.

102. Guichard, pp. 170–71.

103. Albaret, p. 235.

104. Guichard, p. 169; Sachs, pp. 278–81.

105. Albaret, p. 236.

106. Ibid., p. 235.

107. Sachs, pp. 278–79.

108. Ibid., p. 279.

109. Cf. ibid., pp. 284–85.

110. Quoted in Guichard, pp. 169–70.

111. Painter, *The Later Years*, pp. 268–70; Sachs, p. 285.

112. Painter, *The Later Years*, p. 268; Sachs, p. 285.

113. Painter, *The Later Years*, p. 268.

114. Ibid.

115. For a disclaimer of the stories about the rats and the pictures see Albaret, pp. 238–39.

116. Albaret, p. 239 and passim.

117. Painter, *The Later Years*, p. 268, n. 2 and passim.

118. Albaret, pp. 239–40.

119. Ibid., pp. 240–41.

120. *Hommage à Marcel Proust*, p. 285.

121. James Robert Hewitt, *Marcel Proust*, p. 106.

122. Albaret, p. 234.

123. *Pastiches et mélanges,* pp. 66–67; cf. 3: 382.

124. Vigneron, p. 115.

125. *Correspondance générale,* 6: 89.

126. *Lettres à André Gide,* p. 38.

127. *Correspondance générale,* 6: 242.

128. Ibid., 6: 244.

129. Quoted in Bonnet, p. 202; italics Proust's.

130. *Correspondance générale,* 2: 193; dated by Vigneron, p. 97.

131. Lucien Daudet, *Autour de soixante lettres de Marcel Proust,* p. 65.

132. *Correspondance générale,* 6: 122; dated March 1913 by Vigneron, p. 97.

133. *A un ami,* pp. 223–24.

134. Painter, *The Later Years,* p. 206.

135. Quoted in Maurois, pp. 131–32; cf. Painter, *The Later Years,* pp. 206–07.

136. Lucien Daudet, p. 76.

137. *Correspondance générale,* 2: 204.

138. Léon Pierre-Quint, *Proust et la stratégie littéraire,* p. 96.

139. *Correspondance générale,* 4: 61.

140. Ibid., p. 1: 248.

141. Albaret, p. 232.

142. *Correspondance générale,* 6: 242.

143. Vigneron, p. 106.

144. *Correspondance générale,* 6: 242.

145. Ibid., 1: 270–71.

146. *Lettres à André Gide,* pp. 38–39.

147. *Correspondance générale,* 5: 92.

148. Pierre-Quint, p. 131.

149. See for instance Hewitt, p. 107; Albaret, p. 234; and cf. Painter, *The Later Years,* p. 209.

150. Quoted in Bardèche, 1: 299, n. 1; and Bonnet, pp. 197–98.

151. Plantevignes, pp. 637–38; and Bonnet, p. 196.

152. Quoted in Bardèche, 2: 37, n. 1; and Bonnet, p. 198.

153. Bonnet, pp. 199, 195.

154. Quoted from Notebook 33 in Bardèche, 2: 34–35.

155. Quoted in Bardèche, 2: 35.

156. Bardèche, 1: 298–300; 2: 13, n. 1, and 32–35.

157. Vigneron, pp. 100–15 and passim.

158. Painter, *The Later Years,* pp. 208–9. The sources Painter mentions as proof that Proust had conceived the story of Albertine before 1913 do not, in fact, mention Albertine at all. They are *Marcel Proust et Jacques Rivière: Correspondance,* p. 3; and *Francis Jammes-Arthur Fontaine: Correspondance,* pp. 286–87.

159. Philip Kolb, ed., *Le Carnet de 1908,* pp. 8, 49, and cf. p. 50.

160. *Correspondance générale,* 5: 230–31; and Painter, *The Later Years,* p. 222.

161. *Correspondance générale,* 5: 234.

162. Ibid., 5: 234–41; rpt. in *Essais et articles,* pp. 559–64.

163. Bardèche, 1: 301.

164. Ibid., 2: 72–75.

165. Translated from the photograph of the telegram reproduced in Bonnet, facing p. 188.

166. Albaret, p. 233.

167. I have quoted the poem from Stéphane Mallarmé, *Œuvres complètes,* pp. 67–68, restoring an omitted line in Proust's quotation. The poem, which is untranslatable, might be roughly rendered as follows:

The virginal, the long-lived and the beautiful today
Will it lacerate for us with a blow of its drunken wing
This hard, forgotten lake which, underneath its frost, is haunted
By the translucent glacier of flights never flown!

A swan of days gone by remembers that it is he
Who, magnificent but hopeless, frees himself,
Because he did not sing of the region in which to live
When the tedium of sterile winter was resplendent.

With his whole neck he'll shake off this white agony
Inflicted by space on the bird that denies space,
But not the horror of the ground in which his plumage is held fast.

He is a phantom, his pure brilliance assigns him to this place,
Motionless amid the cold dream of scorn
Which the swan dons amid useless exile.

168. *Lettres retrouvées,* pp. 97–101.

169. My discussion of the two letters is heavily indebted to Philip Kolb's notes in *Lettres retrouvées,* pp. 101–4, and to Henri Bonnet's analysis in *Marcel Proust de 1907 à 1914,* pp. 194–95.

170. *Lettres retrouvées,* pp. 106–8.

171. Léon Daudet, *Memoirs of Léon Daudet,* p. 265.

172. Albaret, p. 231.

173. Painter, *The Later Years,* p. 287.

174. Jacques Porel, "Marcel Proust chez Réjane," pp. 93–94.

3 · A DREAM OF ART

1. Cf. Bardèche, 2: 230.

2. *Les Plaisirs et les jours,* p. 36.

3. *Jean Santeuil,* pp. 812–13.

4. Ibid., pp. 676–77, 718–19.

5. Gregh, p. 9; Painter, *The Early Years*, pp. 216–18; Appignanesi, p. 173.

6. *Les Plaisirs et les jours*, p. 92.

7. See John Lauritsen and David Thorstad, *The Early Homosexual Rights Movement (1864–1935)*, p. 33.

8. The original French editions of *Les Plaisirs et les jours* and their English version (*Pleasures and Regrets*, tr. Louise Varese) do not contain "Avant la nuit." The story is, however, included as an appendix to the 1971 Pléiade edition of *Les Plaisirs et les jours*.

9. There have been, so far as I can determine, only two previous translations of "Avant la nuit," one of them published while this study was being written. They are by Abigail Sanford (1960) and Richard Howard (1977).

10. For remarks on this well-known and much-criticized tradition see Arnie Kantrowitz, "Homosexuals and Literature," p. 327.

11. Under section 330 of the French penal code homosexual acts were treated in the same way as heterosexual acts: they were punishable only when they outraged public decency, employed violence or force, or involved minors or someone not able to give valid legal consent. This liberal policy held true for all European countries whose penal codes were based on the Code Napoléon (it was written into the Italian penal code in 1889). See Edward Westermarck, "Homosexual Love," in Donald Webster Cory, ed., *Homosexuality*, pp. 121–22; and John Addington Symonds, "A Problem in Modern Ethics," in Cory, p. 97.

12. On the sin of Sodom see Derrick Sherwin Bailey, *Homosexuality and the Western Christian Tradition*, pp. 1–28.

13. Quoted in André Gide, *Corydon*, p. 49, n. 1.

14. Painter, *The Early Years*, p. 246.

15. Garde, pp. 658–59.

16. H. Montgomery Hyde, *The Trials of Oscar Wilde*, p. 76.

17. Until 1861 the penalty for homosexuality in England was death. In 1861, with the passage of the Offences Against the Person Act, the penalty was reduced to imprisonment for from ten years to life. Then, in the Criminal Law Amendment Act of 1885, the penalty was further reduced to a "term not exceeding two years, with or without hard labor." See Bailey, pp. 151–52; Karlen, p. 255, n.; and Hyde, p. 167.

18. Quoted in Karlen, p. 255.

19. Quoted in Hyde, p. 201.

20. Ibid., p. 272.

21. Ibid., p. 273. As is often pointed out, a sentence of two years at hard labor was almost the equivalent of a death sentence, given the brutal prison conditions in England at that time.

22. Rowse, pp. 165–68.

23. Karlen, p. 256.

24. On *Der Eigene* see James Steakley, *The Homosexual Emancipation Movement in Germany*, p. 23.

25. Garde, p. 671. This account also draws on John Montgomery, "The Truth About 'Fighting Mac,' " *Gay News* (London), no. 150 (7–20 September 1978), p. 24.

26. Karlen, p. 256.

27. Quoted and translated in Steakley, p. 32.

28. Cf. Karlen, p. 256.

29. Quoted and translated in Steakley, p. 33.

30. Johannes Haller, *Philip Eulenburg*, 1: 279–388; 2: 169–87.

31. Quoted in Haller, 2: 174–75.

32. Haller, 2: 150–51.

33. Ibid., 2: 203.

34. Ibid., 2: 195–96.

35. Quoted in Henri de Weindel and F.-P. Fischer, *L'Homosexualité en Allemagne*, p. 47.

36. Quoted in Weindel and Fischer, p. 48.

37. Adolf Brand, "Paragraph 175," in Jonathan Katz, ed., *Documents of the Homosexual Rights Movement in Germany*, p. 1 of the original German document. See also Lauritsen and Thorstad, p. 21 and passim.

38. Quoted in Haller, 2: 214.

39. Ibid., 2: 217–18.

40. Ibid., 2: 219.

41. See Haller, 2: 219.

42. Haller, 2: 255 and passim.

43. Ibid., 2: 269.

44. Painter, *The Later Years*, p. 105.

45. Haller, 2: 269.

46. Garde, p. 683.

47. In addition to the works footnoted during the course of the discussion, this account of the Eulenburg affair draws upon Steakley, Vigneron, and Maurice Baumont, *L'Affaire Eulenburg et les origines de la guerre mondiale*.

48. Haller, 2: 253.

49. Westermarck in Cory, p. 126; and John Lauritsen, *Religious Roots of the Taboo on Homosexuality*, p. 7.

50. Bailey, pp. 73–76; and Lauritsen, *Religious Roots*, pp. 10–11.

51. Edward Gibbon, *The Decline and Fall of the Roman Empire*, p. 94 (Chapter 44, Section IV).

52. The practice was not limited to the Middle Ages. Until the enactment of the Code Napoléon people could be burned at the stake in France for homosexuality, in accordance with the penalty of *vindices flammae* in Roman and medieval law. The penalty was last carried out just before the French Revolution—and thus less than a hundred years before Proust was born. See Lauritsen, *Religious Roots*, pp. 11–14; and Havelock Ellis, *Sexual Inversion*, in *Studies in the Psychology of Sex*, 1: 346–47.

53. On this see especially Churchill, pp. 205–7; and Tripp's chapter "The Politics of Homosexuality," pp. 202–42.

54. Vigneron, p. 70, n. 1 and passim.

55. Weindel and Fischer, p. 1; and Vigneron, p. 72.

56. Vigneron, pp. 71–72; Painter, *The Later Years*, p. 106; Billy, p. 176; and John Grand-Carteret, *Derrière "Lui,"* pp. 1–21.

57. Billy, p. 176; cf. pp. 174–75, 216. Cf. also Plantevignes, pp. 609–11.

58. Billy, p. 175.

59. The possibility that Kaiser Wilhelm II himself was homosexually inclined was the great unspoken throughout the Eulenburg affair; it is a question German historians are only now beginning to entertain. See for instance John Röhl, ed., *Philipp Eulenburgs politische Korrespondenz*, I; see also the review of this book entitled "Eulenburg-Affäre: Briefe, die das Licht scheuten," *Der Spiegel* (1976), 30(40): 209–18.

60. On Charlus's scatological language see Justin O'Brien, "An Aspect of Proust's Baron de Charlus."

61. M. de Charlus is, of course, interested in the garrison town of Doncières not for purposes of espionage but because Morel is stationed there.

62. Tripp, p. 208.

63. On the kaleidoscope image see Victor E. Graham, *The Imagery of Proust*, p. 75.

64. Vigneron, p. 70, n. 1 and passim.

65. Henri Albert, "Lettres allemandes," pp. 560–61.

66. *Essais et articles*, pp. 550–52.

67. Binet-Valmer, *Lucien*, pp. 75, 94. Subsequent references to *Lucien* are given in the text by page number.

68. Quoted in Vigneron, pp. 83–84.

69. Soupault, p. 197.

70. *Lettres à la N. R. F.*, p. 103. Binet-Valmer's *Lucien*, a work of capital importance in the literature of sexuality, has never been translated into English and, as far as I know, never discussed in any other context as the pivotal document it is. It deserves greater attention.

71. *Correspondance générale*, 4: 234–35.

72. Robert Dreyfus, *Souvenirs sur Marcel Proust*, p. 239.

73. *Correspondance générale*, 4: 234, n. 2.

74. Cf. Proust's similar discussion of Wilde and Lucien de Rubempré in *"Contre Sainte-Beuve" précédé de "Pastiches et mélanges" et suivi de "Essais et articles,"* p. 273 and note. In *A la recherche* Proust has Charlus quote Wilde's remark about Rubempré and attribute it to an anonymous "man of taste" (2: 1,050). George Painter supplies the following annotation: "Wilde's remark occurs in his dialogue 'The Decay of Lying,' which Proust had read in one of the two French translations of *Intentions* published in 1906. 'One of the greatest tragedies of my life,' says Vivian, 'is the death of Lucien de Rubempré. It is a grief from which I have never been able completely to rid myself.'" Painter, *The Later Years*, pp. 107–8, n. 2. See also *Le Carnet de 1908*, pp. 48–49.

75. "Marcel Proust et la Bourse," p. 16.

76. It is also rejected by the editors of *"Contre Sainte-Beuve" précédé de "Pastiches et mélanges" et suivi de "Essais et articles,"* pp. 821–22.

77. Jean Milly, ed., *Les Pastiches de Proust,* p. 18 and passim.

78. Bonnet, p. 61 and passim.

79. Vigneron, p. 83.

80. Bardèche, 1: 162; and Kolb, "Introduction" to *Le Carnet de 1908,* p. 11 and passim.

81. Bardèche, 1: 163.

82. *Le Carnet de 1908,* pp. 66, 63. Proust here spells the name "Eulembourg."

83. Bardèche, 1: 216–17.

4. THE GOOD FAITH OF A CHEMIST

1. Painter, *The Later Years,* p. 107. Painter's reference is to *"Contre Sainte-Beuve" suivi de "Nouveaux mélanges,"* pp. 247–66 ("La Race maudite"). Cf. Bardèche, 1: 162.

2. *Marcel Proust et Jacques Rivière: Correspondance,* p. 3.

3. "Swann is my friend, but truth is a greater friend." The Latin proverb, which derives from a comment attributed to Aristotle, is "Amicus Plato, amicus Socrates, sed major veritas" ("Plato is my friend, Socrates is my friend, but truth is greater").

4. *Correspondance générale,* 3: 10.

5. Louis de Robert, *Comment débuta Marcel Proust,* pp. 63–64; cf. *Lettres à André Gide,* p. 40.

6. Robert, p. 66.

7. Colette, *Le Pur et l'impur,* p. 346; Maurois, p. 218; Milton Hindus, *The Proustian Vision,* p. 242; and cf. Bonnet, p. 187.

8. Gide, *Journal, 1889–1939,* p. 705.

9. J. Z. Eglinton, *Greek Love,* p. 407.

10. Jacques J. Zéphir, *La Personnalité humaine dans l'œuvre de Marcel Proust,* p. 166.

11. Lucien Daudet, p. 64.

12. On Proust's father's association with Tardieu and Brouardel see Painter, *The Early Years,* pp. 5, 401; Painter, *The Later Years,* p. 49; *Correspondance, 1880–1895,* 1: 60, 62, 67, 239; and *Correspondance, 1896–1901,* 2: 15, 135. On the reputations of Tardieu and Brouardel as authorities on homosexuality see Karlen, pp. 185, 217; and Weindel and Fischer, p. 5.

13. Miller, p. 148, n. 6.

14. Karlen, pp. 185–86.

15. Paul Moreau, *Des aberrations du sens génésique,* pp. 71–72; and Richard von Krafft-Ebing, *Psychopathia Sexualis, With Especial Reference to the Antipathic Sexual Instinct,* pp. 223–24, 226, and passim. Krafft-Ebing's work first appeared in German in 1886. It was translated into French in 1895

as *Psychopathia sexualis, avec recherches spéciales sur l'inversion sexuelle* and was enormously popular in various languages all over Europe. Before Krafft-Ebing died in 1902, he saw his book through twelve editions. On Krafft-Ebing's thought and influence see also Karlen, pp. 191–96.

16. Moreau, pp. 122–24.

17. P[aul] Brouardel, *Les Attentats aux mœurs*, p. 4; cf. the theories of Casper and Tarnowsky as described by John Addington Symonds, "A Problem in Modern Ethics," in Cory, pp. 19, 29.

18. Havelock Ellis, *Love and Pain*, p. 156.

19. Krafft-Ebing, tr. Klaf, pp. 414, n. 9, 88.

20. On this idea see Symonds in Cory, p. 30.

21. On this see especially Benjamin Tarnowsky, *Anthropological, Legal, and Medical Studies on Pederasty in Europe*, where we read that patients afflicted with senile dementia "have a special fondness for demoralizing youngsters and depraving them" (p. 103). Tarnowsky was a professor at the Imperial Academy of Medicine in Saint Petersburg, and his opinions on homosexuality were highly influential in the medical community of the late nineteenth and early twentieth centuries. A French version of his treatise on sexual aberration appeared in 1904 as *L'Instinct sexuel et ses manifestations morbides au double point de vue de la jurisprudence et de la psychiatrie*. On the taste of senile old men for young boys see also Krafft-Ebing, tr. Klaf, p. 374, and Moreau, p. 77. Proust speaks of the *ramolissement* [*sic*] of Charlus in *Le Temps retrouvé* (3: 1,019).

22. The portrait of Charlus in later life sometimes reads as if it were a cento of observations and case histories taken from Krafft-Ebing. Krafft-Ebing writes that *"old and decrepit debauchees . . . prefer boys"* but also observes that "for want of better material" any homosexually oriented man can "become dangerous to boys" (Klaf, tr., pp. 241–42). He describes the case of a man with homosexual preferences and says that "it was possible for him—though but an overgrown child, and incapable of personal independence—to live in society . . . under the care and guidance of normal individuals" (p. 261)—a description which recalls the relationship of nursemaid and "big baby" maintained by Jupien and Charlus in *Le Temps retrouvé*. Further, Krafft-Ebing reports the case of one T., who, like Jupien (2: 628), was interested only in older men and who "conceived a violent love for an old man whom he accompanied for years on his daily walks" (pp. 244–45).

23. Margaret Mein, "Le Thème de l'hérédité dans l'œuvre de Proust," p. 96.

24. Cf. Gourmont, "L'Amour à l'envers," p. 475.

25. Alfred C. Kinsey et al., *Sexual Behavior in the Human Female*, p. 448; cf. Churchill, pp. 60–69 and 100–20; Tripp, pp. 12–21 and 36; and Weinberg and Williams, pp. 6–7.

26. Freedman, pp. 14–15.

27. Tripp, p. 36.

28. Edward Carpenter, "The Intermediate Sex," in Cory, p. 152.

29. Tarnowsky, tr. Gardner, p. 129.

30. The linking of such traits with a homosexual orientation survives even in very recent psychoanalytic theory. For a summary and a refutation see Freedman, pp. 87–90.

31. There are, of course, other precedents for Proust's portrayal of the multiple self, among them the theme of the double as it appears in the work of such writers as Stevenson, Poe, Wilde, Maupassant, and Dostoevsky.

32. Karlen, p. 185.

33. Moreau, p. 154.

34. Brouardel, p. 11.

35. Rupert Hart-Davis, ed., *The Letters of Oscar Wilde*, pp. 401–02.

36. Quoted and translated in Steakley, p. 48.

37. Gide, *Corydon*, p. 38; and *Journal, 1889–1939*, p. 693.

38. Antoine Bibesco, p. 424.

39. Porel, p. 87.

40. The evidence against viewing homosexuality as an illness is by now overwhelming and is amplified yearly. As Weinberg and Williams point out, in much current sex research "homosexuality is not seen as ipso facto pathological but rather as a variant of sexual expression. It is assumed that there are many types of homosexuals, some with fewer psychological problems than others; and on the part of those with more problems, homosexuality is not necessarily a symptom or cause" (p. 6). In Britain the highly influential *Wolfenden Report* (1957) concluded that "homosexuality cannot legitimately be regarded as a disease, because in many cases it is the only symptom and is compatible with full mental health in other respects" (p. 32). In *Society and the Healthy Homosexual* (1972) George Weinberg predicted that the time would come when "prevailing psychiatric opinion will be that homosexuals are not all sick men and women" (p. 35). And two years later the American Psychiatric Association voted to remove homosexuality from its list of mental disorders. The evidence, both inductive and theoretical, continues to accumulate. For instance, a recent empirical study of 140 college-educated men who had a homosexual orientation and were not psychiatric patients indicated no significant differences in psychopathology between this group and a comparison group composed of heterosexually oriented people (T. Clark, "Homosexuality and Psychopathology in Nonpatient Males," pp. 163–68). See also Howard B. Roback et al., "Self-Concept and Psychological Adjustment Differences Between Self-Identified Male Transsexuals and Male Homosexuals," pp. 18–19.

41. *A la recherche* seems to contradict itself on the question of whether homosexuality can be "cured." In *Sodome I* the narrator first speaks of homosexuality as "an incurable sickness" (2: 616). But a little later he promises that "we shall see that inversion is curable" (2: 625). Despite this promise, we never see any instances of "curable" homosexuality in the novel. At one point

the narrator does speak of homosexually oriented people who, for one reason or another, are able to "detach" themselves from homosexual practices (3: 780). But this seems to be a matter of self-control, not of changing one's preferences. Proust's position on the curability of homosexuality is perhaps made clearer in a passage in the notebooks, where he states: "In certain homosexuals, extremely rare, the illness is not congenital; [and] in this superficial case it can be cured. Sometimes. . . . its cause is a feeling of disgust for women, a repugnance caused by their smell, by the texture of their skin—a repulsion which can be overcome, as in certain children who get sick when they see oysters or cheese and end by liking them very much; but, most often, those who are born with a taste for men die this way. On the surface their way of life can change; their vice no longer appears in their everyday habits; but nothing is lost; a hidden jewel is always found again; when the quantity of a sick man's urine diminishes, he perspires more copiously, but it is still necessary that the excretion be accomplished. A homosexual man seems cured; contrary to the laws of moral physics, the quantity of sensual energy which had seemed to be annihilated has simply been transferred elsewhere" (quoted in Maurois, p. 214; cf. A la recherche, 2: 625).

Like most other speculation on whether homosexuality can be changed or "cured," this passage assumes that homosexuality is an illness. When the illness fallacy is dismissed, such speculation becomes irrelevant; and it also becomes obvious why therapy has never been able to "cure" homosexual urges (Freund, "Should Homosexuality Arouse Therapeutic Concern?," p. 237; Tripp, p. 252). Such therapy tampers with a fundamental trait of human nature, existing, to be sure, in different people to different degrees but present wherever there are human beings. It tampers with what Thorkil Vanggaard calls "the homosexual radical." "A radical," Vanggaard writes, "is something inherent in humans, something which . . . exerts a powerful pressure, and which therefore has to be dealt with either by being given discharge in some form, or by being suppressed in one way or another" (Phallós, p. 16). Denouncing homosexual urges and attempting to change them makes, as John Money says, "as much sense as condemning a left-handed person for not being right-handed. The analogy between handedness and sexuality is not as farfetched as it may seem. Earlier in this century, left-handedness was condemned, and left-handed pupils were punished for not using the right hand. The outcome was impairment of all learning, not an increase of dextrality. Likewise, condemnation of homosexuality induces impairment of all sexuality rather than an increase of heterosexuality" ("Bisexual, Homosexual, and Heterosexual," pp. 230–31). Proust is right, then, when he says that homosexuality generally cannot be changed into heterosexuality and that its "sensual energy" cannot be annihilated. But he is right for the wrong reason, since his conclusion proceeds from the erroneous supposition that homosexuality is a disease.

42. Gourmont, "Variétés," p. 100.

43. Moreau, p. 165, n. 1.

44. Symonds in Cory, p. 25.

45. For further thoughts on this idea see Tripp, pp. 67–68.

46. *Great Dialogues of Plato*, pp. 133–34; *A la recherche*, 2: 614 ff., especially 623–26.

47. Symonds in Cory, p. 4.

48. Quoted and translated by Symonds in Cory, p. 19.

49. Symonds in Cory, p. 19; Tarnowsky, tr. Gardner, p. 120; and Paolo Mantegazza, "The Perversions of Love," in Cory, p. 259.

50. Richard Burton, "Terminal Essay: *The Book of the Thousand Nights and a Night*," in Cory, p. 218; Edward Carpenter, "The Intermediate Sex," in Cory, p. 155.

51. Quoted and translated in Richard Lewinsohn, *A History of Sexual Customs*, tr. Alexander Mayce, p. 342.

52. George Weinberg, p. 64.

53. Quoted and translated in Steakley, p. 82.

54. Deleuze, p. 9.

55. Weindel and Fischer, pp. 62–80; see also Kinsey, Pomeroy, and Martin, *Male*, pp. 618–20; and Lauritsen and Thorstad, pp. 60–61.

56. Kinsey, Pomeroy, and Martin, *Male*, pp. 650–51.

57. Churchill, p. 49.

58. Kinsey, Pomeroy, and Martin, *Male*, p. 626.

59. The first comprehensive survey of sexual practices in America after Kinsey was carried out by a group funded by the Playboy Foundation. The results were reported in a *Playboy* article entitled "Sexual Behavior in the 1970's" and in a book with the same title. Both article and book were written by Morton Hunt. The *Playboy* study tried to quarrel with the Kinsey figures on homosexuality and did so at the cost of some misrepresentation of Kinsey's research. The article states that "our guarded conclusions . . . are that some 20 to 25 percent of all American males have at least one homosexual experience and that this figure is about the same as an educated downward correction of Kinsey's exaggerated incidence" (p. 194). The article goes on to state that "much of the homosexual experience included in both Kinsey's figures and our own is early or adolescent play or experiment" (p. 194). Hunt thus implies that the inclusion of adolescent homosexual experience somehow mitigates or invalidates his and Kinsey's findings—as if there were some difference between adolescent homosexual contacts and "real" homosexuality (see also Hunt, *Sexual Behavior in the 1970's*, p. 306). Kinsey's point, however, is that homosexuality is homosexuality. For Kinsey there are no "homosexuals"; there are only homosexual acts and homosexual feelings occurring with varying degrees of regularity in different individuals. In light of the *Playboy* study's attack on Kinsey's methods and conclusions, it should be emphasized that Kinsey's figure of 50 percent homosexual feeling and/or ex-

perience includes only males who have reached sexual maturity (i.e., males between adolescence and old age) and that, as Churchill points out, "if the homosexual activities of . . . younger males were counted the figures would be substantially higher" (Churchill, p. 49).

The Kinsey study of male sexuality was based on responses from 5,300 males; the *Playboy* study was based on responses from roughly 982 males. Kinsey and his associates state that their study is "an attempt to accumulate an objectively determined body of fact about sex which strictly avoids social or moral interpretations of the fact" (Kinsey, Pomeroy, and Martin, *Male*, p. 5); the *Playboy* study condemns "sex researchers and sexual liberals [who are] loath to make any value judgments about . . . sexual behavior" (*Sexual Behavior in the 1970's*, p. 295). The underlying premises of the two studies—and their relative scientific value—should be clear.

Tripp (pp. 232–40) has an instructive discussion of the efforts which were made after the publication of Kinsey's research to distort and devalue it on moralistic or quasi-scientific grounds. The *Playboy* study shows that these efforts are still continuing.

60. Karlen, p. 512; Fritz A. Fluckiger, rev. of *The Homosexual Matrix*, by C. A. Tripp, p. 170.

61. Kinsey, Pomeroy, and Martin, *Male*, p. 617.

62. William C. Carter has also noticed that Charlus's statistics coincide with those of Kinsey. See the synopsis of his research in the *Proust Research Association Newsletter* (1973), no. 10, pp. 24–25.

63. Ellis, *Sexual Inversion*, p. 28, n. 1.

64. Carpenter in Cory, p. 195.

65. Timothy d'Arch Smith, *Love in Earnest*, p. 191.

66. *Essais et articles*, p. 630.

67. Quoted in Painter, *The Later Years*, p. 120, n. 1.

68. Smith, p. 193.

69. *Lettres à André Gide*, pp. 38–39.

70. For more on class distinction and homosexuality see Tripp, pp. 168–69.

71. Hyde, p. 201; *The Letters of Oscar Wilde*, p. 402; Karlen, p. 257; Krafft-Ebing, tr. Klaf, p. 192 and passim; Ellis, *Sexual Inversion*, p. 119 and passim; Steakley, p. 61.

72. George Domino, "Homosexuality and Creativity," pp. 261–67.

73. Ambroise Tardieu, *Etude médico-légale sur les attentats aux mœurs*, p. 216; Carpenter in Cory, pp. 150–51; Krafft-Ebing, tr. Klaf, pp. 252, 258 ff.; Tarnowsky, tr. Gardner, p. 19; cf. Churchill, pp. 39–41.

74. *"Contre Sainte-Beuve" suivi de "Nouveaux mélanges*," p. 261.

75. Cf. the statement of a homosexually oriented doctor quoted by Krafft-Ebing: "I know about 120 'aunts' personally. Most of them—particularly myself, who possess the instinct to a very high degree—have the

ability of being able to tell immediately whether another is also a pervert"
(Klaf, tr., p. 252). Tarnowsky also asserted that the homosexual man "is at
once recognized by his appearance" (Gardner, tr., p. 19).

76. On Ulrichs's influence see Eglinton, p. 372; Steakley, pp. 3–17; and
Weindel and Fischer, p. 272.

77. Karl Heinrich Ulrichs, *Memnon*, p. vii and passim; Steakley, pp. 6,
8, 16. Steakley (p. 8) explains that Ulrichs took the term *Urning* from "Plato's
Symposium, in which the patron goddess of men who love other men is identified as Aphrodite Urania" [the heavenly Aphrodite].

78. *Lettres à André Gide*, p. 39.

79. Tarnowsky, tr. Gardner, p. 23.

80. Carpenter in Cory, p. 152; Charles Godfrey Leland, *The Alternate
Sex*, pp. 41, 51.

81. Quoted in Maurois, pp. 208–9.

82. "*Contre Sainte-Beuve*" suivi de "*Nouveaux mélanges*," p. 261, n. 1.
On the use of gender confusion as a source of "simplistic amusements" see
Tripp, pp. 26–27.

83. Kinsey, Pomeroy, and Martin, *Male*, p. 647.

84. Tripp, pp. 22–23, 35, 98, 127.

85. Apparently, however, masculine traits in women do not always
equal lesbianism. There are, the narrator says, certain women whose masculine traits have caused them to marry homosexually oriented men. This is the
case with Mme de Vaugoubert, of whom the narrator says, "Mme de Vaugoubert was a man" (2: 645), without, however, suggesting that she might also
have lesbian inclinations. The same is true of the wife of M. d'Huxelles, a
man whose homosexuality was mentioned by Saint-Simon. Charlus discusses
Mme d'Huxelles in the same terms the narrator applies to Mme de Vaugoubert, and it is Charlus who formulates the rule that "in general, the wife of an
Aunt is a man" (3: 304). In neither case is there any hint that these masculine
wives of homosexually oriented men have lesbian tendencies. Indeed, the
narrator proposes a complicated series of reasons for the mannishness of such
women, among which lesbianism is conspicuous by its absence (2: 645–47).

86. Symonds in Cory, pp. 16–17.

87. On this see Freud's letter to the mother of a homosexually inclined
son, where he states that homosexuality "cannot be classified as an illness; we
consider it to be a variation of the sexual function produced by a certain arrest of sexual development." Quoted in Bieber et al., *Homosexuality*, p. 275.

88. Tripp, p. 162.

89. D. A. Begelman, rev. of *The Homosexual Matrix*, by C. A. Tripp, p.
168.

90. Churchill, p. 113.

91. George Weinberg, p. 26.

92. Cf. Tripp, p. 29.

93. Weinberg and Williams, p. 158; cf. Freedman, p. 97; and Tripp, p. 162.

94. See for instance the reminiscences in René Boylesve, *Feuilles tombées*, pp. 266–67 and Edmond Jaloux, *Avec Marcel Proust*, p. 11.

95. Quoted and translated in Lauritsen and Thorstad, p. 24.

96. Cf. Maurois, pp. 211–15.

97. *Lettres à André Gide*, p. 39.

98. Louie Crew and Rictor Norton, "The Homophobic Imagination," p. 283.

99. He mentions them in *A la recherche* (3: 709; 2: 229). The passages from Gautier and the Sâr Péladan are quoted in A. J. L. Busst, "The Image of the Androgyne in the Nineteenth Century," pp. 41, 57.

100. Kupffer is quoted and translated in Steakley, p. 46; Friedländer is quoted and translated in Lauritsen and Thorstad, p. 50; Gide, *Corydon*, p. 36.

101. Quoted in Lauri Goodman, "Transsexual Crisis Resolved in Surgery," p. 2.

102. Jan Morris, *Conundrum*, pp. 26, 11, 22.

103. *Le Carnet de 1908*, p. 63; Maurois, p. 211.

104. Morris, pp. 24, 62; Richard Green, *Sexual Identity Conflict in Children and Adults*, pp. 50–51 and passim; Deborah Heller Feinbloom, *Transvestites & Transsexuals*, pp. 175–76 and passim.

105. George Weinberg, pp. 65–68.

106. Robert J. Stoller, *Sex and Gender, I: The Development of Masculinity and Femininity*, pp. 126–30, 97; Green, pp. 18–21, 227–29; Morris, p. 8.

107. Stoller, p. 190.

108. The term "transsexual" does not occur before 1949, when, as Arno Karlen points out, "Dr. David O. Cauldwell described a woman who wanted to be a man and called it a distinct syndrome, which he named *psychopathia transsexualis*" (p. 372). The term "homosexuality" was coined in 1869 by the Hungarian doctor Károly Mária Benkert (1824–82). The origin of the term "sexual inversion" is not known. Havelock Ellis speculates that it perhaps first appeared in English and was then adopted by the Romance languages (*Sexual Inversion*, pp. 2–3). See also Steakley, pp. 11–12.

109. Thorkil Vanggaard, *Phallós*, p. 12 and passim; see also Hans Licht [pseud. of Paul Brandt], *Sexual Life in Ancient Greece*, pp. 440–98.

110. Gide, *Corydon*, p. 9, n. 1.

111. On the Sacred Band see Paul Brandt, pp. 442–43.

112. Shattuck, p. 124.

113. Lauritsen and Thorstad, pp. 78–79.

114. Leo Bersani, *Marcel Proust*, p. 71.

115. *A un ami*, p. 149.

5 . MONSTERS OF TIME

1. Maurice Samuel, "The Concealments of Marcel," p. 14 and passim; Melvin Seiden, "Proust's Marcel and Saint-Loup," p. 240 and passim; Marcel Muller, *Les Voix narratives dans la "Recherche du Temps perdu,"* pp. 13, n. 22, and 144–56.

2. See for instance Moreau, pp. 97–121; Krafft-Ebing, tr. Klaf, pp. 223, 230, 259.

3. See for instance Krafft-Ebing, tr. Klaf, p. 192 and passim.

4. Tarnowsky, tr. Gardner, p. 46; cf. Krafft-Ebing, tr. Klaf, pp. 223–24 and passim; and Moreau, p. 123.

5. Kinsey and his associates found that for two-thirds (68.4 percent) of preadolescent boys "self masturbation provides the first ejaculation." Kinsey, Pomeroy, and Martin, *Male,* p. 499.

6. Krafft-Ebing, tr. Klaf, pp. 188–90 and passim; cf. Moreau, who comments that "everyone is familiar with the physical disorders which are the fatal consequence of unbridled masturbation: dizzy spells, blackouts, insomnia, painful or voluptuous dreams, sudden awakenings, palpitations, ringing in the ears, weakening of vision, loss of appetite, pain in the back, loss of muscle tone . . . etc." (pp. 173–74).

7. Moncrieff translates: "I explored, across the bounds of my own experience, an untrodden path which, I believed, might lead me to my death, even—until passion spent itself and left me shuddering among the sprays of flowering currant which, creeping in through the window, tumbled all about my body" (*Remembrance of Things Past,* 1: 121). Moncrieff omits the reference to seminal fluid and the comparison of the fluid to "the track of a snail."

8. Krafft-Ebing, tr. Klaf, p. 384.

9. O'Brien, "Albertine the Ambiguous," p. 941; cf. p. 939, n. 9.

10. Weindel and Fischer, p. 7.

11. Burton in Cory, pp. 224, 221. See also the Koran 11: 77–84; and 15: 58–74.

12. Jean Milly, "Le Pastiche Goncourt dans *Le Temps retrouvé,*" p. 833.

13. Shattuck, p. 131.

14. *Marcel Proust et Jacques Rivière: Correspondance,* p. 2.

15. H. Kopman, *Rencontres With the Inanimate in Proust's "Recherche,"* p. 24.

16. Roland Barthes, "Une Idée de recherche," p. 27.

17. Burton in Cory, p. 244.

18. In making Gomorrah the mythical homeland of women who love women, Proust is partly following the lead of Alfred de Vigny's poem "La Colère de Samson," from which he took the second epigraph for *Sodome et Gomorrhe* ("Woman will have Gomorrah and Man will have Sodom").

19. For a consideration of this pattern from a different perspective see Marcel Muller, "*Sodome I* ou la naturalisation de Charlus," p. 476 and pas-

sim. Muller defines it as "initial accord, inevitable separation, necessary reconciliation."

20. *Great Dialogues of Plato*, pp. 131–34.

21. For further thoughts on the relationship of homosexuality and Jewishness in *A la recherche* see Barbara J. Bucknall, *The Religion of Art in Proust*, pp. 145–46.

22. Marcel Muller has previously noticed the equation of Sodom with Eden in *Sodome I*, and this detail supports his argument. See his "*Sodome I*," pp. 474–75.

23. Edmund Wilson, *Axel's Castle*, p. 181.

24. The mention of an embassy staffed by men with homosexual tastes is almost certainly an allusion to the rumors current during the Eulenburg affair that homosexuality was especially rampant in the field of diplomacy. Eulenburg had distinguished himself in the German foreign service. On this see Lewinsohn, p. 341 and Garde, p. 679.

25. Carolyn G. Heilbrun, *Toward a Recognition of Androgyny*, pp. 5, 89–90, 87.

26. Deleuze, pp. 146–48; Appignanesi, pp. 205–15.

27. A. J. L. Busst, "The Image of the Androgyne in the Nineteenth Century," p. 10 and passim; see also Françoise Cachin, "Monsieur Vénus et l'ange de Sodome: L'androgyne au temps de Gustave Moreau."

28. Charles Darwin, *The Descent of Man*, p. 339.

29. For a more detailed consideration of the difference between the Freudian and Jungian conceptions of androgyny and bisexuality see June Singer, *Androgyny*, pp. 90–100.

30. C. G. Jung, *The Archetypes and the Collective Unconscious*, p. 71.

31. *Correspondance générale*, 5: 190–91; *Essais et articles*, p. 336; cf. *Lettres à Reynaldo Hahn*, p. 206; and Princesse Bibesco, *Au bal avec Marcel Proust*, p. 34.

32. Marie Delcourt, *Hermaphrodite*, pp. 72–74, 81–83, 101; and June Singer, *Androgyny*, pp. 90–100.

33. Cf. O'Brien, "Albertine the Ambiguous," p. 950.

34. *Essais et articles*, p. 534.

35. Delcourt, pp. 22, 11–12, and passim; Walter F. Otto, *Dionysus*, p. 176; Aristophanes, *Frogs*, 45–46, 96; and see Cedric H. Whitman, *Aristophanes and the Comic Hero*, p. 236.

36. Otto, pp. 176, 110.

37. Weinberg and Williams, pp. 177–78.

38. Eric Bentley, *Theatre of War*, pp. 341–42.

39. Jean Gillibert, "L'Acteur, médian sexuel," pp. 71–72.

40. Northrop Frye, *A Natural Perspective*, p. 83.

41. Krafft-Ebing, tr. Klaf, p. 226; cf. Ellis, *Sexual Inversion*, pp. 311 ff.

42. Quoted from Victor Hugo, *Œuvres poétiques*, 1: 964–65. This allusion escapes the usually astute eye of Jacques Nathan, who fails to identify it

in his *Citations, références et allusions de Marcel Proust dans "A la recherche du temps perdu."* The source in Hugo was pointed out to me by Professor Jeffrey Meyers. Proust is probably quoting, as usual, from memory, and he makes a slight mistake, writing *être* ("creature") where Hugo has *âme* ("soul"). The poem might be roughly translated as follows:

> Since here below every soul
>   Gives to someone
> Its music, its flame,
>   Or its fragrance;

> Since here below everything
>   Always gives
> Its thorn or its rose
>   To the things it loves;

> Since April to the oak trees gives
>   A charming sound;
> And night gives to griefs
>   The forgetfulness of sleep;

>   .   .   .

> I give you, in this hour,
>   As I bend down to you,
> The best thing
>   I have within me!

> Receive, then, the gift of my thought,
>   Which is, moreover, sad,
> And which, like the dew,
>   Comes in sobs to you!

>   .   .   .

> [Receive] my transports of intoxication,
>   Purified of distrust,
> And all the caresses
>   Of my songs!

43. *Great Dialogues of Plato*, p. 150.

44. Ibid.

45. Rina Viers, "Evolution et sexualité des plantes dans *Sodome et Gomorrhe*," pp. 105–7.

46. Charles Darwin, *The Different Forms of Flowers on Plants of the Same Species*, p. 138.

47. Havelock Ellis, *Analysis of the Sexual Impulse*, in *Studies in the Psychology of Sex*, 1: 34. Ellis is summarizing a paper by the nineteenth-century naturalist James Bladon.

48. Brooke, p. 16; Maurois, p. 218; cf. Brooke, p. 18.

49. Bardèche, 2: 60.

50. Ibid., 2: 60 and passim.

51. Alfred de Vigny, *Œuvres complètes*, p. 197.

52. Serge Gaubert, "Proust et le jeu de l'alphabet."

53. Bersani, p. 137.

54. Appignanesi, pp. 161, 169, 190, 205, and passim. Appignanesi does concede at one point that "the experience of maleness is also important to the formation of the total artist" (p. 203). But the burden of her argument is that femininity overshadows masculinity in the narrator's development.

55. Brooke, p. 15.

56. The source is identified by the editors of the Pléiade edition of *A la recherche* (2: 1,198). The text by Leconte de Lisle, from which Proust's quotation diverges at certain points, can be found in *Hésiode; Hymnes orphiques; Théocrite; Bion; Moskhos; Tyrtée; Odes anacréontiques*, tr. Leconte de Lisle (Paris: Lemerre, n.d.), p. 90.

57. Robert Graves, *The Greek Myths*, 1: 30. See also *The Oxford Classical Dictionary*, 2nd ed., s.v. "Phanes."

58. Cf. Appignanesi, p. 196.

59. Bersani, p. 55; cf. *Le Carnet de 1908*, p. 69.

60. Delcourt, pp. 82–83, 101.

61. On these myths see Edward Carpenter, *Intermediate Types Among Primitive Folk*, pp. 71–83; Delcourt, pp. 67–83; and Singer, pp. 55–66 and passim.

62. Quoted in Delcourt, p. 71.

63. *Le Carnet de 1908*, p. 80.

6 . EPILOGUE

1. Jonathan Katz, *Gay American History*, pp. 6–7.

2. Richard Poirier, *The Performing Self*, p. vii.

3. Poirier, p. xv.

BIBLIOGRAPHY

WORKS BY MARCEL PROUST

A la recherche du temps perdu. Edited by Pierre Clarac and André Ferré. 3 vols. Paris: Gallimard, Bibliothèque de la Pléiade, 1954.

"Before Dark" ["Avant la nuit"]. Translated by Richard Howard. In Seymour Kleinberg, ed. *The Other Persuasion: An Anthology of Short Fiction About Gay Men and Women.* New York: Vintage, 1977.

Carnet de 1908, Le. Edited by Philip Kolb. Cahiers Marcel Proust, Nouvelle Série, vol. 8. Paris: Gallimard, 1976.

"Contre Sainte-Beuve" précédé de "Pastiches et mélanges" et suivi de "Essais et articles." Edited by Pierre Clarac and Yves Sandre. Paris: Gallimard, Bibliothèque de la Pléiade, 1971.

"Contre Sainte-Beuve" suivi de "Nouveaux mélanges." 14th ed. Paris: Gallimard, 1954.

"In the Twilight" ["Avant la nuit"]. Translated by Abigail Sanford. *The Ladder* (1960), 5: 4–8.

"Jean Santeuil" précédé de "Les Plaisirs et les jours." Edited by Pierre Clarac and Yves Sandre. Paris: Gallimard, Bibliothèque de la Pléiade, 1971.

Past Recaptured, The [*Le Temps retrouvé*]. Translated by Andreas Mayor. New York: Vintage, 1971.

Pastiches de Proust, Les: Edition critique et commentée. Edited by Jean Milly. Paris: Colin, 1970.

Pleasures and Regrets [*Les Plaisirs et les jours*]. Translated by Louise Varèse. New York: Crown, Lear Book, 1948.

297

Remembrance of Things Past [*A la recherche du temps perdu*]. Translated by C. K. Scott Moncrieff and Frederick A. Blossom. 2 vols. New York: Random House, 1934.

CORRESPONDENCE OF MARCEL PROUST

A un ami: Correspondance inédite, 1903–1922. Paris: Amiot-Dumont, 1948.

Choix de lettres. Edited by Philip Kolb. Paris: Plon, 1965.

Correspondance de Marcel Proust, 1880–1895. Vol. 1. Edited by Philip Kolb. Paris: Plon, 1970.

Correspondance de Marcel Proust, 1896–1901. Vol. 2. Edited by Philip Kolb. Paris: Plon, 1976.

Correspondance générale. 6 vols. Edited by Robert Proust, Suzy Mante-Proust, and Paul Brach. Paris: Plon, 1930–36.

Lettres à André Gide, avec trois lettres et deux textes d'André Gide. Neuchâtel and Paris: Ides et Calendes, 1949.

Lettres à la N. R. F. Les Cahiers Marcel Proust, vol. 6. Paris: Gallimard, 1932.

Lettres à Reynaldo Hahn. Edited by Philip Kolb. 7th ed. Paris: Gallimard, 1956.

Lettres retrouvées. Edited by Philip Kolb. Paris: Plon, 1966.

Marcel Proust et Jacques Rivière: Correspondance, 1914–1922. Edited by Philip Kolb. Paris: Plon, 1955.

"Marcel Proust et la Bourse: Trois lettres inédites au marquis d'Albufera." *Le Figaro*, 9 July 1971, p. 16.

WORKS ABOUT MARCEL PROUST

Albaret, Céleste. *Monsieur Proust.* Edited by Georges Belmont. Paris: Robert Laffont-Opera Mundi, 1973.

Appignanesi, Lisa. *Femininity and the Creative Imagination: A Study of Henry James, Robert Musil, and Marcel Proust.* New York: Harper, Barnes and Noble, 1973.

Bardèche, Maurice. *Marcel Proust, romancier.* 2 vols. Paris: Sept Couleurs, 1971.

Barthes, Roland. "Une Idée de recherche." *Paragone* (1971), no. 260, pp. 25–30.

Bergler, Edmund. "Proust and the 'Torture-Theory' of Love." *The American Imago* (1953), 10: 265–88.

Bersani, Leo. *Marcel Proust: The Fictions of Life and of Art*. New York: Oxford University Press, 1965.

Bibesco, Antoine. "The Heartlessness of Marcel Proust." *The Cornhill Magazine* (1950), no. 983, pp. 421–28.

Bibesco, Princesse. *Au bal avec Marcel Proust*. 1928. Reprint. Cahiers Marcel Proust, Nouvelle Série, vol. 2. Paris: Gallimard, 1970.

Billy, Robert de. *Marcel Proust: Lettres et conversations*. Paris: Editions des Portiques, 1930.

Bonnet, Henri. *Marcel Proust de 1907 à 1914*. Rev. and enl. ed. Paris: Nizet, 1971.

Boulanger, J.-B. "Un Cas d'inversion coupable: Marcel Proust." *L'Union Médicale du Canada* (1951), 80: 483–93.

Brooke, Jocelyn. "Proust and Joyce: The Case for the Prosecution." *Adam: International Review* (1961), 29(297–98): 5–66.

Bucknall, Barbara J. *The Religion of Art in Proust*. Urbana: University of Illinois Press, 1969.

Carter, William C. "A Synopsis of Proust's Remarks Concerning Homosexuality." *Proust Research Association Newsletter* (1973), no. 10, pp. 22–25.

Daudet, Lucien. *Autour de soixante lettres de Marcel Proust*. Les Cahiers Marcel Proust, vol. 5. Paris: Gallimard, 1929.

Deleuze, Gilles. *Proust et les signes*. Paris: Presses Universitaires de France, 1971.

Doubrovsky, Serge. *La Place de la madeleine: Ecriture et fantasme chez Proust*. Paris: Mercure de France, 1974.

Dreyfus, Robert. *Souvenirs sur Marcel Proust, accompagnés de lettres inédites*. Paris: Grasset, 1926.

Ferré, André. *Les Années de collège de Marcel Proust*. 4th ed. Paris: Gallimard, 1959.

Gaubert, Serge. "Proust et le jeu de l'alphabet." *Europe* (1971), no. 502–3, pp. 68–82.

Graham, Victor E. *The Imagery of Proust.* New York: Barnes and Noble, 1966.

Gregh, Fernand. *Mon amitié avec Marcel Proust: Souvenirs et lettres inédites.* Paris: Grasset, 1958.

Guichard, Léon. *Introduction à la lecture de Proust.* Paris: Nizet, 1969.

Hewitt, James Robert. *Marcel Proust.* New York: Ungar, 1975.

Hindus, Milton. "The Pattern of Proustian Love." *New Mexico Quarterly* (1951), 21: 389–405.

—— *The Proustian Vision.* 1954. Reprint. Carbondale and Edwardsville: Southern Illinois University Press; London: Feffer and Simons, 1967.

Hommage à Marcel Proust. Les Cahiers Marcel Proust, vol. 1. Paris: Gallimard, 1927.

Jaloux, Edmond. *Avec Marcel Proust, suivi de dix-sept lettres inédites de Proust.* Paris: La Palatine, 1953.

Jones, David L. "Dolorès Disparue." *Symposium* (1966), 20: 135–40.

Kolb, Philip. "Historique du premier roman de Proust." *Saggi e ricerche di letteratura francese* (1963), 4: 217–77.

Kopman, H. *Rencontres With the Inanimate in Proust's "Recherche."* Paris: Mouton, 1971.

Levin, Harry and Justin O'Brien. "Proust, Gide, and the Sexes." *PMLA* (1950), 65: 648–53.

Maurois, André. *A la recherche de Marcel Proust.* 1949. Reprint. Paris: Hachette, 1970.

Mein, Margaret. "Le Thème de l'hérédité dans l'œuvre de Proust." *Europe* (1971), no. 502–3, pp. 83–99.

Miller, Milton L. *Nostalgia: A Psychoanalytic Study of Marcel Proust.* Boston: Houghton, 1956.

Milly, Jean. "Le Pastiche Goncourt dans *Le Temps retrouvé.*" *Revue d'Histoire Littéraire de la France* (1971), 71: 815–35.

Muller, Marcel. *Les Voix narratives dans la "Recherche du Temps perdu."* Geneva: Droz, 1965.

—— "*Sodome I* ou la naturalisation de Charlus." *Poétique* (1971), 8: 470–78.

Nathan, Jacques. *Citations, références et allusions de Marcel Proust dans "A la recherche du temps perdu."* Rev. and enl. ed. Paris: Nizet, 1969.

O'Brien, Justin. "Albertine the Ambiguous: Notes on Proust's Transposition of Sexes." *PMLA* (1949), 64: 933–52.

—— "An Aspect of Proust's Baron de Charlus." *Romanic Review* (1964), 55: 38–41.

Painter, George D. *Proust: The Early Years.* Boston: Little, 1959.

—— *Proust: The Later Years.* Boston: Little, 1965.

Pierre-Quint, Léon. *Proust et la stratégie littéraire, avec des lettres de Marcel Proust à René Blum, Bernard Grasset, et Louis Brun.* Paris: Corrêa, 1954.

Plantevignes, Marcel. *Avec Marcel Proust: Causeries-Souvenirs sur Cabourg et le Boulevard Hussmann.* Paris: Nizet, 1966.

Porel, Jacques. "Marcel Proust chez Réjane." *La Table Ronde* (1950), no. 34, pp. 82–97.

Quennell, Peter, ed. *Marcel Proust: A Centennial Volume.* New York: Simon, 1971.

Robert, Louis de. *Comment débuta Marcel Proust: Lettres inédites suivi de souvenirs et confidences sur Marcel Proust et de réflexions sur Marcel Proust.* Rev. and enl. ed. Paris: Gallimard, 1969.

Samuel, Maurice. "The Concealments of Marcel: Proust's Jewishness." *Commentary* (1960), 29: 8–22.

Sansom, William. *Proust and His World.* New York: Scribners, 1973.

Seiden, Melvin. "Proust's Marcel and Saint-Loup: Inversion Reconsidered." *Contemporary Literature* (1969), 10: 220–40.

Shattuck, Roger. *Marcel Proust.* New York: Viking, 1974.

Souday, Paul. *Marcel Proust.* Paris: Kra, 1927.

Soupault, Robert. *Marcel Proust du côté de la médecine.* Paris: Plon, 1967.

Viers, Rina. "Evolution et sexualité des plantes dans *Sodome et Gomorrhe.*" *Europe* (1971), no. 502–3, pp. 100–13.

Vigneron, Robert. "Genèse de *Swann.*" *Revue d'Histoire de la Philosophie et d'Historie Générale de la Civilisation* (1937), 5: 67–115.

Wilson, Edmund. *Axel's Castle: A Study in the Imaginative Literature of 1870–1930.* New York: Scribners, 1931.

Zéphir, Jacques J. *La Personnalité humaine dans l'œuvre de Marcel Proust: Essai de psychologie littéraire.* Paris: Minard, 1959.

WORKS ABOUT SEXUALITY AND
HOMOSEXUALITY

Allen, D. G. MacDonald. *The Janus Sex: The Androgynous Challenge.* Hicksville, N.Y.: Exposition, 1975.

Bailey, Derrick Sherwin. *Homosexuality and the Western Christian Tradition.* New York: Longmans, 1955.

Baumont, Maurice. *L'Affaire Eulenburg et les origines de la guerre mondiale.* Paris: Payot, 1933.

Begelman, D. A. Review of *Beyond Sexual Freedom*, by Charles W. Socarides. *Journal of Homosexuality* (1976), 1: 322–25.

—— Review of *The Homosexual Matrix*, by C. A. Tripp. *Journal of Homosexuality* (1976–77), 2: 167–69.

Bentley, Eric. "An Interview With Eric Bentley." Conducted by Rictor Norton. *College English* (1974), 36: 291–302.

Bieber, Irving, Harvey J. Dain, Paul R. Dince, Marvin G. Drellich, Henry G. Grand, Ralph H. Gundlach, Malvina W. Kremer, Alfred H. Rifkin, Cornelia B. Wilbur, and Toby B. Bieber. *Homosexuality: A Psychoanalytic Study.* New York: Basic Books, 1962.

Bieber, Irving, Paul Goodman, Richard H. Kuh, Dick Leitsch, Phyllis Lyon, Marya Mannes, Judd Marmor, Ted McIlvenna, Morris Ploscowe, William Simon, and Kenneth Tynan. "Playboy Panel: Homosexuality." *Playboy* (1971), 18(4): 61–92, 164, 178–91.

Binet-Valmer, [Jean-Gustave]. *Lucien.* 19th ed. Paris: Ollendorf, 1910.

Brand, Adolf. "Paragraph 175." 1914. Reprinted in *Documents of the Homosexual Rights Movement in Germany, 1836–1927.* Edited by Jonathan Katz. New York: Arno Press, 1975.

Brandt, Paul [Hans Licht]. *Sexual Life in Ancient Greece.* Translated by J. H. Freese. Edited by Lawrence H. Dawson. 10th ed. London: Abbey Library, 1971.

Brouardel, P[aul]. *Les Attentats aux mœurs.* Cours de Médecine Légale de la Faculté de Médecine de Paris. Paris: Baillière, 1909.

Brown, J. A. C. *Freud and the Post-Freudians.* Baltimore: Penguin, 1964.

Buchen, Irving, ed. *The Perverse Imagination: Sexuality and Literary Culture.* New York: New York University Press, 1970.

Busst, A. J. L. "The Image of the Androgyne in the Nineteenth Century." In *Romantic Mythologies.* Edited by Ian Fletcher. London: Routledge, 1967, pp. 1–95.

Cachin, Françoise. "Monsieur Vénus et l'ange de Sodome: L'androgyne au temps de Gustave Moreau." *Nouvelle Revue de Psychanalyse* (1973), no. 7, pp. 63–69.

Carpenter, Edward. *Intermediate Types Among Primitive Folk: A Study in Social Evolution.* London: Allen; Manchester: Clarke, 1914.

Churchill, Wainwright. *Homosexual Behavior Among Males: A Cross-Cultural and Cross-Species Investigation.* New York: Hawthorn, 1967.

Clark, T. "Homosexuality and Psychopathology in Nonpatient Males." *American Journal of Psychoanalysis* (1975), 35: 163–68.

Cochran, William G., Frederick Mosteller, John W. Tukey, and W. O. Jenkins. *Statistical Problems of the Kinsey Report on Sexual Behavior in the Human Male: A Report of the American Statistical Association Committee to Advise the National Research Council Committee for Research in Problems of Sex.* Washington: American Statistical Association, 1954.

Cory, Donald Webster, ed. *Homosexuality: A Cross Cultural Approach.* New York: Julian Press, 1956.

Crew, Louie and Rictor Norton. "The Homophobic Imagination: An Editorial." *College English* (1974), 36: 272–90.

Delcourt, Marie. *Hermaphrodite: Myths and Rites of the Bisexual Figure in Classical Antiquity.* Translated by Jennifer Nicholson. London: Studio Books, 1961.

Domino, George. "Homosexuality and Creativity." *Journal of Homosexuality* (1977), 2: 261–67.

Eglinton, J. Z. *Greek Love.* New York: Oliver Layton Press, 1964.

Ellis, Havelock. *Analysis of the Sexual Impulse.* 1903. Reprinted in *Studies in the Psychology of Sex,* vol. 1. New York: Random House, 1936.

—— *Love and Pain.* 1903. Reprinted in *Studies in the Psychology of Sex,* vol. 1. New York: Random House, 1936.

Ellis, Havelock [and John Addington Symonds]. *Sexual Inversion.* 1896. Reprinted in *Studies in the Psychology of Sex,* vol. 1. New York: Random House, 1936.

Feinbloom, Deborah Heller. *Transvestites & Transsexuals: Mixed Views.* New York: Delacorte Press/Seymour Lawrence, 1976.

Fluckiger, Fritz A. "Research Through a Glass, Darkly: An Evaluation of the Bieber Study on Homosexuality." *The Ladder* (1966), 10(10): 16–26, (11): 18–26, (12): 22–26.

—— Review of *The Homosexual Matrix,* by C. A. Tripp. *Journal of Homosexuality* (1976–77), 2: 170.

Freedman, Mark. *Homosexuality and Psychological Functioning.* Belmont, Calif.: Wadsworth, Brooks/Cole, 1971.

Freund, Kurt. "Should Homosexuality Arouse Therapeutic Concern?" *Journal of Homosexuality* (1977), 2: 235–40.

Garde, Noel I. *Jonathan to Gide: The Homosexual in History.* New York: Vantage Press, 1964.

Gide, André. *Corydon.* 56th ed. Paris: Gallimard, 1948.

Gillibert, Jean. "L'Acteur, médian sexuel." *Nouvelle Revue de Psychanalyse* (1973), no. 7, pp. 71–77.

Goodman, Lauri. "Transsexual Crisis Resolved in Surgery." *The Cavalier Daily* (University of Virginia), 28 March 1973, p. 2.

Gourmont, Rémy de. "Dialogues des Amateurs, L: L'Amour à l'envers." *Mercure de France* (1907), 70: 474–77.

—— "Dialogues des Amateurs, LII: Variétés." *Mercure de France* (1908), 71: 98–100.

Grand-Carteret, John. *Derrière "Lui": L'Homosexualité en Allemagne.* Paris: Bernard, 1908.

Green, Richard. *Sexual Identity Conflict in Children and Adults.* New York: Basic Books, 1974.

Hatterer, Lawrence J. *Changing Homosexuality in the Male: Treatment for Men Troubled by Homosexuality.* New York: McGraw-Hill, 1970.

Heilbrun, Carolyn G. *Toward a Recognition of Androgyny.* New York: Knopf, 1973.

Hirschfeld, Magnus. *Les Homosexuels de Berlin: Le Troisième Sexe.* Paris: Rousset, 1908.

—— *Sappho und Sokrates: Wie erklärt sich die Liebe der Männer und Frauen zu Personen des eigenen Geschlechts?* 1896. Reprinted in *Documents of the Homosexual Rights Movement in Germany, 1836–1927.* Edited by Jonathan Katz. New York: Arno Press, 1975.

Hunt, Morton. "Sexual Behavior in the 1970's." *Playboy* (1973), 20(10): 85–88, 194, 197–207.

—— *Sexual Behavior in the 1970's.* Chicago: Playboy Press, 1974.

Hyde, H. Montgomery. *Famous Trials: Seventh Series: Oscar Wilde.* 1948. Reprinted as *The Trials of Oscar Wilde.* New York: Dover, 1973.

Jones, Ernest. *Essays in Applied Psychoanalysis.* Vol. 1. London: Hogarth, 1951.

Jung, C. G. *The Archetypes and the Collective Unconscious.* Translated by R. F. C. Hull. 2nd ed. Princeton: Princeton University Press, 1968.

Kantrowitz, Arnie. "Homosexuals and Literature." *College English* (1974), 36: 324–30.

Karlen, Arno. *Sexuality and Homosexuality: A New View.* New York: Norton, 1971.

Katz, Jonathan. *Gay American History: Lesbians and Gay Men in the U.S.A., A Documentary.* New York: Crowell, 1976.

Katz, Jonathan, ed. *Documents of the Homosexual Rights Movement in Germany, 1836–1927.* New York: Arno Press, 1975.

Kinsey, Alfred C., Wardell B. Pomeroy, and Clyde E. Martin. *Sexual Behavior in the Human Male.* Philadelphia: Saunders, 1948.

Kinsey, Alfred C., Clyde E. Martin, Wardell B. Pomeroy, and Paul H. Gebhard. *Sexual Behavior in the Human Female.* Philadelphia: Saunders, 1953.

Krafft-Ebing, Richard von. *Psychopathia Sexualis, With Especial Reference to the Antipathic Sexual Instinct: A Medico-Forensic Study.* Translated from the twelfth German edition by Franklin S. Klaf. New York: Bell, 1965.

―― *Etude médico-légale: Psychopathia sexualis, avec recherches spéciales sur l'inversion sexuelle.* Translated from the eighth German edition by Emile Laurent and Sigismond Csapo. Paris: Carré, 1895.

Lauritsen, John. *Religious Roots of the Taboo on Homosexuality: A Materialist View.* Privately printed, 1974.

Lauritsen, John and David Thorstad. *The Early Homosexual Rights Movement (1864–1935).* New York: Times Change Press, 1974.

Leland, Charles Godfrey. *The Alternate Sex, or The Female Intellect in Man, and the Masculine in Woman.* New York: Funk, 1904.

Lewinsohn, Richard. *A History of Sexual Customs.* Translated by Alexander Mayce. New York: Bell, 1958.

Masters, William Howell and Virginia Johnson. *Homosexuality in Perspective.* Boston: Little, 1979.

Money, John. "Bisexual, Homosexual, and Heterosexual: Society, Law, and Medicine." *Journal of Homosexuality* (1977), 2: 229–33.

Moreau, Paul. *Des aberrations du sens génésique.* 2nd ed. Paris: Asselin, 1880.

Morris, Jan. *Conundrum.* New York: Harcourt, 1974.

Pomeroy, Wardell B. *Dr. Kinsey and the Institute for Sex Research.* New York: Harper, 1972.

Raffalovich, Marc-André. *Uranisme et unisexualité: Etude sur différentes manifestations de l'instinct sexuel.* Lyon: Storck; Paris: Masson, 1896.

Roback, Howard B., Donald S. Strassberg, Embry McKee, and Jean Cunningham. "Self-Concept and Psychological Adjustment Differences Between Self-Identified Male Transsexuals and Male Homosexuals." *Journal of Homosexuality* (1977), 3: 15–20.

Rowse, A. L. *Homosexuals in History: A Study of Ambivalence in Society, Literature and the Arts.* New York: Macmillan, 1977.

Saint-Paul, Georges [Dr. Laupts]. *Tares et poisons: Perversion et perversité sexuelles.* Paris: Carré, 1896.

Schumann-Arndt, Oskar. *Wir vom dritten Geschlecht.* Leipzig: Sattler, 1907.

Singer, June. *Androgyny: Toward a New Theory of Sexuality.* Garden City, N. Y.: Anchor/Doubleday, 1976.

Smith, Timothy d'Arch. *Love in Earnest: Some Notes on the Lives and Writings of English "Uranian" Poets from 1889 to 1930.* London: Routledge, 1970.

Steakley, James D. *The Homosexual Emancipation Movement in Germany.* New York: Arno Press, 1975.

Stoller, Robert J. *Sex and Gender, I: The Development of Masculinity and Femininity.* New York: Aronson, 1974.

Tardieu, Ambroise. *Etude médico-légale sur les attentats aux mœurs.* 7th ed. Paris: Ballière, 1878.

Tarnowsky, Benjamin. *Anthropological, Legal, and Medical Studies on Pederasty in Europe.* [Translated by Paul Gardner]. 1933. Reprint. North Hollywood, Calif.: Brandon House, 1967.

—— *L'Instinct sexuel et ses manifestations morbides au double point de vue de la jurisprudence et de la psychiatrie.* Paris: Carrington, 1904.

Tripp, C. A. *The Homosexual Matrix.* New York: McGraw-Hill, 1975.

Ulrichs, Karl Heinrich. *Memnon: Die Geschlechtsnatur des mannliebenden Urnings.* Schleiz: Hübscher-Heyn, 1868.

Vanggaard, Thorkil. *Phallós: A Symbol and Its History in the Male World.* Translated from the Danish by the author. New York: International Universities Press, 1972.

Weinberg, George. *Society and the Healthy Homosexual.* New York: St. Martin's, 1972.

Weinberg, Martin S. and Colin J. Williams. *Male Homosexuals: Their Problems and Adaptations.* New York: Oxford University Press, 1974.

Weindel, Henri de and F.-P. Fischer. *L'Homosexualité en Allemagne: Etude documentaire et anecdotique.* Paris: Juven, 1908.

Wolfenden, John. *The Wolfenden Report: Report of the Committee on Homosexual Offenses and Prostitution.* Authorized American Edition. New York: Stein and Day, 1963.

OTHER WORKS

Albert, Henri. "Lettres allemandes." *Mercure de France* (1907), 70: 559–63.

Bentley, Eric. *Theatre of War: Comments on 32 Occasions.* New York: Viking, 1972.

Boylesve, René. *Feuilles tombées.* Paris: Dumas, 1947.

Colette. *Le Pur et l'impur.* In *Œuvres complètes de Colette: Edition du centenaire.* Vol. 7. Paris: Flammarion, 1973.

Darwin, Charles. *The Descent of Man and Selection in Relation to Sex.* 1871. Reprint. Edited by Robert Maynard Hutchins. Great Books of the Western World, no. 49. Chicago: Encyclopaedia Britannica, 1952.

—— *The Different Forms of Flowers on Plants of the Same Species.* 1877. Reprint. New York: Appleton, 1897.

—— *Des différentes formes de fleurs dans les plantes de la même espèce.* Translated by Edouard Heckel. Paris: Reinwald, 1878.

Daudet, Léon. *Memoirs of Léon Daudet.* Edited and translated by Arthur Kingsland Griggs. New York: Dial, 1925.

Daudet, Lucien. *Le Chemin mort.* Paris: Flammarion, 1908.

"Eulenburg-Affäre: Briefe, die das Licht scheuten." *Der Spiegel* (1976), 30(40): 209–18.

Frye, Northrop. *A Natural Perspective: The Development of Shakespearean Comedy and Romance.* New York: Columbia University Press, 1965.

Gibbon, Edward. *The Decline and Fall of the Roman Empire.* 1776–88. Reprint. Edited by Robert Maynard Hutchins. Great Books of the Western World, no. 41. Chicago: Encyclopaedia Britannica, 1952.

Gide, André. *Journal, 1889–1939.* Paris: Gallimard, Bibliothèque de la Pléiade, 1951.

Graves, Robert. *The Greek Myths.* Vol. 1. Rev. ed. Baltimore: Penguin, 1960.

Haller, Johannes. *Philip Eulenburg: The Kaiser's Friend.* Translated by Ethel Colburn Mayne. 2 vols. New York: Knopf, 1930.

Hugo, Victor. *Œuvres poétiques, I: Avant l'exil, 1802–1851*. Edited by Pierre Albouy. Paris: Gallimard, Bibliothèque de la Pléiade, 1964.

Jammes, Francis. *Francis Jammes-Arthur Fontaine: Correspondance, 1898–1930*. Edited by Jean Labbé. Paris: Gallimard, 1959.

Jullian, Philippe. *Prince of Aesthetes: Count Robert de Montesquiou, 1855–1921*. Translated by John Haylock and Francis King. New York: Viking, 1967.

Mallarmé, Stéphane. *Œuvres complètes*. Edited by Henri Mondor and G. Jean-Aubry. Paris: Gallimard, Bibliothèque de la Pléiade, 1945.

Nabokov, Vladimir. *Ada or Ardor: A Family Chronicle*. New York: McGraw-Hill, 1969.

—— *Pale Fire*. New York: Putnam's, 1962.

Otto, Walter F. *Dionysus: Myth and Cult*. Translated by Robert B. Palmer. Bloomington: Indiana University Press, 1965.

Plato. *Great Dialogues of Plato*. Translated by W. H. D. Rouse. Rev. ed. New York: New American Library, 1970.

Poirier, Richard. *The Performing Self: Compositions and Decompositions in the Languages of Contemporary Life*. New York: Oxford University Press, 1971.

Röhl, John, ed. *Philipp Eulenburgs politische Korrespondenz*. Vol. 1. Boppard am Rhein: Boldt, 1976.

Sachs, Maurice. *Le Sabbat: Souvenirs d'une jeunesse orageuse*. Paris: Corrêa, 1946.

Vidal, Gore. *Two Sisters: A Memoir in the Form of a Novel*. Boston: Little, 1970.

Vigny, Alfred de. *Œuvres complètes*. Edited by F. Baldensperger. Paris: Gallimard, Bibliothèque de la Pléiade, 1950.

Whitman, Cedric H. *Aristophanes and the Comic Hero*. Cambridge, Mass.: Harvard University Press, 1964.

Wilde, Oscar. *The Letters of Oscar Wilde*. Edited by Rupert Hart-Davis. New York: Harcourt, 1962.

INDEX

NOTE: *There are separate entries for "Heterosexuality," "Stereotypes of heterosexuality," "Homosexuality," and "Stereotypes of homosexuality." I have distanced the phenomenon and its corresponding stereotypes alphabetically, just as I have tried to distance them philosophically in the foregoing discussion.*

After assembling the many listings for the "Stereotypes" categories, I saw that they form a narrative in their own right. A glance at these entries will reveal the extent to which, throughout history, we have used the concept of "the homosexual" as a means of excusing, explaining, ignoring, or propitiating whatever we do not understand about the world and whatever we most fear and despise in our own natures, just as we have used the concept of "the heterosexual" as an image of clarity, progress, and social and cosmic harmony. These are not the only symbolic roles these concepts have played, but they are highly influential ones, and they emerge very clearly from the juxtaposition of ideas in these two index entries. The two entries that begin with "Stereotypes" should, then, be regarded as dealing with myth in the broadest sense of the term.

"Stereotypes of homosexuality" is by far the longest entry, and "Stereotypes of heterosexuality" is one of the longest. And, of course, the two categories are intimately intertwined: the one generates the other. That we have had to address such an extensive list of traditional sexual fictions in order to understand Proust shows once again that his confrontations with and transmutations of his own sexuality were, in fact, confrontations with and transmutations of a major branch of Western history and myth.

Principal page references are in boldface type.